RISKS OF
UNINTENTIONAL NUCLEAR WAR

RISKS OF UNINTENTIONAL NUCLEAR WAR

DANIEL FREI
with the collaboration of
CHRISTIAN CATRINA

Published in cooperation with the
United Nations Institute for Disarmament Research

ROWMAN & ALLANHELD
Totowa, New Jersey

ROWMAN & ALLANHELD PUBLISHERS

Published in the United States of America in 1983
by Allanheld, Osmun & Co. Publishers, Inc.
(A Division of Littlefield, Adams & Company)
81 Adams Drive, Totowa, New Jersey 07512

Copyright © 1983 by United Nations Institute for
Disarmament Research

Library of Congress Cataloging in Publication Data

Frei, Daniel.
    Risks of unintentional nuclear war.

    Bibliography: p.
    1. Atomic warfare. 2. Atomic weapons and disarmament.
I. Title.
UF767.F774   1983   355'.0217   82-16333
ISBN 0-86598-106-X

Published in 1983 in Great Britain by

Croom Helm Limited
Provident House
Burrell Row
Beckenham
Kent BR3 1AT

ISBN (U.K.) 0-7099-1030-4

83 84 85 10 9 8 7 6 5 4 3 2

Printed and bound in the United States of America

CONTENTS

PREFACE

The awareness of the threat posed by nuclear weapons today has penetrated deep into the consciousness of people who realize that there is no choice but to halt the arms race and proceed to disarmament or face annihilation.

A consensus has emerged today in the world that the accumulation of weapons, particularly nuclear weapons, constitutes much more a threat than a protection for the future of mankind and therefore the time has come to put an end to this situation, to abandon the use of force in international relations and to seek security in disarmament, that is to say, through a gradual but effective process beginning with a reduction in the present level of armaments.

The most acute and urgent task of the day is that of elimination of the danger of nuclear war. Among the measures that could serve this goal, the General Assembly of the United Nations included "the prevention of attacks which take place by accident, miscalculation or communications failure, by taking steps to improve communications between governments, particularly in areas of tension, by the establishment of 'hot lines' and other methods of reducing the risk of conflict".

It is against this background that the United Nations Institute for Disarmament Research — UNIDIR — has undertaken the study of the risks of unintentional nuclear war.

UNIDIR was established by the General Assembly of the United Nations to conduct scientific research aimed at encouraging efforts towards disarmament and to facilitate the access of a large number of states, in particular the developing ones, to existing information, studies and research on disarmament. It is thus mandated to carry out research for the purpose of assisting negotiations and providing a general insight into the problems involved.

The institute was set up on 1 October 1980 within the administrative framework of UNITAR, for the period until the second special session of the General Assembly devoted to disarmament. It is located at the Palais des Nations, in Geneva. Its budget is financed by voluntary contributions from governments, intergovernmental organizations, foundations and individuals.

This volume is the outcome of an immense amount of work carried out with diligence over a short period of time by Professor Daniel Frei, with the collaboration of Christian Catrina, both from the University of Zurich, Switzerland. UNIDIR is most grateful for the outstanding quality of their research and their devotion to the cause it is serving. We are also indebted to all those in the research community and the officials in the Soviet Union and the United States of America whom Professor Daniel Frei has consulted and those, who, at the invitation of UNIDIR, made comments and suggestions on the manuscript.

This study forms part of the research programme approved by the Advisory Council of UNIDIR and the Board of Trustees of UNITAR. Its content is the responsibility of the authors and not of UNIDIR or UNITAR. Although UNIDIR takes no position on the views and conclusions expressed by the authors of its studies, it does assume responsibility for determining whether a study merits publication.

UNIDIR commends this study to the attention of all those who have responsibilities in the disarmament field or are interested in it — government officials, academics, journalists, members of non-governmental organizations and students. By publishing it, UNIDIR hopes that the study will help to better understand some issues at stake in the current wide debate on nuclear weapons, thus contributing to the cause of disarmament.

Davidson NICOL
Executive Director, UNITAR

Liviu BOTA
Director, UNIDIR

SUMMARY

The possibility of a nuclear holocaust being triggered unintentionally is a matter of growing concern. Large sectors of the public are increasingly alarmed by the traumatic prospect of a system of strategic deterrence getting out of control and suddenly confronting mankind with a doomsday nightmare.

Ever since the film *Dr. Strangelove* portrayed such a prospect, it has become quite popular to worry about insane colonels ordering an unauthorized missile launch, hapless officers pushing the wrong button, the self-activation of an electronic guidance system, blips on a radar screen showing a flock of geese, which is mistaken for attacking missiles, and so on. Yet popular belief in these and other nuclear-war-by-accident scenarios does not necessarily mean that such scenarios are relevant.

Although the dangers of possible nuclear accidents and incidents must certainly not be underestimated, the conclusion cannot be avoided that the focus on the risk of nuclear war by accident may misrepresent the problem and draw attention away from more serious risks. While redundant and efficient safeguard systems practically rule out any serious possibility of human and technical failure, international crises pose a far greater danger. As the following analysis will show, it is quite conceivable that an acute international crisis may act as a catalyst to trigger a nuclear war not in fact intended by the Governments concerned.

What is being envisaged here is not accidental nuclear war, but rather nuclear war based on false assumptions, i.e. on misjudgement or miscalculation by the persons legitimately authorized to decide on the use of nuclear weapons. Substandard performance by decision-makers in crisis situations is particularly common: more than two decades of crisis research have provided ample evidence of all kinds of individual and organizational failures, such as misperceptions, erratic behaviour under stress, the improper handling of information, the escalation of hostilities by mirror-image mechanisms, the hazards of "group-think", the failure to implement decisions due to their overwhelming complexity, confusion due to organizational bottlenecks and the inflexibility of standard operating procedures.

This creates many opportunities for the adoption of fatally wrong decisions. Some authors have recently referred to the 1914 analogy, which in fact continues to constitute a frightening example of the cumulative effect of such mistakes in an acute crisis confrontation. To-day, similar situations might involve States armed with nuclear weapons and hence would very likely mean nothing less than the beginning of a nuclear holocaust.

Why unintentional nuclear war?
The anatomy of the danger

When referring to international crises as the possible catalysts of an unintentional nuclear war, it would be quite simplistic to claim that any crisis creates a trigger-happy situation involving the risk of nuclear war. The risks do not originate in the crisis situation alone; they are generated by the crisis if and only if the strategic system has a certain propensity to become destabilized. Strategic instability and a crisis as a catalytic cause are necessary and sufficient conditions for triggering an unintentional nuclear war. It is their combination which creates a synergistic effect that may lead to a nuclear war.

Strategic instability can be said to exist if the Governments facing an international crisis feel that it is extremely urgent to decide on the use of nuclear weapons. The urgency in turn depends on the vulnerability of their strategic weapons and C^3 (command, control and communications) systems. If the strategic forces and/or the command channels which carry the threat of retaliation are vulnerable to sudden destruction, this threat can be removed by a pre-emptive attack aimed at those forces. On the other hand, strategic stability exists if the overall relation of forces leads potential opponents to conclude that any attempt to settle their conflict by using nuclear weapons entails a clearly unacceptable risk. Related to this is the concept of Mutual Assured Destruction (MAD), which implies that neither country's strategic nuclear deterrent force should be vulnerable to a first strike by the other; therefore, neither country has any incentive whatever to strike first. Some authors very pertinently prefer to replace the term "strategic stability" by the term "crisis stability", meaning a configuration of strategic forces which, in a situation of international crisis, allows each side to wait without any great disadvantage in case the other side attacks. By contrast, crisis *in*stability leads to pre-emption by creating an urge for timely action and the first use of nuclear weapons.

Strategic or crisis stability is a central concept of strategic thinking in both East and West. Although Soviet sources do not use this term as explicitly as is the case in official American sources, the issue of strategic stability can rightly be said to be a matter of common concern. The two major powers formally acknowledged its importance in the Joint Statement of Principles and Basic Guidelines for

Subsequent Negotiations on the Limitation of Strategic Arms, signed on 18 June 1979 in the context of the SALT II negotiations. In this Statement, the two signatories reaffirmed that "the strengthening of strategic stability meets the interests of the Parties and the interests of international security". They agreed to "continue for the purpose of reducing and averting the risk of outbreak of nuclear war to seek measures to strengthen strategic stability".

The nature of crisis stability can be further described and illustrated by two familiar paradigms offered by games theory. Under conditions of strategic stability, both opponents recognize that the use of nuclear weapons would inevitably entail destruction and death on both sides and, possibly, mutual annihilation. Therefore, both sides have an interest in choosing a co-operative strategy, i.e. avoiding the use of nuclear weapons. Thus the situation tends to stabilize itself; this is the typical outcome of so-called "chicken" game situations.

If, on the other hand, there is a premium on pre-emptive attack, i.e. if, by a preventive first strike, the opponent's capability to retaliate can be successfully knocked out and if both sides perceive the situation this way, they feel a strong urge to launch a disarming first strike. Under these circumstances peculiar to the so-called "prisoner's dilemma" game, the strategic system is highly unstable. In such a situation, a crisis confrontation is liable to trigger a nuclear war even if the Governments concerned do not intend to do so. It is the simple fear that the opponent might strike first which creates a powerful incentive for each side to keep at least one step ahead on the escalation ladder.

In order to assess the risk of unintentional nuclear war, two main questions have to be asked:

(1) What factors tend to affect crisis stability in the contemporary international system?
(2) What are the prospects of the use of force as a "continuation of politics by other means" generating acute international crises?

Account might also be taken of the institutions set up and the multilateral and bilateral agreements signed with a view to mitigating the risks of crisis instability and crisis avoidance and/or crisis management:

(3) How do existing agreements help to counter the risk of unintentional nuclear war?

Factors affecting crisis stability

When trying to assess the probability of averting crisis instability, three aspects of the current evolution of the strategic system have to be envisaged: (1) the arms race; (2) the development of strategic doctrines; and (3) nuclear proliferation. These three issues involve serious challenges to future crisis stability.

The current arms race implies the danger that the vulnerability of the strategic systems deployed by the two major Powers will be constantly jeopardized by technological improvements. Qualitative changes thus play a more important role than the quantitative arms race: the retaliatory forces of the other side are being threatened and a pre-emptive first strike becomes potentially feasible as a result of developments such as the introduction of multiple independently targetable re-entry vehicles (MIRVs), higher-yield warheads, the higher accuracy of delivery systems and the improved certainty with which the location of targets can be determined. At the same time, the invulnerability of potential targets is challenged by the development of anti-satellites capable of interfering with early-warning and C^3 systems and even more so by potential breakthroughs in anti-submarine warfare jeopardizing the relative invulnerability of sea-based deterrent forces. Furthermore, the feasibility of launching a disarming surprise attack is supported by the ability to fire missiles whose flight time is just a few minutes, owing either to increased speed or to the close stationing of the launchers. A grave threat is thus also posed to the invulnerability of C^3 systems, thereby giving rise to fears of a "decapitation" surprise attack against command centers and communications facilities. These prospects may in turn make it tempting to adopt launch-on-warning policies or predelegation measures giving subordinate commanders the competence to decide on the release of nuclear weapons. Finally, new technologies contribute to the strengthening of the defensive protection of strategic forces, especially land-based intercontinental ballistic missiles (ICBMs), as well as civilian targets. If it were possible to establish an operational anti-missile defence system, the first Power having such a system might be tempted to launch a disarming strike against its opponent, which would in such a case be deprived of the capability to punish the attacker by a retaliatory second strike.

Recent official United States and Soviet publications offer ample proof that both sides are afraid that their opponent is acquiring or intends to acquire first-strike capability. They tend to have precisely the same fears, suspicions and nervous attitudes. Their expectations and allegations fuel the arms race, regardless of whether they are correct or false. They prevent the arms race from becoming stabilized; arms-race stability can be said to exist if there appears to be no way for one side to achieve an overwhelming advantage over the other by quickly acquiring any feasible quantity of some weapon and, thus, there is no really strong incentive to do so.

Much has been written about the causal factors that determine the dynamics of the arms race. The armaments process seems to be largely governed by an intrinsic inertia having its own momentum independently of conscious decisions taken by policy-makers. There is also a tendency towards mirror-imaging; scientists and engineers often do not wait for a potential enemy to react, but, operating on "worst case" assumptions, react against their own brain-children by designing counter-weapons designed to neutralize weapons developed previously. The arms race is progressing on an incremental step-by-step basis without proper national, let alone international, control. Whatever the causes of the arms race, it cannot be denied that the arms race instability prevailing in the contemporary international system undermines crisis stability.

This does not mean that the arms race has already succeeded in destroying crisis stability. It must not be overlooked that there are also some mitigating factors. The nuclear Powers are extremely sensitive about and attentive to the potential vulnerability of their retaliatory capacity and C^3 systems; consequently, they make enormous efforts to forestall potential "windows of vulnerability". New weapons technologies also require testing because no sane decision-maker would be inclined to launch a pre-emptive attack with a new weapon without having determined its reliability; however, testing mitigates the danger of being surprised by a technological breakthrough achieved by the opponent. The MAD relationship continues to prevail and will do so for the foreseeable future. The risks of arms-race instability are not at present liable to upset crisis stability. Yet they are utterly alarming in the long run.

Destabilizing effects of doctrinal developments

The international strategic system is determined by what Soviet authors call "objective factors" — arms — and "subjective factors" — doctrines. Strategic doctrines are sets of operational beliefs, values and assertions that guide official behaviour with respect to strategic research and development, weapons choices, acquisitions policy, force deployment, operational plans, force employment, arms control, etc. Notwithstanding their high degree of sophistication, they ultimately rest on complex and indissoluble political judgements and are thus subject to all kinds of fallacies, distortions and misjudgements. This has particularly dangerous consequences for United States—Soviet strategic relations because United States strategic doctrine is characterized by a bewildering array of partly contradictory conceptions, while Soviet strategic doctrine is surrounded by a high degree of secrecy. There is every reason to assume that strategic doctrines in East and West are mismatched.

This mismatch has its origin in deep-rooted differences in philosophical and national traditions. Assumptions such as permanent conflict or the "ultimate triumph of socialism" and misrepresentations of the Soviet concept of surprise in the battlefield can hardly be said to promote mutual understanding and harmony in matters of strategic doctrines. Linguistic difficulties only make this problem worse. For instance, the English word "stability" cannot be adequately translated into Russian by the word *stabilnost;* while "stability" in the Western sense corresponds to crisis stability as defined above, the Russian term *stabilnost* seems to be synonymous with "balance" or "parity" in general. In the context of the United States, the debate about "parity", "superiority" and "sufficiency" is a particularly confusing aspect of strategic thinking; the practical usefulness of these terms is rather doubtful.

Mismatch and confusion in the field of strategic doctrine challenge crisis stability in two ways: they lead either to underestimation or overestimation of the opponent's intentions in a situation of acute international crisis.

Underestimating the opponent's intentions means that the deterrent ceases to be credible. A may assume that B is bluffing and thus underestimate B's resolve to honour its commitment; or A may assume that it would be irrational for B to carry out the threat to retaliate. Hence deterrence fails and a crisis may easily escalate into a nuclear war in which the attacker may realize too late that his action was based on miscalculation. On the other hand, overestimating the opponent's intentions is a result of "worst case" assumptions resulting from a strategic relationship dominated by ambiguity and a lack of proper mutual understanding of each other's strategic doctrines. "Worst case" thinking may lead A to infer from everything it sees and hears that B is engaged in preparations for launching a disarming first strike; hence it feels a strong urge to prevent impending disaster by quickly attacking B by surprise according to the logic of "use it or lose it". Again, this kind of reasoning would have disastrous consequences if it prevailed in decision-making during an acute international crisis.

The dilemma generated by the asymmetric and fuzzy nature of strategic doctrines of East and West has particularly grave consequences for the strategic situation in Europe. The Governments of the NATO countries realize that the strategic situation in Europe is characterized by a marked conventional imbalance favouring the Warsaw Treaty Organization (WTO). Since the NATO countries do not, for various reasons, feel in a position to redress this imbalance by an appropriate build-up of conventional armaments, NATO strategy basically refuses to rule out the use of nuclear weapons (mainly tactical nuclear weapons) to counter a WTO attack carried out by conventional or nuclear means against the territory of a NATO ally should NATO's conventional defence be overrun. This doctrine makes it highly uncertain that it would be profitable to attempt to exploit conventional superiority by launching a tank "blitzkrieg" for example.

NATO's strategy creates a two-fold credibility problem: first, the Soviet Union firmly rejects the idea that a nuclear war, once started by NATO's first use of nuclear weapons, could be kept limited or controlled; secondly, Soviet sources threaten to launch a "full-scale devastating and annihilating" retaliation strike against the homeland of the United States, thus casting doubts on the credibility of extended deterrence implying nothing less than the incineration of Chicago and New York for the sake of Hamburg and Hannover. On the other hand, NATO tries to enhance the credibility of its concept of extended deterrence and nuclear deterrence against any kind of attack by introducing a land-based intermediate range nuclear force (INF) in Western Europe; however, this policy is promptly denounced by WTO as an attempt to achieve first-strike capability and even the capability of surprise attack against Soviet strategic forces and C^3 installations by launching highly accurate INF missiles with an extremely short flight time (6 to 8 minutes). By placing emphasis on such prospects and uncertainties, the West's deterrence is in turn being deterred, thus eroding the credibility of the United States "nuclear umbrella" over Europe and, at the same time, accusing the West of preparing a disarming first strike. Both aspects are clear indications of doubt about the crisis stability of nuclear armament and strategic doctrines in and for Europe. It would be naïve to assume that the problem could be solved and stability redressed by suggesting common understanding of strategic doctrines. On the contrary, it seems that the mutual rejection of strategic concepts is part of a deliberate and conscious effort to manipulate each other's deterrence posture and, in particular, its doctrinal underpinnings.

When assessing the risks involved in the problem of strategic doctrines, the mitigating factors should not be overlooked. Nor should tendencies and potential dangers be confused with the actual state of affairs. Doubts about credibility do not automatically lead to a complete breakdown of credible deterrence. For the time being, the threat of retaliation and, thus, the expectation of incalculable damage is still effective and credible. No nuclear Power can expect to escape retaliation if it launches a pre-emptive strike against its opponents unless its Government engages in insane risk-taking behaviour. Although they are far from satisfactory, strategic doctrines do not destroy crisis stability. Yet this situation of relative stability will not be safe indefinitely. It should also be borne in mind that doubt and the erosion of the credibility of deterrence by the evolution of strategic doctrines tend to generate low-key crises and limited probes which in turn involve a risk of escalation.

Precarious stability in a world of many nuclear Powers

In the very near future, a considerable number of countries might acquire nuclear weapons. The efforts made to halt nuclear proliferation may eventually prove to be insufficient, particularly if the nuclear-weapon States themselves do not start a genuine process of nuclear disarmament. In the context of this contribution, it must be asked whether more nuclear Powers will mean more nuclear wars or a greater risk of international crises triggering nuclear conflagration. When trying to answer this question the problem has to be seen in terms of the likelihood of the outbreak of nuclear war between countries emerging as nuclear Powers, on the one hand, and in terms of the likelihood of a new nuclear Power triggering an all-out nuclear war among other nuclear Powers and, in particular, the United States of America and the Soviet Union, on the other hand.

As far as the first problem is concerned, the arguments put forward in the rapidly growing literature on nuclear proliferation are very controversial. Some specialists argue that an increase in the number of nuclear Powers would reduce the probability of war by providing an additional restraining force and increasing uncertainty about the others' reaction. Other authors, however, refer to the delicate situation of regional crisis instability that exists when a nation is about to become a nuclear Power. As a State develops a nuclear capability, there will be a temptation for its potential enemies to attack it before its nuclear delivery system is operational. That was the rationale underlying the "surgical strike" executed by Israel against Iraq's Osirak research reactor. A similar incentive to pre-empt may also be generated after two regional rival countries have acquired nuclear weapons, which, in the initial stage, will be characterized by a high degree of vulnerability that creates a temptation to launch a pre-emptive strike. Hence there is some probability that local crises will escalate into local nuclear wars.

The second problem relates to the possibility that such a local nuclear war might ignite a general nuclear war. One might assume that the two major Powers would behave with utmost care and circumspection in any such conflict. They might even be tempted to exert pressure on their respective clients not to use nuclear weapons. Nevertheless, any generalized conclusion would be misleading. The outcome of a conflagration of this kind would probably be determined by the nature of the involvement and commitment of the two major Powers. Hence the evolution of a crisis would be different in different regions.

The future of international crises

Since unintentional nuclear war may result from the cumulative effect of inherent crisis instability and acute crisis confrontation, the prospects for future crises must be examined. In particular, two aspects have to be analysed:(1) the impact of nuclear armaments and nuclear strategy on the nature of crises; and (2) the propensity of the international system to generate crises.

The nature of crises in the nuclear age

According to a familiar definition crises are the result of a threat to basic values, the high probability of involvement in military hostility and awareness of a time limit for response to the external threat. There is hardly any need for further explanation in order to conclude that the existence of nuclear weapons and the evolution of nuclear strategic doctrines inevitably intensify the gravity and urgency of crisis situations. The nature of nuclear threat establishes a completely new order of magnitude of a danger never heard of before, virtually leading to terror. (It should be noted, in this context, that the term "terror" has the same etymological root as the term "deterrence".) At worst, terror tends to upset firmly established role structures and traditional patterns of perception and behaviour, thus making it extremely difficult to think clearly and decide properly. In other words, the element of terror inherent in any nuclear threat may cause unsuitable behaviour both in individuals and in organizations faced with an international crisis.

Furthermore, any tendency of nuclear-weapon systems to create urgency due to vulnerability in turn helps to aggravate a crisis. The more serious a crisis, however, the more the decision-makers' capability of making an appropriate, rational analysis of the situation is reduced. This is highly unfortunate at a time when strategic doctrines are becoming increasingly complex and are based on a variety of weapons with different performance characteristics. It must therefore be asked whether the political leaders of the countries concerned, in the hectic situation of a crisis emergency, will still be capable of deciding and acting fully in accordance with the requirements of the complex and infinitely subtle logic of nuclear crisis strategy. Decision-makers may become victims of urgency and commit all kinds of mistakes, miscalculations and misperceptions.

In other words, the propensity of the strategic system to become unstable has additional consequences that aggravate the risk of unintentional war by increasing the probability of inappropriate decisions. Thus, crises in the nuclear age are far more dangerous than in the pre-nuclear age. Of course, contemporary political leaders still remember Hiroshima and therefore adopt a very cautious attitude towards the use of nuclear weapons. Yet the general trend may, in the long run, offset these restraints.

The use of force: tendencies and prospects

Despite the threat of nuclear disaster, the frequency of international crises has not declined in the nuclear age. "Coercive bargaining" is and continues to be a dominant factor in international politics. The symbolic use of force is general practice in the international system. The use of force for the purpose of conveying signals to the opponent in a situation of coercive bargaining may easily produce incidents of all kinds which have a propensity to escalate. This risk is even more serious if nuclear weapons serve as demonstrations of resolve; there are reports of measures such as putting missiles on various levels of alert status, deploying strategic bombers, placing more bombers in the air on airborne alert, deploying tactical nuclear weapons near the crisis area, sending more nuclear submarines on patrol, etc.

The danger inherent in this type of manipulation of the risks of nuclear war naturally leads statesmen to behave with much more caution whenever nuclear weapons are involved. Both the United States and the Soviet Union are known to be placing more emphasis on the central control of their systems. Also, as soon as a crisis escalates, the political leaders of the countries concerned tend to pay much more attention to minute tactical details than in periods of "normalcy". Nevertheless, the fact that it is very difficult to convey messages credibly through this kind of manipulation of force in a situation dominated by distrust must not be disregarded. There is a possibility of misunderstanding and hence of miscalculation in every step made in this delicate field.

There are many reasons to expect cases of coercive bargaining to continue and even increase. Whenever a situation of rivalry between two nuclear Powers is characterized by a high degree of ambiguity, it invites provocation, i.e., all kinds of "limited probes" and "controlled pressure". Ambiguity is presently growing in third world regions where the two major Powers are increasingly inclined to engage in all kinds of poorly defined commitments. Unlike "classical" alliance commitments, this new type of commitment implies a great deal of uncertainty and unpredictability. This gives the two major Powers more opportunities to "test" each other by means of crisis confrontation and coercive bargaining. Hence the risks involved in unintended consequences of such behaviour become proportionately greater.

Existing agreements to counter the risk of unintentional nuclear war

Confronted with the risk of unintentional nuclear war, the Powers and especially the two major Powers undertook efforts to mitigate this risk by arms control and related agreements. A general evaluation of the measures agreed upon so far tends to lead to rather gloomy, if not sarcastic, conclusions. Some authors do not hesitate to call them "futile, ineffective and outside the main thrust of great Power military efforts". There are two main groups of agreements: those open for accession by all States and bilateral agreements (or agreements with limited membership). The following agreements in the first group are relevant for the prevention of unintentional nuclear war:

> Antarctic Treaty (1959)
> Limited Test-Ban Treaty (LTBT) (1963)
> Outer Space Treaty (1967)
> Treaty of Tlatelolco (1967)
> Nuclear Non-Proliferation Treaty (NPT) (1968)
> Seabed Treaty (1971)
> Confidence-Building Measures (CBMs) of the CSCE Final Act (1975)

Among the bilateral agreements the following have an immediate bearing upon the problems discussed:

Hot-Line Agreement (1963)
Agreement to Reduce the Risk of Nuclear War (1971)
Agreement on the Prevention of Incidents on the High Seas (1972)
Basic Principles (1972)
SALT I (Interim Agreement) (1972)
Anti-Ballistic Missile (ABM) Treaty (1972)
Prevention of Nuclear War Agreement (1973).
SALT II (1979).

Although it is not possible, in the present context, to offer a detailed evaluation of these agreements and treaties, a summary assessment may lead to some tentative conclusions. In the following table, each agreement is examined in the light of the contribution it makes to the strengthening of crisis stability and to the containment of future international crises. The symbols used are:

+ The provisions of the agreement or treaty are capable of *fully* coping with the risk involved.

(+) The provisions *partly* cope with the risk involved or *mitigate* it.

(−) There are *doubts* about the utility of the provisions; they may even slightly impair efforts to contain the risk involved.

— The provisions are entirely *counterproductive.*

Agreements	Risks				
	Crisis instability			Future crises	
	Arms-race instability	Destabilizing doctrines	Nuclear proliferation	Gravity of crises	Frequency of crises
Antarctic Treaty	(+)				
LTBT	(+)		(+)		
Outer Space Treaty	(+)				
Tlatelolco Treaty	(+)		(+)		
NPT			(+)		
Seabed Treaty	(+)				
CBMs		(+)		(+)	
Hot Line				(+)	
Risk of Nuclear War Agreement				(+)	
Naval Incidents Agreement				(+)	
Basic Principles					(+)
SALT I (Interim)	(−)	(+)			
ABM	(+)	(+)			
Prevention of Nuclear War Agreement				(+)	
SALT II	(+)	(+)			

The results of the analysis presented in the table are quite revealing, even though they are tentative and somewhat impressionistic. The conclusion cannot be avoided that the existing agreements cope with a small fraction of the risks only and do so in a very incomplete and hence unsatisfactory way. Nevertheless, it would be misleading to conclude that the existing provisions are simply worthless.

They are in fact capable of controlling some of the risks. More important, their existence reflects widespread awareness of the risks involved in contemporary crisis politics.

Practical conclusions

The risk of an international crisis escalating into an unintentional nuclear war requires energetic efforts at the unilateral, bilateral and multilateral levels. The foregoing analysis may lead to the following practical conclusions:

With regard to coping with arms-race instability:

(1) The inclusion of additional issues in the agenda of international arms control negotiations, e.g. prevention and prohibition of anti-satellite and anti-submarine developments;

(2) Increased emphasis on the qualitative aspects of the arms race and the development of appropriate verification and inspection procedures;

(3) Efforts to achieve strategic stability at the lowest possible level.

With regard to the destabilizing consequences of strategic doctrines:

(4) Talks among military experts from the major Powers on strategic doctrines with a view to finding areas of common understanding;

(5) Negotiations on possible solutions to the problem of extended deterrence, e.g. an agreement on no first offensive use of nuclear weapons.

With regard to the destabilizing consequences of nuclear proliferation:

(6) Satisfaction of the legitimate security needs of threshold countries by non-nuclear means;

(7) Priority for regional arms control measures as compared with universal approaches.

With regard to the aggravation of crises by nuclear strategy:

(8) The improvement of quick and efficient communications between opponents in the event of crisis;

(9) Restraint in using nuclear alerts and deployments for demonstrations of resolve.

With regard to the future frequency of crises:

(10) Avoiding additional, and reducing existing, commitments by the major Powers to the third world;

(11) Bilateral and multilateral restraints on arms transfers to the third world which cause new commitments;

(12) Discussions on "crisis conventions" with a view to agreeing on minimum standards of behaviour when using force.

It goes without saying that the lasting and proper answer to the problem can only be general and complete disarmament and the establishment of a peaceful international order, i.e., an effective system for the international settlement of disputes. In the absence of these two ultimate goals, however, these and other specific short-range measures deserve further examination.

AUTHOR'S PREFACE

This study sets out to analyse one of the most disquieting and controversial aspects of the current arms race. In the current discussions on this subject, the risk of unintentional nuclear war is being assessed differently according to the way in which this phenomenon is conceived. While the public discussion tends to focus attention on spectacular accidents involving nuclear weapons or causing false alarms, experts conceptualize the risk of unintentional nuclear war in a broader context by pointing to the synergetic effect of catalytic events in a situation of general strategic instability.

The United Nations General Assembly, at its first special session devoted to disarmament, also felt alarmed by the prospects of unintentional war. In paragraph 93[1] of the Final Document it recommended that, among the measures yet to be agreed upon, the following should be undertaken:

> "The prevention of attacks which take place by accident, miscalculation or communications failure by taking steps to improve communications between Governments, particularly in areas of tension, by the establishment of 'hot lines' and other methods of reducing the risk of conflict".

The threat of unintentional nuclear war, and of an inadvertent nuclear global holocaust arising therefrom, has been felt from the very beginning of the modern strategic system. Concerned scientists in many fields of study have made efforts to clarify its nature and to develop ways and means of coping with it. For this reason, a considerable thesaurus of specialized literature is available.

The main purpose of this study is twofold: (1) to discern the underlying structure of the problem and to identify those areas of knowledge where a consensus can be said to exist; and (2) to provide a systematic survey of factors aggravating the risk of unintentional nuclear war and factors reducing it. Particular emphasis is also laid on those aspects which still seem to be subject to dissenting assessment. By presenting the different views put forward, the author of this study hopes to contribute to a further stimulation of a discussion which deserves to be pursued on a large scale and by intensive efforts. The focus of the study is on the strategic forces of the United States of America and of the Soviet Union. While the general problem of proliferation is also examined, the special problems presented by the nuclear deterrents of France and the United Kingdom are not included in the analysis.

The study was written with a view to informing diplomats, government officials and members of the general public interested in the subject. Although it does not aim at making available to the professional expert any new information or interpretation, it is hoped that the study will be found useful.

The analysis is based primarily on a critical evaluation of the literature available; so far, about 500 titles can be identified, the overwhelming majority of which are American or West European. This is subsequently reflected in this study. The knowledge gathered from the literature was supplemented by information collected in the course of consultations held with Government agencies and academic institutes in both Washington D.C. and Moscow. The main rationale of this study is to collect, connect and integrate a widely dispersed multitude of perspectives and pieces of information. When quoting various sources, the author does not necessarily imply agreement with the substance of the respective references.

It is hoped that these efforts will lead to the presentation of a comprehensive, systematic and hopefully exhaustive and coherent picture and evaluation of the dangers that may lead to an unintentional nuclear war. The wide variety of theoretical insights and theoretical evidence on the nature of these risks will also allow a number of practical conclusions with regard to their prevention.

The approach underlying this study focuses on the risk of unintentional nuclear war only. The respective problems are examined on the assumption of a continuing arms race. Of course, the lasting and proper answer to the problem of unintentional nuclear war is general and complete disarmament. The author of this study is deeply convinced that, in the long run, there is no other way out of the frightening dilemma of the nuclear age than to engage on a course leading to true disarmament. But pending the attainment of this ultimate goal, full attention has to be devoted to what may seem an expedient yet has the utmost relevance for the very survival of mankind.

A similar remark is called for with regard to another of the central concepts of this study: crisis stability. When examining the risks inherent in crisis management and advocating improved policies of crisis management, again the author does not purport to suggest a permanent solution to this problem. Rather he discusses this issue as part of a broader effort directed towards the creation of a peaceful international order. The ultimate aim continues to be that proclaimed by

Article 1 of the Charter of the United Nations:

> "To maintain international peace and security, and to that end: to take effective collective measures for the prevention and removal of threats to the peace, and for the suppression of acts of aggression or other breaches of the peace, and to bring about by peaceful means, and in conformity with the principles of justice and international law, adjustment or settlement of international disputes or situations which might lead to a breach of the peace".

Providing security through disarmament and providing security through collective arrangements such as the United Nations system are of course interrelated and should be pursued in parallel (cf. United Nations General Assembly 1981e: 54f.). But as for the time being neither objective can easily be met, there is no alternative but to deal with the issue of unintentional nuclear war and other issues on the basis of the conditions offered by the contemporary international political system. To neglect this reality and to fail to draw appropriate conclusions would be a fatal error.

ACKNOWLEDGEMENTS

For organizational reasons this study had to be written within the brief time-span of three months and the author was obliged to perform this task in addition to his various duties as a university professor and head of a research institute. In pointing this out, however, the author is not trying to offer an easy excuse for the obvious shortcomings of this study but wishes to stress that the task of writing it in such a short time would have been quite impossible without the generous help of many persons competent in the field under consideration.

First of all the author wishes to thank Mr. Christian Catrina, research associate, who showed extraordinary application, skill and ingenuity in helping him to collect, read and analyse the vast amount of literature available on this subject. Mrs. Aurelia Boermans, the author's highly efficient secretary, typed and partly rewrote the manuscript and saved the author from a crash in what must virtually be said to be a crash programme.

The first draft of the study was carefully read by Dr. Philipp Sonntag (Science Centre Berlin), who in addition contributed several paragraphs to the manuscript; his experience as both a physicist and a social scientist represented a very welcome support.

The manuscript or parts of it were also read by Dr. Liviu Bota (UNIDIR), Rikhi Jaipal (Committee on Disarmament), Professor Klaus Ritter, Dr. Hubert Feigl and Mr. Axel Strehlke (all at the Stiftung Wissenschaft und Politik, Ebenhausen), Dr. Milton Leitenberg (Swedish Institute of International Relations), and Dr. Albert A. Stahel (Swiss Federal Institute of Technology, Zurich). The comments offered by these distinguished specialists were crucial in shaping the final version presented here.

The author also wishes to express his gratitude to a number of government officials and distinguished scholars in both Washington D.C. and Moscow who gave him an opportunity to receive first-hand information from the two main vantage points of the strategic central balance. In Washington D.C. the author was able to have discussions with Miss A. Bohlen, Colonel J. Pappageorge, Mr.

J. Martin, Mr. D. Schwartz (all at the Department of State), Mr. F. Miller, Mr. R. Hanmer (at the Department of Defense), Mr. S. Riveles (Arms Control and Disarmament Agency) and Dr. B. Blechman (Carnegie Endowment for International Peace). In Moscow he consulted Professor O. Bykov, Professor V. Razmerov, Professor A. Nikonov and Mr. A. Kamynin (all at the Institute of World Economy and International Relations/USSR Academy of Sciences), Dr. E. Kutovoi and Dr. A. Vavilov (both at the Foreign Ministry of the USSR), Professor G. Shakhnazarov (President, Soviet Political Science Association), Dr. I. Tyulin, Dr. V. Lukov, Mr. M. A. Chrustalev, Dr. V. B. Zukov, Dr. A. V. Zagorsky, Dr. I. I. Kusnetsov, Dr. V. Sergeev, and Miss Z. N. Vlovitchenko (all Moscow State Institute of International Relations). The author also gratefully acknowledges comments offered by Ambassador V. L. Issraelyan, Mr. B. P. Prokofiev and Mr. G. Berdennikov (Soviet delegation to the Committee on Disarmament, Geneva).

Last but not least, the author feels very much obliged to Dr. Liviu Bota, Director of the United Nations Institute for Disarmament Research (UNIDIR), for having kindly offered him the privilege of his confidence. Dr. Bota also suggested a multitude of important ideas. Through his easy mastery of all administrative and publishing problems, he made the author's co-operation with UNIDIR a true pleasure.

While the author gratefully acknowledges all the help so kindly offered to him by so many persons, he would like to emphasize that all shortcomings of this study must of course be attributed to him and to the problem of his yield/time ratio which he has tried to solve to the best of his ability: *Ultra posse nemo obligatur.*

GLOSSARY

AAM	Air-to-Air Missile
ABM	Anti-Ballistic Missile
ACDA	Arms Control and Disarmament Agency (United States)
ACIS	Arms Control Impact Statements (United States)
AFB	Air Force Base
ALCC	Airborne Launch Control Center
ALCM	Air-Launched Cruise Missile
ALCS	Airborne Launch Control System
ASAT	Anti-Satellite
ASBM	Air-to-Surface Ballistic Missile
ASW	Anti-Submarine Warfare
BAS	Bulletin of the Atomic Scientist
BMD	Ballistic Missile Defence
BMEWS	Ballistic Missile Early Warning System
BOOB	Bolt out of the Blue
C^3	Command, Control, and Communications
CAT	Conventional Arms Transfers
C^3I	Command, Control, Communications, and Intelligence
CBM	Confidence-Building Measures
CD	Command Destruction Design
CEP	Circular Error Probable
CINC	Commander-in-Chief
CINCSAC	Commander-in-Chief Strategic Air Command
CJCS	Chairman of the Joint Chiefs of Staff
CMP	Counter Military Potential
CSCE	Conference on Security and Co-operation in Europe
CTB	Comprehensive Test Ban
DB	Deep Basing
DoD	Department of Defense (United States)
ECM	Electronic Counter Measure
ELF	Extremely Low Frequency
EMP	Electromagnetic Pulse
ER	Enhanced Radiation
EWS	Early Warning System

FBS	Forward Based Systems
FOBS	Fractional Orbital Bombardment System
FY	Fiscal Year
GCD	General and Complete Disarmament
GLCM	Ground-Launched Cruise Missile
GPS	Global Positioning System
IAEA	International Atomic Energy Agency
ICBM	Intercontinental Ballistic Missile
INF	Intermediate Range Nuclear Force
IRBM	Intermediate Range Ballistic Missile
JCS	Joint Chiefs of Staff (United States)
LAA	Launch on Attack Assessment
LCC	Launch Control Center
LNO	Limited Nuclear Option
LoADS	Low Altitude Defense System
LOI	Launch On Impact
LOW	Launch On Warning
LRTNF	Long Range Theater Nuclear Forces
LTA	Launch Through Attack
LTBT	Limited Test Ban Treaty
LUA	Launch Under Attack
MAC	Military Airlift Command
MAD	Mutual Assured Destruction
MAP	Multiple Aim Point
MARV	Maneuverable Re-entry Vehicle
MBFR	Mutual and Balanced Force Reductions
MIRV	Multiple Independently Targetable Re-entry Vehicle
MPS	Multiple Protective Shelter
MRBM	Medium Range Ballistic Missile
MRV	Multiple Re-entry Vehicle
MT	Megaton
MX	Missile Experimental
NATO	North Atlantic Treaty Organization
NAVSTAR	Navigation Satellite Timing and Ranging
NCA	National Command Authorities (United States)
NEACP	National Emergency Airborne Command Post
nm	nautical mile
NORAD	North American Air Defense
NPT	Non-Proliferation Treaty
NSC	National Security Council (United States)
OAS	Organization of American States
P	Probability
PAL	Permissive Action Link
PD	Presidential Directive
PGM	Precision-Guided Munitions
PLU	Preservation of Location Uncertainty
PNET	Peaceful Nuclear Explosions Treaty
PRP	Personnel Reliability Programme
psi	Pounds per Square Inch

PTBT	Partial Test Ban Treaty
R&D	Research and Development
RDF	Rapid Deployment Force
RDT&E	Research, Development, Test and Evaluation
REM	Roentgen Equivalent Man
ROA	Ride Out Attack
RV	Re-entry Vehicle
SAC	Strategic Air Command (United States Air Force)
SAFE	Survivability, Assured Destruction, Flexibility and Essential Equivalence
SALT	Strategic Arms Limitations Talks
SAS	Sealed Authenticator System
SCC	Standing Consultative Commission
SIOP	Single Integrated Operational Plan
SIPRI	Stockholm International Peace Research Institute
SLBM	Submarine-Launched Ballistic Missile
SLC	Strategic Laser Communications
SLCM	Sea-Launched Cruise Missile
SOP	Standard Operating Procedures
SOSUS	Sound Surveillance System
SSBN	Ballistic Missile Submarine, Nuclear-Powered
SSN	Submarine, Nuclear-Powered (Attack)
TAC	Tactical Air Command (United States)
TERCOM	Terrain Contour Matching
TNF	Theater Nuclear Forces
TNW	Tactical Nuclear Weapons
TTBT	Threshold Test Ban Treaty
USAF	United States Air Force
VLF	Very Low Frequency
WTO	Warsaw Treaty Organization
WWMCCS	World-Wide Military Command and Control System

I. INTRODUCTION

A. Popular Views of the Problem

There is a growing public concern about the possibility of a nuclear holocaust triggered off unintentionally by error, miscalculation or simply by accident or mischief. Ever since the beginning of the nuclear era, people have been concerned about what the popular film "Dr. Strangelove" presented as a horror fiction of a system of strategic deterrence getting out of control and confronting mankind suddenly with a Doomsday nightmare: a mad colonel ordering an unauthorized missile launch, an unfortunate officer pushing the wrong button, signals on a radar screen reflecting a group of geese mistakenly interpreted as attacking missiles.

The mere existence of nuclear weapons caused many people to think about their inherent risks. Doubts as to the safety and control of these systems never ceased to be expressed although it seemed in the late 1960s and the early 1970s that arms control agreements were contributing to the establishment of a deterrence system less prone to the risk of becoming inadvertently destabilized.

In addition, large segments of the American public felt alarmed by the trauma of a surprise attack out of the blue which seemed theoretically feasible after 1957, when the Soviet Union launched the first satellite and became the first Power to achieve an intercontinental ballistic capability. The late 1950s and the early 1960s were virtually dominated by a kind of "nuclear fever" (Mandelbaum 1981:219). In the meantime this "nuclear fever" has become universal.

In the contemporary world and in the foreseeable future the arms race has developed a new momentum, and the relative stability is thus seriously challenged. This gives renewed cause for fearing the outbreak of unintentional nuclear war. "Thinking the unthinkable" has again become the preoccupation not only of concerned scientists but of a large concerned segment of the general public as well. Reports about accidents and incidents involving nuclear weaponry—called "broken arrows" and "bent spears" — receive increasing attention, and the same can

1

be said about scenarios based on events such as the failure of radar equipment and computers of early warning systems, the occurrence of false alarms, mechanical failures, malfunctioning of safeguards, theft by terrorists, unauthorized launching of missiles and the like (cf. e.g., *Newsweek*, 5 October 1981; *Der Spiegel*, 23 June 1980). The titles of books such as *Nuclear Nightmares* (Calder 1980), *Apocalypse* (Beres 1980), *World War against One's Will* (Lutz 1981) are indicative of a growing mood created by the disquieting prospects offered by the future of nuclear weaponry. More importantly, many people have doubts about the reliability and credibility of the deterrence system, and many people also feel anxious about the possibility of a "probe" through the launching of a surprise attack.

The public awareness of this issue does not necessarily and automatically imply an appropriate understanding of the matter at stake. Exaggeration and distortion may be as probable as underestimates and lack of appreciation. It cannot be denied that the general public tends to perceive the risks of accidents as the main danger capable of leading to unintentional nuclear war, neglecting the pitfalls that lie in the decision-making structure concerned with the planning and execution of a nuclear war. Yet, there are parallels also on the official side which often simply points to the many technical and organizational safeguards established to protect warheads and launchers against accident and misuse. The emphasis on these aspects may also be somewhat incomplete and disregard other and possibly more crucial factors that might lead to unintentional nuclear war.

Furthermore, as far as the general public's understanding of the problem is concerned, there may be a tendency to confuse the specific question of the risk of unintentional nuclear war with a general antipathy to nuclear weapons and to the idea of nuclear war, rooted in moral considerations. Rejection of nuclear weapons on moral grounds often leads to short-cut conclusions about the dangers presented by these weapons. The same must be said about the distrust of any form of "runaway technology" (Mandelbaum 1981: 226), which sometimes leads people to have generalized misgivings about any technological progress, including any type of arms improvement irrespective of its own merits or demerits.

It is also important to differentiate between the situation prevailing in the 1950s and the early 1960s and today's situation: It cannot be denied that the technological specifications and the doctrinal concepts underlying nuclear armaments are not the same today as two or three decades ago. Much of the public's concern seems to be directed to problems which no longer constitute any danger. For understandable reasons, there is always a certain time-lag between the present state of technological progress and the realization of its implications by the public. With reference to the problem of unintentional nuclear war, it is important to note that as early as 1962 and 1963 the 18-Nation Disarmament Committee dealt with

2

measures to prevent the accidental outbreak of war. Both the United States and the Soviet Union made proposals for reducing the risks of war through accidents, miscalculation or failure of communication, and the Committee devoted much attention to these issues (United States Arms Control Disarmament Agency: *Documents on Disarmament*, 1962, vol 1:142f.; vol 2: 1214f.; 1963: 127f.). These discussions resulted in the agreement to establish a "hot line" communication facility between Washington and Moscow. Although some of the issues raised in the 1962/1963 discussions may still be relevant, one must not disregard the fact that in the meantime additional problems have considerably changed the whole task of preventing unintentional nuclear war.

B. Terminological Preliminaries

Discussion of the topic to be covered by the present study reveals a considerable amount of terminological confusion or at least terminological vagueness. There is a variety of terms being used in this context. Many of them are meant synonymously by some authors while other authors attribute distinct meanings to different terms. The terms to be found in the literature can be summarized as follows:

> *Accidental war:* War resulting from a malfunction of some weapons system or from human error, not including errors in judgement (Schwarz/Hadik 1966: 117).
> Other definitions of this term include:
> War resulting from failure to foresee the consequences of military actions or the accumulation of irreversible threats in the heat of crisis (Schelling/Halperin 1969: 46).
> War initiated by the belief that war has already started or has become inevitable (Schelling/Halperin 1969: 47).
> *Inadvertent war, unintentional war, unpremeditated war* (used as synonyms): Armed conflict arising from error of political judgement.
> War that starts without explicit decisions by the responsible leaders of the participating nations (Schwarz/Hadik 1966: 117; Ignatieff 1979: 69).
> *War by miscalculation or misunderstanding:* War due to failure adequately to think through the consequences of actions (Kahn 1962: 44).
> *Pre-emptive war:* War initiated in the expectation that attack is imminent (Schelling/Halperin 1969: 43f.).
> *Preventive war, premeditated attack* (used as synonyms): Attack initiated in the belief that war is fairly likely sooner or later and that the conservative course would be to initiate it on the best possible terms (Schelling/Halperin 1969: 46).
> *Catalytic war:* A deliberate plot by some third country or countries to precipitate war between major Powers (Schelling/Halperin 1969: 46).

Apart from the terms *catalytic war* and *preventive or premeditated war*, referring to clearly separate phenomena, all other terms appear as somehow interrelat-

3

ed, partly identical (synonymous), partly overlapping. The use of these terms also varies from author to author; thus no coherent practice can be discerned.

The main consideration underlying the various definitions can easily be identified: it is whether the war results from mischief (in the technical field, in communications or in the command structure) or from an error of political judgement. This distinction may be somewhat artificial because it is conceivable that a Government might make an error of political judgement in response to an accident caused by mischief. For this reason, and as this study wishes to avoid any premature narrowing of the scope of analysis, the most general term and the most comprehensive definition will be taken as a starting-point, i.e., the term *unintentional nuclear war*. It is defined in the present study as covering the following types of war:

(1) A nuclear war initiated independently of any explicit decision by the legitimate authorities;

(2) A nuclear war initiated deliberately and voluntarily by legitimate authorities but based on false assumptions;

(3) A war of greater intensity and scope than was envisaged by those who made the decision to use force, e.g., a war escalating from conventional warfare into a nuclear exchange not foreseen by the opposing sides.

The characteristic of being "unintentional" thus refers to the occurrence of war (i.e., to the unintentional triggering of a war according to types (1) and (2)) as well as to the unexpected evolution of a war (i.e., its unintentional nature or intensity according to type (3)). As will be shown below, these two aspects are closely interrelated.

Furthermore, it is important to note that certain factors affecting the likelihood of one type of unintentional nuclear war may at the same time also have an impact on the occurrence or intensity of the other types. Therefore an approach rigidly differentiating between the three types would hardly be adequate, given the complexity of the problem. For this reason, this study does not summarily ascribe specific causes to specific effects in the field of unintentional nuclear war but it endeavours to examine the various sources of risks on their own merits, assessing the significance of each type of risk for each type of unintentional nuclear war. Based on these considerations, and in conclusion, an overall assessment of the risk of unintentional nuclear war in general will be offered.

C. Why Unintentional Nuclear War?
The Structure of the Problem

As this study aims at a systematic rather than a case-oriented analysis of the risk of unintentional nuclear war, a theoretical framework is required in order to map the various elements under consideration in a coherent and meaningful way.

The basic assumption serving as a starting point for all subsequent lines of argument is that, in order to explain any type of unintentional nuclear war and in order to assess any risks conducive to unintentional nuclear war, two main perspectives have to be taken into account simultaneously.

The first is a general predisposition of the strategic system of deterrence; depending on its characteristics, the system is more or less likely to produce an unintentional nuclear war and thus has a certain propensity for unintentional nuclear war.

The second necessary condition for unintentional nuclear war is a cause triggering such a war at a specific moment, i.e., a catalytic cause such as an acute international crisis confrontation. The overall structure of the problem can therefore be summed up in the following arrow diagram (the arrows representing causal relationships):

predisposition of the
deterrence system
                    unintentional nuclear war
catalytic cause

Going beyond this very general model and trying to elaborate on it, one may wish to shed some light on factors determining the predisposition as well as factors producing catalytic causes.

Strategic Stability

The crucial factor affecting the propensity of a system to produce unintentional nuclear war is the *urgency* with which the decision must be made; this in turn depends on the *vulnerability* of both the strategic weapons and the communication and command channels. This hypothesis rests on the assumption that a nuclear Power tends to be preoccupied with the urgency of attacking where evidence exists that another nuclear Power is about to, if, in the event that war occurs, the strategic system gives an advantage to the side that starts it (Schelling/Halperin 1969:43). If the strategic forces and/or the command channels which carry the threat of retaliation are vulnerable to sudden destruction, the deterrent threat can be removed or sharply reduced by a pre-emptive attack aimed at those forces (Steinbruner 1978:413).

Such a situation is called *strategic instability* (Steinbruner 1978:411ff.; von Baudissin/Lutz 1981:15). According to a generally accepted definition, strategic stability can be said to exist if the overall relation of forces leads potential opponents to conclude that any attempt to settle their conflict by military means constitutes a clearly calculable unacceptable risk. The United States concept of strategic stability is defined as "a condition in which incentives inherent in the arms

5

balance to initiate the use of strategic nuclear forces (...) are weak or absent''. An official source (FY 1982 ACIS: 22) defines strategic stability as "the maintenance as far as possible of conditions such that neither the US nor the USSR would feel compelled to use its nuclear forces". Salomon (1977: 255) offers still another definition of the United States concept of strategic stability:

> "In the United States stability was regarded as the existence of invulnerable strategic forces such that neither the United States nor the Soviet Union could destroy the other's ability to retaliate with a devastating blow, if attacked with nuclear weapons".

Thus, strategic stability is closely connected with the survivability of forces designated for retaliation (Steinbruner 1978: 413).

Related to this is the concept of Mutual Assured Destruction (MAD) which holds as minimum requirements that:

> "(a) neither country's strategic nuclear deterrent force should be vulnerable to a first strike by the other, and (b) neither country should so protect its population and industry as to deny the other the certainty of wreaking a high absolute level of destruction; and, moreover, that strategic systems be configured such that, in a crisis situation, neither country has any incentive whatsoever to strike first'' (Ball 1977: 24).

In the United States, authorities and strategic thinkers seem to be very much and conspicuously preoccupied with the idea of strategic stability. The introduction of new elements, for example the MX missile, is to a large extent discussed in terms of the impact it would have on strategic stability (see, for example, FY 1982 ACIS: VII). Schilling (1981: 68) notes that the maintenance of strategic balance providing strategic stability has been one of the United States' most important strategic objectives.

The relevance of the notion of strategic stability has not been affected in any way whatsoever by the changes and shifts in emphasis that have taken place in the basic conceptions of United States strategic doctrine. For instance, the United States has partly abandoned former strategic concepts based on mutual deterrence and has introduced some flexibility in strategic planning, first with changes announced by Secretary of Defense Schlesinger in 1974, later by the public declarations regarding the so-called "countervailing strategy". Secretary of Defense Brown emphasized the importance of the concept of stability when presenting the countervailing strategy (DoD Annual Report, FY 1982: 44—45) and mentioned stability as a factor contributing to deterrence. The United States, according to Brown, is committed to strengthening stability by increasing the survivability of the strategic forces and of the C³ (Command, Communications, Control) systems. Secretary Brown has described strategic stability as resting on four pillars: survivability, assured destruction, flexibility, and essential equivalence (Guertner 1979: 29), abbreviated SAFE. Survivability of the forces and the related C³ systems does not require further elaboration. Assured destruction refers to the ability of United States nuclear weapons to retaliate, in order to deter. Flexibility should procure deterrence across the spectrum of possible provocations (Ermarth 1978: 148). Essential equivalence is intended to preclude political exploitation of perceived or real weaknesses. After having enjoyed superiority for a long time, "essential equivalence" was the new United States assessment of the strategic balance. It is an "essential" equivalence because the balance is composed of different elements, and the balance between the major nuclear Powers is not the same in all the components.

The United States position with regard to strategic stability is aptly and authoritatively summarized in Secretary of Defense Weinberger's Annual Report to the Congress:

> "The United States will maintain a strategic nuclear force posture such that, in a crisis, the Soviets will have no incentive to initiate a nuclear attack on the United States or our allies. U.S. forces will be capable under all conditions of war initiation to survive a Soviet first strike and retaliate in a way that permits the United States to achieve its objectives. Nuclear weapons systems will not be funded merely to make our forces mirror Soviet forces according to some superficial tally of missiles or aircraft deployed in peacetime (...) Instead, our goal will be to gain and maintain a nuclear deterrent force which provides an adequate margin of safety with emphasis on enduring survivability". (DoD Annual Report, FY 1983: I—17).

While the concept of strategic stability is considered absolutely central by United States authors concerned about the prevention of unintentional nuclear war, the importance of this concept in Soviet strategic thinking seems less evident at first glance. Some Western observers (e.g. Ermarth 1978:145) actually doubt whether it means anything in a Soviet perspective. Yet there are official Soviet statements that tend to disprove this assertion. According to the Soviet author Trofimenko (1981: 39),

> "the Soviet Union, which is content with the state of strategic parity and does not strive for superiority, has agreed to conclude SALT II, because Moscow sees it as an opportunity to really stabilize the strategic balance, even if it is based on the MAD principle, for want of something better".

The Soviet Union, however, does not hold that a situation based on the balance of fear is one of genuine stability.

> "We hold that it is necessary to move away from such a macabre balance as soon as possible to a more stable situation through arms cuts" (Trofimenko 1981: 35).

Soviet acceptance of the United States doctrine of mutual assured destruction was to some degree assumed after conclusion of SALT I, particularly after the signing of the ABM agreement.

7

It seems that the concern for strategic stability is shared by both major Powers similarly. Although Soviet authors do not consider a first strike feasible, they draw attention to "the increasing risk of a dramatic fatal mistake under conditions of acute international crisis" (Arbatov 1979: 151). Arbatov explicitly talks about "the danger of nuclear war even though no Government may want such a war or plan deliberately to unleash one". The issue of strategic stability can be justly said to be a matter of common concern.

The two major Powers explicitly acknowledged the importance of this concept in the Joint Statement of Principles and Basic Guidelines for Subsequent Negotiations on the Limitation of Strategic Arms, signed on 18 June 1979, in the context of the SALT II negotiations. In this Statement, the two signatories reaffirmed that "the strengthening of *strategic stability* meets the interests of the Parties and the interests of international security". They agreed to

> "continue for the purposes of reducing and averting the risk of outbreak of nuclear war, to seek measures to strengthen *strategic stability* by, among other things, limitations on strategic offensive arms most *destabilizing* to the strategic balance and by measures to reduce and to avert the risk of surprise attack".

They also expressed their intent to "consider other steps to ensure and enhance *strategic stability*" (emphasis ours).

It should also be noted that both major Powers, in their history, have been traumatized by the experience of surprise attacks. What the German offensive of June 1941 means to the Soviet Union, Pearl Harbor means to the United States. For the generation of Soviet and United States leaders currently in office these two cases of surprise attack have had a decisive influence in shaping their conception of security and stability.

Crises as Catalytic Causes

As has already been pointed out, the risk of unintentional nuclear war greatly increases as a function of the intensity and frequency of *catalytic causes* that may *trigger* the potential instability inherent in a strategic situation. Generally speaking, these catalytic causes can be summed up under the general concept of *crisis behaviour*. There is reason to fear that in times of mounting political crisis, vulnerable weapons systems with a first-strike capability might provoke their own first use, to avoid the danger of being wiped out (Senghaas 1981: 322). In addition, the degree of tension involved in all crisis situations tends to generate a variety of suboptimal adaptation and reaction processes which involve considerable risks of misinterpretation, misunderstanding and miscalculation and also risks of organizational failure sufficient to overthrow the potentially instable strategic system.

The more refined basic model thus looks as follows:

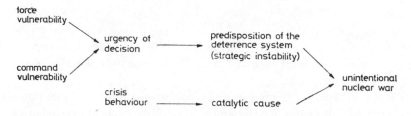

So far this model has little explanatory power. Being hardly more than a crude framework, it cannot offer any indications about the nature and the imminence of the risks of unintentional nuclear war existing in the real politico-strategic situation at a given moment. Nevertheless it is useful inasmuch as it can now serve as an organizing tool for asking and answering more relevant questions.

These questions may be grouped into two major clusters, the first pertaining to factors aggravating the risks, the second pertaining to factors dampening the risks. In each cluster, a further distinction may be made with regard to the level of analysis by looking for aggravating/dampening factors on the level of (i) the individual decision-makers subject to stress in an acute crisis situation, (ii) the level of the organizational decision-making structure and (iii) the level of the international strategic system. Using this framework as a heuristic instrument offers a possibility to obtain a comprehensive and exhaustive survey of elements conducive or detrimental to the prevention of unintentional nuclear war:

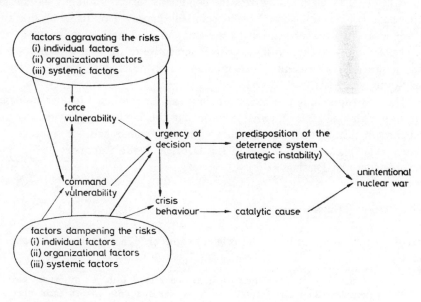

D. The Logic of Crisis Stability

As the worries about strategic stability are closely linked with the occurrence of international tension and crises, some authors prefer to replace the term "strategic stability" by *crisis stability* (Afheldt 1978: 273; Garwin 1979: 94) which is obviously quite a pertinent concept.

Crisis stability is a situation in which neither side forgoes crucial options and waits instead of delivering a pre-emptive strike. Under conditions of crisis instability, on the other hand, there are strong incentives to strike first if the occurrence of war is perceived as real possibility, i.e., in a situation of international crisis. Crisis stability allows each side to wait without incurring great disadvantage in case the other side attacks. Crisis instability is conducive to pre-emption thereby abruptly eliminating time which could be used to defuse the crisis by communications and moves of restraint.

A policy aimed at securing crisis stability is one of preventing the outbreak of war triggered not by real intent, i.e., not by a conscious and deliberate decision, but rather by the desire to minimize the losses deemed intolerable. More specifically, strategies with heavy emphasis on retaliation, based on deterrence rather than on delivering a debilitating first blow to the adversary forces, seem to be an element conducive to crisis stability. A key ingredient is the quality, i.e., the survivability due to hardening, dispersal, and concealment, of the nuclear weapons and of the related control and command system.

Afheldt (1978: 273) summarizes the conditions for crisis stability as "the position where neither side should be substantially improved by its being first to go to war in a crisis (no prevention or pre-emption premium)". On the other hand, the urge for timely action during a crisis is indicative of the loss of crisis stability and the pressure to strike first is tantamount to giving military considerations primacy over policy (Afheldt 1979).

The precarious nature of crisis stability can be elucidated further by describing it in terms of games theory. In particular two kinds of games deserve to be examined in this context: the so-called "Chicken" game and the so-called "Prisoner's Dilemma" game (Brams 1975; Deutsch 1968; Rapoport 1974; Smoke 1979; Snyder and Diesing 1977).

The "Chicken" Game

According to Kahn (1965: 10) the original game of 'Chicken' can be described as follows:

> "'Chicken' is played by two drivers on a road with a white line down the middle. Both cars straddle the white line and drive toward each other at top

speed. The first driver to lose his nerve and swerve into his own lane is 'chicken' — an object of contempt and scorn — and he loses the game. The game is played among teenagers for prestige, for girls, for leadership of a gang..."

However, this analogy has to be changed slightly (Kahn 1965: 12) in order to fit the strategic situation:

"'Chicken' would be a better analogy to escalation if it were played with two cars starting at an unknown distance apart, travelling toward each other at unknown speeds, and on roads with several forks so that the opposing sides are not certain that they are even on the same road. Both drivers should be giving and receiving threats and promises while they approach each other, and tearful mothers and stern fathers should be lining the sides of the roads urging, respectively, caution and manliness".

In its second version the game is complicated by several facts and uncertainties. Communication is introduced, and there are domestic groups pressing the decision-makers to exercise restraint or urging them to be unyielding. And then, there is at least the possibility that the escalation may not lead to disaster.

By contrast to the simple original version of the "Chicken" game, and as indicated by this second version, even "Chicken" game situations are not immune from a catastrophic course of action. A kind of unintended disaster may still happen.

Although some reservations regarding the stability of a "Chicken" situation may be legitimate, it is still basically valid. The emergence of nuclear weapons had the effect of widening the gap between the interests at stake in conflict and the possible cost of war (Snyder and Diesing 1977: 450—452). The constraints of war-avoidance have thus been strengthened. As has been very aptly observed by Holsti, "perhaps nuclear capabilities, and the recognition in both Washington and Moscow that their use would entail destruction without parallel in history, served as a constraint against undue provocation of the adversary" (Holsti 1972: 193). Generally speaking, Chicken game-like situations tend to stabilize themselves, and there is a good chance that the process of escalation taking place in such a confrontation will come to a halt.

The Prisoner's Dilemma Game

On the other hand, Prisoner's Dilemma situations bear very high risks of escalation once a confrontation starts. The respective matrices according to the usual notation of game theory situations are:
(The numbers indicate the respective pay-offs. 4 is the most preferred pay-off, 1 is the least preferred pay-off.)

11

The Chicken Game

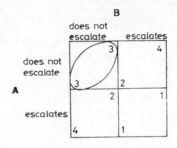

The Prisoner's Dilemma Game

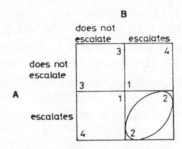

The decisive difference between Chicken confrontation and Prisoner's Dilemma confrontation lies in the difference between the pay-offs in the case of mutually non-co-operative behaviour (i.e., escalation) and mutually co-operative behaviour (i.e., no escalation). If, as in the Chicken game situation, mutually non-co-operative behaviour inevitably leads to a clash amounting to mutual annihilation, the two opponents will almost certainly prefer a mutually co-operative course of action. If, on the other hand, as in any Prisoner's Dilemma situation, mutually non-co-operative behaviour does not constitute the worst outcome, and if the really worst pay-off must be expected in the case of one's own co-operative behaviour combined with the opponent's non-co-operative behaviour, a further escalation of hostilities becomes inevitable.

However, a constructive approach to the analysis of systems stability in the context of the problem of nuclear confrontations is offered by game theory research done on the factors which, notwithstanding the inherent impossibility of solving the Prisoner's Dilemma, tend to offer at least some way out of the dilemma. The openness of the time horizon has been identified as the most crucial factor in this context. If the time horizon is open, or in other words, if the game is not just a "one shot" game but consists of several tit-for-tat steps it is much easier to avoid an escalation and to try to use accommodative steps or at least measures aimed at stabilizing the situation and avoiding its additional heating-up. Playing the game in several sequences means offering an opportunity for reciprocity. Once the principle of reciprocity is established, there is no longer any need to escalate or to trigger a showdown by a pre-emptive attack (Bonoma 1975; Frei 1982; Howard 1971; Rapoport and Chammah 1965). That is what has been found out by the so-called "metagames theory", which offers a sound solution to the problem and points to a way out of the psychological trap established by the cruel logic of the original Prisoner's Dilemma situation.

Metagames theory also has found out that communications can be interpreted as a substitute for time. If the opponents have an opportunity to contact each other between each step of the game, they gain time. Thus, the opportunity to communicate offers an opportunity to make conditional steps: "I won't escalate any further, provided you don't escalate either", or: "My next step will constitute limited escalation and I am acting with deliberate restraint which, however, I may abandon if you do not act in a reciprocal way". In practical terms, the question has to be asked to what extent current weapons technology and current strategic doctrines allow for the utilization of time or its substitute, communication.

Nuclear Strategy and Games Theory

When interpreting the strategic situation in terms of games, the basic assumptions of contemporary mutual deterrence can be said to be still valid. They do in fact correspond to a game between two players, each rationally calculating the expected pay-off of his actions across the range of possible consequences (Steinbruner 1976). The players are assumed to be fundamentally hostile toward each other, and therefore one expects that each of them will act to minimize the damage that his opponent might do to him in the course of play. Deterrence consists in one player's threatening his opponent with such severe retaliation that the rationally calculating opponent will always choose not to attack. Mutual deterrence is said to exist when both players exercise such a threat against each other. The calculations for force planning are made very conservatively, under such rigid criteria that even an opponent "with only a very tenuous hold on rationality" will reach the desired conclusions (Steinbruner 1976: 225, 227). The structure of deterrence has to be sufficiently evident to transcend cultural differences.

There is, however, a problem: "Though it is assumed that strategic forces, in order to deter, must have a real capacity to retaliate massively, such retaliation is not at all what the rational calculator would undertake in the actual event of war" (Steinbruner 1976: 231). He would rather prefer to hold back nuclear weapons in order to deter any residual capacity of his opponent. This problem is very bothersome and has been dealt with in the context of counter-deterrence, self-deterrence and "Called Bluff" games.

This problem, however, is mitigated by the fact, that one cannot assume perfect rationality on both sides, i.e., the attacker could not be completely sure that the opponent would not retaliate even if strict rationality would point to this option. This uncertainty seems sufficient to make any nuclear attack unattractive from the rational point of view (see Steinbruner 1976: 231—232).

On the other hand, a strategic confrontation with nuclear weapons where the delivery systems are mutually vulnerable to a first strike has a marked similarity to the Prisoner's Dilemma once the outbreak of a war has become probable (Snyder and Diezing 1977: 88). If war seems unavoidable, there may be advantages for the side striking first, if possible by a surprise strike. One has of course to remember that this situation exists in its pure form only under conditions of complete vulnerability of the forces assigned for retaliation and under the assumption that striking the adversary is a net gain. This insight, however, can trigger a nuclear war if one side perceives the actions of the adversary as being in preparation for a nuclear attack. The danger lies in the conviction that war has become inevitable, and, given this fact, it is best to strike first.

However, this interpretation may be different if strategic doctrines emphasize the second strike capability and if there are weapons which survive a first strike able to perform this task. The fact that nuclear war can not only be conceived as a single exchange of devastating all-out attacks but as consisting of a number of discrete events in escalating order, complicates the situation further. While, in the situation just described, the alternatives are "strike — don't strike", the real choice may have a different shape: to escalate or to not escalate. Once an escalation has been started, the probability of a mutually undesirable outcome may be higher than in a scenario with just one decisive step from crisis to all-out nuclear war. It is important to have many rungs in the escalation ladder, or, to put it another way, to be able to play many games one after the other, because there are in such a case more possibilities to stop the exchange at a level with less unfavourable consequences than in a case where after a few decisions the ultimate intensity of warfare has been reached. An example of an escalation ladder has been suggested by Kahn (1965: 39).

Another possibility of changing the inherently dangerous situation described in terms of the Prisoner's Dilemma is to change the outcomes of the alternatives: increase the incentives for co-operative behaviour and/or decrease the gains of non-co-operative behaviour or increase each side's expectation that the other will co-operate (Jervis 1978: 171). The possession of relatively invulnerable nuclear weapons facilitates co-operative behaviour because the effects of non-co-operative behaviour by the other player are not as grave as under conditions of vulnerable weapons. Once more, the stabilizing effect of an assured second-strike capability is evident.

The expectation of co-operation also depends on the possibility of communicating during a crisis. While it may be conceivable that a tacit understanding would suffice, a clearly communicated signal of restraint might be preferable.

Another refinement regarding the logic of a strategic relationship which is genuinely identical with a Prisoner's Dilemma situation has been suggested by Jervis (1978: 211—214) by distinguishing the offence from the defence. A highly unstable situation exists when the offence has the advantage and the offensive weapons are not distinguishable from the defensive ones. The offence has a certain advantage if the weapons are vulnerable to a surprise attack. For instance, a situation in which both sides relied on MIRVed Intercontinental Ballistic Missiles (ICBMs) of a high degree of accuracy would generate great dangers because of the high premium on the first strike. The defence would have the advantage, if there were no MIRVed missiles. The effect of MIRVing is that the number of warheads may be increased and even multiplied without a concomitant increase in the number of aim points. In such a case, several warheads may be targeted at the same aim point, for example an ICBM, thus producing a higher kill probability. Assuming the absence of MIRVs, it would take more than one attacking missile to destroy one of the adversary's. Because each warhead has a kill probability of less than 100 per cent (varying with accuracy, yield and size and hardness of the target), more than one warhead would have to be assigned to each target. If both sides had an equal number of single-warhead missiles, the attacking side could destroy the missiles of the adversary (perhaps 900 out of 1,000) by launching the entire nuclear force. However, the situation is entirely different with MIRVed ICBMs. In this case, a portion of the attacker's missiles may be sufficient to destroy a very high percentage of the targets. From this the conclusion must be drawn that the introduction of MIRVed missiles has added instability to the nuclear balance, as it has increased the expected gains of the attacking side, thus enhancing the validity of the Prisoner's Dilemma paradigm.

To sum up, the doctrines of nuclear warfare, based on the concept of guaranteed second-strike capability and mutual assured destruction (MAD), generally tended to transform nuclear confrontations into Chicken game situations, characterized by a high degree of stability. For both opponents, the best outcome is where both wait and do not attack (Russett and Starr 1981: 369), even in the uneasy and tense situation of escalating crisis confrontation. On the other hand, any development of strategic doctrines and strategic capabilities shifting the logic of the situation toward a Prisoner's Dilemma-style confrontation severely jeopardizes the overall stability of the system. The question therefore is: to what extent do the current strategic doctrines and weapons systems transform Chicken situations into Prisoner's Dilemma situations?

Before trying to answer these questions (in chapters II and III) a word of caution is necessary regarding the kind of logic which is meant when one talks about the logic of crisis stability in terms of game theory. In particular, one has to ask to what extent the assumption of rationality underlying the whole concept of strategic interaction as represented by game theory really holds true. There are at least five reasons to doubt its validity, as pointed out by Russett and Starr (1981: 373—376). First, one must not forget that, more often than not, decision-makers do not make a decision on its own intrinsic merits but, rather, tend to consider the new situation in terms of prior experience; the assessment of prior experience may be selective or otherwise one-sided. Secondly, governments, cabinets, politburos and the like do not act as single "gamblers"; the assumption of a unitary actor making a cool and rational assessment of a given situation is highly improbable; "group-think" and internal rivalry may be equally important factors determining the outcome of a decision-making process in which decision-makers may be willing to settle for one of the first acceptable solutions, instead of continuing to search for a still more preferable alternative (satisficing instead of optimizing). Thirdly, the options available may be numerous, but the essential factor is the perception of the situation, which does not exist objectively but is seen through many different eyes; also, the data available may be poor and inconclusive. Fourthly, the assumption of symmetry in values very often simply does not hold true. In addition, decision-makers are faced with the necessity of comparing different outcomes, ordering their preferences and calculating estimates of gain and loss. Trade-offs between conflicting values may be necessary (Stein 1978: 319—322). Finally, one has to keep in mind that decisions about peace and war, especially nuclear war, can hardly be considered as taking place under "normal" conditions. The individuals engaged in such fateful decisions will be subject to intensive stress; as will be shown in chapter V, stress tends to generate a number of consequences that preclude or impinge on a rational decision-making.

E. Programming Unintentional Nuclear War: Launch-on-Warning (LOW) and Predelegation Policies

The nature of strategic or crisis instability can be further illustrated by two typical conclusions which might hypothetically be drawn from a strategic situation perceived to be inherently unstable. The first is the adoption of launch-on-warning (LOW) and related procedures; the second is the predelegation of authority in the release of nuclear weapons. Both policies aim at adapting to the potential reality of crisis instability by programming practical procedures to implement decisions regarding the use of nuclear weapons.

It must be made plain, however, that so far no nuclear Power has engaged in a LOW or predelegation policy. Yet the relevant considerations are constantly being elaborated, and there can be no doubt that once crisis instability is perceived, these policies will be given high priority. They would have grave consequences, greatly enhance the risk of unintentional nuclear war, and inevitably contribute to a further deterioration in crisis stability. The description presented in this subsection may increase awareness of the pitfalls lurking in the type of logic employed in the context of strategic considerations and scenario building.

Both policies constitute a response to the growing urgency generated by the shrinking of the time available between warning and impact of offensive missiles. This time has been rapidly dwindling in recent years as a result of technical innovation. It is said to be about 20—30 minutes for land-based ICBMs, 15 minutes for SLBMs, but between 3 and 8 minutes only for Intermediate Range Ballistic Missiles (IRBMs) such as SS-20 and Pershing-II. The requirements for decision timelines are described by the United States Office of Technology Assessment (1981 a: 163) as follows: "Depending on the circumstance, the amount of time available for deciding on a response to Soviet attack could range from an upper limit of 20 minutes to no time at all. Meeting this timeline would probably require at least some provisional advance planning by the President and other NCA".

Launch-on-Warning

For these reasons, one might be tempted to replace the launch-on-impact principle (LOI) by the LOW principle in order to save time and to protect retaliation forces by firing at the earliest possible moment. This, in turn, would render any misunderstanding or false alarm highly dangerous. It also provides an incentive for the original attacker to launch his second wave of weapons before they are destroyed *(Newsweek,* 5 October 1981) according to the logic of "use them or lose them" (Garwin 1980: 118 f.).

LOW is considered a possible launch mode mainly for land-based ICBMs as the vulnerability of the SLBMs is assumed to be much lower and the long-range bombers are able to scramble at short notice of an impending attack and put a sufficient distance between themselves and the bases, preventing heavy damage. The bombers are a recallable weapons delivery system, whereas the ICBMs or SLBM lack this important characteristic. LOW becomes a real possibility only in cases of vulnerability of weapon-systems which cannot be launched and recalled. There are several similar but distinguishable concepts to be mentioned in the context of LOW:

> *Launch on warning* (LOW) is defined by the United States Air Force (definitions and a very large part of the information given in this subsection are derived from Garwin 1980) as "a launch in response to sensor indication of an attack on the continental United States".

Launch under attack (LUA) is "a launch after high-confidence determination that [the continental United States] is under massive attack".

Launch on (or after) *impact* (LOI), means "a launch after nuclear explosions on or above ICBM fields".

Launch on attack assessment (LAA): "a launch after determination of the intent and extent of the attack, including the degree of threat to ICBM silos".

Launch through attack (LTA) is adopted if the attacking missiles are launched with a timing appropriate for sequential hitting of the targets. Under such circumstances, the attacked power might decide to ride out the first wave of incoming ICBMs in order to assess the intent and extent of the attack, and then launch a counterstrike through the follow-on salvos of the attacker (Gray 1977: 14—15).

Each of these procedures has its advantages and shortcomings. For example the pin-down effects of nuclear explosions on or near an ICBM field must be considered when speaking about LOI or LTA. While LOW has great advantages in respect of assured second-strike capability, the danger of accidents by adopting LOW is rather sobering. LUA is described by Garwin (1980) as a possible means of redressing the vulnerability of the aging Minutemen, the main component of American ICBMs. The functioning of LOW depends on specific characteristics of both the hardware and procedures. It requires a net of sensors capable of identifying the launch of an attack by very few or a great number of hostile ICBMs. It goes without saying that the reliability must be secured beyond any doubt. The sensors must be able to discriminate between real launches and other sources emitting fire and heat. They have to communicate the findings very rapidly to the NCA empowered to make decisions about peace and war. The decision-makers need to have a certain amount of time to assess the imminent attack. Furthermore, they require proper equipment and procedures to communicate the authorization to launch the ICBMs assigned for LUA. The order to launch has to reach the ICBM sites in time to allow the missiles to fly out before impact of the attacking missiles and without suffering damage from the blast, heat or electromagnetic pulse (EMP) caused by nuclear explosions.

LOI would reduce a source of error inasmuch as the sensing of the launches would not be absolutely necessary. Instead ground-sensors at the ICBM sites would in the last instance provide information as to whether an attack has really occurred. These sensors have to survive and still work in the environment of exploding nuclear warheads, which requires extreme reliability and robustness. (Of course sensors to detect the launch would be useful in giving about 20 minutes' warning time to the decision-makers, but under LOI they would wait for the definitive confirmation of the attack, i.e., the impact on the ICBMs fields.) Under present circumstances the ability to launch the ICBM after impact of attacking ICBMs may be questioned due to the vulnerability of vital systems within the ICBMs.

The deterrence value of a LOW posture is high because of the certainty that even a surprise attack would meet with a response in kind. Garwin (1980) argues that the ICBM assigned for a launch-under-attack mode should be targeted against highly valued installations or assets (countervalue), so as to have an optimal deterrence value. Targeting the missiles against ICBMs would not make very much sense, for it would probably trigger a second wave launched in a LOW mode by the adversary; also the targeted silos might be empty, or their hardening would limit the effect.

Garwin does not attribute a higher danger of unauthorized or accidental launch to a LUA posture (Garwin 1980: 124). One must recall that so far neither the United States nor the USSR have adopted the LOW posture, but this is a field where even the slightest doubts weigh very heavily. Garwin argues that even after a hypothetical adoption of LOW procedures, one might envisage making the system inoperable during periods of high confidence by removing certain central components. But the more advanced launch modes proposed by Garwin would include only minimum human participation, as most parts of the system would work automatically.

There is a second risk for a Power adopting LOW tactics. The adversary might decide to trigger a launch by launching a small fraction of his ICBMs and then declare it an accident once the Power with the LOW posture had fired off its missiles, prompting it to disarm the warheads in flight. Of course this scenario is only thinkable if the ICBMs assigned to LOW were launched unarmed and armed in flight and if the adversary had reliable knowledge of this fact. Garwin (1980: 125) suggests limiting a LOW to a maximum of about 50 ICBMs to be launched as a response to an attack; an erroneous launch would in this case not reduce the ICBM force significantly (about 5 per cent).

As mentioned above, there are several conceivable solutions to the problem of a launch followed by the sudden revelation that there is no real attack. While the missiles currently in the arsenal of the major Powers are assumed to be irrevocably armed once launched, Garwin suggests developing devices whereby it would be possible to launch a missile unarmed but with the option of arming it in flight (or launching it armed subject to disarming in flight). While the danger of accidents would be minimized by selecting the first option (arming in flight, positive command of arming required), the danger of destruction of the necessary transmitters is to be considered, however, it seems feasible to multiply the transmitters and protect them sufficiently to assure the transmission of the "arm" command.

The second version (launch armed, disarming in flight) seems to be rather more accident-prone while still preferable to adopting a LOW posture with Minutemen or other ICBMs launched armed without any possibility of disarming them in flight. In order to avoid disastrous unintended consequences, the launch would take place only after assessment of a massive attack, not just one or two incoming missiles. In the event of the adoption of LOW or LUA, the role of the sensors (satellites in geostationary position) becomes crucial. An attack on such a satellite could well be treated as the equivalent of an all-out attack. This situation could be improved by positioning several satellites covering the same area or placing "dormant" satellites in the space. Sensors sometimes have difficulties in distinguishing a technical malfunction from an attack by advanced anti-satellite (ASAT) capabilities. Garwin acknowledges (1980: 136) that a LOW mode might have undesirable consequences in case of an accident leading to a false alarm. However, he argues that the adoption of LUA would have the advantage of turning Soviet (if written by a United States author) military programmes away from the capability of destroying the land-based missile force. Gray (1977: 14) also sees a limited role for LOW: "As an operational firing tactic, it would be a monumental folly, but as a veiled suggestion of the 'we refuse to rule it out' variety it should not be despised". Garwin (1980: 139) suggests limiting human involvement in the LUA procedure essentially to the top decision-makers assessing the attack. The decision to launch should be largely automatic, the role of the National Command Authority being limited "to an endorsement of the assessment that a massive raid is indeed in process".

As indicated above, the adoption of a LOW or LUA posture may be especially tempting when warning time is extremely short. The deployment of missiles capable of hitting hard targets with a high kill probability after a flight time of only 5 to 10 minutes in this respect entails some risks. The considerations of LOW and LUA are generally influenced by the perceived vulnerablility of the strategic weapons delivery systems. One should not forget, however, that the threat is mainly directed at the ICBMs; the SLBMs and the bomber force are still assumed to be safer. Hence the temptation to introduce LOW policies is substantially countered. It should also be noted that there are some intrinsic doubts regarding the feasibility of LOW. Betts (1981b: 91) is not sure whether LOW would work at all: "Too many things would have to happen within twenty-five minutes or less": tactical warning would have to be processed, the President would have to be informed, believe it and authorize the response, the authorization would have to be transmitted to the launch control centres and confirmed. The missile crews would have to believe it and (if the electronic devices had been unlocked in time) turn their keys. In the environment of ultimate panic, the smooth functioning cannot be taken for granted. False alarms of which there have been quite a few (see United States Department of Defense Annual Report FY 1972: 120—121) are apt to increase doubts as to whether the launch orders are to be executed promptly.

Nevertheless, the mere thought of introducing such accident-prone launch modes as LOW and the possibility of false alarms during crises is nightmarish (Feld 1980; Dumas 1978: 127; Carter 1975: 29). However, the assumption that the other side has adopted LOW may lead to increased caution in dealing with counter-force capabilities and strategies. Douglass and Hoeber (1979: 77) cite Soviet authors as saying that a United States LOW capability is a major concern.

LOW has one important characteristic in common with the concept of mutual assured destruction of which it can be an integral part in case of ICBM vulnerability. It may increase deterrence by reducing the incentives for a first strike, but it is not an operational guideline once deterrence has failed; if LOW is really to be executed, it has already failed to serve its purpose.

Generally speaking, the adoption of LOW tactics due to a high vulnerability of land-based ICBMs would have a detrimental effect on crisis stability. The presence of SLBMs mitigates the danger of being caught by surprise, but there are targets which only ICBMs are capable of hitting (high time-urgency and high-accuracy requirement; the bombers need several hours to reach the targets, while SLBMs lack currently the accuracy). Even with an unarmed launch, the danger of accidents seems much greater than in the case of riding out an attack and deciding afterwards on the appropriate response.

Predelegation

As in the case of the possible adoption of a LOW policy, the principle of predelegation, too, is connected with the exigencies of vulnerability and urgency. It is generally assumed that the release of nuclear weapons has to be authorized by the highest command authorities in each country. Little is known about the arrangements made by the countries whose forces are equipped with nuclear weapons. Available information is practically limited to the United States.

In the United States, only the President is authorized to release nuclear weapons. As Miller (1979: 56) explains, he cannot do this without the Secretary of Defense and the Chairman of the Joint Chiefs of Staff (CJCS) "being totally involved in the decision". If the Secretary of Defense is not available, a chain of command is provided. There are rumours that the Commander of the North American Air Defense Command (NORAD) originally used to hold delegated authority in order to assure the appropriate military response to an unexpected attack. Such an authorization, however, seems to be constrained, and Miller (1979: 56) asserts that it is highly doubtful that the NORAD commander still retains such delegated authority.

On the other hand, Fried (1981: 25) assumes the *power* (as opposed to the authority) to use nuclear weapons to have been delegated in a number of ways. More especially he expects the "military commanders in various parts of the world, including commanders of submarines" to have the power to decide on the use of nuclear weapons, as a result of geographically widespread responsibilities assumed by the major nuclear Powers. It is, however, not fully clear whether the power to use nuclear weapons can be equated with the authority to use nuclear weapons.

In connection with the delegation of authority and ability to use nuclear weapons without authority, many critics focus on the SLBMs carrying submarines. The arrangements made for certain contingencies, say, the attack by a hostile submarine on an SSBN, are not known, yet they might entail a delegation of authority. As far as the land-based components of the strategic triad are concerned, the information available from United States sources suggests that they are equipped with electronic locks, permissive action links systems (PALs), and thus cannot be used without authorization by the President. By contrast, the difficulties of transmitting signals to SSBNs at great depths and distances impede the use of such locks, requiring predelegation; progress in communications technology could alter the situation.

As a consequence of the hypothetical adoption of LOW or similar procedures, due to perceived vulnerability and the urge to remove the missiles from their silos before they are destroyed, predelegation may become necessary. As Kissinger (1979: 266) pointed out, "launching strategic forces on warning can be accomplished only by delegating the authority to the proverbially 'insane Colonel' about whom so many movies have been made". Nevertheless, such predelegation cannot be excluded completely. According to Brown (1979: 126) the Soviets "would have to consider the possibility of our having launched the Minuteman force before their ICBMs arrived, even though we have not made 'launch under attack' a matter of policy". Considering these statements and the number of steps required from the reception of the warning of an attack to the firing of ICBMs, LOW seems to entail a sort of predelegation; this could be altered by adoption of largely automatic procedures, whereby human involvement would essentially be reduced to a presidential endorsement of the assessment reached by the warning systems (cf. Garwin 1980).

The predelegation of authority to release nuclear weapons is of course crucial, because nuclear weapons are considered completely different from conventional armament. Even by reducing the yield and increasing the accuracy (the "conventionalization") of tactical nuclear weapons, this threshold would probably still hold. For this reason, Frye (1980: 100) advocates the replacement of small-yield battlefield weapons (especially anti-tank weapons) by modern conventional weapons (PGM), because conventional weapons can be released for use at the discretion of the commander on the scene and can be fired at the first sight of the enemy force, under standing orders which entail no delays for consultation with political authorities.

The dilemmas that are posed by the characteristics of LOW and predelegation policies discussed in the preceding paragraphs clearly demonstrate how sensitive the international strategic system is with regard to any tendencies which might contribute to its destabilization. Once crisis stability has begun to crumble, additional steps would be taken which would inexorably lead to its precipitated and complete breakdown.

II. THE ARMS RACE AND STRATEGIC STABILITY

A. Arms Race Instability Versus Crisis Stability

Destabilizing Consequences of the Qualitative Arms Race

Many experts are alarmed by the tendency of the current arms race to undermine the credibility of nuclear deterrence (e.g. Barnaby 1980: 37f.) and thus strategic or crisis stability. Once the deployment of very accurate missiles and effective anti-submarine warfare enables one side to destroy so much of the opponent's retaliatory force, it would no longer be able to deter an attack effectively. Worse, it is sufficient for one side merely to perceive that the other side has the capability of destroying its retaliatory forces. Long-term advances in military technology may create incentives to strike first — out of fear that the other side might do it. Then the original situation existing in the 1950s would be restored, ironically at immense costs and with much more deadly precision jeopardizing and denying the capability to retaliate.

Such a hypothesis, however, must be said to be highly improbable, at least for the foreseeable future. Although it cannot be denied that in the 1980s the vulnerability of land-based ICBMs and the bomber force may theoretically be growing, neither major Power is likely to be able to execute a totally disarming first strike (Gray 1981b: 64).

Still, perceptions of particular asymmetries in strategic capability could have a very negative impact on both pre-war and intra-war deterrence. According to Gray (1981b: 64f.) there is also good cause for alarm about the survivability of submarines and manned bombers. Furthermore, one cannot deny that the premises upon which the present strategic stability is based are no longer assured (Bertram 1981a: 100). Hence, in a very general way one cannot but make the point that the current arms race entails the danger that the vulnerability of the strategic systems deployed by the two major Powers is periodically jeopardized by technological

23

improvements. In this respect, the two sides are thinking with precision along the same lines of strategy. As was pointed out by the Soviet specialist Arbatov (1981: 166), the United States strategic concepts, officially postulating the need to "counter" the alleged "threat of a Soviet counter-force strike" mean, in fact, developing exactly such a threat by the United States itself. "The forces created by the Pentagon supposedly for 'retaliation' can be used for a preemptive missile attack as well", Arbatov asserts. Statements like this indicate that even if no pre-emptive strike whatsoever is intended, the technological innovations of each side may lead the other side to *infer* that the opponent is actually planning to attain a first-strike capacity.

Steinbruner (1978: 414) has very aptly summarized the parameters affecting strategic stability. The most notable parameters are the number of strategic launchers, the number of independently targetable warheads they carry, the yield of the warheads, the accuracy of the delivery systems, the certainty with which the location of targets can be determined, and the resistance of these targets to damage from the effects of nuclear explosions. According to Steinbruner, from these parameters probabilities of damage inflicted by each strategic force on the other are calculated and the residual retaliatory capabilities — i.e., the damage to be expected from the opponent's maximum pre-emptive attack — are then estimated. Thus far these calculations have yielded a positive result, i.e., strategic stability still seems to be guaranteed.

Yet, as has been said, it is constantly being challenged. What particular new products of technology tend to affect the vulnerability of deterrent forces? According to a survey presented by Bertram (1981a: 100—104) the following general developments may be relevant in this context:

— Extraordinary accuracy due to greatly enhanced precision-guidance capacities: this provides the missiles with a true counterforce capability.
— Changes in the technology of explosives and warheads: increase of destructive potential, choice yield and detonation bombs, enhanced radiation bombs: these developments increase the practical applicability of nuclear weapons by a range of additional options.
— Improvements of C^3 technologies, data-processing, and re-targeting increase the ability to launch nuclear strikes of a very limited and selective nature, including also controlled sequential exchanges.
— Development of anti-satellites (ASAT) capable of interfering with verification and reconnaissance, early warning and C^3.
— Potential breakthroughs in anti-submarine warfare (ASW), jeopardizing the relative invulnerability of the sea-based deterrent.

— Possibility to develop a viable ballistic missile defense (BMD), based on the charged-particle ("directed energy") beams principle, undermining the fundamental "deterrence through mutual vulnerability" concept.

In addition and as has specially been highlighted by Soviet authors, the ability to launch missiles with a flight time of just a few minutes (due either to close stationing of the launchers or to the increased speed) will deny the potential adversary any chance of making a simultaneous retaliatory strike. Hence a pre-emptive strike is made considerably more tempting. According to the Soviet view, this prospect is a matter of concern with regard to new theatre nuclear weapons and cruise missiles (Soviet Committee for European Security and Co-operation 1981: 24). A similar concern is also expressed with regard to improved guidance systems based on NAVSTAR, i.e. the United States Navigation Satellite Timing and Ranging System. Soviet sources also see some destabilizing tendencies in the possible re-introduction of some BMD elements; they find these tendencies particularly disturbing because they feel that in this field the United States has a clear lead in R&D. Similar concerns were expressed regarding United States plans to deploy the MX system which, according to a Soviet specialist, has "the task of destroying the nuclear weapons systems of the hypothetical enemy in a manner depriving him of a chance to respond with a retaliatory blow" (Sergeyev 1981: 35).

Thus, the concern about the destabilizing consequences of the qualitative arms race can be said to be mutually shared by both major Powers. This has been amply reflected in the United States publication *Soviet Military Power* (1981) and its Soviet companion publication *Whence the Threat to Peace* (1982). The United States publication points to Soviet capabilities of seizing the initiative through a pre-emptive attack, reducing the impact of a retaliatory strike (*ibid.*: 54). According to United States assumptions, the mission of the Soviet strategic rocket force is to destroy an enemy's means of nuclear attack, military-industrial production facilities, civil and military command and control capabilities and logistics and transport facilities.

On the other hand, the Soviet publication *Whence the Threat to Peace* (1982) rejects the allegations that the Soviet Union counts on winning a nuclear war by means of a pre-emptive strike (*ibid.*: 11), while accusing the United States of arming for delivery of a pre-emptive nuclear strike. Pre-emptive functions are ascribed to the United States ICBMs (*ibid.*: 17), particularly to the projected MX, which is said to be intended "for hardened targets, that is, for delivering a 'nuclear knockout' " (*ibid.*: 30). In the Soviet publication, the new Trident III missile is also described as a "first-strike weapon" (*ibid.*: 34), and the plans for the new strategic bomber "Stealth", according to the Soviet publication, also constitute a proof of first-strike strategies (*ibid.*: 34). In the same context, concern is expressed about United States efforts to develop "active means for hitting space objects" (*ibid.*:36) and "plans to use the manned Shuttle spaceship as a space attack system" (*ibid.*:36). The Soviet publication concludes: "The agreed schedule of the Pentagon plans for building up strategic offensive armaments and deploying anti-missile and space defense systems is timed to complete the development of a so-called first-strike potential in the 1980s" (*ibid.*: 36).

The inescapable conclusion is that the plague of strategic or crisis instability to a large extent results from the plague of arms race instability. This is the idea behind two definitions suggested by Barnaby (1978: 215). He holds crisis stability to exist if "in a military crisis, one side cannot add much to its chances of survival by striking first and so there is no strong inducement to do so". Arms-race stability, on the other hand, as defined by Barnaby, exists if "there does not appear to be any way for one side to achieve an overwhelming advantage over the other side by quickly acquiring any feasible quantity of some weapon, and so again there exists no really strong inducement to do so". In fact, the absence of arms-race stability constantly and continuously gives new momentum to the challenges to crisis stability. Experts in East and West agree that it is mainly modern scientific and technological developments which have virtually shifted the problem of the arms race from the context of quantitative accumulation to that of qualitative improvement of weapons (Petrovsky 1980 : 147; Huntzinger 1980: 29).

The Causes of the Arms Race

Much has been written about the causal factors determining the dynamics of the arms race. Myriads of possible causes have been suggested. According to Barnaby "the military-scientist is the key actor here. His activity alone fuels the Soviet-American nuclear arms race (at least qualitatively), destroys nuclear deterrence policy, and stimulates nuclear-war fighting ones" (Barnaby 1981: 11). Such statements on the role of the scientists working on nuclear arms projects point to a potential source of armaments dynamics outside conscious decisions taken by policy-makers. Attention is also to be drawn to the intrinsic inertia of the armaments process (Kaliadine 1981: 26). Barnaby goes so far as to say that military techno-logy "is now totally out of the control of the political leaders". This is, of course, one view; as Barnaby acknowledges, a number of scientists would strongly disagree and claim just to satisfy the demands of politicians. The debate on the military-industrial-scientific complex is not very new, but it nevertheless is to be mentioned as a possible causal factor behind the technological progress sometimes threatening established strategy. Gallagher and Spielmann (1972: 10) cite Senator Albert Gore as suggesting that the scientists engaged in the MIRV development in the United States were probably inspired more by technical challenges than by the evidence of Soviet deployment of an ABM system. Senator Gore "mused that

26

a scientist's response to a technical challenge could be likened to a mountain climber's response to an unscaled peak" (cf. also Dewitt 1981). As pointed out by a Soviet scholar, the arms race has been taking an increasingly qualitative form:

> "The scientific potential of a country increasingly emerges as the key concept of its military potential. The ratio between civilian and military, or paramilitary, research is steadily changing in favour of the latter, especially insofar as investment is concerned" (Gvishiani 1980: 55).

Offering a more general interpretation of the arms race, Tsipis (1975b) develops the proposition that the arms race between the United States and the Soviet Union has common characteristics with "the practice of posturing, a phenomenon that is only readily observable in the animal world". There are three ways to resolve conflicts: combat, negotiation, or posturing. Combat, of course, provides a clear way of deciding the confrontation by establishing one's superiority over the other. Negotiation depends heavily on the mutual acknowledgment of legitimate desires. Posturing seems to be based on a desire to avoid combat but to resolve the conflict by determining which of the two opponents is the more competent (Tsipis 1975b: 79). The major nuclear Powers seek to avoid nuclear war as a means of conflict resolution; the arms race, however, is continuing.

Morgan (1977: 192f.) has drawn attention to the fact that in an arms race, as in a lengthy prolonged crisis, the two opponents may engage on a collision course without paying due attention to the risk inherent in such a course. "The arms race acquires an incrementalist basis, allowing full play for such factors as the attraction of technological imperatives, bureaucratic politics, domestic politics, and so on. And it can culminate in war on a step-by-step basis". This may lead to extremely dangerous situations because the possibility of being cautious and having time encourages an illusion of proper management of the arms race while setting the stage for the two sides to gradually perceive the approaching war as probably inevitable. One of the origins of this danger is very probably deeply rooted in the nature of technological innovation; Soviet Academician Markov draws attention to this fact by stressing "the unpredictability of the sometimes rather distant but none the less real future results of its development. History shows that our technical and scientific imagination is capable of penetrating only a very short way into the future" (Markov 1981: 11f.).

Another problem, different from the general drive of scientists and engineers to improve the characteristics of the weapons design, but also partly beyond the control of the political decision-makers, is what might be called "mirror imaging". As Epstein (1976: 28) puts it, scientists do not wait for a potential enemy to react, but, operating on the "worst case" theory, themselves "react against their own brainchildren". This leads from a new weapon to a counter-weapon designed to neutralize this development if adopted by the adversary, and then to counter-

27

counter-weapons in order to ensure the effects desired by deploying the original weapon.

Mirror-imaging, surely, happens not only within the scientific laboratories; Governments are also subject to such considerations, reacting, in order to minimize the potential losses and the threat, on the basis of a worst-case scenario and thus fuelling the arms race. The uncertainty about the effectiveness of newly developed weapons will most probably be interpreted very differently by different Governments. Whereas the side in possession of a new development will be rather doubtful about its effects, the other side, lacking exact details and impact assessments, will tend to act very cautiously and assume high effectiveness. The secrecy surrounding military research is not conducive to halting such speculation, which promotes the technological, qualitative arms race (Panofsky 1981: 49—50). This mirror-imaging does not seem to be confined to countries with a specific social structure; the problems exist within the defence establishments (military, military-scientists) of both the major nuclear Powers (Gallager and Spielmann 1972:76ff.).

The Ambivalent Nature of Arms Control

The crisis stability of armaments deployed by the major Powers can be influenced by arms control measures, provided that there is a basic consensus about which developments may lead to crisis instability and are therefore to be considered contrary to the interests of all participants in the qualitative arms race. In fact, the major nuclear Powers have made some attempts to co-operate in preventing the deployment of weapons introducing strong crisis instability. A salient example of this kind of co-operation is the ABM Agreement (1972). On the other hand, the development and deployment of MIRVs is an often cited example of a missed opportunity to stop a destabilizing technological innovation.

By countering the tendencies that might affect the invulnerability of the strategic system, arms control contributes to reducing the probability of war; this concern represents one of the three goals of arms control, the other two being the reduction of damage if war occurs and the reduction of the cost of preparing for war (Garwin 1978: 98).

The United States approach to arms control can largely be explained as being guided by the concept of strategic stability, which in turn is based on the possession of a secure second-strike capability by both the Soviet Union and the United States (Kober 1981; Steinbruner 1978: 416). It has to be acknowledged that this concept is part of the strategy of mutual deterrence, and arms control can be viewed as an instrument for assuring proper perception of mutual deterrence. According to Kober, the Soviet Union also supports the concept of arms control as a means to provide strategic stability. But it is hard to prove that the Soviet Union and the United Stated pursue arms control only for the sake of crisis stability. Arms control attempts may be viewed by one side as unjustified attempts to stabilize a balance strongly in favour of the party proposing an agreement. However, SALT-type agreements, with their heavy emphasis on numbers, neglecting limits on qualitative aspects, are viewed by some as fuelling the arms race and thereby contributing to the deterioration of crisis stability.

Some critics also question the assumption that arms control may ever lead to crisis stability (Burt 1979: 37). They view the absence of any shared consensus between the United States and the Soviet Union over the meaning of strategic stability as a serious obstacle. Burt even writes that the "growing vulnerability of American ICBMs was probably viewed in Moscow as a stabilizing rather than a dangerous development" (Burt 1979: 37).

Of course, the concept of crisis stability has to be seen in connection with strategic doctrines. But, on a general level, enhancing the ability to wait during a high-tension situation, without incurring the risk of rapid military defeat, is certainly something desirable. Disagreements over the effects of certain moves and situations will, however, persist. But arms control can at least help to minimize risks considered undesirable by consensus.

Carter (1975) views a United States counterforce capability against Soviet ICBMs as "more likely to create an incentive for the Soviet Union to adopt a hair-trigger, launch-on-warning posture" (Carter 1975: 29), thereby reinforcing crisis instability. The counterforce role of ICBMs depends on the achievable accuracy. Carter proposes a strict limit on the number of missile tests as a means of impeding accuracy improvements or at least limiting them (Carter 1975: 30). However, such limits conflict with the desire not only to test new missiles but also to ascertain the accuracy and the range of missiles already deployed.

Frye (1977: 18—19) makes the same proposal, adding that such missile tests could be restricted to missiles already deployed or firmly scheduled for the near future. He envisages agreed-on test ranges and prior notification. Such limits on the number, location and timing of missile tests could constitute part of an arms-control package designed to limit accuracy. However, since this proposal was made, half a decade has passed, and the limitation would very probably not make the same sense today because the accuracies achieved are considered sufficient for counterforce applications; particularly the ICBMs, but more and more also the SLBMs, seem to have the capabilities with destabilizing effects.

As the battle to prevent threatening improvements of accuracy seems lost, arms control could focus on the prevention of anti-satellite warfare (ASAT) deployments (Frye 1977: 20); however, this is also a very urgent undertaking, since the Soviet Union and the United States are considered to already be developing ASAT capabilities leading to command vulnerability which may result in just the same problems as force vulnerability, i.e., in the temptation to pre-empt as long as the capability to strike still exists. The Vought Corporation in the United States is reported to be testing a full-scale engineering model of a miniature homing vehicle ASAT system developed by the Air Force's Space Division (Smith 1981: 24).

The prospects for arms control as a means of preserving crisis stability are rather gloomy if one looks at the failure to prevent MIRVing, the very high accuracy of ICBM warheads, and ASAT. Frye's (1977: 19—20) proposal to prohibit tracking of SSBNs and to create sanctuaries for SSBNs focuses on what may be the last opportunity to prevent one more destabilizing technological development which threatens to render obsolete the relative invulnerability of the sea-based nuclear forces. The risks are steadily rising. Crisis stability seems to be threatened. Nevertheless, arms control is as yet not applied very extensively to those systems which obviously play a crucial role in the future preservation of crisis stability. One can only deplore the absence of any serious effort to try to put a lid on the Pandora's box of the strategic arms race, which so far is producing nothing but an ongoing competition in the development of weapons, counter-measures and counter-counter-measures.

One major reason for the regrettable impasse in arms control is certainly the lack of reliable methods and institutions for verifying the agreements. Both the United States and the USSR Governments are aware that the traditional verification procedures, especially the "verification by national means" (i.e., by satellite observation and conventional intelligence), although constantly being improved, may, in the foreseeable future, become insufficient and lag behind the increasing complexity and sophistication of the strategic weapons systems. This concern is, for instance, expressed by Arbatov (1981: 171), who notes that "the qualitative characteristics of a number of new weapon systems, such as cruise and mobile ballistic missiles, complicate reciprocal control over the observation of possible agreements on their limitation". Similarly, Eugene Rostow, Director of the United States Arms Control and Disarmament Agency (ACDA), deplored that "verification has been a more and more troublesome aspect of arms control in recent years", and he indicated that the United States Government believes that co-operative measures to supplement national technical means will be necessary (Rostow 1981). The Final Document of the first special session on disarmament, under paragraph 31, also calls for "adequate measures of verification (...) in order to create the necessary confidence...". Therefore it might be wise not to expend too much effort, which may be illusory, on the invention of new disarmament measures only and on new fields of applying the disarmament approach, but also on new procedures of verification. In view of the increasingly complex technical specifications of the new weapons systems, new techniques and procedures of verification seem to constitute one of the keys to any substantial progress in the field of arms control.

B. The Challenge to Force Survivability

The New Vulnerability

When discussing the vulnerability of strategic weapons in terms of strategic or crisis stability, the central issue at stake is obviously the urgency it produces — urgency with respect to making a decision to launch a punitive strike *before* the missiles or aeroplanes capable of performing this strike are destroyed at their emplacements.

Although the preoccupation of the two major Powers with this issue is understandably very basic, it must not be forgotten that they have been living with the problem ever since 1959. In the case of the United States, the Soviet SLBMs off the Washington coastal region constituted a threat establishing a high degree of urgency in case of an enemy attack; a similar situation was experienced by the Soviet Union, which is basing a large part of its strategic forces on fixed silos on land.

In spite of this situation, however, the two major Powers never felt a degree of urgency such as to induce them to take corresponding precautions, such as the introduction of LOW policies and the like. This attitude is determined by the fact that they have so far always succeeded in making urgency a non-vital issue. They were always in a position to rely on systems which were less vulnerable or even invulnerable to any attack and which therefore did not generate urgency in the sense of "use it or lose it". For the foreseeable future urgency obviously continues to be of concern, but it also seems that for the foreseeable future it will not be a burning issue. Both major Powers constantly make all possible efforts to reduce the urgency problem by taking appropriate armaments decisions.

Nevertheless, the nuclear Powers have every reason to worry about the challenges posed by the development of new arms to their retaliatory forces. Crisis stability depends to a high degree on the confidence the authorities can place in the survivability of their nuclear weapon systems:

> "Crisis stability requires that each side believes that if its opponent launched a surprise attack, it would be able to launch a devastating retaliatory attack with its surviving forces. Otherwise, the side that had forces vulnerable to being destroyed in a surprise attack might fear such an attack during a crisis and decide to launch a preemptive strike in order to limit the damage it would otherwise suffer" (Staff of the Carnegie Panel on U.S. Security and the Future of Arms Control 1981a: 56).

Survivability being a central requirement of crisis stability, discussion has focussed on the vulnerability of the elements of the strategic triad and of the C^3 installations, more particularly the ability to launch a second strike.

The most pressing issue, in this context, is the problem of ICBM vulnerability. Some commentators are inclined to express their respective worries in very unambiguous terms. For instance, Rosen thinks that within the next five years, the Soviet ICBM force will be able to destroy the bulk of the United States' land-based missiles in their silos (Rosen 1979: 109). Such bleak statemenst can be found explicitly or implicitly underlying many discussions on the danger posed to ICBMs by a hypothetical surprise attack. The other two legs, SLBMs and bombers, are not considered to be as vulnerable because they are mobile and, as far as SSBNs are concerned, not easily detectable for the time being.

The "windows of vulnerability" jeopardizing fixed ICBMs depend on several criteria. They are all constantly changing as a consequence of technological developments in the relevant fields: hardness of the silos (measured in psi), yield of the warheads, kill radius, accuracy (measured in metres circular error probable [CEP]), reliability, and, finally, number of warheads which might be directed against a given number of missile sites (see, for example, Speed 1979: 33—36; Anderson 1981; Paine 1981). The combined effect of improvements of these variables has resulted in a vulnerability assessment quite different from that of the early 1970s. Missile silos have been hardened up to a resistance against 1,000 psi (Speed 1979: 39), mitigating the vulnerability, but improvements in accuracy (down to 0.1 nm CEP or less) and the increase in numbers (partly due to MIRVing) of re-entry vehicles (RVs) have resulted in greater vulnerability, or, to put it the opposite way, in greater confidence of the attacker. Based on an evaluation of each factor contributing to vulnerability, Speed (1979: 44) arrives at the conclusion that it is only a matter of time before the present land-based ICBM force becomes vulnerable. His argument, like most of the other statements available in this context, deals with the threat of a Soviet attack to the United States ICBMs, but one has to consider that the opposite threat may be comparatively greater because the accuracy of the United States ICBMs and SLBMs is considered greater and the Soviet Union has a greater part of its nuclear weapons deployed on land-based ICBMs.

The perception of ICBM vulnerability has led to calculations about how many United States ICBMs would survive a surprise attack under some assumed specifications. Such scenarios, differentiating between being attacked under day-to-day-alert as against generated alert and tactics of riding out the first strike as against adoption of LUA, can be found, for example, in the United States Military Posture for FY 1982 (p. 30; cf. also Staff of the Carnegie Panel on U.S. Security and the Future of Arms Control 1981a: 71, 72, 74), presenting the expected outcome for different years under specified assumptions (programmes MX, Trident, ALCM deployment, etc.). The United States authorities perceive a situation of parity to be no longer in existence after 1985 if calculating the consequences of Soviet pre-emption, especially if surprised by day-to-day alert and not having adopted LUA. Without doubt, similar considerations could also refer to the opposite case, i.e., the Soviet strategic forces being surprised by United States pre-emption. In sum, the developments under way lead an expert to the conclusion that by the mid-1980s to late 1980s, neither super-Power will be able to retain sufficient confidence in the ability of its fixed-site ICBM force to ride out a surprise attack and remain a secure second-strike instrument (Gray 1977: 1).

The United States Joint Chiefs of Staff (JCS) testified before the Committee on Armed Services of the House of Representatives in 1981:

> "The major improvements underway in the Soviet ICBM force, incorporating greater throw-weight, more warheads per missile and increased accuracy, pose a growing threat to our fixed silo ICBM forces. The Soviets now possess a clear and growing advantage in the ability to destroy hard targets, such as ICBMs. Because of these Soviet advances, Minuteman survivability is expected to be as low as 10 percent by the mid-1980's against a severe Soviet attack.
> Furthermore, the estimated rate of decline is accelerating as Soviet strategic capabilities improve" (Hearings on Military Posture 1981, Part 1: 260).

But in the same hearings, Major General Browning of the United States Air Force testified that the

> "higher yield and improved fuzing of the MK-12A coupled with the newly developed guidance software will provide Minuteman with an improved capability against targets designated by the single integrated operational plan" (Hearings on Military Posture 1981, Part 1: 435).

Thus the ICBM vulnerability of both sides seems to be growing, despite silo upgrading programmes under way or completed (FY 1982 ACIS: 2). The MK-12A RV

> "was designed to be employed against the total spectrum of targets but increasingly has been planned for employment against a growing Soviet hardened target system, where its combination of yield and accuracy could be used to military advantage" (FY 1982 ACIS: 3).

Some critics, for example Steinbruner and Garwin (1976), question the validity of the standard calculations used for assessing ICBM vulnerability. To them, the apparent vulnerability is a consequence of a principle of conservative force planning and of the test procedures which provide the only empirical data available (Steinbruner and Garwin 1976: 142). There are difficult problems of reliability, interference and timing to be taken into account. In sum, "even a highly aggressive development of the Soviet forces under the Vladivostok regime (...) still would not render the Minuteman force vulnerable under reasonable assumptions" (ibid.: 159). The "relative vulnerability of land-based missiles can be constructed only on the basis of a narrow and rigid criterion of analysis, one which requires that any technically conceivable threat to the missiles be covered" (ibid.: 168).

Even modest shifts in the assumptions are sufficient to shift the apparent advantage from the attacker to the defender.

Similar doubts have been expressed by Anderson (1981), who thinks that the probability of success of a first strike is very low, for three reasons: firstly, the collateral damage of a counterforce attack would be so devastating as to affect also the attacker; radioactive dust would circle the earth, cooling the atmosphere and decreasing also the attacker's crop production. Secondly, assuming even an optimistic probability of all the missiles functioning as expected and assuming even a high accuracy, the kill probability of the missiles fired is considerably below 100 per cent. Thirdly, "fratricide" problems such as the destruction of incoming warheads by preceding nuclear explosions would also affect the chances of success. Anderson concludes that, aiming at a fleet of 1,000 Minuteman missiles, an enemy attacker must realize that the first strike would still leave 600 Minuteman missiles. Hence he must expect a devastating response. For these reasons the strategic relationship characterized by the principle of "mutual assured destruction" (MAD) still continues to represent the very basis of the system of deterrence (Keeny and Panofsky 1981).

The Impact of MIRVing

Despite such reservations, the ongoing arms race has continued to cause strategists' concern about the dangerous vulnerability of the land-based ICBM force. Perry (1979: 133) maintains that "by far the largest strategic force vulnerability problem facing us today is that associated with our ICBM". The main rationale for such expectations and fears must be seen in the development of MIRVs. In the absence of MIRVs an aggressor would have had to expend, in order to destroy a given number of adversary missiles, more missiles than he could hope to destroy, due to a kill probability far below 1.0 for each missile equipped with only one warhead.* This effect is called "self-disarmament", because it would leave the attacker with greater losses in nuclear weaponry than the victim — a situation which made it completely impracticable to attack and did not generate any temptation to launch a first strike.

However, while under no-MIRV circumstances the incentives for a counterforce attack were small, MIRVs had the effect of multiplying the available RVs without a similar multiplication of aim points. Whereas more than 100 one-warhead missiles were necessary to destroy with very high probability 100 adversary missiles, MIRVing lowered the number of missiles necessary for such a strike below 100, changing the outcome in favour of the side attacking first. A situation where the

---

* The basic assumption is that each one warhead will not have a kill-probability of 1.0 against hardened targets, especially ICBMs within their silos. A kill probability of 1.0 would mean that there would be absolute certainty that each warhead would destroy one target. This kill probability grows with the yield of the weapon. To a large extent it depends on the accuracy of targeting, as expressed by CEP (circular error probable) which refers to the median deviance of the warhead from its target. A comparative evaluation of different calculation modes is presented in Lutz (1981 a): 25 ff. and 46 ff.

34

major nuclear Powers would rely only on MIRVed ICBMs would create strong incentives to pre-empt in a crisis (Jervis 1978: 212).

It is important to note that improvements of accuracy by a certain factor will have a greater effect than the increase of yield by the same factor (cf. United Nations General Assembly (1980 a): 10—11). At present, the kill probability is well below 1.0. It varies, of course, for each missile and even for different generations of warheads (the equipping of the Minutemen with the MK-12A warhead decreased the CEP). In such an environment, it takes more than one attacking warhead for there to be a very high probability of an ICBM site being destroyed.

At the time when only single-warhead ICBMs were in the arsenals of the major nuclear Powers, an attack by ICBMs against ICBMs was senseless for the attacker, as he had to launch more ICBMs than he could realistically hope to destroy, leaving him with a comparative disadvantage (Jervis 1978: 213). Thus pre-emption would have been unattractive.

The introduction of MIRVs, however, has changed the situation much to the worse in the sense that it has made the first strike against ICBMs, formerly unattractive, a viable means of achieving military advantages. The main problem is that, in an ICBM vs. ICBM scenario the means of attack are simultaneously the targets of the other side (Lutz 1981a : 20—21). If one is to assume that each side had, say, 1,000 missiles, each one with three warheads, then an attack by 600 missiles (= 1,800 warheads = 1,800 RVs) must be expected to destroy a very large proportion of the attacked 1,000 ICBMs, leaving the aggressor with several hundred ICBMs and denying the adversary the option to retaliate, as he has to expect an annihilating third strike.

The basic problem is that MIRVing multiplied the capacity to attack by a factor of at least two (some missiles are equipped with many more warheads), while the number of targets remained relatively stable. Hence the means vs. target-ratio was considerably altered because the destruction of an unlaunched ICBM would mean the destruction of several warheads. "Since the advantage lies with whoever strikes first, 'MIRVing' turns out to have been one of the most dangerous steps in the history of weapons technology" (Calder 1980: 119). Garwin (1979: 94—95) agrees that the MIRVing had such unfortunate effects, because an "ICBM with a single warhead can destroy no more than one of the opponent's ICBMs, and by reason of imperfect accuracy and reliability, can do considerably less. But a force of MIRVs can in principle destroy a numerically equal or superior force of MIRVed missiles, thus leading to crisis instability". No serious effort was made to reach an agreement preventing the MIRVing process. Yet, as Garwin (1979: 94) argues, there is no such thing as "crisis instability of the MIRVed ICBM force" when that force is embedded in a complex of other strategic offensive forces, launch-on-warning options, and the like.

While it may be true that the destabilizing effects of MIRVs are mitigated by the presence of SLBMs and bombers, MIRVs nevertheless pose a great danger to the land-based elements. The adoption of a LOW posture is a rather alarming suggestion, as it might increase the danger of unwanted developments. Tammen (1973: 133) points to still another problem for the victim of a MIRV pre-emptive strike and says that the attacked country does not know which silos have been fired or refilled and therefore must continue to target the entire enemy force. The effects of MIRVing on strategic stability are summarized in the Comprehensive Study on Nuclear Weapons (United Nations General Assembly 1980 a: 9, paragraph 20): MIRV has raised the spectre that a fraction of one side's ICBMs forces may in a first strike destroy the opponent's ICBMs still housed in hardened silos. "This situation is therefore considered unstable, since in time of crisis each side may consider launching its missiles rather than risk their destruction".

In addition, the introduction of MIRVs has had far-reaching consequences on other aspects of the arms race and strategic doctrine. This has been pointed at by the Soviet author Arbatov who argues that military planners had to "seek a rationale for the 'redundant' warheads" (Arbatov 1979: 150), turning to counterforce strategies. The public mentioning of counterforce features, in turn, was one of the main incentives to discuss LOW tactics.

Arbatov uses this example of MIRV leading perhaps to LOW to illustrate the point that the arms race will "destabilize the strategic situation and increase the risk of a dramatic, fatal mistake under conditions of acute international crisis" (Arbatov 1979: 151). He stresses that the arms race is unlikely to result in any long-term advantages for either side, but instead will increase the danger of unintentional nuclear war.

When interpreting Soviet statements on this subject, it should be borne in mind that the Soviet Union, due to reasons of geography and history, has a much greater part of its RVs placed on ICBMs than does the United States. This generates some problems. The Soviet Union may perceive its strategic forces to be more vulnerable, and indeed Soviet authorities have repeatedly expressed their concern about United States capabilities to launch a pre-emptive strike *(Whence the Threat to Peace* 1982: 34ff.). On the other hand, the basing mode of Soviet strategic forces permits an attack on the opponent's ICBMs with a great numerical advantage of RVs; this is a prerequisite for a successful counterforce surprise attack. There is a United States interest that the perception of vulnerability by the Soviet authorities may lead them to deploy a greater part of the strategic nuclear weapons in less vulnerable basing modes, thus mitigating the incentives for pre-emption in crisis (FY 1982 ACIS: 52).

Surprise Attack
by Intermediate-Range Nuclear Forces (INF)?

Another new threat to force survivability arises in the context of the regional arms race in Europe. According to a decision taken by NATO, the United States will, from 1983 on, deploy a number of mobile Pershing-II launchers capable of launching missiles with a nuclear warhead at a range of about 2,500 km with high accuracy (CEP = 35—40 m). Soviet publications (e.g., *Whence the Threat to Peace* 1982: 58—60) repeatedly emphasize that the plan to deploy Pershing-IIs must clearly be seen in the perspective of massive pre-emptive strike intentions by the United States against the USSR:

> "In Pentagon thinking, surprise attacks with high-accuracy Pershing-II missiles (flight time of 5—6 minutes) on the Soviet Union's strategic weapons would reduce the impact of a retaliatory blow against the USA in the event of aggression against the USSR". (*ibid.*: 60).

Similar conclusions are drawn with regard to cruise missiles whose specific trajectory can penetrate all kinds of defences (Markov 1981: 43).

The careful wording of this allegation deserves attention. The Soviet authors do not assume the *prevention* of a retaliatory blow against the United States; they explicitly talk about a *reduction* of its impact only. This would probably not be questioned by United States planners: they can in fact not — and hence certainly will not—have confidence in being able to launch a surprise attack on Soviet territory which would completely "knock out" Soviet retaliatory power. Hence the term "pre-emptive attack", if referring to such an incomplete "disarming strike", does not seem at all meaningful. The logic of a surprise attack or disarming first strike leads to a dangerous situation only if the chances of wiping out the opponent's retaliatory forces are either close to 100 per cent certainty or very high.

This is in fact conceded by other Soviet authors. For instance, Bykov convincingly concludes:

> "The approximate parity of forces, which exists in the key areas of the military confrontation, is maintained through a mutual balance of the material means of warfare, above all the nuclear missiles (...) In any war with the use of such weapons the aggressor cannot ward off powerful strikes in retaliation. Even under the most unfavourable conditions the other party is capable of inflicting irreparable damage on the initiator of the conflict with its surviving strategic forces. Hence, it is impossible to deliver a pre-emptive strike and go unpunished" (Bykov 1980: 132).

Bykov also asserts that it is practically impossible to make the existing balance unstable:

> "If the existing balance is upset by one party, the other, using its economic, scientific and technical potential, is capable of catching up by boosting up its military might, thus making all advantages temporary and partial" (Bykov 1980: 132).

Similarly, Academician Markov comments on the hopes of gaining a military advantage:

> "Scientific and technological progress is featureless as it serves any opposing sides in the same way. And it is no secret that these sides carefully follow each other's 'successes'" (Markov 1981: 40).

It therefore seems that the allegation that Pershing-II is a pre-emptive strike weapon must be seen in a somewhat relative way.

As a matter of fact NATO planners tend to assume that the deployment of Pershing-IIs contributes to strengthening deterrence and crisis stability. As summarized by Bertram (1981b: 308 f.), United States nuclear forces in Europe will be a more credible and more proportionate demonstration of the link between the United States deterrence and deterrence of attacks on Western Europe. Furthermore the mobility of these nuclear forces should enable them to survive a Soviet attack, so that the danger of slipping inadvertently into an all-out nuclear exchange would be minimized. According to Bertram, these forces do not provide an offensive option against the Soviet Union; the cruise missiles require a flight time of two or three hours to reach their targets and hence are hardly suitable for a surprise attack, while the Pershing-IIs are well below the quantitative levels required for an effective disarming strike against Soviet military targets (Bertram 1981b: 309).

Countering the Challenge:
Ballistic Missile Defence (BMD)

The perception of ICBM vulnerability leads to deliberations about what to do against this threat. There are at least five propositions (FY 1982 ACIS: 44ff.): change the basing mode of ICBMs; do nothing (assuming that sufficient retaliatory capabilities would survive a first counter-silo strike); place more emphasis on sea-based nuclear forces; adopt LUA; or adopt a mix of forces, hard-target-kill and others. LUA can be discounted due to its destabilizing effect. While deterring a deliberate attack, it would be undesirable in a crisis situation as it might produce accidental war (FY 1982 ACIS: 48). Other proposals focus on defensive protection of the ICBMs, i.e., on BMD development. An effective silo defence based on BMD is limited and practically precluded by the ABM treaty signed by the United States and the USSR. The discussions about defensive measures to protect the ICBM force are characterised by a broad scope of techniques examined in this context.

The techniques envisaged include such unorthodox measures as "bed-of-nails defence" against ground-burst fuzing and "pebble-curtain defence" against airburst and ground-burst (Garwin 1976); a third technique is called "dust defence". The first solution can be described as follows:

> "(...) should each Minuteman silo be provided with a thicket of steel palings arranged 1 meter apart in east-west rows 600 meters long, with about 150 rows at 5 meters north-south spacing (the palings being a quarter-inch-diameter (...) steel reinforcing rod 2 meters long, driven 0.6 meters into the ground), it is unlikely that the *fuze* would strike either the ground or one of the palings. Rather, the RV at hypersonic velocity would destroy itself (without nuclear detonation) by contact with one of the palings" (Garwin 1976: 54).

Another way to destroy RVs without provoking a nuclear explosion is the pebble-curtain defence. This installation is described by Garwin (1976: 54) as "an East-West line 300 meters north of each Minuteman silo and 300 meters long, consisting of propellants emplaced in the ground to project a curtain or fan of pebbles up to 300 meters in the air". The principle is similar to the bed-of-nails defence: destroy the RV by contact with the pebbles. This defence would, as opposed to the bed of nails, also be viable by air burst. The curtain of pebbles would be activated by an upward-looking radar, deployed well forward, which would detect incoming RVs.

These BMD measures would be relatively cost-effective; the bed of nails would contain some $ 60,000 worth of steel, and the pebble curtain would consist of 10 tons of steel pellets worth about $ 2,000 (Garwin 1976: 54). Such defences would be effective mainly against low-drag RVs with a small angle of attack. The use of high-drag RVs, however, is nearly precluded by the influence of unpredictable winds on accuracy.

There remain, however, several problems. The proposed defence installations might be targeted prior to an attack on the ICBMs. This would require very accurate timing, as it would surely be taken as a sign of imminent attack on the ICBMs. Still, techniques like the bed of nails are of some interest because they can be assumed to be permitted under the ABM treaty.

Another quite exotic technology discussed in the context of BMD is "dust defence", i.e., a concept evaluated for endoatmospheric ballistic missile defence.

> "Dust defense — also called environmental defense — provides for burying 'clean' nuclear weapons in silo or MPS fields and exploding them shortly before attacking RVs arrive. The dust and debris lofted into the air would destroy approaching RVs either by direct collision with large earth fragments or by dust erosion of the RV's heat shield. The detonations would be placed so as not to damage the ICBMs in their silos or shelters" (Office of Technology Assessment 1981: 126—127).

"Dust defence would be based on nuclear weapons buried north of each silo or shelter, exploding seconds before RV arrival, or throughout the field to be exploded several minutes before RV arrival. In the first case, debris and fragments of earth would have to absorb the RV, as the dust would form a little later. In the second version, the dust alone would have to suffice, the dust cloud formed by a small nuclear weapon could be tens of miles wide and protect many silos.

The drawbacks of the dust defence system are described as the need for warning, the need for multiple explosions if the attack occurs in waves, and the risk of error. The dust slowing down and finally destroying RVs without causing nuclear explosion of its nuclear material could conceivably influence the reliability of the weapons protected if they had to be launched a short time after the dust defence had been activated.

The discussion of BMD and its utility against a perceived threat to the land-based ICBMs in the United States was also linked to the multiple protective shelters (MPS) basing mode considered for the MX ICBMs to be deployed in the near future. The evaluated BMD system consists of two elements, the low altitude defence system (LoADS) and an 'overlay' element (Keeny and Panofsky 1981: 299—301). LoADS would, in effect, consist of hardened radars and small missiles serving as interceptors. The operating area would be the lower atmosphere, at an altitude between 5,000 and 20,000 feet (Starsman 1981: 29). The entire LoADS system would be concealed and activated only in case of attack. It would then break through the roof of the shelter with the radar face and the interceptor canister. The radar would locate the in-coming RV, the data processing devices would calculate the intercept point, and the interceptor would be launched. Destruction of the RV would be performed by nuclear explosion. The concealment of the LoADS system is to be seen in the context of MPS basing.

MPS basing, according to the most advanced planning, was projected to include 200 sites, each containing 23 shelters but only one MX missile, which was to be shuttled around the shelters in an unsystematic way as to preserve location uncertainty (PLU). In case of massive counterforce attack, the opponent would be forced to target each shelter in order to destroy the missile, this would result in an RV exchange ratio of 2. 3: 1, since 23 warheads would have to be directed against the 23 shelters containing one MX ICBM equipped with 10 warheads.

The addition of LoADS to MPS basing would further increase the exchange ratio in favor of the defender, as the attacker would have to attack with at least 2 RVs targeted on each shelter, resulting in an exchange ratio of 4.6: 1. However, only the one shelter containing the missile would be equipped with the LoADS system. This would result in major savings as compared with the equipping of all 23 shelters with LoADS. The precondition, of course, would be that LoADS would be shuttled from shelter to shelter along with the MX missile. MPS equipped with LoADS thus has the capability of changing the ratio of RVs expended or destroyed in favour of the defender. (For a description of LoADS, see, for example, Office of Technology Assessment 1981: chapter 3; Starsman 1981; Ruina 1981). LoADS would be most suited for missile defence, as it operates with nuclear interceptors.

Each LoADS system would have only two interceptors, the first to be used for defence of the LoADS installation, the second only for defence of the missile site. Thus, attacking the (concealed) LoADS system first would result in one expended interceptor but not in a defenceless missile (Starsman 1981: 31). An alternative approach to surmount LoADS would be to attack each shelter with one RV each and then detect by the LoADS system pushed through the roof of the shelter which one really contained a missile, followed by a second attack directed only against the shelters containing the MX missile. This, however, would be a very risky choice, since it is rather improbable that the attacked side would wait for the second attack before launching the missiles (Office of Technology Assessment 1981: 125).

The United States plan to pursue a vigorous R&D programme to provide an active defence of land-based missiles. The LoAD programme will be restructured to accelerate development of an advanced terminal defence for ICBMs (DoD Annual Report, FY 1983: III—65).

The other BMD system currently under study in the United States is the "overlay" system. It is designed to intercept RVs outside the atmosphere and destroy them by conventional means. This system seems to offer better prospects for area coverage, but the problem of leakage is to be considered. As the "overlay" system is not as far advanced as LoADS, the description cannot be very detailed (see Office of Technology Assessment 1981: chapter 3; Keeny and Panofsky 1981: 300 f.).

Beyond the technical problems, still more important questions have to be considered, as these systems might have the potential of radically changing the strategic environment, presenting a danger to stability and perhaps even changing the basic assumptions governing strategic decisions today.

BMD of fixed-site ICBMs would not fundamentally alter the strategy based on deterrence by punishment. It would, in fact, only serve to increase the confidence in the survivability of land-based strategic weapons. The reduced vulnerability could even enhance crisis stability and would render options like LOW unnecessary. This is not to suggest that LOW would be feasible and necessary, but missile BMD would be a further argument against LOW. At any rate, in the perspective of crisis stability, the protection of the retaliatory weapons may seem functional and positive. One might even envisage BMD systems for the protection of urban industrial areas without destabilizing strategic stability. According to Gray (1981a), the United States defence and arms-control community has come to the conclusion that the Soviet Union "does not hold to a concept of strategic stability that is at all recognizable in Western terms". Thus, he maintains, the coverage of a large amount of urban-industrial targets may not even be necessarily a requirement of Soviet strategic doctrine. Hence the deployment of BMD for cities would not influence strategic stability.

It deserves to be noted that the development and testing of ABM components at designated test ranges is not prohibited by the ABM Treaty. A United States BMD programme was at the R&D stage in 1982, concentrating on low-altitude defence capability and a high-altitude capability, pending major decisions at a later moment. The use of this R&D effort as a "very important chip in future negotiations" was also contemplated. The BMD programme was kept at a funding level of about $ 250 million to $ 300 million in the FYs 1980 and 1981 (Hearings on Military Posture 1981, Part 1: 267). The planned funding for 1982 is $ 462 million, the proposed funding for 1983 $ 870 million (DoD Annual Report, FY 1983: III—66).

The United States BMD programme is considered to have "no adverse arms control impact" (FY 1982 ACIS: X). Its purposes are described as keeping the United States abreast of BMD technologies as a precautionary measure against and discouraging of Soviet breakout from the ABM-Treaty:

> "A continuing R&D program within the terms of the ABM treaty serves to promote global and regional stability. Absent the U.S. BMD R&D program, the prospect for Soviet advantages in BMD technology, or perceptions of Soviet advantages, could be increased" (FY 1982 ACIS: X).

The United States Government still seems to be quite sceptical with regard to BMD, as expressed in the latest DoD Report:

> "For the future we are not yet sure how well ballistic missile defenses will work; what they cost; whether they would require changes to the ABM Treaty; and how additional Soviet ballistic missile defenses—which would almost certainly be deployed in response to any U.S. BMD system—would affect U.S. and allied offensive capabilities". (DoD Annual Report, FY 1983: III-65)

The Soviet Union also is said to be undertaking R&D efforts in BMD (FY 1982 ACIS: 38; Davis et al. 1981). Speed (1979: 70) cites sources asserting that the Soviet efforts in BMD were more substantial than on the United States side, the Soviet Union spending about twice as much on ABM R&D as the United States.

On the basis of available information it cannot be ascertained to what extent this holds true and whether technological break throughs have already been achieved. What is more important is the fact that even the mere supposition of Soviet ABM/BMD efforts leads many people in the United States to advocate action to achieve progress in this field in order not to be caught napping should these putative Soviet efforts be a reality.

One may assume that Soviet strategic planning involves the targeting of either force potentials or urban-industrial assets on the United States side (or, more probably, both). The defence of ICBMs by BMD is justified in terms of traditional doctrine (survivable forces do not require fast or pre-emptive action in a crisis), and the denial of urban-industrial targets is justified by the argument that the Soviet

Union does not share the same concept of strategic stability. But one is to assume that the denial of both the force and the urban-industrial targets would surely be considered as rather a dramatic change by strategic planners of the other major nuclear Power.

On ethical grounds, the dominance of the defence in strategic nuclear weapons may perhaps seem preferable. But the transition from the present offensive-dominated situation to that situation would most probably entail a phase in which one major nuclear Power had a high capability of denying the other the second strike. This situation would necessarily be highly unstable.

The deployment of the "overlay" system, if only designed for the defence of fixed-site missiles, would produce a problem for stability, as the long-range interceptors could defend a large area and thus disturb the mutual hostage relations inherent to most strategic doctrines (Rosen 1979: 119). Gray (1981a) argues that a serious multilevel deployment of BMD would reduce United States self-deterrence and help to enhance credibility of extended deterrence. He maintains that BMD deployment could even slow down the arms race inasmuch as it is caused by the reliance on the offensive. BMD for hard-target defence (fixed-site ICBMs) may be perceived as enhancing crisis stability by mitigating ICBM vulnerability (i.e., by forcing a better RV exchange-ratio; an attempt to reverse the effects of MIRV). Area defence, however, encompassing urban-industrial targets, albeit preferable on ethical grounds, might, if deployed, lead to a phase of strategic instability due to target denial by the side deploying BMD, resulting in the other side's loss of the second-strike capability.

This is in fact precisely the object of the concern expressed by Soviet authorities. According to a Soviet publication, "the Pentagon has, indeed, set its sights on laying the requisite technical foundations for the deployment of this operational anti-missile system already in the current decade", and it perceives this trend as a proof of United States intentions "to complete the development of a so-called first-strike potential in the 1980s" *(Whence the Threat to Peace* 1982: 36). Whatever the merits or demerits of these assumptions, it cannot be denied that the mere pre-occupation with BMD problems is bound to cause considerable nervousness. It can hardly be said that this nervousness will not affect strategic stability. It is even more alarming in that the fears and the nervousness seem to be increasing on both sides of the central strategic balance. Even if neither major Power has and may never have a first-strike capability close at hand, the mere belief that the opponent is close to it represents a grave danger, especially in tense international situations.

Finally, the question must be raised whether any efforts undertaken in the field of BMD will not ultimately be futile. All important steps made by one side in this direction will very probably be emulated immediately by the other side. And, most important, it is hardly conceivable that one day one will be able to invent a BMD system that is not penetrable.

Countering the Challenge: MPS Basing

Other proposals advocate MPS basing modes. MPS basing, commonly known in connection with the planned United States MX missile, would result in a vast increase of shelters which the opponent would be forced to target in case of attack without a concomitant increase in the number of missiles. The MX MPS system of the United States was originally planned to consist of 200 MX ICBMs. Each ICBM would be shuttled around 23 shelters linked by a road. The precise location of the missile at a given point in time would not be known to a potential attacker, who would thus have to target all 23 shelters in order to be sure of hitting the missile. The exact features of the MX project are public knowledge, so we may restrict the discussion of the MPS basing mode to the essentials.

The most important feature of MPS is the exchange ratio resulting for the defender. If two countries each rely on 1,000 single-warhead ICBMs, it will take all ICBMs to launch an attack covering all ICBMs of the opponent. However, due to less than perfect reliability, unforeseen influences, etc., the number of ICBMs destroyed will be less than 1,000 (depending on hardening, accuracy, yield, etc.). Thus, there is no incentive for a first strike, because it would leave the attacker in a weaker position than the attacked. The introduction of MIRV has changed the calculation. If two countries each rely on 1,000 MIRVed ICBMs (three or more RVs per missile), an attack with a high chance of success can be launched with only a portion of the ICBMs. Each "successful" RV will destroy at least three hostile RVs, and it will on average not take three RVs to destroy a missile. Thus the defender is weakened more than the attacker.

The emergence of MPS could lead back to the more stable time of single-warhead ICBMs. It provides for a multiplication of targets which the aggressor has to attack without entailing a vast increase in ICBMs.

If one ICBM is deployed in one of the 23 shelters of an MX site, the attacker will have to target all 23 shelters because the position of the missile is not known and the distance between the shelters is sufficient to ensure survival of the missile if only neighbouring shelters are destroyed. Assuming the MX missile is equipped with 10 warheads, this results in an exchange ratio of 2.3:1 in favour of the defender. BMD is able to increase the ratio to 4.6:1. Thus 23 or 46 warheads have to be expended in order to destroy 10 warheads, which is comparable to the situation given only single-warhead ICBMs or even more favourable to the defender.

The stabilizing consequences of MPS are evident. An obstacle to the introduction of such systems is the impact they have on the environment (they need much space), as well as their high cost. Another and perhaps more serious question is whether such a huge and complex system can be adequately controlled and commanded; this is hard to estimate. Also, given the long span of time required for the system's completion, it is conceivable that 10 or 20 years from now, efficient counter-measures might be available neutralizing its stabilizing advantages. Therefore the MPS basing scheme envisaged by the United States Government was cancelled by the President in October 1981; this decision was based on the assumption that an MPS system would not be adequately survivable over the long term, since the potential adversary could deploy additional warheads as fast as the United States could build shelters (DoD Annual Report, FY 1983: III—57).

As an alternative, United States planners are assessing deep basing (DB) as a possible long-term MX basing mode, i.e., placing MX missiles in chambers below the ground to make them invulnerable to direct hits by nuclear weapons on the surface (DoD Annual Report, FY 1983: III — 58). To-date the most recent proposals focus on the so-called "dense pack" basing mode which means in essence arranging several shelters in close neighbourhood; the detonation of a first attacking warhead would probably impede additional attacking missiles from hitting their targets ("fratricide").

The improvement of retargeting and control systems must also be seen in the context of the concern for ICBM vulnerability. The purpose of such measures is to have more options and a higher degree of precision with fewer ICBMs, assuming that the number of surviving ICBMs would be decimated.

Two hundred Minuteman III ICBMs of the United States will in future be capable of retargeting from the air, providing much flexibility for rapid changes in targeting. These could be utilized for counterforce strikes not planned in advance, particularly for a limited response to a limited attack, provided the locations of the opponent's "empty silos" are known within a short time, allowing the surviving force to be targeted on ICBMs still within their silos.

> "When the currently approved portion of the Airborne Launch Control System Phase III program is completed, the airborne aircraft will be able to receive Minuteman status data directly from 200 of 550 MM III missiles via an automatic data link with the launch facilities, and will also have the capability to insert target data into the memory of these 200 missiles" (FY 1982 ACIS: 4).

It is not currently planned to extend this system to all Minuteman missiles.

Invulnerability of the Strategic Triad?

Critics have argued that — notwithstanding the high degree of sophistication in the discussion on measures to counter ICBM vulnerability — the debate is flawed and one-sided. For instance, Schilling (1981: 70) complained that "the strategic debate has focussed on numbers of missiles and warheads as if they were living creatures whose survival was of value in their own right (...)". He advocates a broader view, taking into account the other two legs of the strategic triad, which are not considered to be endangered to a similar degree; in essence: ICBM vulnerability need not necessarily translate into crisis instability as long as the other components can be relied upon.

In fact the discussions about ICBM vulnerability, leading sometimes to the consideration of whether LOW would be necessary in the near future, seem to omit some very basic facts about strategic stability. Although it is the perceptions of decision-makers which count and not the "real" situation, discussions about ICBM vulnerability must be complemented by a broader view of the vulnerability of strategic nuclear weapons in their entirety.

The major nuclear Powers have their strategic forces split between three different kinds of deployment: land-based ballistic missiles, sea-launched ballistic missiles, and long-range bombers. This diversification with respect to basing modes complicates the planning of an attack and also provides a safeguard against obsolescence, as the obsolete leg may be modernized while the other two provide security.

> "This strategic Triad severely complicates Soviet offensive and defensive planning and provides a hedge against Soviet technological breakthroughs or the catastrophic failure of any one element of the Triad to perform its assigned wartime missions" (FY 1982 ACIS: 21).

At any rate it is a good insurance against "nasty technological surprises" (Bundy 1979: 10).

The nuclear forces of the United States are currently considered highly invulnerable, provided that the entire strategic triad is the frame of reference. "Properly balanced and modernized, the Triad poses insurmountable problems to an aggressor" (Hearings on Military Posture 1981, Part 4: 208). This is due to the mutually reinforcing effect of the different modes of deployment. One leg might be neutralized at any given time, but to attack all three simultaneously with high confidence of success is very unlikely (see Hearings on Military Posture 1981, Part 4: 375). The increasing vulnerability of the land-based fixed-site ICBMs is to be seen against the background of overall low vulnerability. At present, the three strategic "legs" are protecting each other against a surprise attack. This may be illustrated by two possible scenarios.

In case of an ICBM attack against the land-based forces (ICBM sites and air bases), there is a warning time of 20 to 30 minutes, allowing a fraction of the bombers to take off and be a safe distance away by the time of impact. Without LOW, a large portion (especially counted in throwweight) of nuclear weapons would survive even a massive attack.

The warning time available in case of attacking ICBMs would suffice to protect a large part of the second "leg", while the SLBMs are considered, at present, nearly invulnerable.

Yet there is also a different scenario: SLBMs attacking bomber bases from short range: "The comparatively short flight time of SLBMs directed at bomber bases (as low as six minutes) could in theory prevent a large portion of the manned bomber force from attaining its safe escape points, but in practice such a salvo would provide ample warning time for the launch of the Minuteman wings" (Gray 1977: 3).

The rejection of both scenarios as not attractive for a potential attacker rests largely on the assumption that the SLBMs are not able to destroy hard targets, but will only suffice for soft targets like airbases. This assumption, however, will not hold true indefinitely, and there are some who doubt its correctness even for the present time (Langer 1977; Ball 1977). The introduction of Trident-type SLBMs and the accurate navigation provided by GPS-like systems entails an enhanced first-strike role for SLBMs. SLBMs would in the corrected scenario be targeted on ICBM sites and bomber bases simultaneously (accurate timing provided) and either destroy the ICBM silos or perhaps render ICBM wings unable to launch due to a pin-down effect. Even under such assumptions, the SLBM force would still be able to retaliate and even hit hard and time-urgent targets.

Guaranteeing Invulnerability? The SLBM Force

Therefore one may readily agree with Steinbruner (1978: 414), who notes that "strategic missile submarines have emerged as the most stable force element, and any increase in the proportion of strategic forces deployed in submarines is considered a stabilizing development". He bases his judgement on the fact that submarines at sea cannot readily be located "under the current and clearly foreseeable state of technology" and it is "more difficult to achieve extreme accuracies with missiles launched from a submarine platform". This fact is apt to lessen the danger of pre-emption during a crisis, as it lessens even the threat to land-based nuclear delivery systems.

Tsipis (1975a) even wrote that "nuclear missile-carrying submarines are an ideal deterrence weapon since they ensure the national security of countries that possess them without destabilizing world peace" (Tsipis 1975a: 36). He added that the communication with SSBNs, "at best laborious and at worst impossible" (Tsipis 1975a: 39) impedes fast retargeting and the co-ordination necessary for a surprise attack.

However, improvements in navigation aids and in antisubmarine warfare (ASW) have changed the very two criteria for which the SSBNs are commended:

invulnerability is being increasingly reduced while the accuracy of SLBMs is being enhanced to an extent which would allow covering of hard targets. In addition, SLBMs have the potential to perform a first strike because they can be moved much closer to their targets than ICBMs (Langer 1977: 45), thus reducing warning time. SLBMs could be used to "flush out" the enemy ICBMs (Langer 1977: 46); this action could not be carried out by ICBMs because of the possibility of LOW. The SLBMs could be used to produce a "pin-down effect", delaying the launching of the ICBMs and allowing time for the arrival of other nuclear weapons capable of destroying the residual ICBMs: "However, some use could be made of even relatively inaccurate SLBMs, to 'pin-down' enemy ICBMs so that they cannot be launched until friendly ICBMs and manned bombers arrive to finish them off" (Langer 1977: 48).

This scenario has, however, a certain weakness in failing to take account of the enemy's SSBNs, which, assuming rudimentary communication is possible, would probably not remain idle until both land-based legs of the strategic triad were "finished off". The simultaneous destruction not only of the different ICBM fields and the bomber bases, but also of the SSBNs spread over several oceans is a task which could (at least in 1977) not be envisaged realistically. Ball (1977), like Langer, considers that SLBMs are approaching a stage where they could be called a real counterforce weapon and urges a re-thinking.

Fast progress in ASW would add one more destabilizing factor to the arms race. ASW could perhaps (in a co-ordinated way) be utilized to reduce the threatening nuclear potential to a certain degree; however, the taking out of SSBNs would very probably be taken as a signal of nuclear attack, triggering the launch of the residual nuclear weapons. In this context, it is rather difficult to see how an ASW capability could deny a first-strike capability (Ball 1977: 36); rather, the possession of it would give a boost to the first-strike capability by targeting not only land-based components but simultaneously also the sea-based leg and thus removing a very great part of retaliatory capacity.

Tsipis (1975a: 45—46) proposes "areas in the oceans accessible only to submarines of one nation" in order to ensure the second-strike capability necessary in order to have stability in a mutual deterrence structure. The ASW capabilities are subject to fast change. The statements of 1975 or 1977 may rapidly become obsolete. Wilkes (1979b: 427), writing only a few years later, said that combined developments may soon make it possible to detect, locate and destroy all adversary missile submarines within a time period so short as to effectively eliminate the adversary's sea-based retaliatory capability. ASW indeed presents a rather disquieting prospect (Pott 1981: 209 ff.). Although Navy planners hope to escape the dangers of new

ASW technologies by constructing quieter submarines which are harder to detect, there are some doubts as to whether these improvements might not be rendered meaningless by advances in detecting enemy submarines by non-acoustic methods such as monitoring nuclear contaminants in the wake of submarines or spotting "submerged wakes", i.e., the trail of disturbed water which ultimately rises to the surface (Beck and Martin 1982; Wilkes 1979b). ASW could invalidate the very foundations of the basic strategy of mutual deterrence. Wilkes (1979b: 449) describes the dilemma which would arise if constantly improved ASW systems, even though only originally intended for tactical use, resulted in a kind of first-strike capability. If this capability is reached, there will be a temptation to use it. The other side, of course, would perceive the threat and this would result in destabilization of the "use them or lose them" kind not only for land-based nuclear weapons but for sea-based nuclear weapons as well. Therefore it seems urgent to place limits on ASW by agreement, as proposed by Ruina (1975: 55), Pott (1981: 222 f.) and others.

But it is not only the danger of destruction of the SSBNs that matters. Wilkes mentions the equally important condition that communication systems be reliable enough to guarantee that orders to launch SLBMs will get through to the submarines (Wilkes 1979 a: 389). The C^3-problems with respect to SSBNs are well known, and the command stability of this weapons system could be questioned. Guaranteeing secure transmission of orders to the submarines is much more difficult than it is for the land-based missiles (Wilkes 1979a: 394), due to the mobility and the greater distances. There are, of course, a number of communications systems, providing ample redundancy, but they have only a limited chance of being functional after heavy attack. The projected systems of Extremely Low Frequency (ELF) transmitters only partly mitigate this problem. In sum, the role of SLBMs in nuclear strategy is affected by increased vulnerability of the submarines, increased accuracy of the warheads carried, and doubts about the ability to command a retaliatory strike after an attack targeted on vital communications installations. According to Wilkes (1979a: 390), if survivability of neither the submarines nor their communications systems can be guaranteed, then there will be an increased temptation to adapt the SLBM system as a whole for use in a first-strike counterforce role (Wilkes 1979a: 390). The accuracy of the SLBM is affected by two sources of error: the navigational error and the inaccuracy due to incalculable influences during the flight. Fixed-site ICBMs have, of course, only the second component, and thus normally have greater accuracy. However, the navigational error has been diminished by improved systems to update the inertial navigation (Wilkes 1979a). The result is a hard-target kill capacity of such systems as Poseidon or Trident on the United States side. The Soviet SLBMs are assumed to have a somewhat lesser accuracy; however, the available information does not allow the accurate assessments which are needed in a field where performance has risen dramatically.

An overall assessment of the position of the sea-based leg in a strategic system based primarily on deterrence must certainly include the facts that (1) invulnerability is seriously in doubt; (2) the reliance on SLBMs as a means for retaliation suffers from uncertainties about the survivability of the communications systems necessary to trigger such a second strike; (3) the acquisition of hard-target kill capacity due to greater accuracy allows for the assignment of tasks to the SLBMs formerly reserved for ICBMs and bombers. Increased accuracy alone would not endanger the second-strike capability and thus not be very much destabilizing, even though it might facilitate counterforce options.

An analysis of current trends in armaments technology affecting strategic stability leads to the conclusion that the nature of the overall strategic balance is undergoing a fundamental change. This change clearly points in the direction of greater instability due to increasing force vulnerability. Yet on the other hand, United States and Soviet experts independently conclude that at the present moment and in the foreseeable future neither major Power can seriously assume itself capable of launching a disarming strike against the opponent's forces. They are also anxious to counter any such tendency by intensive efforts to close possible "windows of vulnerability".

C. The Challenge to C^3 Survivability

The Crucial Significance of C^3

The urgency aggravating the risk of unintentional nuclear war by creating an incentive to strike pre-emptively depends to a considerable degree on the vulnerability of command, control, and communications ($=C^3$) systems. According to Steinbruner (1978: 418) the danger of losing central command over strategic options shortly after the initiation of warfare is very great indeed; Steinbruner thinks that there is good reason to believe that communication systems, and hence the military command structure, are vastly more vulnerable to attack than individual force elements *(ibid.: 420)*. This view is shared by Bundy (1979: 14), who thinks that "the greatest single threat to the strategic deterrent is the threat to its nervous system and its brain". As a matter of fact, both major Powers are known to prepare C^3 targeting in their nuclear planning. Strategic stability thus also means command stability.

The need for survivable C^3 systems as a prerequisite for command stability was publicly acknowledged and emphasized by United States Secretary of Defense Brown. He said that the national C^3 system must provide the NCA with flexible operational control of the strategic forces at all levels of conflict, during or after enemy attack. Thus, survivable tactical warning and assessment of enemy attack, survivable command centres for decision-making and the direction of the forces are needed. Survivable communications to transmit retaliatory orders to the launch control centres are no less important. The C^3 system also has to facilitate termination of nuclear conflict by securing communications with adversaries. The United States Secretary of Defense announced the countervailing strategy requiring capabilities to conduct a controlled exchange of some duration. It was urged that survivability, endurance and flexibility of the C^3 systems should match that of the strategic forces (DoD Annual Report FY 1982: 52).

As a consequence of these and other considerations within the comprehensive programme for revitalizing the United States strategic deterrent, the improvement of the communications and control system is considered as "the most urgently needed element", especially if these systems are to survive, endure, and be usable (DoD Annual Report, FY 1983: I—39).

The emphasis on the need to counter C^3 vulnerability is even more important if one takes account of the fact that there are already problems with C^3 in peacetime. According to a Report by the United States Comptroller General (1981: 34), the performance of the World-Wide Military Command and Control System (WWMCCS) "is so poor that rapid improvements are necessary to minimize continuing critical shortfalls in capability, particularly during times of crisis". It seems that a major cause of these problems is the continued use of computers whose circuitry was not designed to function in an on-line environment by the command and control function. These problems obviously increase the risk of failure. Source information provided by WWMCCS is also said to be not timely, accurate, or complete enough for managing time-constrained situations *(ibid.*: 7). Furthermore, command facilities and supporting information systems are not considered capable of surviving civil strife, sabotage, or war *(ibid.*: 8).

The severe challenge to C^3 survivability arises primarily from the fact that the highest national authorities in the United States are not protected from sudden attack. A change in this situation is hardly possible and very unlikely. There are probably procedures for conducting nuclear war if the highest authority is one of the first casualties (chain of succession, predelegation for certain contingencies, etc.). However, this is only part of the problem; nuclear explosions may destroy or interfere with large parts of the C^3 system. The main vulnerabilities of communications systems include:

        Physical destruction
        Electromagnetic pulse (EMP)
        Ionospheric disruption
        Jamming
        ASAT threats
(see Office of Technology Assessment 1981: 281—283).

51

It would be very hard to maintain command and control over nuclear weapons once both landlines and radio links are affected.

A similar, although less specific concern about C³ vulnerability is expressed by Soviet sources, which explicitly accuse the United States of planning a massive nuclear strike at, among other targets, "seats of political, state, and military power (...), transport and communications, and the main administrative centers in the USSR" *(Whence the Threat to Peace* 1982: 58).

Potential Destabilization by ASAT Developments

Among the developments undermining the stability of C³ systems, those related to satellite technology undoubtedly have the most severe impact, at least in the hypothetical future. Many applications of satellite technology (cf. Jasani 1978; Garwin 1981) are of crucial importance for communications with long-range nuclear weapons, mainly ICBMs and SLBMs, but to a certain degree others as well (for example, the geodesy is of maximum importance for the programming of the TER-COM guidance system in the cruise missile). Satellites in space are described as "force multipliers" (Schneider 1981: 13) because they constitute a crucial link for executing any military action. The destruction of the most important satellites would not only preclude a response to an attack, it would also make it very difficult to reliably assess attack and damage. Photographic, electronic and nuclear-explosions detection reconnaissance is necessary in order to verify compliance with arms-control agreements as long as such treaties are based on verification by national technical means.

Early warning given by photographic and infra-red reconnaissance represents the first indication of an attack by ICBMs or SLBMs. Jasani (1978: 44—45) describes how the warning time (of ICBM attack) has been doubled by the introduction of artificial earth satellites as opposed to reliance on radar systems. The infra-red sensor will detect the very hot exhaust of the ICBM boosters, and TV cameras allow the ground observer to determine the origin of the infra-red radiation. Thus the early-warning satellites play a crucial role in crisis stability by procuring (in case of intercontinental attack) 10 to 15 minutes' additional warning time. If LOW is ever to be applied, it will also depend on the signals from early-warning satellites.

Satellites can be used not only to detect ICBM and SLBM launches but also to assess the attack. "The geostationary satellites of the Defense Support Program detect rocket launches and, in conjunction with ground-based radars, can be used to estimate the size and direction of a Soviet missile attack" (Karas 1981: 8—9).

52

These uses for reconnaissance purposes seem to stabilize the strategic situation and offer no incentives to pre-empt by launching ICBMs. An accurate damage assessment satellite, however, would diminish the number of warheads required for successful attack on hostile ICBMs: if quick damage assessment reports were available, the initial attack would need to use only one warhead per silo, followed, if the warhead were to fail, by another directed at the same missile silo (Karas 1981: 9). The environment resulting from nuclear blasts, however, gives rise to some doubts as to whether it would be feasible to conduct photographic reconnaissance in time to order a second attack.

Yet there is another kind of satellite reconnaissance which has a clearly desta-bilizing impact: ocean surveillance. According to Karas (1918: 12) there is some speculation that in the future satellites may utilize techniques that render the oceans transparent, making it impossible for submarines to hide at all (Karas 1981: 12).

Communications are heavily dependent on satellites, especially for long dis-tances as may be usual with SSBNs. Karas (1981: 12) asserts that the use of satellites for assisting long-range communications may reduce their vulnerability by extending the areas of the ocean in which the SSBNs can hide. Communication satellite links may be disturbed by jamming of the uplink to the satellite or the downlink at the ground-based receiver (Garwin 1981: 49). The United States World-Wide Military Command and Control System (WWMCCS) is based on satellites, and the Soviet Union as well has deployed a high number of communication satellites. The use of satellites for navigational purposes allows the accuracy of the SLBMs to be increased.

United States fleet ballistic missile-submarines, if equipped with NAVSTAR Global Positioning Satellite receivers, could hit targets with 30 to 50 per cent greater accuracy (Schneider 1981: 13). This is due to the ability to define very accurately the position of launch, minimizing this source of error, leaving only the unpredic-table flight irregularities to influence deviation from the target. The United States has already deployed part of its new Global Positioning System (GPS); in its final form it should consist of 18 or 24 NAVSTAR satellites. Their performance is impressive as they will tell a user within 0.1 second his position in three dimen-sions to an accuracy of 10 metres, and vector velocity to about 1 centimetre per second (Garwin 1981: 49). For the fixing of the position of sea-based force components, a smaller number of satellites would suffice, as the position in one of the three dimensions (the altitude) can be supplied by other devices in this case. GPS "will provide submarine-launched ballistic missiles with accuracy at least as good as those projected for the land-based MX missile" (Garwin 1981: 49).

It goes without saying that these applications of satellite technology are not necessarily desirable from the point of view of maintaining strategic stability. The counterforce potential will not be limited to land-based systems, and of the two reasons given for the particular usefulness of SLBMs (invulnerability, inaccuracy),

53

the second one will be lost. In case of NAVSTAR, it is the receiver who can be jammed, not the satellite (Garwin 1976: 69).

Space might also be used for ballistic missile delivery (Garwin 1981: 50), but the Outer Space Treaty states that

> "Parties to the Treaty undertake not to place in orbit around the earth any objects carrying nuclear weapons or any other kinds of weapons of mass destruction, instal such weapons on celestial bodies, or station such weapons in outer space in any other manner" (article IV).

Because satellites positioned in orbit play a crucial role in attack assessment and in directing the nuclear forces, the possibility of ASAT has been recognized and evaluated. As Garwin wrote (1976: 68), it would be physically possible for the Soviet Union to launch anti-satellite vehicles, which could reach synchronous orbit in six to eight hours and in principle destroy individual satellites ...

The development and deployment of ASAT weapons in space is *not* prohibited by the Outer Space Treaty, and the SALT I agreements, by acknowledging the crucial role of national technical means for verification, do not seem to include all the satellites, but probably only reconnaissance satellites (see Jasani 1978: 167). From a purely military standpoint it is highly desirable to have a unilateral ASAT option in wartime, as Schneider (1981: 13) notes; the risk will increase, especially in crises, as the early warning, communications, navigation and surveillance satellites become vulnerable. A strike against such satellites would be an act of war. Yet the military advantages of striking first might be tempting in a deteriorating crisis situation. Particularly if retaliatory weapons are highly vulnerable, the destruction of early warning facilities may be considered as an equivalent to a massive attack and be responded to accordingly (for a discussion in the context of LOW, see Garwin 1980). Thus, the interference with or attack on satellites crucial for deterrence could be defined as tantamount to trigger retaliation in the form of a nuclear attack. This would, however, entail the danger of misinterpretation of technical problems, e.g., if a satellite ceases to function due to a technical defect.

It is therefore important to find ways and means of controlling or prohibiting future ASAT developments. The Soviet Union, in 1981, proposed a draft Treaty on the Prohibition of the Stationing of Weapons of Any Kind in Outer Space. The proposal to conclude such a treaty was supported by most of the delegations at the thirty-sixth session of the United Nations General Assembly. The United States did not vote against it; however, it preferred to abstain from voting on this resolution and suggested the conclusion of an agreement on the narrower question of ASAT systems (Batsanov 1982: 152—158). Although the United States and the USSR may differ in this approach to coping with the ASAT threat to strategic stability, there seems to be a commonly shared concern about this issue.

The two major Powers are reported to be undertaking R&D in the field of ASAT. The Soviet Union, according to Garwin (1981: 50), has tested a vehicle carrying a rocket-propelled homing vehicle. The destruction of satellites can be achieved by a high-explosive warhead or with pellets. According to testimony by the Chief of Research and Engineering of the United States Department of Defense at a hearing before the House Armed Services Committee, the Soviet Union may be ready to put into orbit laser weapons capable of destroying United States spy and communications satellites (*Time*, 15 March 1982: 24). Meanwhile, the United States 1983 budget proposes that $ US 218.3 million be spent on space defence, with a further $ US 115.7 million for laser research and $ US 40.6 million for a space-laser program. In summer 1982, the United States is to test a small ASAT vehicle to be launched from F-15 fighter aircraft at high altitude and then homing directly to the attacked satellite (direct-ascent intercept) (see Smith 1981; Garwin 1981: 50). It is 17 ft long and about 20 inches wide, weighing about 2600 lb. The satellites of the present generation are not armoured. Even rather low impact might so impair their function as to render them useless. The development and deployment of ASAT weapons launchable from widely dispersed aircraft would pose a very great threat to the satellites in case of war, with possibly fatal consequences: the nuclear weapons might get out of control, as the field commanders would be cut off from communication. In-built redundancy may mitigate this danger.

More exotic space weapons — laser weapons and more generally beam weapons — are not at a very advanced stage of R&D. The United States is currently assessing the technical feasibility of space-based laser weapons (DoD Annual Report, FY 1983: III—65). The United States Space Shuttle could also be utilized for military purposes, for example for orbiting satellites which would replace the ones impaired by attack, or to capture enemy satellites in order to put them out of order and/or inspect them. However, this danger could easily be avoided by equipping the satellites with "a small explosive charge, which would be armed some days after launch, to detonate whenever the satellite is subject to accelerations not induced by its own rocket motors" (Garwin 1981: 51). According to Soviet sources, the Shuttle technology is perceived as a grave threat to Soviet satellite systems.

The launching of "dormant" satellites which would take over the functions of a satellite that had been destroyed might be a means of mitigating the ASAT threat. Furthermore, alternative means of communication could be constructed. The blinding of early warning systems would, in any case, provoke extreme alert.

The Decapitation Nightmare

Ultimately, the absence of command stability, or the vulnerability of control systems, can offer an incentive for a pre-emptive strike against C^3 systems — what in strategic terminology is sometimes sarcastically called "decapitation" (Steinbruner

1981: 18; Ball 1981: 14). The C^3 in fact constitute the most vulnerable and valuable target (Steinbruner 1981: 18f.) According to Ball, at the present moment such a decapitation strike against the United States' national command system would require only about 50 to 100 warheads (Steinbruner 1981: 18); by contrast, the Soviet Union would need to expend thousands of warheads in any comprehensive counterforce attack against United States strategic weapons (Ball 1981: 35). C^3 vulnerability has at least two unfortunate destabilizing consequences: if a Power judges that nuclear war can no longer be avoided, it is a rational defensive act to launch a pre-emptive decapitation strike. Yet this very logic produces powerful incentives on the part of the potential decapitation victim to conduct full-scale strategic operations at the outset of any serious engagement, thus immediately escalating any "limited" nuclear war (Steinbruner 1981: 19—23).

The author of a comparative analysis of United States and Soviet strategic command and control capabilities (Ball 1981: 43—45) comes to the conclusion that the vulnerability of these capabilities is greater in the case of the United States than in the case of the Soviet Union, which has a more extensive system for protecting the top political and military leadership and a higher degree of redundancy and dispersion of communication links. However, while it would be easier to isolate the United States national commanding authority from its strategic forces than in the case of its Soviet counterpart, the Soviet strategic forces depend to a much larger extent on central orders, and lower commanders are probably left no room for initiative where nuclear weapons are concerned; this might easily constitute an Achilles' heel of the Soviet forces in a war. Soviet specialists in fact tend to assume therefore that Soviet C^3 systems are more vulnerable than United States C^3 systems, especially in the event of a deployment of Pershing-II missiles in Western Europe, which would leave only a short warning time.

It is important to note that most studies regarding C^3 vulnerability focus on the central balance and start from scenarios assuming the risk of an attack against the homelands of one of the two major nuclear Powers. This is, however, only part of the picture. One must not forget that the same problems necessarily arise at the regional level as well, and perhaps even more dramatically. For instance, it is conceivable that the system of regional nuclear deterrence postures, as existing in Europe, may also become the framework for anti-C^3 warfare. If at that level the C^3 systems are vulnerable, it is hard to imagine how a "limited" nuclear war could be waged. The same problem might also be relevant in the context of newly emerging nuclear Powers in the third world.

It is outside the scope of this study to make a detailed examination of technological and other factors affecting the stability of command and communication systems. Special studies in this context usually point at nuclear effects (blast, radiation, in particular degradation of electrical and electronic systems as a result of EMP, sabotage, vulnerability of C^3 systems with regard to conventional bombing,

56

human error, natural phenomena such as northern lights, equipment failure, jamming, deficient communications security and the like) (Ball 1981, chapter II). The risk of failure of redundant complex systems is very hard to estimate. However, most of these factors affect the C^3 structure in a situation where a nuclear war has already been started. This problem may be different from the original problem of command stability.

In general, it is hard to prove that C^3 systems are vulnerable to the extent of offering an easy target for a "decapitation" attack. In addition, both major Powers are working on programmes to enhance the survivability of their C^3 systems by developing back-up systems, new systems (airborne command posts and mobile terminals on the ground) and upgrading the old systems in order to enhance their survivability (Schilling 1981: 61; Hearings on Military Posture, Part 4: 213, 1158—1161; DoD Annual Report, FY 1982: 44—45 and 1983: III-79; Steinbruner 1981: 21).

Upgrading C^3

Worries about C^3 vulnerability have led the United States government to allocate more funds for upgrading these systems (Steinbruner 1981: 25). The United States plans to construct an Extremely Low Frequency (ELF) system for communications from operation headquarters and the national command authority to SSBNs and nuclear attack submarines operating at maximum speeds and depths in all operational areas. The submarines would not need to use trailing antennas or buoys. It is planned to construct the antenna required for ELF transmission in Michigan; it would be underground, 130 miles long. However, "ELF would be a (. . .) system for day-to-day operations only, since it is vulnerable and not expected to survive in wartime" (FY 1982 ACIS: 87).

The United States is also undertaking some R&D on Strategic Laser Communications (SLC):

> "The goal of the strategic laser communications program is to develop those technologies of blue-green laser communications through clouds and water to submerged submarines in a one-way direction. (. . .) We believe this will provide a wartime capability C^3 link to the SSBN forces". (Hearings on Military Posture 1981, Part 4: 85; see also pages 86—90, 122—123).

Yet, at present these technologies are not operational. In order to communicate the submarines have to come up near the surface or stick an antenna through the surface or tow a long wire within a few feet of the surface (Hearings on Military Posture 1981, Part 4: 27). The communication with land-based manned bombers seems comparable with that of the ICBMs. However, in crisis situations, dispersal of the bomber fleet in order to lower the vulnerability would cause problems of command and control (Steinbruner 1978: 423). It is planned to equip the United

States bomber force with very low-frequency receivers to enhance their ability to communicate (DoD Annual Report, FY 1983: I-40). More generally speaking, the United States also plans to upgrade the so-called "Defense-Wide C³", which includes five major classes of systems which provide the infrastructure for navigation and position-fixing; base and support communications; common-user communications; communications security; and information systems (DoD Annual Report, FY 1983: III-83).

So far, no nuclear Power can have enough confidence in its ability to wipe out the C³ systems of the opponent. If one Power were really interested in such a policy, it would have to test new weapons suitable for this mission in order to find out whether those weapons are really reliable and whether they deserve confidence. This testing could hardly be performed without being detected by the other side.

Similar reservations seem appropriate with regard to the probability of a scenario which is sometimes labelled the "BOOB" attack scenario. It refers to a decapitation strike comparable to a "bolt-out-of-the blue sky" launched as a pre-emptive surprise attack. Although this scenario appears to be quite attractive in theory, it must not be forgotten that in practice it can hardly occur other than in the context of an acute crisis. In such a situation, however, the Governments concerned would be in a state of alert which would render meaningless any attempt to launch a "BOOB" attack, because surprise would then be practically unfeasible.

Nevertheless, the nightmare of the decapitation scenario has a certain relevance for the problem of unintentional war because the more one thinks about it, the more one may be tempted to adopt LOW postures. This of course is highly undesirable from the point of view of strategic stability. More generally speaking, any system which could force a Government into a hasty decision is *ipso facto* undesirable (Bundy 1979: 14).

As mentioned previously, one should not underestimate the incentive for preemptive destruction of the United States command structure in the specific situation where the Soviet Union was already involved in a war or had to reckon with a fully committed United States attack. According to Steinbruner (1978: 426; 1981: 19), in such a situation a pre-emptive attack against the United States command structure would have the advantage of offering a slight chance of escaping with very low damage and of precluding the worst-case destruction which would occur in a fully coordinated United States attack. It seems that the United States authorities are increasingly concerned with the endurance of the C³ systems *after* the beginning of a nuclear war (Perry 1979: 133). Verne Orr, Secretary of the United States Air Force, testified before the House Committee on Armed Forces that the ground communication installations are highly vulnerable to attack:

> "During the first half-hour of a nuclear attack launched today, many ground-based sensors and communications centers would be destroyed or rendered inoperable" (Hearings on Military Posture 1981, Part 1: 1369).

Also, the ASAT threat cautions against relying too much on satellite-based communications systems.

Another unfortunate consequence of command vulnerability has been identified by Steinbruner (1978: 424), who notes that

> "the most serious threat of war under current circumstances probably lies in the possibility that organizationally and technically complex military operations might override coherent policy decisions and produce a war that was not intended".

Steinbruner complains about the exclusive concern of United States force planners over vulnerability in the traditional sense (i.e., force vulnerability). The more efforts are undertaken to improve this situation (e.g., by avoiding two-way communication with submarines and strategic bombers), the more command stability is undermined by the very same measures. There is, in other words, a trade-off between the vulnerability of force elements and the stability of command channels (Steinbruner 1978: 423). It is difficult to see a way out of this dilemma.

Conclusions: Risks of Unintentional Nuclear War Generated by the Arms Race

The risks:

1. *The qualitative and quantitative arms race continuously generates new military options. Thus the delicate strategic stability is constantly challenged and undermined. The arms race may, e.g., create a propensity of the international strategic system to collapse due to incentives to pre-empt and to adopt LOW policies. In other words, it affects the crisis stability of the international system, thus aggravating the risk of nuclear war by miscalculation.*
2. *The secrecy surrounding new weapons developments leads the nuclear Powers to infer the "worst case" and to overreact; thus the arms race is accelerated.*
3. *The risks involved in the current technological arms race derive mainly from:*
   Enhanced accuracy and yield (mainly due to MIRV) of anti-ICBM weapons, thus jeopardizing ICBM invulnerability;
   ASW developments jeopardizing the SLBM "leg" of the strategic triad;
   Shrinking warning time due to forward basing.
4. *Efforts to counter ICBM vulnerability by reconsidering possible BMD measures may be misunderstood by the opponent.*
5. *Even if the strategic systems are not as vulnerable as some observers assume, the mere perception of their vulnerability may lead to misjudgement and miscalculation.*
6. *A grave threat is posed to the invulnerability of C^3 systems; this may offer temptations to launch a pre-emptive first-strike attack or to adopt LOW policies and*

predelegation measures, which aggravate the risk of unauthorized initiation of nuclear war.

7. *To a considerable extent the arms race is progressing on an incremental step-by-step basis lacking proper national let alone international control. It thus produces results that are often highly dysfunctional to both national security interests and international concerns for strategic stability.*

Mitigating factors:

1. *The nuclear Powers are extremely sensitive and attentive to potential vulnerabilities of their retaliatory capacity and C^3 systems; as a consequence they undertake huge efforts to forestall potential "windows of vulnerability".*
2. *New weapons technologies require testing, which offers an opportunity to detect new dangers in due time; this might mitigate the danger of being surprised by a technological breakthrough achieved by the opponent.*
3. *So far and for the foreseeable future the arms race between offensive and defensive systems is led by the offensive systems. This fact helps the "mutual assured destruction" relationship to continue to prevail.*
4. *Arms control agreements may help to minimize threats to strategic stability by consensus.*

Risk assessment:

It is clear that the risks arising from the arms race are not efficiently countered or checked by the mitigating factors. Although in the absence of an acute international crisis these risks are not liable to overthrow strategic stability at the present moment or in the foreseeable future, they are extremely alarming in the long run.

III. DOCTRINAL DEVELOPMENTS
AND STRATEGIC STABILITY

A. The Mismatch of Strategic Doctrine
of East and West

The Risk of Fallacies

The following chapter is devoted to issues of strategic conceptions or doctrines. Recent years have witnessed an astonishing and, to some extent, quite bewildering growth of strategic thinking. The qualitative arms race has had a most significant impact on the nature of strategic doctrines. Some specialists are even inclined to assert that

> "policies are changing because military technology has produced more precise weapons; once available, weapons are usually deployed, and policies then have to be modified to justify (i.e., rationalize) the deployment" (Barnaby 1980: 5).

At least in Western countries, a new profession seems to be emerging, the strategic expert, and like all professional subcultures, the field of strategy is increasingly becoming specialized and characterized by an abundant use of technical terminology which sometimes makes it difficult for outsiders to understand what is involved.

Yet one should avoid being confused or mystified by this development. As has rightly been noted by critics of contemporary strategic thinking (e.g. Green 1966: 259), it must not be forgotten that assertions in the field of strategy, notwithstanding the apparent degree of sophistication of this thinking, ultimately rest on complex political judgement, i.e. on an expression of beliefs based on experience. Of course this fact implies considerable risks, since judgement can be correct or fallacious. In the last resort, even central concepts such as "strategic balance" ultimately depend on beliefs — beliefs concerning what each country might be able to undertake and the outcome of such undertakings, beliefs concerning what each nation can or cannot do, both militarily and politically. As Goldhamer points

61

out in his study on thep erceptions of the United States—Soviet balance, these considerations may lead observers to include elements as fuzzy as national will in perceptions of the military balance (Goldhamer 1978: 9). Strategic doctrine can therefore be defined as

> "a set of operative beliefs, values, and assertions that in a significant way guide
> official behavior with respect to strategic research and development (R&D), weapons
> choice, forces, operational plans, arms control, etc." (Ermarth 1978 : 138).

Furthermore, as suggested by Leitenberg (1980a: 10) it may also seem appropriate to distinguish between employment policy, declaratory policy, acquisition
policy and deployment policy. In particular, the difference between "real" strategic
doctrine and publicly expressed doctrine must not be neglected; but unfortunately,
due to problems of access to information, it is hardly helpful in scientific research.

An important and possibly crucial question to be asked in connection with
strategic doctrines refers to the degree of congruity or incongruity existing between
strategic perceptions held by major Powers (Chari 1979: 155). It cannot be denied
that the strategic debate suffers from serious deficiencies in this respect. One of the
two major Powers is not always explicit about its concepts, perceptions and intentions, thus offering broad scope for idle speculation of all kinds which is typical of
situations characterized by uncertainty. The other major Power, in turn, may be
said to be far too explicit at one time or another, increasing uncertainty by frequent
changes of terminology and concepts. A Soviet author (Gerasimov 1982: 56) says
that American strategic thinking follows a kind of "zig-zag" course; it cannot be
denied that this point may be valid.

This state of affairs also results in a tendency to distort or misrepresent actual
capabilities and intentions. Soviet spokesmen, for example, deplore this tendency as
"the artificial prime cause of many of the fears" (Soviet Committee for European
Security and Co-operation 1981: 6). Another Soviet author also complains about
the tendency, in Western strategic thinking, to refer to alleged "Soviet experts"
without giving proper reference, and to misquote Soviet sources (Gerasimov 1982: 5).
Certainly everybody may agree with the conclusion expressed in a Soviet publication that "now, as at all other critical junctures of history, it is highly important
for Governments and nations to have correct knowledge of each other, especially
where it concerns war and peace" (Soviet Committee for European Security and
Co-operation 1981: 7). This is in line with what a United States author had in mind
when he warned that the "failure to recognize them [the differences] has had dangerous consequences for the United States—Soviet strategic relationship" (Ermarth
1981: 67).

"The concept of military doctrine is used in somewhat different ways by the
major military Powers" (United Nations General Assembly 1980a: 94). In the
West, military doctrines are similar to operational concepts guiding the use

of force (Schwarz 1978; Schwarz 1981: 63ff). In the Soviet Union, however, strategic doctrine has a broader meaning encompassing also political, economic and technological considerations (Schwarz 1978b; Schwarz 1981: 70ff). In the United States a community of strategic thinkers, to a great degree not professionally involved with the armed services, has formulated and continues to formulate very differentiated and fine-tuned strategies for the employment of strategic nuclear weapons. These writings do not lack clarity and display a diversity of views.

As for the Soviet Union, the circumstances are different:

> "Soviet nuclear doctrines are generally not as openly expressed as is the case in the United States. Soviet thinking on the subject to a large extent has to be deduced from very general statements, from military force dispositions, and from Soviet military writing" (United Nations General Assembly 1980 a: 103).

The high degree of secrecy surrounding Soviet strategic doctrine, or at least a certain reluctance to reveal much about Soviet strategic thinking, has something to do with historical traditions which are different from those of the United States. From the Soviet point of view, the strategic doctrine underlying Soviet force deployment and employment is sufficiently clearly outlined. Yet, it should also be borne in mind that, from the Soviet point of view, secrecy is also part of the Soviet strategic posture.

This difference has led to much discussion of the difference of doctrines between the major nuclear Powers: According to Legvold (1979: 9), the essential difference is that the United States has, or aspires to have, a strategic doctrine: the Soviet Union does not. She persists with only the operational concepts of war. The broader setting of Soviet military doctrine, including political, economic, and technological considerations, sometimes leads Western observers to conclude that there is a lack of precision in Soviet strategic writings. Also the very basis of strategic reasoning is considered to be different. United States theory of deterrence seems to be a theory of bargaining; the Soviet notion of deterrence seems to be without a theory and substitutes instead the science of war (Legvold 1979: 8).

Such doubts, however, are not always justified because the USSR's central strategic concepts, by contrast with those of the West, are not laid down in an elaborate strategic literature; they are expressed in authoritative statements by the Soviet leaders (e.g. Brezhnev 1982a, 1982b, 1982c; Ustinov 1981).

The major cause of misunderstandings, however, can easily be identified in the confusion of Soviet military doctrine and the Soviet theory of combat by Western observers. Actually, Soviet writers clearly distinguish between these two levels of theory: On the one hand there is what they call "doctrine or military policy" which they assert to be of a purely defensive nature. On the other hand, they speak about aspects of combat, such as battlefield tactics, which involve offensive operations (cf. Soviet Committee for European Security and Cooperation 1981: 10f.). Another current distinction refers to "military art" (the theory and practice of preparing and conducting military operations) on the one hand and "military science" (the system of knowledge about the character and laws of war) on the other hand. According to this distinction, strategic thinking is part of military science (Leebaert 1981: 14 f.)

There are some indications that Soviet strategic thinkers have an understanding of United States strategic doctrines which differs from the intentions of United States authors. Perhaps, the twists in strategic declarations and writings are to be considered as attempts to maximize the psychological impact of a given force structure on the adversary (see, for example, Trofimenko 1981; Legvold 1979). "Soviet observers regard them [parts of doctrines] as ill-considered attempts to rationalize the use of nuclear weapons" (Legvold 1979: 9), and, more generally, accuse the United States of manipulating the threat of war in order to maximize apparent or real edges over the Soviet Union. The United States' strategic nuclear doctrine was constantly based on the premise of deterrence; after the Soviets caught up, it was mutual deterrence which resulted in the doctrine of mutual assured destruction (MAD). The Soviet acceptance of this doctrine was a topic of intense speculation, particularly after the conclusion of SALT I, as the acceptance of anti-ballistic missile (ABM) limitation was considered to indicate Soviet concern for maintaining mutual vulnerability, a crucial prerequisite of deterrence by punishment (see, for example, Garthoff 1978a, 1979, 1981; Lambeth 1979; Brennan 1979).

In the meantime, however, a considerable number of authoritative Soviet statements indicate that the Soviet leadership is familiar with this concept although using a different terminology mainly focused on terms such as "nuclear stalemate" (Gerasimov 1982: 49), and "equality and equal security" (Brezhnev 1981b: 4; Ustinov 1981: 23). This conclusion is also supported by repeated Soviet assertions expressed in official sources that in a nuclear war there can be no victory (Gerasimov 1982: 48) and that the Soviet Union never seeks military superiority (Ustinov 1981: 28).

As was indicated at the beginning of this section, the overall assessment of Soviet strategic doctrine by Western authors is subject to much speculation and guessing based on controversial evidence. It cannot be denied that this state of affairs generates some risks because the very situation of an adversary relationship tends to breed fallacies. As Garthoff (1978b) has pointed out, there is, in any strategic relationship between two opponents, always a problem in estimating and ascribing intentions. Among the many fallacies which Garthoff cites, three have an immediate relevance to the problem of unintentional war.

The first fallacy is what might be called worst-case thinking. Prudence determines estimates. As very much is at stake — possibly the very survival of the nation — one tends to inflate both the capabilities and intentions ascribed to the opponent. Garthoff argues that this approach, as a guiding concept, is highly pernicious and carries its own often unrecognized perils: it may have a distorting effect on the opponent's perceptions if he is led, by gross overestimates on the part of the other side, to conclude that the side applying the worst-case thinking has hostile intentions. It may also have an impact on the range of options examined, reducing them because overestimates suggest that some options are excluded prematurely for fear of a grossly exaggerated enemy reaction.

A second fallacy according to Garthoff (1978 b: 24) is the inclination to eschew analysis of intentions and to stress only measurable capabilities; in fact, once engaged in this line of thought, one ceases to estimate intentions and infers intentions from capabilities. The danger here lies in the temptation to assume implicitly maximum intentions.

Thirdly, there is the mirror image (Garthoff 1978 b: 25), i.e. projecting onto the subject of the estimates one's own views, perceptions, values, and behaviour. Garthoff makes the criticism that this thinking led United States strategists to impute specific intentions to the Soviet leaders: belief in mutual deterrence and mutual assured destruction, support for the global status quo and the like. It seems, however, that more often than not these mirror-images are simply substitutes for dire ignorance of the other side's motives and bases for action.

Keeping in mind these reservations and caveats, one might nevertheless try to examine the principal elements of United States, and Soviet strategic doctrines. This will be done with a view to identifying problems which might arise from a possible mismatch of strategic doctrines and which might be conducive to mutual misunderstandings and thus jeopardize strategic stability.

It should be noted, however, that for reasons explained above, the following sections are somewhat unbalanced as far as the material presented about United States and Soviet strategic doctrines is concerned. As more information is available on United States doctrine than on Soviet doctrine, it is also much easier to make critical comments on United States doctrine. In fact, many aspects of United States strategic doctrine are the subject of heated controversy taking place in publicly available newspapers and journals. Nothing comparable can be discerned in the Soviet Union. For this reason the present study offers only a small amount of information on Soviet strategic doctrine; the scarcity of critical comments on this subject does not necessarily imply approval or disapproval of these doctrines by the author.

Deterrence or War-fighting ?

Probably the most central issue of contemporary nuclear strategy is the debate about deterrence and war-fighting. The crucial question is: are the nuclear arsenals intended only for deterring a potential opponent or can they also be used for waging — and eventually winning— a war? It must be doubted whether any satisfactory answer to this question will ever be found. The dialectics of nuclear doctrine suggest that in order to deter, a nuclear potential must seem to be usable and nuclear war thus thinkable. The ability to fight a war is generally considered one of the more reliable ways to deter aggression (Simes 1981: 82). However, once the use of nuclear weapons for war-fighting appears to be conceivable, it is hard to deny that the nuclear threshold is considerably lowered and the risk of nuclear war increased. The delicately contradictory nature of this issue has given rise to all kinds of confusion misunderstandings and misrepresentations of intentions and assumptions.

For instance, American thinking on strategic doctrine is widely dominated by guesses about how the Soviet Union might interpret these concepts. The controversy on the issue seems to be never-ending. Garthoff emphasizes that in Marxist-Leninist ideology military power is not seen as a decisive element in advancing historical progress, and that the use of military power is sanctioned only if it is expedient in advancing the socialist cause (Garthoff 1978 a: 113). But he makes the point that the Soviet strategists see war-fighting and war-winning capabilities as providing the most credible deterrent, as well as providing against the contingency of war actually breaking out. Nitze (1977: 125) also thinks that Soviet spokesmen see deterrence and a war-winning capability "as complementary, not opposing concepts". According to Nitze a Soviet force capable of defeating any attacker and going on to win the resulting war is clearly better able to deter the other side than any lesser force. Lambeth (1979: 27) states that the Soviet Union rejects the concept of "mutual vulnerability" and appears persuaded that, in the nuclear age no less than before, the most reliable way to prevent war is to maintain the appropriate capacity to fight and win it should it occur. This orientation might be labelled "unilaterally assured survivability".

The difference between a strategy of (mutual) deterrence and one of war-fighting is presumed to be reflected in the characteristics of weapons. Whereas inaccurate but relatively high-yield missiles and warheads are considered to indicate a strategy based on deterrence (if they are sufficiently invulnerable to a first strike), the acquisition of weapons with high accuracies is taken to point to a war-fighting strategy based on strikes against the adversary's nuclear delivery systems. The targeting of hostile ICBMs has the main purpose of damage limitation, should a war indeed become inevitable.

Indisputably, the capability to fight a war will deter potential aggressors; however, the main question with respect to Soviet strategy is whether the concept of MAD is accepted. Of course one must bear in mind the change of doctrines over time as a result of changed perceptions of the environment and the development of the relevant technology. Garthoff (1979: 198) summarizes his findings on Soviet

66

views with respect to acceptance or rejection of MAD. He assumes the Soviet leaders to think

> "(1) that Soviet deterrence of the West is their principal military task ; (2) that there is a 'nuclear balance', strategic 'parity', and a reciprocal capability for overwhelming retaliation by either side if attacked ; (3) that this balance of mutual retaliatory capability should be maintained ; (4) that nuclear parity, rather than superiority, is the goal of Soviet military policy ; and (5) that negotiated strategic arms limitation is a desirable means to contribute to this maintenance of parity and balance",

and concludes: "I call this acceptance of mutual deterrence."

There is by no means unanimity in the assessment of Soviet strategy. According to Salomon (1977: 260 f.) Soviet thinking, as reflected in strategic force planning, behaviour at SALT negotiations and military doctrine, has, on the contrary, emphasized war-fighting capability and war survivability rather than deterrence in the MAD sense. Brennan (1979) also expresses serious doubts concerning the assumption that the Soviet Union had adopted a kind of MAD doctrine.

Accordingly, if both sides are able to maintain a capacity to retaliate after having been attacked, the basic requirements are met. However, each side may well strive for stronger deterrence and perhaps even some damage limitation through the targeting of some elements of the opposing nuclear force. As the required technology is not available at present, the Soviet Union no less than the United States is obliged to accept the reality of MAD. The Soviets would risk incalculable damage in a general nuclear war with the United States, and there is no reason to believe that their leadership is insensitive to these risks (Buchan 1981: 17). However, the state of technology is changing, and options not now available may be valid tomorrow.

There are some signs that even the United States, where the MAD strategy was "invented" is abandoning some central tenets of this doctrine, for example, the public emphasis on counter-city second strikes. According to Simes (1981: 80) there is indeed some convergence in United States and Soviet strategic concepts. And it may appear that instead of "educating" the Soviet Union about the virtues of MAD, the United States has moved closer to the Soviet view that there can be no credible difference without the capacity to fight in the case of its failure. Similarly to the position of the United States, the Soviet Union may perceive an increased vulnerability of the land-based Inter-Continental Ballistic Missiles (ICBMs) due to greater accuracy of the new warheads (MK-12A for Minuteman III, in the future MX) developed in the United States. Garthoff (1978a: 131) sees Soviet inclinations towards a Launch-on-Warning (LOW) concept as a possible consequence of the perception of United States counterforce capabilities.

Essentially, according to Legvold, the Soviet Union means to practise "a strategy of damage limitation" (1979: 10) by having the capability to destroy at least a portion of the ICBMs targeted at the USSR, once war seems inevitable. The efforts towards civil defence could be interpreted as another step to secure at least some damage limitation. Legvold considers the ABM treaty as an exception (renunciation of defence) proving the rule.

The picture presented by the current strategic debate among Western specialists is thus utterly confusing. The situation becomes even more difficult to understand if official Soviet sources are taken into account. Rightly or wrongly, Soviet strategists refuse to reason about the use of military force in the abstract quasi-mathematical manner of Western analysis (Calder 1979: 130). The number of authoritative Soviet statements about these issues is therefore very limited. The problem is aggravated by the fact that Eastern and Western doctrinal statements, although referring to the same phenomenon, i.e. nuclear war and its prevention, do not exactly coincide in their terminology. The key concepts used in doctrinal statements largely differ. For this reason, many Western authors quoting Soviet sources may unintentionally misrepresent the views actually conveyed in the statements they quote. This seems to be an unavoidable consequence of the mismatch of strategic terminology and doctrine.

When trying to assess the Soviet position regarding the contradiction between deterrence and war-fighting, and when trying to find out whether or not the Soviet Union accepts the doctrine of MAD, it should be noted that the Soviet authors never directly touch on these questions. Their doctrinal statements tend to be more encompassing and broader in scope, i.e. they refer to the use of nuclear weapons in general. This is expressed in the Soviet booklet *The Threat to Europe*:

> "Western political and military writers content that Soviet military doctrine is based exclusively on the belief that a world nuclear war can be won. But that is a simplistic and distorted view of our approach. In fact, the Soviet Union holds that nuclear war would be a universal disaster, and that it would most probably mean the end of civilisation. It may lead to the destruction of all humankind. There may be no victor in such war, and it can solve no political problems. As Leonid Brezhnev pointed out in his reply to a Pravda correspondent on 21 October 1981, 'anyone who starts a nuclear war in the hope of winning it has thereby decided to commit suicide. Whatever strength the attacker may have and whatever method of starting a nuclear war he may choose, he will not achieve his aims. Retaliation is unavoidable. That is our essential point of view'. Soviet people are not thinking in terms of winning a nuclear war, but of averting such a war by all means".
> (Soviet Committee for European Security and Cooperation 1981: 9)

Related to this are two additional elements salient in Soviet nuclear doctrine: the concept of retaliation (as opposed to pre-emption) and the rejection of the idea of limited nuclear war. As to the first concept, the official Soviet booklet *The Threat to Europe* says:

> "Soviet military doctrine, which has always reposed on the principle of retaliatory, that is, defensive action, says nothing at all in the new conditions of the 70s and early

80s of nuclear war being winnable and, more, lays the accent still more emphatically than before on preventing it, on maintaining the military equilibrium, and on lowering the level of military confrontation by means of military detente. 'There is no task that we intend to accomplish by armed force,' Leonid Brezhnev said in an interview to *Vorwärts*, the weekly of the Social-Democratic Party of Germany. It is extremely important to understand the essence of Soviet military doctrine if you want an objective picture of the political and military situation of the present-day world, and a bad blunder to mistake concepts of the 60s, however true they may have been in their time, for the content of Soviet military doctrine today". (Soviet Committee for European Security and Co-operation 1981: 11f).

This is also confirmed by the USSR Minister of Defence, D. F. Ustinov, who in turn refers to Leonid Brezhnev:

"Our strategic doctrine, as Leonid Brezhnev has said, has a thoroughly defensive orientation. This is reflected in the Constitution of the USSR. The essence of Soviet military doctrine is that, guided by the principles of Leninist foreign policy of peace and international security, it aims at defending the Soviet Union and other socialist states and at preventing imperialist aggression. Preventive expansionist wars of any type and scale and the concepts of pre-emptive nuclear strikes are alien to Soviet military doctrine." (Ustinov 1981: 27)

The idea of limited nuclear war is unanimously and constantly rejected in Soviet strategic doctrine. According to Leonid Brezhnev,

"if a nuclear war breaks out in Europe or elsewhere, it will necessarily and unavoidably become universal."

And

"only naïve people who are aloof from reality can suppose that the thermonuclear catastrophe will spare their homes if they are situated at a great distance from the place of disaster." (Brezhnev 1982a)

Referring to American conceptions regarding supposed "rules of the games" operative in case a nuclear war breaks out, D. F. Ustinov strongly emphasizes that any such concept is not acceptable to the Soviet Union:

"None but utterly irresponsible individuals can claim that nuclear war can be fought under some rules established in advance whereby nuclear missiles will go off under a 'gentleman's agreement', only at specific targets without hitting the population in the process." (Ustinov 1981: 7).

These and other Soviet statements on strategic doctrine offer the great advantage of being very explicit, coherent and clear.

Yet again it must be noted that Soviet and American statements do not refer to identical concepts, let alone reflect identical strategic doctrines, although seemingly the texts deal with identically the same subject.

Therefore the conclusion cannot be avoided that despite the abundant strategic discussion in the West and despite the concise nature of Soviet statements on strategic doctrine, the crucial problems are not resolved. The asymmetry of concepts and the mismatch of strategic doctrines continues to exist. It should also be noted that this situation is not simply the result of some transitory misunderstanding which can easily be overcome by goodwill and some intellectual effort aimed at a clarification and clear definition of terms and concepts. As a matter of fact, any such hope would be tragically misleading and naïve. On the contrary, it has to be borne in mind that the mutual rejection, misunderstanding and misrepresentation of strategic concepts is part of an effort to influence each other's deterrence posture and in particular its doctrinal underpinnings.

However, this situation may be extremely dangerous in moments of acute international crisis when only minutes are left for making fatal decisions on war and peace and when a kind of instant dialogue and mutual understanding between the adversaries armed with nuclear weapons is most urgently required. The mismatch of strategic doctrines cannot but impede the rationality of decision-making and the prospects of averting an imminent danger of nuclear war through a quick exchange of views about intentions and capabilities.

Differing Perspectives on Europe

Additional problems arise with regard to Soviet strategy in the more specific context of a potential European war theatre. The French strategist Pierre Gallois, analysing Soviet concepts and doctrines, highlights the emphasis placed by Soviet authors on surprise attack. He quotes the Soviet treatise *Scientific Technical Progress and the Revolution in Military Affairs* , which states that "surprise is achieved by confusing the enemy of one's intention, keeping secret the overall purpose of the forthcoming actions and preparations for them, the unexpected use of weapons, and particularly nuclear weapons" (Gallois 1978: 15). Other authors, also relying on official Soviet sources, similarly underline the importance of surprise in Soviet strategic doctrine. There are repeated assertions by Soviet authorities that a nuclear strike is the faster and most feasible avenue to victory (Coutrot *et al.* 1979: 148). Gallois concludes that, in view of the heavy emphasis laid by Soviet doctrine on the element of surprise, no credence can be given to the official NATO assumptions which suggest that Soviet forces would rely simply on their great numerical superiority in the conventional field. Rather, the Soviet Union would be inclined towards beginning a war with a nuclear attack — provided that United States forces no longer guarantee Europe's security. Gallois is afraid that, should the United States withdraw from Europe and were it to be sure that there would be no United States retaliation, the Soviet Union, after the necessary testing time, might decide to use force (Gallois 1978: 17). In other words, Gallois argues that there is an incentive for a pre-emptive nuclear strike against Western Europe once the United States "umbrella" loses its credibility.

That is how, as pointed out by Calder (1980: 39) the mismatch of military doctrine between East and West engenders inevitable misjudgements of the opponent's intentions. According to Soviet doctrine, once an attack against the Soviet homeland or against Soviet allies has been identified, it must be countered by military superiority. On the other hand, according to NATO doctrine, a few nuclear weapons would be used, in the first instance, as a signal of resolve and in order to harness Soviet military operations at specific points. This is in turn vehemently criticized by Soviet spokesmen, who sometimes seem unwilling to accept the proposition that the first use by the United States of nuclear weapons against selected targets would be a response to Soviet tactical, conventional gains in a situation where Western conventional defence breaks down in Central Europe. They tend to equate this type of defensive first use with pre-emption and charge the United States with seeking to blur the distinction between nuclear and conventional warfare (Deane 1978: 87f.). On the other hand, United States Government officials complain about the Soviet Union not having adopted a doctrine of stability and of maintaining a credible second-strike capability (cf. also Rostow 1981b: 3).

The asymmetry of perceptions and doctrine is therefore particularly great with regard to "tactical" nuclear weapons. Are the two major powers therefore on a "collision course" leading to nuclear war, as asserted e.g., by LaRoque (LaRoque 1981: 369)?

As far as Soviet doctrine is concerned, the rare strategic statements by Soviet authorities are perhaps less indicative than the capabilities which the Soviet Union deploys. By contrast to Soviet doctrinal statements, the Soviet capabilities so far deployed point to preparations for waging a limited nuclear war in much the same sense as it is made explicit in the case of NATO's concept of flexible response. Missiles for intermediate-range and tactical purposes (SS-20, SS-21, SS-23), dual-capability aircraft and artillery capable of firing small nuclear warheads, torpedoes armed with a nuclear weapon, etc., may lead to the inference that the Soviet Union quite systematically envisages situations in which a nuclear war does not necessarily escalate into an all-out "spasmic" nuclear war of mutual annihilation. Obviously the Soviet Union is not basing its strategic planning only on one option but is envisaging various kinds of limited nuclear options at the theatre and, perhaps, at the strategic level (Ermarth 1981: 62; Klein 1979: 39).

Soviet doctrinal statements, on the other hand, which still maintain total nuclear war to be inevitable once the threshold between conventional fighting and nuclear fighting has been passed, may be designed to serve other, mainly political, purposes. If these assumptions are correct, it would not be meaningful to speak of a mismatch between strategic doctrines; it seems more appropriate to conclude that there exists a certain difference between strategic doctrines and strategic practice on the Soviet side (cf. Krell 1981: 6; Stratmann 1981: 173—181, 244).

Yet this fact nevertheless has serious implications for many aspects of nuclear strategy, especially for the Western concept of extended deterrence (see below, chapter IV B). According to a Western analyst, Soviet military doctrines can be seen realigning in a triadic mode: massive nuclear capabilities are to neutralize and stabilize Soviet relations with the West; Soviet theatre forces, both conventional and nuclear, are to enhance deterrence but also to serve as a warfighting capability in the event deterrence fails; and the conventional forces are to serve as the vital political and military element (Kolkowicz 1981: 84).

Still, some doubts regarding the degree of compatibility or incompatibility of United States and Soviet nuclear strategies continue to exist, particularly with regard to the European continent. Some authors (for example, Senghaas 1981: 322) argue that, in principle, the Soviet image of war — in case deterrence fails — is a short war with massive use of weapons, fought on the opposite side of the border, for example in the Federal Republic of Germany, whereas NATO has based itself on the possibility of limited warfare and controlled escalation from conventional to tactical nuclear war and finally to strategic nuclear war. The problem arising from this and related questions will be dealt with in chapter IV.

B. The Debate about "Superiority", "Parity" and "Sufficiency"

A particularly disquieting — and perhaps also destabilizing — aspect of strategic doctrine has to do with the arguments about superiority, parity and sufficiency, although the practical implications of these terms may be rather doubtful (Clemens 1981: 8). As the United States was first to introduce nuclear weapons, it had a clear lead. This strategic superiority, however, was eroded by the major growth of the Soviet Union's strategic nuclear warfare capability. United States President Nixon introduced the term "strategic sufficiency" into the discussion, defining it as "strategic forces strong enough to inflict the damage needed to deter strategic attacks on the United States and its allies". Strategic sufficiency was centered on four objectives:

> "(1) having a second-strike capability adequate to deter an all-out surprise attack on U.S. forces; (2) assuring there was no incentive for the Soviet Union to strike first in a crisis; (3) preventing the Soviet Union from having greater ability to do urban-industrial damage to the United States than the U.S. could do to it; and (4) being able to defend against small attack or accidental launches" (Rosen 1979: 151—152).

One might ask what nuclear superiority was and how one could use it (Kissinger, cited in Epstein 1976: 32); sufficiency would do for defensive purposes. The problem of extended deterrence necessitated the introduction of some flexibility. Parity, according to Schilling (1981: 61—63) has not substantially affected United States plans and capabilities for assured destruction, the credibility being the same after conceding equality to the Soviet Union. In the United States, it was sometimes suggested that efforts should be made to restore United States nuclear superiority ("superiority for stability", Gray 1979: 85), but generally such attempts were considered unrealistic. The then Secretary of Defense Brown relied on essential equality when he pronounced the countervailling strategy (DoD Annual Report, FY 1982: 43—44). The SAFE formula for strategic deterrence also included "essential equivalence" (Guertner 1979: 29).

The acceptance of parity with the Soviet Union on the strategic nuclear level, however, entailed some problems for the United States, as commitments relying on extended deterrence may be questioned. The threat of escalation to a higher level was somewhat less credible than in the era of unquestioned superiority. The introduction of flexibility by planning limited nuclear options and counterforce application was considered to reconcile the requirements of extended deterrence with the realities of strategic parity (Salomon 1977).

The Soviet Union, according to Soviet writer Trofimenko (1981: 39) "is content with the state of strategic parity and does not strive for superiority ". A United States author, analysing Soviet writings relevant in this context (Garthoff 1981: 92), concludes that the Soviet political and military leadership has recognized that under contemporary conditions there is a strategic "balance" between the two superpowers and, as a result, mutual deterrence; that the nuclear strategic balance is not transitory, but also not necessarily enduring; but, finally, that in recent years U.S. readiness to accept parity and strategic arms limitations reflecting and perpetuating parity has become increasingly doubtful.

Garthoff (1978a: 140) reports that a leading Soviet spokesman viewed the situation as approximate parity consisting of asymmetries in the diverse fields which one might choose for comparison (numbers of warheads, throw-weight, etc.). Such concepts as parity, equivalence, and balance (being very similar to each other) are, according to Lambeth (1979: 25) unnatural because they imply an enshrinement of the status quo, something alien to every known tenet of Soviet political ideology and historical doctrine. Lambeth says that nowhere in the public record of Soviet utterances is there any indication that the Soviet leadership has endorsed "essential equivalence", at least as it is understood in the United States. This dynamic orientation of Soviet strategy, according to Simes (1981: 81), influences the Soviet interpretation of deterrence. However these assertions are contradicted by authoritative Soviet sources which have repeatedly stressed the importance of maintaining an approximate equilibrium of forces. Thus Garthoff (1978a: 146) reaches the conclusion that the record "indicates that the Soviet political and military leadership accepts a strategic nuclear balance between the Soviet Union and the United States as a fact, and as the probable and desirable prospect for the foreseeable future", because without interference of military power the "decisive social-economic forces of history would determine the future of the world". Another study on Soviet strategy stresses that the Soviet approach is mission-oriented in targeting: Rather than beginning with a detailed list of targets, the Soviets, according to Douglass and Hoeber (1979: 75), appear to begin with the identification of the strategic missions that are to be performed. The foremost initial strategic mission is "the defeat of the opposing military forces, in particular, the nuclear forces" (*ibid.*) The concept of surprise attack as an assumption in planning does not seem to be as important in the Soviet Union as in the United States, and the state of alert is generally lower. However, as Douglass and Hoeber conclude from Soviet literature, modern warfare is different from the past as it is "possible to suddenly, decisively, and unexpectedly change the correlation of forces" (Douglass and Hoeber 1979: 90). The significance of a surprise attack has been limited for a long time due to the relative invulnerability of the nuclear forces. With developments in warhead accuracy and ASW, this situation may be subject to some change.

Also, the specific concept of "peaceful coexistence" developed by Marxist-Leninist thought may shed some doubts on the long-term acceptability of parity (cf. Pankov 1981) and so too do the notions of the "shifting correlation of forces", of perennity of conflict, decline of capitalism and ultimate triumph of socialism and the emphasis on "class hatred against imperialism" and "irreconcilability to bourgeois ideology" (Ogarkow 1981). Western doubts refer to the Soviet rejection of freezing strategic constellations in the overall context of the East-West struggle (Ermarth 1981: 59). Doubts are also reinforced by frequent reference, in Soviet military writings, to Clausewitz's concept of "war as a continuation of politics by other means" (Garthoff 1981: 96 f.). Nevertheless, Soviet sources consistently underline the importance of the "rough strategic military equilibrium" which, in their view, "helps to stabilize peaceful relations between East and West" (Bykov 1980: 131f.; Soviet Committee for European Security and Co-operation 1981: 8; Whence the Threat to Peace 1982).

When discussing Soviet concepts relevant in this context, it should be borne in mind that for conceptual *and* linguistic reasons the seemingly identical terms do not mean the same in the English and Russian languages. For instance, the Russian term *stabilnost* is hardly identical with the English term "stability", as in "strategic stability". Rather, *stabilnost* seems to be synonymous with "balance" or "parity" in general, or more precisely, it is seen to be the outcome of parity. An interesting concept suggested by A. D. Nikonov is "dynamic balance", which implies that some slight changes in the strategic balance are quite normal and will sometimes favour one side and sometimes the other. According to Nikonov it would not be justified to talk about a destabilization of the balance in this case. Only if there is a decisive imbalance may one speak about destabilization.

Finally a caveat is required: the discussions about superiority, parity, and equivalence do not rest on any kind of generally acknowledged measure for strategic forces. Thus, selective information presented to an audience may be used as proof of one's own inferiority in order to stimulate a build-up. At the present moment, both the United States and the Soviet Union express concern about the other side's tendency to aspire to superiority. In particular, Soviet spokesmen repeatedly accuse the United States of intending to achieve superiority in terms of first-strike capability against Soviet strategic forces and C^3 systems (Whence the Threat to Peace 1982: 71; cf. also Schmidt 1982).

The assessment of the strategic balance is open to many interpretations, as the forces consist of a variety of weapons with different characteristics and performance parameters (cf. Stratmann 1981: 43—56; Lutz 1981c; Albrecht *et al.* 1978). Also, the uncertainties about the reliability of C^3 systems and their performance in war make conclusions about parity and superiority almost impossible. At any rate, the time has definitely passed when it was sufficient to compare the number of battalions. Soviet authors usually distinguish between "objective" and "subjective" factors shaping the balance. While "objective" factors refer to performance parameters of the weapons systems, the "subjective" factors refer to the strategic doctrines and perceptions of these doctrines; they are thus more difficult to assess. The "objective" factors are also difficult to compare, since the composition of United States and Soviet strategic forces is different.

These differences in both the composition and quantity of the strategic forces are the source of all kinds of controversial "perceptions", i.e., judgements of a nation's or an alliance's defence capabilities. One may be inclined to agree with Bundy who said that "perception is a word planners often use for things they cannot really see" (quoted in Leitenberg 1981b).

C. The Doctrine of Counterforce Strategy

Shortcomings of Mutual Assured Destruction

A starting-point in the recent evolution of strategic doctrine must be seen in the recognition that the strategy of Mutual Assured Destruction (MAD) has some important shortcomings. One very important shortcoming of MAD is that it holds for attacks on the strategic level only, leaving the lower levels relatively unprotected, as a massive strategic retaliation response cannot be expected in case of low-level incursions. This must erode deterrence. Thus a strategy based on the execution of a rigid plan encompassing the majority of the strategic nuclear weapons was no longer considered appropriate for honouring commitments by the major nuclear Powers, particularly the United States' commitment to deter aggression against Western Europe. Also, the problem of self-deterrence, counter-deterrence or "Called Bluff" was not solved satisfactorily by the adoption of MAD: one side, relying solely on the deterrence of MAD — this was the unsettling scenario — could find itself deterred from the use of the remaining weapons after having suffered a surprise attack because the other side would still have sufficient capabilities to inflict a third strike (Afheldt 1976: 75ff.). MAD has only the capability of pre-war deterrence (Gray 1979: 61), as it is based on a very simple scenario: first strike and second strike. This leaves no possibility for terminating the hostilities on a lower level. Intra-war deterrence could not be expected from the adoption of a pure strategy of Mutual Assured Deterrence (MAD).

The strategy based on MAD was not only criticized for its shortcomings but also because there was some speculation that the Soviet authorities would not share the basic assumptions of MAD (Klein 1979; Howard 1981: 6). Negotiations leading to SALT I and SALT II are considered by some authors to have induced the Soviet acceptance of a strategy of mutual deterrence (Garthoff 1981: 180). The Soviet author Trofimenko explains the position of the Soviet Union in respect to mutual deterrence:

> "We in the Soviet Union do not naturally think that a situation of mutual deterrence through the threat of assured destruction is the highest theoretical achievement" (Trofimenko 1981: 35).

It must be noted that Garthoff and Trofimenko speak only about mutual deterrence, not about Mutual *Assured Destruction*. MAD is, of course, based on mutual deterrence, but it is not the sole conceivable strategy based on this concept.

Buchan (1981: 17) argues, however, that technical constraints lead to acceptance of MAD; he thinks that no less than the United States, the Soviet Union is obliged to accept the reality of MAD. The Soviets, according to Buchan, would risk incalculable damage in a general nuclear war with the United States, and there is no reason to believe that their leadership is insensitive to these risks.

From MAD to Counterforce Targeting

Successive strategic targeting appeared to move United States policy further from the declaratory doctrine of MAD, according to Gray and Payne (1980: 17). The United Nations Comprehensive Study of Nuclear Weapons (United Nations General Assembly 1980a: 98) notes the introduction of intra-war deterrence at the doctrinal level through the concept of flexible response and through selective targeting options currently "being professed by one State". War fighting as a concept has grown in importance. Kissinger urged the United States to acquire a counterforce capability, not least in order to be able to back up its commitments to Western

Europe (Kissinger 1979b: 266—267). Escalation control and domination is not possible without a counterforce capability, particularly if the opponent is assumed to have this capability.

A counterforce strategy is different from a simple deterrence strategy based on the threat of destruction of industrial and economic assets because it has different targeting. Secretary of Defense Brown lists the four categories of targets valid for the countervailing strategy: 1. strategic nuclear forces; 2. other military forces; 3. leadership and control; and 4. industrial and economic base (DoD Annual Report, FY 1982: 41—42). A counterforce capability requires two elements:

> "(a) that the most accurate and destructive U.S. forces must be able to survive a Soviet first strike and (b) that these forces, principally ICBMs with Multiple Independently Targetable Re-entry Vehicles (MIRVs), should be able to destroy Soviet military targets, distinguished as far as possible from civilian targets" (Staff of the Carnegie Panel on U.S. Security and the Future of Arms Control 1981a: 53).

Sukovic (1978: 144) reports a statement by Secretary of Defense Schlesinger in 1974 to the effect that the United States intended to adopt a counterforce strategy in order to have deterrence across the entire spectrum of risks and to achieve intra-war deterrence, preventing uncontrolled escalation. The responses should bear some relation to the provocation. The introduction of limited nuclear options, giving flexibility, was criticized as undermining deterrence and thus making nuclear war more thinkable, acceptable, and respectable. The requirement for accurate Re-entry Vehicles (RVs) able to destroy hardened missile silos was also considered destabilizing (Sukovic 1978: 145). The declaration of Schlesinger, and even the major announcement of the then Secretary of Defense Brown in 1980 that the United States was to adopt a countervailing strategy do not seem, however, to have changed the spectrum of targets covered. Rather, options for discrete use have been created, "packaging" units which might be attacked, thus creating flexibility in use but not attacking new targets formerly not covered. Brown strongly emphasized that the countervailing strategy was no departure from the past and the counterforce targeting was not to be considered an innovation (DoD Annual Report, FY 1982: 38—45). This is confirmed by Leitenberg (1980a; 1981). Rather, one might assume that the declaratory doctrine was adjusted to the employment doctrine (see Leitenberg 1981).

Promoting the adoption of a counterforce posture by the United States, Gray and Payne (1980: 14) emphasize the importance of the recognition that war at any level can be won or lost. Also, the distinction between winning and losing should not be trivial. In the classic MAD scenario, the distinction between winner and loser was hardly possible. Gray and Payne argue for a change, not because they find the idea of fighting a nuclear war attractive but because they believe that the ability to wage and survive a war is vital to the effectiveness of deterrence. Such a posture would provide for intrawar deterrence and perhaps even escalation control and dominance by the United States (Gray and Payne 1980: 18—19).

The targeting policy obviously distinguishes the "war-fighters" from the advocates of pure mutual deterrence; Gray and Payne also propose the targeting of the opponent's bureaucracy, hoping that disintegration or anarchy might result therefrom. As United States strategic thinkers they are understandably preoccupied with the effects of such a posture on the Soviet Union and argue that the "most frightening threat to the Soviet Union would be the destruction or serious impairment of its political system" (Gray and Payne 1980: 21). The first priority of a targeting scheme would be the opponent's military power of all kinds, and the second would be the political (Gray and Payne 1980: 24). They recognize, however, that a functioning Government might be required in order for intra-war deterrence and negotiations to be successful. Heavy emphasis is also placed on the destruction of the capabilities necessary for rapid economic recovery (Gray 1979: 66). The targeting of military forces does not seem to be very different from the past (DoD Annual Report, FY 1982: 38—43; Leitenberg 1980a, 1981), but some difference seems to exist in the scope of the military targeting, "in its ability to cope with a much harder target set than before, and in its design for separation from civil society" (Gray 1979: 79).

The concept of extended deterrence which will be dealt with in the following chapter constitutes an additional argument for strategists wanting to move away from a simple MAD strategy to more elaborate strategies based on flexible options. Theorists whose concept of deterrence is limited to massive retaliation after Soviet attack would have nothing of interest to say to a President facing conventional defeat in the Persian Gulf or in Western Europe (Gray and Payne 1980: 15). United States strategic forces do not exist solely for the purpose of deterring a Soviet nuclear threat to the United States itself, but also for support of commitments (Gray and Payne 1980: 20). To Gray (1979: 70) it seems virtually incomprehensible that a Power like the United States, committed to project power over long distances, should have embraced the "mutual hostage theory of deterrence".

Beside the requirements of extended deterrence, the main argument for counterforce targeting is the desire to avoid the impression that the authorities would back down instead of retaliating against a nuclear attack:

> "If the United States could respond to such an attack only by attacking Soviet cities, Soviet leaders might not believe that the United States would respond at all" (Staff of the Carnegie Panel on U.S. Security and the Future of Arms Control 1981a: 53)

This is the familiar scenario of self-deterrence. The reasoning, however, is somewhat flawed by the fact that the ICBMs and submarine-launched ballistic missiles (SLBMs) were even in the heyday of MAD only partly targeted on "cities". Counterforce targeting seems to be only a question of how selected military targets can be attacked; in addition, some military targets are not to be considered so hard as to require effective hard-target kill capacity. The discussion of counterforce capabilities and strategy is influenced by the tacit assumption that the opponent's ICBMs are the targets, but there are many other targets vital for the hostile forces.

The parameters of the available strategic nuclear weapons allow some conclusions to be drawn about their role. While an attack against urban or industrial centres requires the delivery of a large amount of thermal energy and the creation of modest overpressures over very large areas (Tsipis 1974: 11), the performance requirements for destroying a missile inside a reinforced concrete silo are very different, because the weapons must deliver a very large amount of energy against a very small target, and must therefore be very accurate (Tsipis 1974: 12). Beside the CMP coefficient and the degree of silo hardening another criterion can become of major importance: the quickness of delivery of the warheads, depending on the delivery systems. This is particularly important for a counterforce action in response to pre-emptive attack, as in such a case a number of hard and time-urgent targets would probably be targeted. For a long time ICBMs were considered the only nuclear weapons system capable of such strikes, because of the slowness of manned bombers and the slightly lesser accuracy of SLBMs (Staff of the Carnegie Panel on U.S. Security and the Future of Arms Control 1981a: 53 —54). Improvements in accuracy have rendered a number of weapons instrumental for counterforce application. This holds true even of the SLBM force, which can now be assumed to have a counterforce potential due to increased navigational accuracy of forward-based submarines, improved ballistic guidance and MIRVing (Ball 1977). The uncertainties of interference ("fratricide") of a large number of attacking RVs are raising some doubts about operational reliability in counterforce use, but the expected pin-down effect is considered to make up for this (Tsipis 1974: 13).

There has been some speculation as to whether the Soviet Union has also adopted a counterforce concept. Trofimenko (1981: 29) says that

> "the Soviet Union has emphasized repeatedly that it does not advocate counterforce strategy, as it does not support the first-strike concept".

Western observers partly tend towards different assumptions, as they cannot detect any signs of the Soviet Union having modified its emphasis on a strategy of war-fighting and war-survival intended to both disarm and devastate the adversary with a sudden massive concentration of firepower (Osgood 1979: 58). Dumas, however, notes that the Soviet Union is reluctant to embrace the counterforce doctrine and has clung to the idea of counter-city deterrence (Dumas 1978: 126). Trofimenko (1981: 30—33) concedes that the Soviet Union also has strategic forces capable of precision strikes against hardened point targets; this is an inevitable result of qualitative improvements in strategic armaments. However, he argues that the United States preoccupation with changing nuclear strategies serves other aims than the one proclaimed:

> "American strategists strive to maximize some or other — real or only apparent — U.S. edge over the potential adversary. (...) Washington strives each time to complicate its opponent's strategic planning. It tries to gain some psychological edge ...".

Destabilizing Implications of Counterforce Strategy

The increase of counterforce potentials on both sides and the adoption of counterforce options in official doctrine raise doubts about the future crisis stability of strategic nuclear weapons. Gray (1979: 83) criticizes the criterion of stability in strategic force planning. He deplores the fact that United States strategic (and arms control) policy, since the mid-1960s, has been misinformed by stability criteria which rested (and rest) upon a near-total misreading of Soviet phenomena. The American stability theorem held only for so long as both sides endorsed it. Advocating superiority for stability, Gray (1979: 87) does not seem to worry much about crisis stability. The fact that "the United States might pose a theoretical first-strike threat to much of the Soviet strategic posture should not give aid and comfort to the 'use them or lose them' argument". This argument starts from the assumption that the United States will in no case actually launch a pre-emptive strike. This assumption may not have the same appeal to all observers, and attempts to gain clear-cut nuclear superiority have as questionable chances of success only.

Dumas (1978: 127) warns that the adoption of counterforce doctrines, raising the fear of a pre-emptive first strike in a crisis, would lead to reliance on the "hair trigger" mode of operation and LOW tactics, thus increasing the chance of inadvertent attack or even unintentional nuclear war. The existence of counterforce capabilities puts a premium on pre-emption. Such apprehensions are also confirmed by Soviet statements that a "counterforce strike is a preventive strike" and conditions of counterforce superiority of one side would steadily heighten confrontational tensions. "All this (...) is conducive to a situation where peace hangs by a thread" (Trofimenko 1981: 44—45).

The mutual fear and suspicion surrounding the questions related to these concepts sometimes leads to a kind of mirror-image thinking that must be said to be highly detrimental to the cause of strategic stability. Garthoff (1981: 117) quotes the Soviet General Simonyan who, in 1979, observed:

> "Indeed, a power which sets itself the aim of destroying the 'potential enemy's' military facilities must be the first to deliver a strike because otherwise its nuclear charges will land on empty missile launch silos and airfields".

As can be seen, United States counterforce doctrine leads Soviet authors to infer a United State first-strike intention.

In sum, counterforce targeting policies have a negative impact on the long-term prospects of strategic stability. In addition, as will be demonstrated in the next chapter, a policy based on deterrence — whatever its targets — creates problems of credibility which in turn might jeopardize strategic and crisis stability.

An additional problem to be considered in this context concerns the amount of collateral damage caused by the use of small-yield nuclear warheads. Apart from the possibility of unintentional triggering of nuclear war due to an unstable strategic system, the employment of nuclear warheads, as envisaged by certain strategic doctrines, is likely to have unintentional consequences. According to calculations made by Sonntag (1981: 48—59) the collateral damage of so-called "limited" nuclear warfare is much greater than generally expected and realized. The unintentional and unexpected amount of damage produced by "controlled" and "limited" war may in turn lead to a nuclear escalation, and the war may get out of control and become unlimited although this was not the political intention. For instance, even the small-calibre enhanced radiation (neutron) warhead for the Lance missile still produces the same levels of blast damage experienced at Hiroshima at a little less than one half the distance from the point of detonation (Keeny/Panofsky 1981: 297).

Conclusions: Risks of Unintentional Nuclear War Generated by Developments of Strategic Doctrine

The risks:

1. *Strategic doctrines, as the basis for arms development and deployments as well as for defence postures, rest on extremely fuzzy grounds — guesses, speculations, beliefs, assumptions of all kinds. These can be erroneous and thus lead to inappropriate conclusions jeopardizing strategic stability.*
2. *Differing concepts employed in East and West may give rise to inadvertent misunderstandings which in turn are prone to produce additional distrust. This distrust is liable to fuel both the arms race and the forces undermining strategic stability; in addition, it may also lead to grave misunderstandings in situations of acute international crisis.*
3. *Due to the reluctance of Soviet leaders to make pronouncements on the matter Soviet strategic doctrine is particularly subject to all kinds of speculation by Western observers which is largely based on "worst case" assumptions and hardly conducive to strengthening strategic stability.*

4. *In particular, misrepresentations of the element of surprise in Soviet statements about tactics in the battlefield may lead to the conclusion that the Soviet Union is interested in launching a first strike. Nuclear war by misjudgement may thus become more probable.*
5. *On the other side, United States counterforce targeting policy may specifically lead to the presumption of pre-emptive strike preparations against the Soviet Union. This may also contribute to the risk of nuclear war by misjudgement.*
6. *These problems are particularly grave in the case of strategic doctrines referring to the possible European war theatre.*
7. *Collateral damage caused by "limited" nuclear warfare may exceed any intended limits and thus lead to escalation beyond controlled, limited war.*

Mitigating factors:

1. *Although the strategic doctrines which were enunciated may differ substantially, the strategic capabilities of East and West are largely comparable. If doctrinal intentions are inferred from capabilities, the mismatch seems less marked.*
2. *The threat of retaliation and thus the expectation of incalculable damage is still so effective and currently reinforced by doctrinal refinements of MAD as to make any doctrinal speculation about pre-emptive attack a necessarily idle activity. At the present moment no nuclear Power can expect to escape retaliation if it launches a pre-emptive strike against its opponent.*

Risk assessment:

The mismatch existing in the field of nuclear doctrine cannot be said to constitute a cause of imminent danger. Yet it is constantly fuelling the arms race, thus contributing to the factors that undermine strategic stability in the long run.

IV. THE FAILURE OF DETERRENCE

A. How Stable is "Stable Deterrence"?

How Deterrence Works

A nuclear war may break out as a consequence of inadequate assessment of the other side's resolve to offer resistance.In other words, war may be caused by miscalculation regarding the deterrence posture. In fact, the current efforts undertaken by both major Powers in the field of strategic armaments precisely point to the prevention of any miscalculation of this kind. They are greatly preoccupied with making their deterrence posture credible and enhancing this credibility to the maximum extent possible.

Although the two major Powers, in their overall strategic relationship, quite rightly assume that deterrence works, one must not overlook or neglect the potential risks inherent in such a system of mutual deterrence (Schwarz/Van Cleave 1978). Historical experience suggests that very often a Government underestimating the opponent's capability for effective resistance has launched an aggressive war with unwanted results — either defeat or a failure to attain its strategic goals. In the history of warfare many instances can be found where the Government concerned certainly would not have initiated an attack if it had prior knowledge of the eventual outcome and if it had not completely misinterpreted the existing balance of military forces. Singer/Small (1972: ch. 14) found out that, in the 1815—1965 period, the nations whose forces appear to have made the first overt military moves in strength not only lost the war in nearly one third of the cases, but also with about the same frequency suffered more battle fatalities than did their putative victims *(ibid.*: 370). That means that at least one third of the past wars must be ascribed to a failure of deterrence based upon a gross miscalculation of the opponent's capability and intent. Can this happen again in the nuclear age?

Clearly, both major Powers aim at precluding any such possibility, or at least reducing the propensity of the other side to underestimate the resolve and the capability and thus the meaning of deterrence. Both are undertaking all possible efforts to make clear to the other side that any aggression would meet with a response. This constitutes the very essence of their policy and strategy with regard to each other. It also constantly fuels the arms race which has been going on ever since an adversary relationship emerged after the Second World War . There is no need to expound on that in the present study.

Underestimating the deterrent powers' capabilities and intent in practice means that there is a credibility problem. If A wishes to deter a possible attack by B, a credibility problem may arise under the following conditions (Morgan 1977: 85 f.):

   (1) If it is possible to deceive B on these matters — A might in fact be bluffing and thus B must be convinced that A's threat is no bluff;
   (2) If it would be irrational to carry out the threat;
   (3) If A is too irrational to carry out the threat — if it is "scared" or highly irresolute, for example;
   (4) If B does not correctly perceive A's intentions and/or capabilities.

Such credibility problems, especially the problem (2), tend to arise particularly in situations of mutual deterrence. If the nuclear weapons are relatively invulnerable, and as the total number of nuclear weapons available rises, it becomes increasingly difficult to find a rational justification for retaliation (Morgan 1977: 93). This conclusion belongs to the classical inventory of strategic thinking and has been referred to by Kahn in his book *On Escalation* (1965: 57f.). Kahn laconically says: "In most deterrence situations, once deterrence has failed, it is irrational to carry out the previously made warnings and threats of retaliation since that action will produce an absolute or net loss to the retaliator". In other words, "deterrence collapses just when it was needed. And it collapses precisely because of the damage each side can do to the other — not in spite of it" (Morgan 1977: 94).

On the other hand, it might be argued that one who threatens retaliation may be moved by profound passions in responding to an attack (Morgan 1977: 114). Thus there is at least uncertainty as to whether the threatener will eventually retaliate. Irrespective of the justified doubts regarding the credibility of his deterrence posture, the state to be deterred cannot take it for granted that the threatener will not honour his commitments, even if these appear to be hardly rational. For deterrence to be credible, not rational political judgement but insane vindictiveness or some unthinking "doomsday" device must be seen to be in control (Boserup 1981).

In the context of this study the question must be asked whether there are any tendencies in the current evolution of nuclear strategy which might contribute to making the deterrence of one side or the other less credible, and which thus might be conducive to a war by miscalculation. At any rate, one may draw attention to some problems which seem to make the issue of credible deterrence more difficult.

Deterrence, i.e., the use of threats of harm to prevent someone from doing something one does not want him to do (Morgan 1977: 17), is said to be a very old concept.

> "The phenomenon of deterrence probably existed already at very early stages of human existence. It is based essentially on the threat of use of force to prevent someone from carrying out his intentions. It can take the form of either a threat to inflict severe consequences in case a certain act is carried out: deterrence by punishment, or of a threat to prevent by force the actual implementation of the act: deterrence by denial. The principle of deterrence has in all times served as a basis for military doctrines for the defense of States" (United Nations General Assembly 1980a: 95, paragraph 285).

Two kinds of deterrence must be distinguished (Speed 1979: 7; Segal and Baylis 1981; Morgan 1977: 18 f.). Generally, punishment is assured by the ability to retaliate, while deterrence by denial can be achieved only through a good defence; in the latter case, the potential aggressor will be deterred by the probability that he will not succeed. In the nuclear age, defence is considered as not (yet) feasible; in such a case, there remains only the possibility of deterring by punishment. Deterrence has also changed in two other ways: the effects of attack and punishment are much greater and they can be carried out in a very short time (United Nations General Assembly 1980a: 95, paragraph 286). This emphasis is certainly correct in the context of the so-called "central balance", i.e., the adversary relationship between the United States and the USSR. For other countries, defence in the sense of "dissuasion" (Beaufre 1964a; 1964b) by rendering too costly the *relative* advantage of conquering a certain territory may seem more adequate. Today's situation is characterized by high vulnerability of each major Power, controlled only by the ability to retaliate:

> "The very cornerstone of what is projected as defense is offensive capability" (United Nations General Assembly 1980a: paragraph 287).

The calculus of deterrence has often been represented in game theory. In the earlier stages of the nuclear armaments, clear-cut distinctions and scenario-building were relatively easy due to relatively simple strategic doctrines based (at least as far as the declaratory doctrines are concerned) mainly on the assumption of a very few, devastating strikes. The introduction of flexibility, a multitude of options and ideas about limited nuclear warfare have very much complicated this context.

Strategies based on mutual deterrence place heavy emphasis on the offensive. In fact, offensive forces sufficiently invulnerable to surprise attack and able to penetrate defences, if such exist, are the centre of defence (United Nations General Assembly 1980a: 95, paragraph 287). Polanyi (1980: 6) links modern developments to Leo Szilard's idea of emplacing nuclear weapons, controlled from each other's command centres, beneath the major cities, respectively. In both cases, the idea is to institutionalize the vulnerability of valued assets in order to ensure the so-called second strike: the retaliation as a response to an attack. The renunciation of defences against ballistic missiles in the SALT I agreement between the United States and the Soviet Union is discussed in terms of assured vulnerability.

The vulnerability of valued industrial and demographic assets is vital to a strategy of deterrence, but the vulnerability of the nuclear weapons designed for retaliation is highly undesirable. The whole idea of exchanging nuclear blows rests also on the assumption that the C^3-installations necessary for assessing the attack and the damage, and for executing a launch order would resist the first attack, at least well enough to allow the transmission of a few relatively simple messages (Ball 1981: 9ff.).

The implications for targeting, in such a simple model, are clear: in order to have maximum deterrence, the assets most valued are to be targeted, sometimes operationalized as a certain percentage of population and industry. However, the developments in nuclear weapons technology and the sophistication of delivery systems have introduced new sources of instability and uncertainty into the nuclear balance: with the vast increase in the number of warheads (partly due to MIRVing) and the subsequent possibility of not only attack and response, but a sequence at strikes, the targeting of nuclear weapons delivery systems ("counterforce") and other primarily military assets has become feasible.

How Deterrence Fails

Strategies of deterrence (pre-war deterrence), while primarily devised to prevent the outbreak of war, have their maximum utility in the pre-war phase. Once nuclear war has erupted, the question of intra-war deterrence becomes more important (United Nations General Assembly 1980a: 97—98, paragraph 297). Intra-war deterrence has been introduced by selective targeting options and the general concept of flexible response.

However, adhering to basic deterrence based on the plan to retaliate in one massive blow entails some problems. One of them can be described in terms of the game theory paradigm "Called Bluff" and self-deterrence, in connection with theories on the "exploitable capability".

According to such scenarios, a massive attack directed against the adversary's nuclear weapons might destroy a great part of them before they are launched. In a MIRV environment, only a small fraction of ICBMs would be needed to perform such a strike, leaving the attacker with still a formidable nuclear potential deterring the party attacked from retaliation, because a third strike would definitely appear to be a real possibility. The victim of the surprise attack against its forces would have to make the choice between launching the remaining missiles and being prepared to receive a second attack, or accepting the situation.

The probability of such a scenario depends on several assumptions: A great part of the forces must be destroyed if the attack is to be successful; this is an expectation still highly unrealistic due to the invulnerability of the SLBMs and the immediate start of the strategic bomber force. Also the effect of a massive attack on the accuracy of the individual missile is not exactly known: even the trajectories used would entail some unknown elements. Furthermore, the side attacked would have a choice only between launching all the remaining force or doing nothing; in reality flexible targeting options differ from this situation.

In addition, the attacker would not be sure whether the attacked missiles were still in their silos at the time of impact of the warheads, because the victim might have adopted LOW or a related quick reaction.

However, all these uncertainties have not prevented strategic analysts from pondering about how the President of the United States might react in such a situation, having absorbed a counterforce blow, with only a small portion of intercontinental nuclear weapons left, while the adversary has expended only a small fraction of his. (If one is tempted to complain that such scenarios are always one-sided in the sense that the United States is attacked, one has to consider that Soviet strategic thinkers either do not publicly contemplate such scenarios or do not see any sense in analysing such hypothetical situations.)

Yost (1980) suggests that the "Soviets would be likely to assume, on the basis of their own psychology, that we [the United States], would retaliate", even if a nuclear attack mostly on cities would be threatened. Buchan (1981) dismisses the speculation that the choice would be between surrender and national suicide, that is, "by attacking Soviet cities with our residual strategic forces and expecting a response in kind". He envisages a different response for the United States in such circumstances — to do nothing. The Soviet strategy would have failed because as a potential attacker, the Soviet Union would have risked a great deal to extract a political concession which was not forthcoming and which they had no way to enforce (Buchan 1981: 15).

It goes without saying that the adoption of such contingency plans by any Government possessing nuclear weapons is out of question for the foreseeable future. However, once deterrence has failed (which is the case after nuclear war on the strategic level has started), it might nevertheless acquire some relevance.

The aforementioned scenario can be named "Called Bluff" because of its resemblance to a game-theory situation in which two players are facing each other and each one has only two options: to co-operate or to defect. In contrast to such games as Prisoner's Dilemma and Chicken, Called Bluff is not symmetrical; it is, in fact, for one player a Prisoner's Dilemma situation, for the other a Chicken situation, resulting in the ability of the first to dominate the second. In

game-theory notation, it would look as follows (the numbers indicating the preferences: 4 as the most preferred, 1 as the least preferred pay-off):

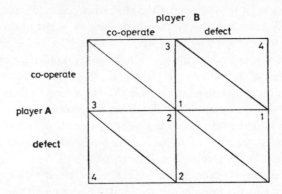

For player A, the rank order of the preferred outcomes is similar to the
one in Prisoner's Dilemma game, but for player B, it is the same as in the Chicken
game.

If player A chooses to defect, player B will nevertheless co-operate, because
this outcome is for him preferable to the result of both defecting. Player A is
dominant in this game, because the opposite does not hold: if B chooses to
defect, A will also defect in order to minimize the losses (Snyder/Diezing 1977: 46).

The crucial question, however, is whether the existing strategic balance could
offer temptations to initiate a scenario like Called Bluff. As has already been pointed
out, the proverbial "Bolt out of the Blue" (BOOB) is generally considered unlikely, but some analysts envisage such scenarios for hypothetical cases: according
to Lambeth, Soviet planners might believe the rational response for the United
States leadership would be to retain its surviving forces as instruments for negotiating a settlement from a position of weakness rather than to execute a SIOP-scale
retaliation against Soviet cities, which would only trigger a devastating Soviet
counter-response in kind (Lambeth 1981: 113). "Self-deterrent" is the knowledge
that a response will only trigger a second blow with still more disastrous consequences. The first strike in such scenarios has been called a counter-deterrence
strike (against deterrent forces) for some time, but this has been replaced by the
somewhat broader concept of counterforce strike.

The Called-Bluff scenario and related scenarios, although highly unlikely under
present circumstances, draw attention to the fact that stable deterrence may be
a less solid base of stability than one might assume. The disquieting conclusion
is, as expressed, for example, by Bueno de Mesquita (1980: 383—393), that there
is no such thing as absolutely stable deterrence.

In addition, one has to bear in mind that even in situations where Called-Bluff scenarios are improbable and where mutual deterrence seems to work, a number of conditions must be fulfilled if the strategic relationship is to be a stable one.

Concepts of deterrence have to be mutually understood and, to some degree, accepted, in order to be effective (United Nations General Assembly 1980a: 97, paragraph 294). More precisely, there must be a generally accepted assessment regarding the adversary's most valued assets: it has to be assured that the adversary will interpret the State's behaviour as it was intended. There should be correct beliefs about the other's strengths and options. The adversary's intentions must be interpreted in a generally correct way (Jervis 1979: 305 ff.). Furthermore (George and Smoke 1974: 522 ff.), the commitment of the defender has to be beyond doubt, otherwise miscalculation is possible. It must be ascertained that the potential adversary will perceive this commitment. It is not sufficient for the real capabilities to exist; it is the adversary's perception that counts. However, the reliability of the commitment alone will not do: the potential aggressor must not be allowed to calculate the risks. The capabilities of the deterrent side should be appropriate and the capability to punish has to be beyond doubt. Not only the capability, but also the motivation of the defender must be made clear to the potential aggressor. There should not only be punishment, but also some incentives for co-operative behaviour: not only the big stick, but also the carrot. The willingness to trade-off different areas of concern will also reinforce the deterrence, as it may contribute to preventing confrontations in areas vital to a particular participant.

The problem of credible deterrence as referred to above is also intensively discussed by French specialists in strategic doctrine in terms of the efficiency of the French nuclear deterrence posture. Emphasis is placed on signalling to a potential aggressor one's own determination to really use the strategic forces. According to de Foïard (1980: 26f.) "occidental rationalists subject to crises of conscience and to the constraints of a consumer society" are particularly vulnerable in this respect. Yet "fortunately", de Foïard concludes, tactical nuclear weapons take care of this vulnerability. The essential task of tactical nuclear weapons, based on this concept, is to provide a "rationally plausible character" for the nuclear threat which, in itself, is absurd and perhaps also unreal; hence it becomes credible and consequently also efficient as a deterrent. Tactical nuclear weapons, on the other hand, offer an instrument for using the nuclear argument in a way not automatically implying suicidal consequences (de Foïard 1980: 27; Lewin 1980a: 25). Soviet proposals to include French nuclear forces in future strategic arms limitation talks are interpreted by French authors as evidence of the fact that the deterrent value of the French strategic forces is perceived to be credible (Poirier 1979: 62). The combination of conventional and nuclear forces has the purpose of demonstrating to a potential aggressor that "all action on his part below the threshold of credibility would be bound to fail, and that all action above this threshold would run a great risk of sending our strategic nuclear force into action against the own territory" (Barre 1977: 227). In order to prevent conventional defeat by an adversary with superior forces, Barre advocated "denying the adversary in advance all hope of keeping the battle's violence on the conventional level" (Barre 1977: 227), in fact preserving the right of first use of nuclear weapons. The new Socialist Government has generally confirmed this doctrine (Hernu 1981: 11). The French strategy of nuclear deterrence is aimed at creating additional risks and uncertainties which any potential aggressor has to take into account (Denis 1981: 91).

The Limits of Rationality

These considerations about preconditions of credible deterrence clearly indicate that all strategies based on deterrence rely on the rationality of the participants. This is the subject of another severe criticism: the execution of the strikes devised to deter would perhaps not fit the criterion of rationality. But one has to remember, at this point, that strategies of deterrence have the primary task of preventing the outbreak of war. The question of what behaviour will really be adopted in war may be quite different.

Holsti (1972: 9) cites a critic who points to the fact that the theory of deterrence derives its effect from frightening the adversary but requires his cool judgement even in crisis situations. The assumption of pure rationality of the decision-makers in crisis can, of course, be questioned.

A strategy of mutual deterrence does not, hovever, deter irrational attack. It is only useful against an adversary weighing soberly probable costs and gains. Such a strategy cannot offer any help against unintentional war in the narrow sense, i.e., where there was no cool judgement by the attacker (Afheldt 1976: 102—104). Jervis (1979: 299 ff.) observes that rationality may not be necessary in every case: "Rationality may be neither necessary nor sufficient for deterrence. When critics talk of the impact of irrationality, they imply that all such deviations will be in the direction of emotional impulsiveness, of launching an attack, or of taking actions that are terribly risky. But irrationality could also lead to a state of passive acquiescence, while a rational grasp of the situation could lead to belligerence". Facing an event such as nuclear war, however, one would prefer to run minimum risks. Rationality, according to Jervis, can also lead to the deliberate causation of a nuclear crisis; the initiator may be sure that the other side will retreat, since the ultimate threat in nuclear deterrent strategies amounts to bringing about the end of civilization.

Generally speaking, there is a somewhat ambivalent use and assumption of rationality in nuclear deterrence strategies. The threat of punishment will deter the rational potential aggressor, but the punishment itself may be a completely irrational act for the side attacked, as it would not mitigate the effects of the attack (except in damage-limitation scenarios), but only serve the purpose of revenge which might perhaps, in the present situation, lead to subsequent attacks (third strikes).

Further doubts about the rationality assumptions underlying deterrence strategies arise from scepticism regarding the intellectual and emotional performance of the top national leaders obliged to make the crucial decisions in case of a real emergency. In the United States the use of nuclear weapons is to be ordered by the President, and the other nuclear powers are expected to have similar arrangements. Usually one assumes an attitude of rationality on the part of these decision-makers. Yet, as Beres (1980: 69) notes, "there is no two-man rule at this level. There is, of course, no human reliability screening either". In the United States, the President alone, to be sure, cannot launch nuclear weapons; he is forced to co-operate with the Secretary of Defense and the CJCS. But he has the authority to order their co-operation, and their resistance would be unlawful. Every launch ordered by the President is an authorized launch, as he is by definition the highest authority in this respect. The main safeguard against irrational use of nuclear weapons by the authorities is to avoid the election of mentally unstable persons to such a position, but this is small comfort when the "security of more than four billion people rests on the continuing rationality of relatively few national leaders" (Beres 1980: 70).

The proliferation of nuclear weapons is further increasing the possibility of irrational use, as Beres (1980: 92) notes by indicating that "many of the new nuclear powers are apt to select their leadership in a fashion that precludes all forms of public scrutiny".

Another critical remark regarding the rationality of deterrence and strategic doctrines in general seems appropriate when looking at these problems from the point of view of comparative political science. There are good reasons to doubt whether Governments behave like cool-minded, completely rational "players" in the strategic "game". Governments, after all, are collective entities, and the more complex a modern government structure is, the more divergent are the various perceptions, interests and reactions to the same, identical challenge. Allison (1971, ch. 5) very aptly suggests that in order to explain why a particular governmental decision was made, or why one pattern of governmental behaviour emerged, "it is necessary to identify the games and players, to display the coalitions, bargains, and compromises, and to convey some feel for the confusion". (Allison 1971: 146).

This point is also highly relevant for the functioning of deterrence. Deterrence may fail for the simple reason that the decision to attack resulted from bargaining in the attacking Government. Miscalculation and confusion may generate foul-ups that yield attack as a resultant.

Allison offers a striking illustration of the inherent propensity of Governments to decide according to this pattern by pointing to the Cuban missile crisis of 1962.

91

There was considerable disagreement among the people involved in the crucial United States decisions, and each of these men fought hard for the course of action he judged to be right, ranging from the discovery and identification of the Soviet threat to the definition of issues and the choices available (Allison 1971: 183-210). Even if men act in a rational way, Governments may not necessarily do so. In conclusion, one cannot but agree with the following statement contained in paragraph 13 of the Final Document of the first special session of the United Nations General Assembly devoted to disarmament:

> "Enduring international peace and security cannot be built on the accumulation of weaponry by military alliances nor be sustained by a precarious balance of deterrence or doctrines of strategic superiority".

The following two sections refer to a highly controversial contemporary application of deterrence theory, i.e., to the strategic relationship established in Europe. For analytical purposes, the two problems implied in this strategic relationship will be dealt with separately. The first problem is caused by the asymmetric deterrence posture, i.e., by NATO's rejection of any commitment not to use nuclear weapons in case of being attacked. The problem basically constitutes a credibility problem which may be summed up in the simple question: how can the threat to use nuclear weapons against nuclear or non-nuclear attacks be made credible? The second problem, although in reality closely intertwined with the first, concerns the credibility of extended deterrence: how can the threat to use nuclear weapons for the defence of third countries (i.e., the European allies of the United States) be credibly maintained if the Power to be deterred in turn might be able to launch a direct retaliation strike against the homeland of the Power offering extended deterrence? The credibility of nuclear deterrence for the protection of Western Europe is seriously challenged by both problems simultaneously.

B. Nuclear Deterrence against Conventional Attacks

The First Use of Nuclear Weapons

Doubts regarding the credibility of deterrence may be raised in those instances where strategic concepts imply the use of nuclear weapons in case of a conventional attack if all means of conventional defence are overridden by the attacker. This in fact is one of the crucial elements of the deterrence concept developed by NATO (Nerlich 1978: 422—428). The Governments of the NATO member States realize that the strategic situation in Europe is characterized by a marked conventional imbalance in favour of the WTO. As the NATO countries for various reasons do not feel in a position to redress this imbalance by an appropriate conventional arms build-up or by arms control negotiations leading to a reduction of WTO superiority in the conventional field, the basic concept underlying NATO strategy is not to exclude the use of nuclear weapons (mainly "tactical" nuclear weapons) to counter any WTO attack carried out by conventional or nuclear means against the territory of a NATO ally. According to NATO's conception, conventional as well as non-conventional attacks by WTO forces have to be deterred by the prospect of suffering damage which would render highly uncertain the profitability of an attempt to exploit the superiority in conventional arms by an attack.

More precisely, NATO's strategy envisages three types of reaction: (1) direct defence by employing the same means as the attacker (conventional means in case of a conventional attack and tactical nuclear weapons in case of an attack including also nuclear weapons); (2) deliberate escalation, i.e., geographical escalation as well as escalation from the conventional level to the nuclear level in order to make the cost and risk disproportionate to the aggressor's objectives and the threat of nuclear response progressively more imminent; and (3) a general nuclear response (Stratmann 1981: 59 f.). According to Alexander Haig, then Supreme Commander of NATO forces in Europe, the precise nature of NATO's response to an attack launched by Warsaw Pact troops is deliberately not publicly defined: "In order to insure credible deterrence, we rely on a flexible response strategy whose core is uncertainty" (quoted in: Stratmann 1981: 63).

The Soviet Union and her WTO allies, on the other hand, strongly emphasize the unacceptability and impracticability of any type of first-strike strategy. According to Soviet sources, in the present conditions "any pre-emptive nuclear strike is senseless unless it destroys or at least substantially weakens the strategic nuclear potential of the other side's retaliatory capability"; this cannot be accomplished (Soviet Committee for European Security and Co-operation 1981: 20 f.). The Soviet Union consequently proposes talks with a view to reaching an agreement on the non-first use of nuclear weapons. As early as 1972, the Soviet Union requested the inclusion in the agenda of the United Nations General Assembly of an item entitled "Non-use of force in international relations and permanent prohibition of the use of nuclear weapons" (*United Nations and Disarmament* 1976: 125—128). On 8 November 1976, the United Nations General Assembly adopted a resolution sponsored by the USSR calling for the conclusion of a world treaty on the non-use of force in international relations (Resolution 31/9) (cf. also Batsanov 1982: 51f.)

In November 1976, the Conference of the Warsaw Treaty Political Consultative Committee approved a proposal to the effect that all States signatories of the Final Act of the CSCE should enter into a commitment not to use nuclear weapons against one another (Brezhnev 1981 a: 37). This proposal highlights one of the inherent weaknesses of the NATO concept, or, as a Soviet author put it,

"an obstacle would be put up to the manoeuvres of those forces who were making plans to use nuclear weapons for various 'selective' and 'preemptive' strikes" (Yefremov 1979: 257).

93

As long as NATO perceives itself as inferior to the WTO in conventional armaments, NATO countries are highly reluctant to accept this proposal, unless it is accompanied by measures to re-establish the conventional balance. Nevertheless, the Soviet Union continues to propose the creation of bilateral and multilateral arrangements imposing legally binding obligations not to make first use of nuclear weapons. Soviet diplomacy asserts that such a commitment will have a stabilizing effect. For this reason the Soviet Union also put forward, in the context of CSCE, a similar proposal that all States participants in the conference should commit themselves not to be the first to use nuclear weapons one against the other (Inozem-tzev 1980: 287; Petrovsky 1980: 149—153).

The Soviet Union also maintains that once a nuclear war broke out it could not be controlled, i.e., it would sooner or later escalate into an all-out nuclear exchange involving also the homelands of the two major Powers. As enunciated very plainly by Arbatov (1981: 167),

> "the aggressor must not doubt that the reply to such a 'selective' strike would be full-scale devastating retaliation, possibly, without waiting for the 'counter-force' attack to hit the target".

Other Soviet sources are even more straightforward about this issue, confirming that any use of nuclear weapons would "immediately and inevitably invite an annihilating response by the victim of the aggressor" (Stakh 1981: 89). Also, Soviet sources constantly ignore or reject any idea regarding the political settlement of a nuclear war by communication with the enemy and a common search for a taming of the escalation process and limitation of damage (Stratmann 1981: 182—189). In a statement made in 1981, the Soviet Chief of Staff, Marshal Ogarkow reconfirmed that the USSR's strategic forces are capable of launching an immediate, annihilating counter-strike against any target on the globe once an enemy employs nuclear weapons against the Soviet Union or other countries of the socialist community (Ogarkow 1981). Several authoritative Soviet sources also clearly and distinctly reject the idea of limited nuclear war as underlying Western deterrence concepts. In an interview in *Pravda* (21 October 1981) Leonid Brezhnev said:

> "Whatever strength the attacker may have and whatever method of starting a nuclear war he may choose, he will not achieve his aims. Retaliation is unavoid-able" (quoted in Soviet Committee for European Security and Co-operation 1981: 9).

Similarly, D. F. Ustinov, Marshal of the Soviet Union, said:

> "Could anyone in his right mind speak seriously of any limited nuclear war? It should be quite clear that the aggressor's actions will instantly and inevitably trigger a devastating counter-strike by the other side" (*ibid.*: 10).

Generally, according to Soviet doctrine, a "limited" war cannot be kept within any limits. There is nothing to guarantee that such a war will not grow into a universal nuclear conflagration (*ibid.*: 10). According to Leonid Brezhnev, the idea of a "limited" use of nuclear weapons is completely inadmissible (Brezhnev 1982 a).

On the other hand, some Soviet writers express concern about keeping limited war limited (Kolkowicz 1981: 79). As the Soviet forces in Eastern Europe are also equipped with low-yield nuclear weapons (nuclear artillery, tactical missiles, etc.) one might ask whether — contrary to declared strategic doctrine rejecting the idea of limited nuclear war — such weapons may not indicate the existence of a concept of limited warfare. One might argue that if the Soviet Union automatically reciprocated any use of nuclear weapons by its opponents by employing heavy intercontinental nuclear arms, it would not deploy small-yield nuclear weapons. Soviet specialists, when asked about this problem, tend to concede that in fact some types of weapons might not be used.

By the emphasis placed on such prospects and uncertainties, the West's deterrence is in turn being undermined to some extent: at least this line of argument tends to erode the credibility of NATO's nuclear commitments (Stratman 1981: 189) because facing the prospect of an all-out nuclear holocaust one may be tempted to ask whether a more or less sizeable conventional attack really is worth such a price, and whether it is appropriate to put the very existence of one's entire population at stake in order to respond to conventional infringement.

At this point, what matters is not whether or not the NATO countries are still convinced about the solidity of their deterrence posture. Rather, the question is to what extent these problems might lead the Soviet Union to *believe* that Western nuclear deterrence against a non-nuclear attack is no longer credible. In such a situation, the risk of making a political miscalculation is rising. Depending on the nature of the risk-taking behaviour, this may, with a remote yet still substantial probability, lead to a nuclear war by miscalculation. Very much depends therefore on the ability of the two major Powers to signal deterrence and to interpret the signals properly, irrespective of the basic asymmetry existing between the force postures and the strategic doctrines in East and West.

The nature of this situation obviously leaves many questions open. In the long run, nuclear deterrence against conventional attacks may increasingly lose credibility. That is why many specialists call for a strengthening of NATO's defence posture in the conventional area in order to have a force sufficient to prevent a surprise operation and to compel the aggressor to carry out a large-scale operation (de Rose 1982a). This would also imply a modification of the "Flexible Response" doctrine such that nuclear strikes against military targets on Soviet territory would be executed only in case of Soviet strikes of this type against Western Europe.

Problems of Countervailing Strategy

The doctrinal basis of this specific type of deterrence strategy is the principle of countervailing strategy, which in the context of United States planning since the 1960s is replacing the concept of mutual assured destruction (MAD) in its pure form. It was codified in the (unpublished) Presidential Directive No. 59 (PD-59) (Leitenberg 1981b; Ball 1981; Lübkemeier 1981: 19—27). According to a statement made by the former United States Secretary of Defense Harold Brown, its principal elements can be summarized as follows:

> "For deterrence to operate successfully, our potential adversaries must be convinced that we possess sufficient military force so that if they were to start a course of action which could lead to war, they would be frustrated in their effort to achieve or suffer so much damage that they would gain nothing by their action ... The preparation of forces and plans to create such a prospect has become to be referred to as 'countervailing' strategy". (Quoted in Beres 1981: 25).

Basically, PD-59 implies limited nuclear options to deter an adversary from general nuclear war and nuclear attacks or coercion in relation to a smaller set of targets as well; furthermore and most importantly, it is intended to contribute also to deterring conventional aggression. The ultimate object is to ensure United States ability to retaliate in a fully credible and convincing manner. To serve this purpose emphasis was laid on nuclear targeting directed against Soviet military targets, in particular the missile force. Secretary of Defense Schlesinger and subsequently the Carter Administration in 1978 and 1979, as announced in 1980, added a new category of targets, namely those Soviet facilities that would aid the USSR in post-nuclear recovery, i.e., primarily economic targets. Secondly and more importantly, relatively small and discrete "packets" of targets were selected for limited attack (Leitenberg 1981b: 314). According to Leitenberg, who has been collecting and analysing all the published evidence available on this subject, emphasis is on limited and discrete use, in contrast to large-scale use, and it has been motivated by the drastic improvements of Soviet nuclear weapon capabilities, both in number and in quality (Leitenberg 1981b: 316). Very probably the countervailing strategy represents no dramatic departure from previous strategic planning; Leitenberg (1980a: 11) asserts that the United States nuclear forces were always targeted at least partly on military installations. He reports that both the United States strategic forces and LRTNF have as their designated targets USSR military installations and weapons systems, both 'soft' and 'hard', and that had always been the case. The Single Integrated Operational Plan (SIOP), devised in the early 1960s, included a very large number of military targets — airfields, defences, missile sites, naval bases — as first priority targets even during the heydays of mutual assured destruction.

The flexibility envisaged under the countervailing strategy includes the development of an ability to devise alternative employment plans at short notice. It is designed to provide escalation control in order to gain leverage for a negotiated termination of the fighting. The survivability of the force components and of the C^3 network necessary for effective control are prime requirements for the adoption of a credible countervailing strategy.

As the concept of countervailing strategy was subjected to much criticism the Secretary of Defense, in order to clarify the meaning of this concept, also stated what the countervailing strategy was *not* intended to be (DoD Annual Report, FY 1982: 42—43):

> "— not a radical departure from the past
> — it does not assume the possibility of winning a limited nuclear war
> — it does not assume that a nuclear war can be limited, however, some gains are seen by reacting in a limited way to limited attack
> — it should not be inconsistent with progress in arms control
> — it is not a first strike strategy, but rather a more credible deterrent".

However, it is increasingly felt that the situation characterized by the principle of countervailing strategy creates a serious dilemma and may even, paradoxically, contribute to a lessening of strategic stability, thus facilitating the risk of an unintentional war. The "morass of paradoxes", as one observer calls it (Talbott 1981), comprises at least three thinkable scenarios; it cannot be denied that they do not entirely belong to the realm of mere fantasy.

Firstly, one might imagine a *"High noon"*-type showdown over some crisis. If the Soviet leadership thought that the United States was about to exercise its self-avowed first-use option, the Soviet might proceed to their own nuclear strike all the more quickly. An unintentional pre-emptive nuclear war would be the consequence. In order words, the United States policy of first use may offer incentives to the Soviet Union to undertake a pre-emptive nuclear strike against the United States (Beres 1981: 42 seq.) or at least to "anticipate" NATO's nuclear response by combining any conventional attack against Western Europe right from the beginning with a nuclear strike (Stratmann 1981: 108 f.).

Similarly, another scenario suggested by a critic of PD-59 (cf. Commentary in: BAS 9/36: 63 f.) supposes that, if the Soviet Union was preparing an invasion of Western Europe, it might fear that such an invasion would provoke the United States into an attack upon its nuclear arsenal. Hence the Soviet Union would be forced to fire its missiles in order to avoid losing them. On the other hand, the mere suspicion that the Soviet Union might behave this way would in turn force the United States into the same "use or lose" syndrome in which the pressures compelling the United States to launch its weapons might prove irresistible (Talbott 1981).

Thirdly, there might be a risk that a flexible response-type first use of small-calibre nuclear weapons would unleash a chain reaction beyond either's side control. The Soviet Union might, in such circumstances, be tempted to make the best of a bad situation by keeping one step ahead on the escalation ladder, being the first to proceed to the next higher level. In this case, a limited nuclear war would be quickly transformed into an unintentional all-out nuclear war where control is highly questionable (Rathjens 1981). Many authors in the West have expressed grave doubts as to the ability to limit nuclear war once the nuclear threshold has been passed (for instance, Ehmke 1981: 210; Barnaby 1980: 46).

All three scenarios, however, imply that the Soviet Union would in fact have a great probability of success in launching a pre-emptive strike, i.e., achieving a complete "splendid disarmament" of the West precluding any subsequent retaliation. This assumption can hardly withstand a sober analysis. NATO's nuclear retaliation capacity would still survive to a degree sufficient to inflict intolerable damage on Soviet population centres and military targets (Stratmann 1981: 148—173, 223—225).

The three scenarios also seem to assume extremely bold risk-taking behaviour on the part of the Soviet leadership, which is rather improbable. In addition, they imply a confrontation in which the United States is left with no option; obviously, United States policy is aimed at achieving a degree of flexibility which would prevent such a situation.

Actually the three scenarios start from an assumption of strategic developments which have already destabilized the overall strategic relationship. This leads back to the question of strategic stability dealt with above. As long as strategic stability is not completely destroyed, the likelihood of the three scenarios becoming reality is rather low indeed.

As long as the Soviet leadership has no firm certainty about either an imminent United States nuclear attack or an uncontrolled escalation of nuclear war once it has started, any decision to pre-empt by conducting a nuclear strike would simply be insane. Admittedly, there may be doubts on the part of the Soviet leadership as to whether the United States President would honour the commitment made. Yet, it is one thing to doubt about the credibility of a commitment, and quite another to deny the existence of this credibility absolutely and decisively. In other words, there is no need to have absolute credibility — sufficient credibility is enough (Rosenkranz/Jütte 1974: 17).

A more serious problem in the context of deterrence against conventional attacks may arise from the amount of collateral damage caused by nuclear defence against a conventional attack, and to be suffered partly by those who are to be defended. At worst, the values to be defended might be destroyed by the very efforts to defend them. Therefore and in order to avoid this awful prospect, the defender might be inclined *not* to resort to the nuclear weapons he has been envisaging using — that is what is called "self-deterrence". If this eventuality is realized by the prospective aggressor, nuclear deterrence against conventional attacks ceases to be credible.

In the context of this study no further attention will be focused on this problem of self-deterrence, because it can be assumed to have no immediate bearing on the risk of unintentional nuclear war. *If* self-deterrence becomes fully effective and *if* for the potential aggressor the deterrence posture consequently loses all credibility, war becomes probable, but it will hardly be a nuclear war. *If*, on the other hand, there is a tendency towards self-deterrence, and *if* the potential aggressor cannot be sure of the effective significance of this tendency towards self-deterrence, he is still faced with a considerable amount of uncertainty, and therefore the deterrence posture has not yet lost credibility completely.

The situation is of course different if self-deterrence works only partly whereas the potential aggressor erroneously assumes it to be fully effective. In such a hypothetical situation, an unintentional nuclear war or a war by miscalculation is likely to happen.

Yet the hypothetical assumptions underlying this scenario must be said to be highly unrealistic, because no sane attacker could dare to launch an attack under conditions of uncertainty as to a nuclear response by the victim. The reverse situation may seem much more probable, i.e., a situation in which the defender in fact would be self-deterred and would not dare to respond by nuclear means whereas the attacker still overestimates the defender's willingness to do so and perceives the possibility of a nuclear response at least as uncertain. The potential attacker therefore will abstain from launching an aggressive war.

C. Extended Deterrence

The "Nuclear Umbrella"

Another source of possible misunderstandings and miscalculations must be seen in the fact that the major Powers relate their nuclear deterrence not only to attacks against their homelands but to attacks against friends and allies as well. The promise or guarantee of retaliation against any attack on an allied third party in the same way as an attack on one's own homeland, i.e., by nuclear retaliation, may for various reasons seem less credible than deterrence aimed at protecting the homeland only. The allies themselves may be tempted to ask whether, in the event of a real emergency, their defenders would be willing to contemplate being drawn into an atrocious nuclear exchange for the sake of a far-away ally. On this premise, de Gaulle argued that no United States President would sacrifice Chicago for Paris (Speed 1979: 103 f.). This is the classic "Mourir pour Danzig?" question which, in its nuclear version, has never ceased to worry NATO strategists ever since the establishment of NATO (Beaufre 1964b: ch. II). If the answer to the question is not affirmative, this may lead to conclusions such as the one drawn by France, which preferred to build up its own deterrent, the *force de frappe*, in order to escape the dilemma implied in that question. The smaller NATO allies may not have the same option at their disposal as does France, yet the question, although being answered affirmatively in official alliance policies, has never lost its pertinence. Some critics assert that the United States nuclear umbrella over Western Europe is dead and that no technological "fix" can revive it (Lodgaard 1981: 330; Freedman 1981: 65). This feeling is increasingly prevalent in the post-Viet Nam era, when the United States is undergoing a period of reconsideration of its overseas commitments (Deibel 1980: 3). In some Western European countries, the question "Red or dead?" seems to be a topic of serious discussion (Fritsch 1981: 209).

This question is also of crucial importance with regard to the subject of the NATO deterrence posture. Will the Soviet Union believe that NATO's conception of deterring any aggression by the commitment of the United States nuclear arsenal is still credible? Or are there any doubts regarding the nature of United States deterrence for the benefit of the NATO allies in Europe? (Lübkemeier 1981: 29 ff.) The discussions about "decoupling" the defence of Western Europe from the United States nuclear guarantee will hardly enhance the credibility of NATO's deterrence posture.

At best, this fact will constantly raise doubts about credibility and thus increase the propensity to destabilize the situation. At worst, it may offer a temptation to try to "test" the seriousness of the United States commitment; again, the likelihood of such a conclusion largely depends on the risk-taking behaviour. In periods of "normalcy" the corresponding risks may be low; however, this may not be the case in situations of high tension and dramatic confrontation. At any rate, Luttwak may be correct in saying that protection obtained from extended deterrence must always be the second-best solution (Luttwak 1980: 32).

The Risk of Brinkmanship

The most critical situation arising from this dilemma might occur if a Government were willing to deliberately engage in a strategy of brinkmanship. Brinkmanship crises are "confrontations in which a state challenges an important commitment of an adversary in the expectation that the adversary will back down" (Lebow

1981b: 14). They are highly dangerous and may lead to unintentional nuclear war due to miscalculation. Brinkmanship may have mainly internal causes (weaknesses of a State's political system and of leaders, intra-elite competition for power) and, as a semi-external cause, the expectation of a dramatic shift in the balance of power. Many brinkmanship challenges were initiated without any good evidence that the adversary lacked resolve to back up his commitments. Brinkmanship, in effect, places the burden of choice on the adversary, as it involves challenging him and expecting him to back down. If the adversary does not back down, the blame of initiating hostilities will be placed on him. In game-theory perspective, it is the attempt to forgo all alternatives, to move oneself into a position where no choice exists, in the hope that the adversary will, by having only the choice between accepting the *fait accompli* and initiating hostilities entailing probable losses, in the last instance calculate that acceptance is preferable to fighting.

Brinkmanship means manipulating the risk of war; as Schelling (1966: 99) put it: "It means exploiting the danger that somebody may inadvertently go over the brink, dragging the other with him". The danger is not very great if the brink is clearly recognizable and both sides are in full control. Schelling illustrates brinkmanship by the example of two climbers tied together. If one of the climbers wants to intimidate the other by seeming about to fall over the edge, there has to be some uncertainty. If each climber is in full control of himself and never gets dizzy, and there are no loose pebbles underfoot and no gusts of wind to catch one off guard, neither can pose any risk to the other by approaching the brink. Brinkmanship is the forgoing of the ability to decide on the course of action (Schelling 1966: 99), compelling the other to take a favourable course of action to defuse the dangerous situation.

Although the prospects of any Government adopting a policy of brinkmanship are remote, it is hard to dispel doubts and uneasy feelings regarding the credibility of extended deterrence. This problem was for instance highlighted by former United States Secretary of State Kissinger in his Brussels speech in 1979. Referring to United States' assurances that it would escalate a war to a nuclear level in case of threatening nuclear defeat of its European allies he said that:

> "these words cannot be true, and if my analysis is correct we must face the fact that it is absurd to base the strategy of the West on the credibility of the threat of mutual suicide" (Kissinger 1979b: 266).

Thus Western Europe should not rely on the United States readiness to go nuclear and invite retaliation on the continental United States in order to redress unfavourable military developments in Europe threatening its allies with defeat. Considerations along these lines have become a standard argument in the public discussions about contemporary security problems (Talbott 1981; Schilling 1981; Hoffmann 1981). Nitze (1977: 131) recalls that as early as in the 1960s there were some doubts as to the political credibility of the United States assurances that it would use its nuclear shield to protect Europe. At that time, the United States had a clear nuclear superiority.

The introduction of tactical nuclear weapons in Europe served to link the conventional level of war with the strategic nuclear level. It was intended to obviate a situation in which the United States had to contemplate the immediate use of strategic nuclear weapons in reaction to impending defeat in a conventional battle in Europe. Thus it closed a gap in the deterrence posture. The threat to escalate on a higher level is, however, only credible if the attacker cannot hope to achieve meaningful ratios of superiority at higher levels.

The Strategy of Flexible Response

The currently valid NATO strategy of flexible response is based on the principle of meeting a provocation first at the same level and of threatening escalation to higher levels in order to achieve early termination of hostilities at a low level and to preclude military disaster if such is seen as a definite possibility. The NATO triad consists of conventional weapons, tactical nuclear weapons, and strategic nuclear weapons, including also a number of United States SLBMs under NATO command. The doctrine of flexible response requires "the credible capability to threaten retaliation one level higher than that at which aggression occurs. Under this doctrine, it is important that no significant gap appears in the escalation ladder" (De Vries 1979: 253). This strategy of threatened escalation relies not only on the threat of first use of nuclear weapons but also on an advantage in theatre nuclear weapons (Hyland 1981: 198). Otherwise, given simple parity in theatre forces, escalation control (DoD Annual Report, FY 1982: 40) would not be assured, a rung in the ladder would be missing. The requirement of superior theatre nuclear forces is of course posing some difficulties for arms control agreements (Klein 1979: 23). The principal purpose of United States nuclear weapons in Europe is to bolster deterrence by coupling the outbreak of conventional war in Europe to the prospect of escalation to nuclear war, initially at the theatre and ultimately at the strategic level (Frye 1980: 99). The one-way escalation threat (and control), however, is doubtful in an age of parity at all levels.

The crossing of the "nuclear threshold" could lead to uncontrollable events. While some maintain that a nuclear war could be limited geographically and qualitatively, others say that the escalation to all-out war would be inevitable. It seems "a fallacy to believe the use of nuclear weapons can be confined to tactical ones. Once war has escalated to this level neither side is likely to give up. And escalation to a full-scale strategic, intercontinental war is likely" (Bethe 1981: 4). Rotblat also perceives the probability of isolating the conflict as very small (Rotblat

1981: 34). It would lead from strikes on military targets to more and more indiscriminate use of nuclear weapons and to attack on the respective homelands of the major nuclear Powers. NATO commander Rogers said that "any exchange of nuclear weapons would quickly escalate to all-out atomic war" *(Internationa Herald Tribune,* 9 November 1981: 2). He described the strategic nuclear force as the "ultimate guarantor".

Countervailing strategy and flexible response implied by NATO doctrine seem to have broad similarities (see Lübkemeier 1981: 29—32): the principle of the countervailing strategy is that selective options for the employment of strategic nuclear weapons, the availability of adequate responses to limited aggression, will enhance the credibility of deterrence due to the perceived greater likelihood of their use in conflict. In addition, intra-war deterrence should allow to stop the hostilities short of mutual devastation. The concept of flexible response encompasses also limited responses to limited attacks, the matching of the threat with an adequate and credible deterrent and the termination of hostilities at the lowest possible level. The availability of selective nuclear options to the United States strategic forces is considered to enhance the credibility of the United States nuclear guarantee for Western Europe (Lübkemeier 1981: 29—32).

The possibility of early termination of nuclear hostilities at an acceptable level is subject to serious doubts, particularly if one considers the targeting of political and military leadership and control. Conceivably, the exchange of strikes could proceed and escalate until the difference between the simple exchange of first and second strikes and a simple MAD scenario would not be noticed. According to Schilling (1981: 72) the present strategy of countervailing power, most recently expressed in Carter's Presidential Directive 59, a strategy denying the Soviet Union any prospect of victory on whatever political or military terms it might care to define it, "has a fine Old Testament ring to it: an eye for an eye, a tooth for a tooth, and, if need be, city for city".

Tactical Nuclear Weapons and Limited Nuclear War

The Soviet and United States doctrines for the use of tactical nuclear weapons seem to differ a great deal (Miettinen 1978: 238). For the United States, tactical nuclear weapons are designed for war-fighting and defence of a friendly country and to delay escalation. For the Soviet Union, they are a deterrent, but, in case war is inevitable, a means to "clear an avenue for a massive offensive".

There is some discussion as to whether the Soviet Union would in fact react as envisaged by NATO doctrine. Soviet military writings in the late 1960s referred to the possibility of a limited *non*-nuclear exchange, but they were hostile to ideas of controlled escalation, intra-war bargaining and limited options (Osgood 1979: 22). The possession of capabilities to implement limited nuclear options later on did not induce the public adoption of controlled escalation scenarios and intra-war bargaining (Osgood 1979: 58). A central question is whether the Western distinction between tactical war and strategic war is shared by the Soviet Union. Thus one cannot be sure that the use of tactical nuclear weapons (under United States command) in a geographically limited war would not lead to counter-strikes against the United States, making a full-scale intercontinental war inevitable (Makins 1981: 159 ff.). The introduction of accurate INF in Europe due to the NATO modernization (Pershing-II and GLCM) has also to be seen in this perspective.

Thus the assumption that it is possible to conduct *limited* and perhaps quite protracted nuclear exchanges seems to be the very centre of the problem. On the other hand, the typical lay image of nuclear war assumes that any use of nuclear weapons by one major Power against the opponent would inevitably and rapidly lead to all-out attacks and consequently to mutual annihilation (Ball 1981: 35). Ball, who has made a thorough study of this problem, comes to the conclusion that the notion of controlled nuclear war fighting is essentially astrategic and that there can be no possibility of controlling a nuclear war *(ibid.:* 36). If these speculations are correct, any limited nuclear war would therefore inevitably escalate into an unintentional all-out nuclear war, getting rapidly out of control.

Yet this view is not shared by all specialists. Rathjens (1979: 144) argues that the chances of terminating a conflict after a few nuclear weapons have been used are better than they were some years ago and will improve further. In a recent study, however, and considering the deployment of new nuclear weapons in Europe, he is inclined to assume that once nuclear weapons are used, control will become questionable (Rathjens 1981: 377). Also, the rapidly progressing blurring of the distinction between tactical and strategic nuclear capabilities seems to point in this direction.

There is now some confusion about what to call the nuclear weapons considered crucial for coupling the defence of Western Europe to the United States strategic arsenal. The expressions "theatre nuclear forces" (TNF), "theatre nuclear weapons" (TNW), "tactical nuclear weapons" (also TNW), "eurostrategic weapons", "grey-zone weapons", and "intermediate-range nuclear forces" (INF) have been used.

Sukovic (1978) discusses how these weapons are defined. One criterion used for distinguishing between strategic and tactical nuclear weapons is the range of the delivery systems, meaning that tactical nuclear weapons are those weapons not able to cover the distance between the two major nuclear Powers. Other criteria include the intentions as to how to use these weapons, or their yield. However, the yield seems rather a confusing criterion, as many RVs on the strategic level are rather low-yield due to very high accuracy. The amount of collateral damage caused does not seem a valid criterion for identifying strategic nuclear systems. Probably, the most frequently used criterion which makes the most sense is the *range*.

New developments in tactical nuclear weapons, especially intermediate-range nuclear forces (INF), tend to blur the distinction with strategic nuclear weapons, as the launch of missiles capable of hitting a part of the Soviet Union from Western Europe (under United States command) could be argued to be strategic. Very small nuclear weapons with a very short range, designed for battlefield use, are sometimes considered to blur the line of distinction between nuclear and conventional weapons (Epstein 1976: 33). Developments in conventional weapons technology have "substantially diminished whatever justification may once have existed for reliance on lower-yield nuclear weapons for actual warfighting purposes" (Frye 1980: 100). The fact that conventional weapons could be released for use earlier and without the authorization process necessary for nuclear weapons seems to support such suggestions to rely more on modern conventional weapons. Therefore Frye asks: "If nuclear weapons are cut down to conventional size, is their military utility sufficient to warrant crossing the threshold to nuclear war?" (Frye 1980: 99).

Crisis of Extended Deterrence?

The situation is quite confusing and this gives rise to the evolution of all kinds of scenarios. One may, for instance, assume that Soviet strategists reach the following conclusion: *if* United States deterrence against a Soviet push towards the West is no longer credible, and if the remaining credibility is further undermined by the improved Soviet ICBM threat against United States cities, and if "realistic forces" among the "ruling circles" in the United States increasingly realize this fact — why not try to exploit the Soviet superiority in conventional armaments? The less credible the United States nuclear guarantees for Europe become — and they do so for a variety of reasons — the stronger are the incentives for the Soviet Union to draw these conclusions. This can in turn lead to confrontations and conflagrations which might easily get out of control and thus paradoxically reinforce the propensity to become entangled in an unintentional nuclear war.

The likelihood of this and related scenarios must be matched, however, against the image of a situation that is presented to Soviet decision-makers. While there cannot be the slightest doubt in the minds of the Soviet leadership about the consequences of an attack on the United States (i.e., a retaliation strike), with regard to attacks on the United States allies the Soviet Union must at least be completely uncertain as to the United States response (Speed 1979: 109). As in every case of a credibility problem, one has to distinguish between doubts regarding this credibility up to the point of being sure that credibility has clearly and completely vanished, on the one hand, and doubts which affect credibility without eroding it completely.

As long as the Soviet leadership cannot be certain that nothing would happen if it attacked Western Europe, extended deterrence still works.

Indications available from Soviet sources suggest that in fact such doubts exist, yet no Soviet speaker has ever expressed certainty about an automatic non-fulfilment of United States guarantees. Furthermore, one has to take into account the nature and degree of risk-taking on the Soviet part. It is simply not justified on the basis of all the evidence available to assume risky behaviour and adventurism as the foundation of Soviet foreign policy. The image of a Soviet leadership playing a nuclear "High Noon" may reflect "Wild West" phantasies cherished by Western authors of those scenarios. But it is virtually absurd to ignore the longstanding attitude of responsibility, prudence and care exhibited by the Soviet Union, particularly with regard to nuclear weapons and nuclear strategy. This fact is duly recognized also by United States students of Soviet foreign policy and strategy (cf. Morgan 1977: 128 f.; Lambeth 1981). For instance, Lambeth (1981: V) sees Soviet crisis behaviour as dominated by "pronounced risk-aversion" and "inherent caution". In addition, one should also not forget that Marxist-Leninist theory considers that caution is often in order and retreat sometimes respectable as well as affirming the idea that one must always adapt to developing conditions (Morgan 1977: 176). Marxism-Leninism is certainly not a theory that encourages a policy threatening disaster and radical departures from the status quo. This inherent attitude is further reinforced by the belief that time is on the side of socialism; as a consequence, Soviet leaders from Lenin onward have consistently been reluctant to "push" history with attempts to garner cheap political gains before the natural development of the right conditions (Lambeth 1981: V).

When examining the problem of extended deterrence, the situation discussed in the context of United States nuclear guarantees for the European members of NATO is by no means the sole case in which nuclear deterrence guarantees for third countries may constitute a risk conducive to the outbreak of war by miscalculation. It is simply the situation which is most widely and articulately discussed. Yet there are an increasing number of similar situations involving one or other of the two major Powers, particularly in the Middle East and in the third world generally. The two major Powers are engaging, with growing frequency, in all types of commitments towards third countries. However, by contrast to the "classical" alliance commitments made within NATO and WTO, these commitments are more often than not poorly defined. The degree of the commitment, the type of contingencies to which it refers and the responsibilities of the giver and the recipient of the guarantee lack precision in most instances.

Even if they are clear to the two parties immediately concerned, they may be less clear to those outside Powers which are to be deterred by the commitment. Such is the case in the arrangement for strategic co-operation between the United States and Israel; furthermore, the political evolution of the Gulf area and in South-

East Asia must be mentioned in this context. Similar uncertainties may be perceived in the Soviet commitment for Afghanistan, Libya and South Yemen. Again, this may lead to misunderstandings and miscalculations regarding the nature and extent of the commitment, and again this may foster the temptation to find out more about it by "testing" the opponent in a dramatic confrontation. If a challenger under-estimates the substance of the commitment, and if the guarantor is willing to go so far as to use nuclear weapons as the ultimate instrument to honour his commitment, when the challenger did not expect this, there is a likelihood that a nuclear war will be triggered by sheer miscalculation.

Conclusions: Risks of Unintentional Nuclear War Generated by the Strategy of Deterrence

The risks:

1. *As the essence of deterrence is credibility, which is a subjective concept, the stability of deterrence depends on all kinds of delicate perceptual and psychological processes which might lead to gross miscalculation; if the threat to retaliate is underestimated, deterrence fails and an unintentional nuclear war would be the consequence.*
2. *The system of deterrence is generally drifting towards becoming unstable, as indicated by the concern for scenarios like Called Bluff.*
3. *The assumptions of rationality underlying deterrence strategies are not justified in every situation.*
4. *The NATO concept of deterring conventional aggression by the threat of a selective nuclear strike is constantly affected by doubts about its credibility and reliability. This concept also seems questionable because a limited nuclear war in Europe might destroy what it is supposed to protect. These doubts are supported by the Soviet refusal to accept the concept of limited nuclear war.*
5. *The NATO concept of extended deterrence (United States nuclear guarantees for European allies) also suffers from problems of credibility thus aggravating the risk of miscalculation.*
6. *The two credibility problems (credibility of nuclear deterrence against conventional attack and credibility of United States nuclear guarantees for Europe) add up to one large credibility problem and reinforce each other. This creates regional crisis instability.*
7. *This may create a temptation to engage in low-key "probes" so as to assess the seriousness of commitments made within the framework of extended deterrence.*

107

8. *The question whether there can be such a thing as a "limited nuclear war", not necessarily escalating into an all-out nuclear war, is extremely controversial. There is at least some likelihood that the "tactical" use of nuclear weapons would inadvertently trigger a full-scale nuclear exchange.*
9. *Very serious risks of miscalculation emerge in third world regions, where the two major Powers have made a multitude of poorly defined commitments in the sense of extended (mainly conventional) deterrence.*

Mitigating factors:

1. *For the foreseeable future, no nuclear Power can rely with certainty on escaping any retaliation if it tries to disarm its opponent by a first strike, unless it has a completely insane risk-taking behaviour overriding any rational considerations which, in principle, will prevent gross misjudgement.*
2. *The same can be said of the specific strategic situation prevailing in Europe, yet the prospects for continuing credibility of deterrence may be less far-reaching in time. Credibility is not absolute, but sufficient.*
3. *The uncertainties about possible disastrous consequences of a "probe" of the deterrence postures in Europe are mutual: the Soviet Union is not sure about its chances of escaping United States retaliation. The United States is not sure about an immediate escalation into an all-out nuclear war by the Soviet Union, once it employs nuclear weapons. This does not exclude, however, low-key "probes".*

Risk assessment:

The risk of unstable deterrence which constitutes the very essence of strategic or crisis instability is currently being aggravated and multiplied by a series of strategic developments at both the global and regional levels. Doubts regarding the credibility of deterrence postures are increasing for a multitude of reasons, and this is conducive to miscalculation or inability to prevent miscalculation by the opponent. Still, credibility, although not absolute, is sufficient to stave off any failure of deterrence. Yet this situation of relative stability is not safe for an indefinite future. It also has a propensity to generate low-key crises of all kinds which in turn imply a risk of escalation.

V. INTERNATIONAL CRISES AS
   CATALYTIC TRIGGERS

A. Unintentional Consequences of Crisis Decision-Making

The arms race and ensuing developments in the technological field, the evolution
of strategic doctrines and deterrence policies and a multitude of additional factors
may contribute to a certain propensity of the international strategic system to generate the risk of unintentional nuclear war. As was pointed out in the introductory
chapter of this study, the propensity or predisposition to generate the risk of unintentional nuclear war must not be confused with the possible occurrence of this
type of war. For such a disastrous event to come about, there must also be a catalytic
cause, i.e., a trigger event which might "blow up the world".

Generally speaking, catalytic causes relevant in this context emerge from situations of crisis confrontation. A crisis might escalate into a nuclear war although the
opponents initially never had such a development in mind. This is held to be a conceivable possibility by many experts (e.g., Barnaby 1980: 3f.). Such escalation processes might be the result of poor management of decision processes typical of
the suboptimal behaviour of men affected by stress. Stress is a genuine feature of
all crisis situations, and it may considerably impair decision-making.

Studies on the risk of unintentional nuclear war increasingly emphasize the
crucial importance of crisis situations as catalytic causes (e.g., Tromp 1981; Rathjens 1981). That is also why many authors are inclined to use the term "crisis stability" synonymously with "strategic stability", thus pointing to the crucial importance
of crisis situations as possible triggers.

Consequences of Crisis Stress

In order to grasp the essence of perceptual and behavioural pathology to be discerned in crisis situations, the concept of stress may serve as an intervening variable.
Stress is determined by the scale of the threat and the degree of time-pressure (Hermann 1972: 13; Brecher 1980: 1).

Very much has been said and written about the consequences of crisis situations and ensuing stress upon the behaviour of individual decision-makers and organizations. Most comments refer to dysfunctional adaptation processes, i.e., to harmful effects impairing the quality and adequacy of the crucial decisions to be taken and thus constituting a serious risk of triggering an unintentional war.

On the other hand, it would be misleading to overlook the positive consequences which exist as well. As pointed out by Morgan (1977: 172), a crisis may foster a heightened sense of risk and uncertainty and a greater sensitivity on the part of top decision-makers to their limited control over the situation. In crisis situations, Governments tend to move most cautiously and prudently. This hypothesis is corroborated by most published accounts of the anatomy of crisis decision-making. There is broad agreement among students of international crises that an acute crisis prompts decision-makers to make a greater effort to behave in accordance with the dictates of rationality in the formal sense of the term (Morgan 1977: 177).

Keeping this reservation in mind, in the following paragraphs an attempt will nevertheless be made to identify those aspects of crisis decision-making which might be subject to suboptimal performance by the individual and organizations concerned. Emphasis will be laid on two aspects: firstly, the likelihood of insufficient or defective perceptions and decision-making behaviour at the individual level; secondly, the various sources of poor performance and error of organizations such as bureaucracies, cabinets, politburos, crisis staffs, etc.

Social science research done in various fields of study (political science, psychology, social psychology, semantics) has devoted much attention to the performance of perception and information-processing during international crises. The particular kind of situations with which decision-makers find themselves confronted in periods of international crisis are liable to lead to defective and biased understanding (Cohen 1979: 161; Holsti 1972: 224; Sonntag 1981: 100—108). Crisis situations tend to amplify tendencies inherent in any cognitive process. Decision-makers then virtually suffer from information processing pathologies. This may have dreadful consequences if the object of misperception is situated in the context of nuclear strategy. Underestimating nuclear deterrence postures or misinterpreting moves by the other side as steps requiring immediate escalation can lead to the disaster of an unintentional nuclear war; in either case, cognitive distortions are at the origin of a process the outcome of which nobody actually wanted. Cognitive theory has produced a considerable amount of insights into the logic of misperception at both the individual and the organizational level. Although cognitive processes at the individual level, i.e., psychologically motivated biases and distortions, are often closely intertwined with cognitive processes rooted in the structure of organizations, i.e., decision-making groups, the two types of cognitive failure will be analysed separately.

110

When reviewing the vast amount of literature available on international crises, crisis behaviour and crisis management, it becomes immediately clear that any simplified conclusions as to the consequences of crisis stress would be misleading. Crisis stress is sometimes beneficial, sometimes detrimental.

Holsti (1979: 99) cites former United States President Nixon as saying that he found crises stimulating for creative mental activity. However, this is only part of the picture. Some degree of stress is considered by Holsti (1979: 107) as an integral and necessary precondition for individual or organizational problem-solving, because it serves as a motivating force. Intense stress, however, seems to impair performance. Thus, performance relates to stress roughly like an inverted U-shaped curve. Low to medium levels of stress enhance performance; but higher levels of stress tend to erode rather than enhance the cognitive abilities required from decision-makers in crisis (Holsti 1979; George 1980: 48).

Before considering the effects of high stress in impairing cognitive ability, the impact of biological variables on the performance of individuals under stress may briefly be examined.

Emotional and physical fatigue tend to increase the stress of decision-makers in international crises (George 1980: 48; Wiegele 1973: 309—313). In a crisis, minutes seem like hours, hours like days, days like weeks. The demands on one's energies and emotions are intense; at the same time, opportunities for rest and recuperation are limited (George 1980: 48). Prolonged stress leads to tiredness, and while the susceptibility to physical fatigue in stress situations may differ markedly between individuals, all will suffer in some measure (Williams 1976: 75). The physical factor becomes more and more important as the crisis progresses:

> "Decisions must be made very rapidly; physical endurance is tested as much as perception, because an enormous amount of time must be spent making certain that the key figures act on the basis of the same information and purpose" (Kissinger in *Time*, 15 October 1979: 71).

Other biological factors influencing the susceptibility for stress include the health of the participants of the decision-making unit. This has a bearing on the capability to withstand stress. Wiegele (1973) goes so far as to say that biological health becomes an extremely important factor in international crises entailing great stress. Sleep deprivation may enhance fatigue. This can also disturb the normal physiological rhythms which are generally adjusted to a 24-hour cycle.

Yet, former Secretary of State Kissinger noted:

> "Some may visualize crisis management as a frenzied affair in which key policy-makers converge on the White House in limousines, when harassed officials are bombarded by nervous aides rushing in with the latest flash cables. I have found this not to be accurate; periods of crisis, to be sure, involve great tension, but they are also characterized by a strange tranquility" (Kissinger in *Time*, 15 October 1979: 71).

However, this need not be the case in every crisis. Robinson (1972: 33) draws attention to the increased risks of personal exhaustion and physical problems. The unusually long working time, perhaps only irregularly interrupted by some sleep, will disturb the normal rhythm, which, in turn, will have an influence on the stress level (see Wiegele 1973). Robinson notes that Theodore Sorensen reportedly worked for several days without a hot meal during the Cuban missile crisis. Stress, however, does influence the way in which decisions are taken. Most importantly, it influences the way in which information is appraised and it also has an impact on the behaviour of senior decision-makers.

The age of the individuals participating in crisis management is also to be taken into account in a discussion on stress effects. "Changes in sense acuity which are the result of aging have the overall effect of reducing alertness" (Wiegele 1973: 315). The most important positions in the units taking decisions in international crises tend to be occupied by men in their fifties or older. However, the differences between individuals are very great, and certain functions do not seem to be impaired in older age at all, for example verbalization and comprehension of data.

The findings of empirical research referring to the general population are perhaps to be interpreted cautiously in regard to political decision-makers, as it may be "that only the biologically and psychologically able can rise to positions of high responsibility" (Wiegele 1973: 307). Shortcomings within the process of information-processing and the preparation of options in crises should be alleviated by the decision-maker's knowledge, farsightedness, and caution. Betts (1978: 83) asserts that leaders should be made self-conscious and self-critical about their own psychologies in order to be less vulnerable to cognitive pathologies. But he also notes that intelligence consumers are "political men who have risen by being more decisive than reflective, more aggressive than introspective, and confident as much as cautious".

Finally, the impact of stress on the cognitive and behavioural performance of decision-makers depends not only on intensity (the level of stress) but also on the duration of stress. The cumulation of stress factors in a crisis (events, threats, time pressure) will tend to hold the stress constantly at a high level, not allowing recovery (Williams 1976: 75).

Stress-Induced Misperception

Intense and prolonged stress tends to lead to cognitive rigidity of the decision-makers involved (Holsti 1979: 106—109; George 1980: 49; Smart and Vertinsky 1979; Brecher 1980: 343). In the field of perception a main source of error is produced by the fact that in a situation characterized by stress-generating factors decision-makers suffer from an overwhelming information overflow. The amount of information reaching the top-level decision-makers actually increases during a crisis. Kissinger recalled that during "fast-moving events, those at the center of decisions are overwhelmed by floods of reports compounded of conjecture, knowledge, hope and worry" (*Time*, 15 October 1979: 71). Intelligence failures are generally not due to any dearth of information but to an incorrect evaluation of the available information (Shlaim 1976: 349). The processing of information by the intelligence bureaucracy has some shortcomings, leading to the emergence of distorted perceptions and in the worst case even to self-fulfilling prophecies.

Even assuming that the problems of distinguishing between signals and "noise" and reading the signals correctly can be solved, the amount of information reaching the decision-makers may preclude any adequate response because the flood of analyses and messages increase the decision-makers' stress. On the brink of the First World War, the flood of information was such that the sheer volume of messages at some point exceeded the ability of foreign-policy organizations and officials to cope with it (Holsti 1972: 81). The amount of information by which these officials were inundated served to inhibit sound policy-making. Even assuming greatly enhanced information-processing capabilities today, such findings suggest that there is a point beyond which additional information impedes decision-making *(ibid.)*.

If confronted with an unprecedented mass of information to be dealt with in an extremely short time, decision-makers tend to various types of maladaptation such as omission, error, queuing and filtering (Miller 1965). To cope properly with an information overflow it would be necessary to select the information according to clearly established criteria and priorities. However, that happens very rarely in such situations, thus leading to an inappropriate perception and perhaps also a distortion of reality.

Apart from selective filtering of information, there is increased reliance on past experience and less attention paid to the side effects of options (George 1980: 49; Holsti 1979: 108—109; Brecher 1980: 343 ff.). The inadequacy of reliance on past experience need not be discussed; this is not to negate the worth of experience in international affairs and crisis management, but it is legitimate to caution against thinking in terms of analogies which might lead to a course of action ill-suited for the actual environment.

When some filtering is necessary, important aspects may be disregarded; conflicting values may be overlooked; the choice of options considered is narrowed; the search for new evidence is directed by preconceptions; the course favoured by superior decision-makers or by organizational considerations is not adequate for the given situation. George (1980: 56—57) mentions some particular characteristics of information processing: beliefs and constructs necessarily simplify and structure the external world; information processing is selective and subject to bias; there is variation between individuals in richness and complexity of existing beliefs; beliefs are relatively stable. Thus, the beliefs held by the participants in a decision-making

113

unit during a crisis or by individuals on their staff charged with the preparation of reports are of great importance.

The information needed in order to arrive at a correct assessment of the opponent's capabilities, actions, and intentions is buried in too much information not relevant to the situation. The filtering out of "noise" is difficult (Jervis 1970: 74; Speed 1979: 21). The individuals involved in handling information during a crisis should approach their task with an open mind (Janis and Mann 1977: 203—218), but preconceptions, biases and wishes enter into the process and influence it. The behaviour of the members of the decision-making unit is also important: bolstering a preferred choice would lead to a very selective information search, hypervigilance to an indiscriminate (but probably rather time-consuming) search, while behaviour tending to shift responsibility will lead to delegation of search and appraisal to others (Janis and Mann 1977: 206).

Besides predispositions, the impact of emotions, ideological commitments and bureaucratic behaviour is to be considered. Stereotypes about an adversary can lead to partial blindness towards facts contradicting long-standing assumptions, and within organizations it seems to be functional to stick to assumptions once they have been accepted (Knorr 1979: 78).

Heuer (1981) offers some interesting insights into information processing and the problems of deception. While these considerations are not limited to information-processing in stress situations, the danger may be greatest in such a setting. According to Heuer (1981: 315—316) the most important biases are as follows:

(1) Perceptions are influenced by expectations. More information and more un-ambiguous information is needed to recognize an unexpected phenomenon than an expected one.
(2) Perceptions are quick to form but resistant to change.
(3) Initial exposure to ambiguous or blurred stimuli interferes with accurate perception even after more and better information becomes available.
(4) Probability estimates are anchored by some natural starting-point, then adjusted in response to new information. Normally they are not adjusted enough.
(5) People have more confidence in conclusions drawn from a small body of consistent data than from a larger body of less consistent information.
(6) Less than perfectly reliable evidence is often processed as though it were wholly reliable.
(7) People have difficulty factoring the absence of evidence into their judgements.
(8) Impressions tend to persist even after the evidence on which they are based has been fully discredited.
(9) Events are seen as part of an orderly, causal pattern. The extent to which other countries pursue a coherent, goal-maximizing policy is overestimated.
(10) The behaviour of others is attributed to the nature of the person or the country, while our own behaviour is attributed to the nature of the situation.

There are remedies against most information-processing pathologies. Nevertheless, the effects of stress as well as the information-processing pathologies which are most likely to persist in situations of high stress have to be considered as catalysts which could trigger nuclear disaster in a situation in which international tension would be at a maximum but no side actually had any interest in beginning hostilities. Besides the avoidance of stress-inducing situations an attempt must be made to mitigate the effects of stress or to introduce organizational devices working against these effects. The assumption of the worst case might trigger pre-emption in an unstable strategic balance characterized by vulnerability of the weapons and counterforce targeting. There is a sad irony in the fact that the cognitive capacity of decision-makers in international politics seems impaired most when it is needed most (Holsti 1972: 199—200). As for information processing, there seems to be agreement that prolonged stress affects its complexity. This makes accurate distinction between relevant and irrelevant information less likely, tends to reduce the search for new information and may lead to suppression of unpleasant inputs (Suedfeld and Tetlock 1977: 170—171). An empirical examination of the relations between communicative complexity and crisis behaviour shows that international crises that resulted in war were characterized by lower levels of communicative complexity than those that were resolved peacefully (Suedfeld and Tetlock 1977: 182). The question is, however, whether the probability of war affected low communicative complexity or whether war was caused by deficient crisis behaviour in the sense of low complexity. Suedfeld, Tetlock and Ramirez (s.d.) found similar results by studying United Nations General Assembly statements concerning the Middle East from 1947 to 1976: complexity of information processing was significantly reduced in speeches made in months preceding the outbreak of war.

Pitfalls of Ambiguity

The uncertainty and ambiguity which are so characteristic of high-stress crisis situations (Lutz 1981b: 23) reinforce these tendencies. In ambiguous situations or in circumstances of information overload, one may also be more likely to screen information and respond in terms of personal predisposition (Holsti 1979: 109). People interpret incoming information in the light of their pre-existing views. The greater the ambiguity of the information, the greater the impact of the established belief (Jervis 1970: 132). Even if the information reaching the decision-makers was intended as a signal, the receiver cannot be completely sure what message the sender was trying to convey because the system is noisy and the signal ambiguous. Decision-makers then tend to reinforce maladaptive processes viewed as reducing cognitive dissonance, and they do so the more the ambiguity of their information received increases (Jervis 1976: 195).

The ambiguity of information reaching an intelligence analyst allows more influence to his wishes and his preconceptions, i.e., his assumptions are not likely to be revised upon receiving inconsistent information (Betts 1978: 70). The ambiguity will not even be a source of cognitive dissonance. Shlaim (1976: 357) notes that images, beliefs, ideological bias, wishful thinking, natural optimism or pessimism, confidence or the lack of it, all play a part in determining which facts the observer will notice and which he will ignore, the weight he will attach to the selected facts, the pattern into which he will fit them, and the conclusions which he will draw from them. In sum, "people tend to fit incoming information into their existing views and theories". Such propensities, of course, lead to a distorted perception, as some signals are amplified, while others are downplayed or even neglected (Jervis 1976: 215). Knorr (1976: 113) mentions the predisposition of inertia, that is, a "preference for escaping the rigors and puzzles of continuously monitoring the environment and of modifying an existing schema if the signals do not fit". In order to induce a person to change a long-held belief, a signal has to be very clear and open to a very limited range of interpretations. Yet the "noise" surrounding most of the signals relevant during a foreign policy crisis will more often than not preclude such clear messages (cf. also Smart and Vertinsky 1977).

Dealing with uncertainty is difficult. There are several impairments which can affect the outcome. George (1980: 37) describes some of them: hypervigilance is a panic-like state that is accompanied by a marked loss of cognitive efficiency. It would entail considerable interest in new information and an intensive search for it. Defensive avoidance is a device "used to escape from current worrying about a decision by not exposing oneself to cues that evoke awareness of a decisional conflict or dilemma that is fraught with potential losses". Defensive procrastination is one type of avoidance. Bolstering is another, and "groupthink", referring to certain conditions within a decision-making unit, is a third which may lead to avoidance. Satisficing and a strategy of incrementalism can also be considered to result in suboptimal decisions. The search for an optimal choice is in each of these cases abandoned in favour of a course of action "that will do".

Furthermore, the temporal and political horizons tend to collapse as stress increases. "Muddling-through" on a short-time basis becomes the dominant approach, with any middle-range or long-term vision, as well as any important consequences of one's choice, being neglected (Pugwash 1978: 6 f.). This attitude may induce decision-makers to opt for short-cut solutions to alleviate the short-run time pressure (Holsti 1979: 109; George 1980: 49), and this may be disastrous if the instrument of nuclear warfare is at hand.

Crisis stress also implies a high degree of intolerance of ambiguity, stereotyping, relative insensitivity to the other's perspective. Hence the probability of finding a solution in a crisis is reduced. Reliance on past experience can lead to concepts inadequate for the present situation. The reduced tolerance of ambiguity may result in simply ignoring information. Stereotyping reduces the other's possibilities

116

of signalling readiness for compromises. One side's insensitivity towards the other's perspective tends to lead to a perception that the adversary has the choice between many different courses of action, whereas it itself is limited to just one. This results in shifting the burden to the opponent by supporting the belief that one's own options are quite limited and that only the other side has the opportunity and hence the responsibility to prevent an impending disaster (George 1980: 49; Holsti 1972: 145 ff.; Holsti 1979; Hermann 1972: 198 ff.). The more stress increases, the more decision-makers tend to interpret their choice as the outcome of necessity rather than the result of a choice among several possible options.

Yet, it seems that in post-Second World War crises deliberate efforts were undertaken to explicitly consider a broader range of alternative courses of action (Morgan 1977: 179). Research based on experimental gaming (Mandel 1977: 618) also showed that the imagination, flexibility, and attentiveness of the participants increased significantly as the crisis progressed — as indicated by the number of policy alternatives considered and differing general approaches to the resolution of policy problems.

Another "pathological" consequence of stress related to intolerance of ambiguity is the tendency inherent in all human beings to reject cognitive inconsistency. One may agree with George (1980: 62), who asserts that in princple striving for consistency is neither good nor bad. But it may become suspect and demands vigilance in order to avoid distorted perceptions

(1) If the beliefs preserved thereby are not well-grounded to begin with; or
(2) If the individual (or organization) relies upon inappropriate beliefs or irrelevant rationalizations in order to ward off incoming information; or
(3) If the assimilation of the new information into pre-existing beliefs involves violations of generally accepted rules of treating evidence; or
(4) If the individual fails to notice events of obvious importance that contradict his beliefs or theories; or
(5) If he displays unwillingness to look for evidence that is readily available which would pose challenges to existing policy beliefs; or
(6) If he refuses to address the arguments of those who disagree with his interpretation of events; or
(7) If he repeatedly shifts rationales on behalf of his policy in response to new factors, (George 1980: 63).

It goes without saying that these and other cognitive pitfalls may be at the origin of fatal misjudgements leading to crucially inappropriate decisions in a crisis. This may have the gravest consequences if the use of nuclear weapons constitutes one of the available options.

Types of Distortion

The impact of stress on decision-makers and its general tendency to distort perceptions provoke highly emotional responses and cripple people's analytical capabilities
is a standard theme in the literature on crises. As reported by Morgan (1977: 186)
and originally presented by Schneider (1974), at least the following 17 hypothetical
effects of stress can be identified:

(1) A shrinkage of the ability to think analytically;
(2) A shrinkage of the ability to think creatively;
(3) A decrease in cognitive flexibility; an increase in rigidity;
(4) Increased stereotyping;
(5) Habituation, an increased commitment to habitual means of solving problems;
(6) Increased selective perception to match preconceptions;
(7) A decrease in probabilistic thinking; an increase in jumping to conclusions;
(8) An increase in ethnocentric we-they thinking;
(9) A decrease in work efficiency;
(10) Tunnel vision: a loss of perspective;
(11) Over-simplification, primitive thinking;
(12) Group conformity increases;
(13) Projections of hostility; scapegoating;
(14) Extreme behaviour; apathy and withdrawal or impulsiveness;
(15) An increase in anxiety and fatigue;
(16) An increase in denial, pretending, and abstraction;
(17) An increase in perceptual distortion, misperception.

Bolstering the preferred alternative is also a form of behaviour leading to
low-quality decisions.

> " 'Bolstering' refers to the psychological tendency under certain conditions of deci-
> sional stress to increase the attractiveness of a preferred (or chosen) option and doing
> the opposite for options which one is inclined to reject (or has rejected)" (George
> 1980: 38; see also Janis and Mann 1977: 91).

Pre-decision bolstering occurs under time pressure when a decision-maker believes
that he will not obtain further relevant information about the issue. Bolstering
mitigates the malaise of making a decision in uncertainty. However, as George
notes, the decision-maker's beliefs that the deadline is approaching fast and that
there is no additional relevant information may both be wrong: In order to cut
short the stress and malaise of a decisional dilemma he may rush his decision,
thereby foregoing the possibility of using the remaining time to obtain still additional information and advice. Thus, it seems to lead to suboptimal choices and
to neglect of information. There are several techniques of bolstering or rationalizing
(George 1980: 39; Janis and Mann 1977: 91—95):

(1) Exaggerating favourable consequences;
(2) Minimizing unfavourable consequences;

(3) Exaggerating the possibilities open for reversing the decision, should it turn out badly;

(4) Re-evaluating the negative consequences and attributing certain longer-range benefits to them;

(5) Wishful thinking that gains may materialize in the short run, undesirable consequences only in the distant future;

(6) Convincing himself or the decision-making unit that in case of failure, the visibility of it will be limited;

(7) Believing that even in case of failure, it will have done enough to be worthwhile;

(8) Exaggerating the remoteness of the action commitment (hoping that it is unnecessary to carry out the decision);

(9) Minimizing personal responsibility.

In sum, the perceptual consequences of stress can be identified quite clearly and distinctly. To what extent are these findings relevant for the risks of unintentional nuclear war? Obviously, when looking at the problem of risks inherent in politico-military confrontations between Powers armed with nuclear weapons, one must not simply refer to such vague concepts as "panicking" or "behaving like a cornered rat". There are precisely identifiable perceptual processes at work, and these processes exert a highly dangerous influence on the behaviour of the persons involved in crisis decision-making. One should also not forget that these various cognitive mechanisms tend to reinforce each other according to the theory of cumulative risks. If human fallibility is combined with nuclear weapons, the outcome may be catastrophic. After all, "decision-makers too are human beings" — the probability must not be underestimated that decision-makers in a situation where a nuclear confrontation might become thinkable will no longer be in a position to arrive at an adequate judgement and to interpret reality properly. As a result, they may launch a nuclear holocaust without being aware of what they are doing. Perceptions of existing reality may be inaccurate; however, false perceptions may also create their own reality. There is always the possibility of a "self-fulfilling prophecy" which, in the context of nuclear war, may virtually be a self-destroying prophecy. As was pointed out by W. I. Thomas many years ago, if men perceive situations as real, these perceptions tend to become real.

Misperception Mutually Reinforced:
The Mirror Image

The problem touched upon in this section is even more serious if account is taken of the so-called reactivity or stimulus-response processes which tend to prevail in conflict situations. According to empirical findings (Zinnes 1972; Tanter 1974; North/Holsti/Choucri 1976), each opponent reacts according to stimuli he receives from the other opponent. Unfortunately, there seems to be a kind of *mirror image logic* at work: the more hostile the stimuli one receives, the more hostile one's reaction is. As this logic applies to both opponents in an identical way, the inclination towards escalation becomes almost irresistible once this feedback process has been initiated.

Finally, such escalation processes tend to be determined by additional processes of distortion and misperception. This implies that more often than not a response intended by the opponent A is perceived differently, as a stimulus, by opponent B. This powerful mechanism distorting the feedback process, for obvious reasons, tends to exaggerate hostile perceptions and to underestimate accommodating gestures and moves. Thus the opponents involuntarily engage in a process of mutual escalation which, if a situation is viewed objectively, may not be justified.

Mitigating Factors

Of course it would be premature and inappropriate to overlook the fact that there are also mitigating factors and that politics provides a defence against these defects (Morgan 1977: 188). Assessing the potential for mistakes and errors on the one hand and the corrective tendencies on the other hand, Morgan comes to the conclusion that, paradoxically, we may be safer in a sudden sharp crisis from the threat of the collapse of deterrence than in the larger, slower developing crisis, where there is more time for thought and decision.

This distinction may also offer a clue for understanding and clarifying the sometimes confusing contradictions presented by empirical evidence regarding the perceptual and behavioural consequences of crises. While a great deal of research done on crisis perceptions and crisis behaviour yielded the findings reported above — i.e., findings regarding distorted perceptions and non-rational behaviour — one must not disregard the fact that there are also divergent findings. For instance, Zinnes (1972: 132 f.) reports that decision-makers do not perceive or behave differently in a crisis. In a crisis as in a non-crisis, they react in proportion to incoming stimuli. This perhaps applies to situations in which decision-makers are still fully capable of dealing with the emergency; yet, if a crisis intensifies or turns into a protracted crisis the disruptive effects of crisis seem to prevail. As pointed out above, performance perhaps relates to stress like an inverted U.

According to Brecher (1979), who also examined the difference in behaviour between rise of stress and decline of stress,

(1) The quest for information about the threatening event(s) tends to become more thorough as stress rises;
(2) The search for options tends to increase with rising stress;
(3) As crisis-induced stress rises, the number and variety of core inputs to decisions increase sharply;

(4) Decision-makers tend to assess their decisions as costly and more and more important as stress rises;

(5) The number and variety of core inputs to choice is reduced after the crisis and the stress level has peaked.

Brecher observed increasing resort to choices without precedent as stress rose. This seems to be at odds with the assumption that decision-makers under stress rely more and more on their past experiences. Research on crisis behaviour based in relatively few cases, however, can neither invalidate nor confirm such hypotheses. Behaviour may vary appreciably from case to case and depending on the decision-makers involved, leading to distinct results. However, the general overall tendency, according to Brecher, is that as stress increases, decision-makers' performance worsens (Brecher 1974: 77). Therefore, it would be unwise to disregard or underestimate the risks involved in the psychological traps and pitfalls once decision-makers are confronted with an acute international crisis.

Inadequate Organizational Response: Less Persons for More Problems

The quality — and the risks — of decision-making in crises depend not only on the cognitive and behavioural performance of the individuals involved. There are reasons to assume that they depend as much on the performance of the organization concerned, and the complex network of interactions among the various branches and agencies involved in shaping the decisions to be made in time of crisis.

First of all, in crisis situations, there is a tendency for decision-making groups to contract. The reasons for this are obvious: on the one hand, decisions have to be made very fast; therefore the top decision-makers wish to handle them at once. And on the other hand, the top decision-makers are exclusively competent to make the important decisions, and they do not wish to delegate them to other units. The contraction process takes place therefore at the highest level and it works by simply excluding or omitting the lower strata of the decision-making hierarchy.

This process seems perfectly understandable. However, one has to bear in mind that this very process means that additional time-pressure is being generated for the simple reason that fewer persons have to handle more information. The information-overload problem facing the decision-makers is thus reinforced rather than eased.

On the other hand, the emergence of an *ad hoc*, small-scale decision unit may lead the participants to put aside personal differences, career concerns, and bureaucratic and domestic interests, thus permitting a dispassionate analysis of possible courses of action "on their merits" (Morgan 1977: 178).

121

Kissinger describes crisis management as follows:

> "Some may visualize crisis management as a frenzied affair in which key policymakers converge on the White House in limousines, when harassed officials are bombarded by nervous aides rushing in with the latest flash cables. I have found this not to be accurate; periods of crisis, to be sure, involve great tension, but they are also characterized by a strange tranquility. All the petty day-to-day details are ignored, postponed or handled by subordinates. Personality clashes are reduced; too much is usually at stake for normal jealousies to operate. In a crisis only the strongest strive for responsibility; the rest are intimidated by the knowledge that failure will demand a scapegoat. Many hide behind a line of consensus that they will be reluctant to shape; others concentrate on registering objections that will provide alibis after the event. The few prepared to grapple with circumstances are usually undisturbed in the eye of a hurricane. All around them is commotion; they themselves operate in solitude and a great stillness that yields, as the resolution nears, to exhaustion, exhilaration or despair" (Kissinger in *Time*, 15 October 1979: 71).

This brief description identifies several elements probably typical of crisis management and the organizational processes evolving: concentration of the decision-making group on just one issue; the contraction of this group; and problems of co-operation within the group. In a crisis situation, the President of the United States, for instance, has an unusual opportunity to lead the policy process (Head et al. 1978: 221). He can define the crisis, initiate organizational procedures to cope with it, set deadlines and guide the process of decision-making. In crisis situations, the control over implementation of decisions is greater than usual. Thus, for the United States system, crises enhance the role of the President, while the Congress, the media and interest groups have less influence than normal. The top decision-making unit tends to be a small (12 to 15 members) group of policy-makers. The President has a major influence on the size of the group. The size of the unit tends to increase with the perceived threat (Head et al. 1978: 239—240; Hermann 1972: 197). While the President of the United States is highly involved in crisis decision-making (see also Hazlewood 1977: 101), the normal channels are short-circuited (Williams 1976: 67). Hazlewood notes that the President was involved as a decision-maker in over 73 per cent of the crises sampled, although this involvement was legally required in only 22 per cent of the cases. There was also extensive interagency co-ordination.

One may well expect that the handling of crises by other major nuclear Powers, particularly if involving the threat of the use of nuclear weapons, would follow a similar centralized pattern. However, as most research on crisis management has been done by United States social scientists, the focus is in most cases on the Government of the United States. The United States experience also suggests that organizational structures tend to change in a crisis, possibly for three reasons: the element of surprise makes it less likely that a standard procedure would do; the need for quick action or reaction limits the number of people involved;

and the seriousness of the situation precludes decision-making at a low level (Williams 1976: 66). These three features create the environment of crisis management: centralization and elevation to the highest level. Below this highest level, however, a broad group of people prepare information for the decision-making unit or implement decisions taken (Milburn 1972: 266). At the lower level, problems are caused by delays due to inadequate communications systems, information overload, loss or misinterpretation of information or confidentiality requirements for sensitive information (Hazlewood 1977: 102). Decisions reached seem often to be delayed in transmission and implementation. The options available to the decision-makers are restricted by a concern for information sensitivity in some cases. In a situation of information overload, decision-makers can be forced to employ fewer channels, thus reducing their alternative information sources and shortening their horizons (Smart and Vertinsky 1977: 5, 11). The most significant changes of the structure in a crisis are:

(1) Centralization of decision-making, sidestepping normal procedures and competences;
(2) The top decision-makers are concerned only with the crisis at hand;
(3) The implementation of decisions taken is carefully monitored.

In the history of United States crisis management, the decision-making units were formed on an *ad hoc* basis on several occasions: the chief executive is surrounded by a small, select circle of advisers most appropriately described as an elite within an elite (Williams 1976: 67). Steinbruner (1979) describes the *ad hoc* Executive Committee of the National Security Council during the Cuban missile crisis. This Committee had centralized authority under the President. He and all top officials set aside all other business. The Committee integrated all policy relevant to the crisis across all the divisions of responsibility. However, this Committee failed to ensure accurate implementation of its decisions; far stronger moves than intended were made by the Navy against Soviet submarines near Cuba, raising worrisome questions about command stability.

The *ad hoc* setting of small committees tends to facilitate dispassionate and sober analysis of the issue because of the absence of organizational and institutional egoisms (Williams 1976: 68), provided that the members of the decision-making unit are compatible, experienced, and effective, "intelligent people with considerable drive and staying power" (Milburn 1972: 267). In addition, according to Milburn they should be articulate, dependable, remain organized regardless of pressures. The decision-making unit should also include people who know "how to get things done": people who write, speak, and think clearly and quickly People of great anxiety are hardly adequate. Knowledge of a variety of cultures and situations would be desirable.

One can hardly contradict Milburn, but one has to remember that these members will surely be appointed partly because the highest authority is pleased with or impressed by them. This may lead to "groupthink" (see below). The contraction of authority in time of crisis to a small high-level group with overriding responsibility has several effects (see Hermann and Brady 1972: 292). It is conducive to:

(1) The search for alternatives;
(2) The search for information;
(3) The location of potential bottlenecks or breakdowns;
(4) The ability to bypass routinized procedures;
(5) The exclusion of other issues from attention;
(6) Freedom of action ;
(7) Commitment;
(8) However, physical fatigue and exhaustion are great with such a limited membership;
(9) The number of channels for communication are minimized.

The duration of a crisis has some impact on the structure of the decision-making unit. Brecher (1979: 476) thinks that the greater is the reliance on group problem-solving processes, the greater is the consideration of alternatives. Also, the longer the duration of the crisis, the greater is the perceived need for effective leadership within decision-making units. Growing threat was accompanied by less formal procedures within the decision-making group (Brecher 1978: 267). As the decision time during the crisis extended, consultation with persons outside the core decision-making unit became wider. The greater the crisis, the more information about it tends to be elevated to the top of the organizational pyramid (Brecher 1979: 476).

The contraction of decision-making groups in time of crisis entails some advantages and some disadvantages with respect to the danger of unintentional nuclear war. The concentration of the highest authorities on just one issue, i.e., the crisis at hand, helps to limit distraction. The overriding competence of a small high-level group mitigates the danger posed in day-to-day operations by standard procedures not adequate for a specific case. The maintenance of control over the armed services is crucial and will probably be given close attention; yet the problem of command stability is to be recognized.

While quick action and effective decision-making requires the limitation of the decision-making unit to a small number of members, the disadvantages of information overload and physical exhaustion have to be taken into account (Hazlewood 1977). Other adverse consequences are: delays in securing adequate facts; decisions or orders that are not transmitted rapidly enough from the highest authority; legal concurrences required from various agencies; inadequate communications systems and facilities; information sensitivity issues hampering the crisis management effforts; and inattention resulting from multiple crises (Hazlewood *et al.*

1977: 102). The need for high level interagency consultations consumes time, and the secrecy may prove counterproductive by precluding available options *(ibid.)*.

Extreme secrecy, information overload, and the need for much interagency consultation will therefore reduce the quality of decisions. As fewer people will have the knowledge on which decisions have to be based, there will possibly be an information overload, and much time will be lost by inter-bureaucracy haggling. Smart and Vertinsky (1977: Table 1) recommend special communications channels, special crisis units for data collection and co-ordination, and the setting up of outside channels of information cutting through the hierarchy in order to prevent time delays in intelligence reporting.

The literature on crisis behaviour contains a vast number of hypotheses as to how, within an organization, the information flow and communication will change during the crisis. Holsti (1972: 82) suggests some hypotheses on communication in crises: the volume of communication will rise; there will be an increasing tendency to rely upon extraordinary or improvised channels of communication; the proportion of inter-alliance communication will tend to decline. Brecher (1979), based on research on the behaviour of Israeli decision-makers during the crises of 1967 and 1973, found evidence supporting the following propositions:

(1) The greater the crisis, the greater the felt need for information;
(2) The greater the crisis, the more information about it tends to be elevated to the top of the organizational pyramid;
(3) In crises, the rate of communications by a nation's decision-makers to international actors outside their country will increase;
(4) As crisis-induced stress increases, the search for information is likely to become more active, but it may also become more random and less productive;
(5) The greater the reliance on group problem-solving processes, the greater the consideration of alternatives;
(6) The longer the decision time, the greater the consultation with persons outside the core decision-making unit (Brecher 1979: 475—476).

Thus, in order to maximize the evaluation of different options, the time available is crucial; group problem-solving processes appear desirable, entailing benefits of — perhaps unorganized — multiple advocacy.

The Hazards of "Groupthink"

Authors studying international crisis decision-making have repeatedly drawn attention to the tendency of top decision-makers to surround themselves with "men whose influence seems significantly related to their capacity to play a psychologically supportive role" (Halper 1971: 215). Such findings suggest that the composition of the decision-making unit, comprising the decision-makers and their advisers, more often than not has shortcomings, in not utilizing the superior knowledge of experts because they are less congenial with the persons deciding who will belong to this unit. Experts already knowledgeable in the field to be dealt with would save time and provide the decision-maker with expertise. According to Halper, United States Presidents often seem almost to regress under the pressure of crisis, reverting to reliance upon a few trusted associates whose familiar presence probably promotes feelings of security and reduces feelings of anxiety (Halper 1971: 214).

Real dissenters, not embedded in a system of devil's advocacy, multiple advocacy of formal options, generally tend to be sacked (Holsti 1972: 208). In the case of United States crisis decision-making, the President does not want to be faced with basic challenges while under stress, and the presidential assistant depends entirely upon his capacity to please one man, and he either succeeds or will leave (Halper 1971: 216). Thus the composition of the decision-making unit does not guarantee that a maximum diversity of options are considered.

In a more general view these processes may be termed "groupthink", i.e., a very strong "team" mentality in crisis situations. Doubts and second thoughts are often submerged in the mutual reinforcement that knits the team together emotionally (Morgan 1977: 180 f.). In an extreme case, this may encourage the group to undertake measures even in the face of ample evidence that such a course of action is unwise.

At the same time what is called a "shift to risk" is taking place (Morgan 1977: 181). Morgan describes an impressive amount of studies in social psychology which suggest that groups are sometimes more likely, when collectively deciding, to take chances and to adopt risky solutions. In addition, they tend towards:

(1) Illusion of invulnerability;
(2) Collective rationalization;
(3) Belief in the inherent morality of the group;
(4) Stereotypes of out-groups;
(5) Direct pressure on dissenters;
(6) Self-censorship;
(7) Illusions of unanimity.

The illusion of invulnerability is conducive to taking high risks. Belief in one's own morality may lead to ignorance of the ethical perspective of proposed courses of action. Stereotypes of out-groups may pose great obstacles to recognizing the full range of options and the possibility for compromise.

"Groupthink" depends on several preconditions. While the members of the decision-making unit certainly do not willingly accept or even promote "groupthink", "this pattern of conformity is a much more subtle and insidious thing than pressure to conform exerted against dissident members of a policy-making group" (George 1980: 93). One of the great problems is not the overt suppression of dissent, but the fact that group members may not even realize that such a suppression process occurs. Mind guards will seldom feel compelled to intervene, because self-censorship precludes dissent in cases where the group decides to take action which the individual member alone would consider much too risky.

The conditions in which "groupthink" may occur are summed up by Janis and Mann (1977: 132):

(1) High cohesiveness;
(2) Insulation of the group;
(3) Lack of methodological procedures for search and appraisal;
(4) Directive leadership;
(5) High stress with a low degree of hope of finding a better solution than the one favoured by the leader or other influential persons.

The effects of "groupthink" on decision-making can be summarized as follows (Janis and Mann 1977: 132):

(1) Incomplete survey of alternatives;
(2) Incomplete survey of objectives;
(3) Failure to examine risks of preferred choice;
(4) Poor information search;
(5) Selective bias in processing information at hand;
(6) Failure to re-appraise alternatives;
(7) Failure to work out contingency plans.

There is something like self-indoctrination of an organization. Compared with an individual, an organization has greater resources and greater access to information. However, the need to co-ordinate the work of a great number of individuals often requires a set of assumptions or preconceptions that guides perceptual activity, and this set may become rigid and resistant to revision. Such a set of assumptions, superimposed over the individual set of an intelligence analyst, will normally not be in open contradiction with his beliefs; rather, they will reinforce each other. Thus, "self-indoctrination results from basic organizational needs" (Knorr 1976: 115). As a consequence, the operating characteristics of large organizations often produce, independent of any conscious decision, a number of situations that may induce decision-makers to take actions which they would otherwise avoid (Kashi 1979: 93).

The maintenance of group solidarity usually constitutes a central value. Its effect is that the members focus attention on one interpretation or option only and stress consensus (Shlaim 1976: 360). Within an intelligence-processing organization or among the members of the decision-making unit, there may be some mind guards: persons who will try to reinforce a certain interpretation or option and will attempt to suppress deviating points of view, thereby curtailing the range of interpretations considered. A special protection for minority views could mitigate this flaw (Smart and Vertinsky 1977: Table 1).

For junior officers analysing intelligence and preparing reports it may be very difficult to express thoughts deviating strongly from the dominant interpretations and theories. Knorr (1976: 115) thinks that it is hard for a member to break away from the beliefs of his group or to express views that are known to be unwelcome to superiors: "The incentive is to tell the superiors what they want to hear". Shlaim (1976: 365) agrees that individuals working for an organization displaying a strong commitment to a particular policy will feel tempted to ignore or downplay uncomfortable facts so as not to risk unpopularity with colleagues and superiors. Halper explains the urge to "tell them what they want to hear" by the different levels of loyalty of a member of a great organization. The first loyalty is very probably to himself; the second to the bureaucratic subunit; and only the third to the whole organization. The subordinate will strive to maximize rewards and minimize punishments within this loyalty structure.

The situation may be slightly different with respect to the role of military advisers in crisis decision-making. While there is a widespread assumption that military advice tends to be more "hawkish" than civilian advice and that military officers would be readier to suggest the use of military force, a systematic study of past cases of United States decision-making in crises failed to confirm that military officers were uniformly more sympathetic than civilian advisers to military intervention. Once military force was involved, however, the pressure for escalation was much greater from the officers, who resented "piecemeal gradualism". The reluctance to become involved was, not surprisingly, greatest among the superior army officers, while the Air Force commanders were the main propagandists of military intervention. Intervention by ground forces (Army, Marines) requires the setting up a complex logistic structure. The preferences of the services for different doctrines and different forms of action also derive from interservice rivalry, from advocating the allocation of resources to one's own service.

It is interesting to note that military advisers often show pessimism before undertaking any action perhaps in order to minimize expectations; but once military force is involved, they tend to transmit optimistic messages. The greatest influence by officers on decisions was not in promoting intervention but in practically vetoing it by stating that the necessary capabilities were lacking.

As was pointed out previously with regard to individuals confronted with a situation characterized by ambiguity, organizations also have an inherent inclination towards "satisficing" and "incrementalism". Satisficing means not looking for the best option available (this might entail a very intensive search), but instead settling for a course of action that is "good enough" (Janis and Mann 1977: 25 ff.; George 1980: 40). The option has to meet a set of minimum requirements, and the decision-makers will not attempt to evaluate all possible courses of action. Satisficing will in most cases lead to suboptima decisions. The search for the option with the highest payoff, however, is often impractical, as the resources may be lacking: too little time, insufficient organization and personnel. A person or an organization satisficing has only to consider some alternative courses and then settle for one which promises satisfactory results (George 1980: 40). The degree of optimization depends on the quality of the search for options and on the number of options evaluated. A sequence of satisficing decisions can have the shape of incrementalism; at each stage where a decision is required, one of the options that "will do" is chosen. The danger in this decision strategy is that the decision-makers will lose sight of long-range aims. The urgency so typical of crisis situations is of course particularly conducive to this kind of maladaption occurring in crisis decision-making.

The Perils of Internal Dissension

Additional problems arise when a serious threat and a high degree of time-pressure trigger internal dissension and conflict. Social-psychology research has found out that, depending on certain variables, a decision-making group facing an enormous external threat under time-pressure tends either to become more united or to be split in what becomes a protracted inner conflict (Lanzetta 1965; Hamblin 1965; Minix 1980; Stein 1976). These variables include the opportunity to divert aggression towards an external enemy or internal scapegoat, the prospects of finding a crisis resolution and the absence of demoralizing surprise (Lang 1964). Generally speaking, the higher the degree of uncertainty created by a crisis situation, the greater the tendency towards demoralization.

As to the behaviour of decision-making groups in real crises, the findings and insights that can be derived from the information available are quite contradictory as far as the divisive or cohesive impact of crises is concerned. Former United States Secretary of State Kissinger found that "personality clashes were reduced; too much is usually at stake for normal jealousies to operate" (Kissinger in *Time*, 15 October 1979: 71). However, other findings indicate that crises raise tensions among the policy-makers involved and heighten the stress and anxiety they experience (Lentner 1972: 133). Brecher (1979: 476) tentatively confirms three related hypotheses (based on Israeli crisis management in the 1967 and 1973 crises):

> The longer the decision time, the greater the conflict within decision-making units;
> The greater the group conflict aroused by a crisis, the greater the consensus once a decision is reached;
> The longer the amount of time available in which to make a decision, the greater will be the consensus on the final choice.

The third hypothesis virtually follows from the first two. Stein (1976) suggests that external conflict (as will be the case in international crisis) does increase internal cohesion under certain conditions: specifically, the external conflict needs to involve

129

some threat and affect the entire group and all its members indiscriminately, and there has to be a solution.

Thus, there are several conditions which determine whether cohesion or disintegration will prevail during a crisis. If no solution to the crisis is in sight, the climate within the decision-making unit will tend to worsen. The *ad hoc* setting of decision-making units will tend to mitigate the influence of bureaucratic and organizational interests which might foster conflicts in an institutional setting (Williams 1976: 68); the members are not responsible to a department but only to the highest authority. In addition, the need for quick action sets limits to the degree of dissent and intransigence to be tolerated (Williams 1976: 69). The day-to-day institutional setting entails incentives for behaviour which must be considered dysfunctional for dealing with a high-risk crisis, as "large organizations are not teams, but coalitions" which share some goals but nevertheless strive to maximize the gains of the subunit.

Inflexibility Due to Standard Operating Procedures

In emergency situations decision-making groups tend to act on the basis of a pre-programmed routine. This may entail several flaws. Most importantly, routine reactions may not be able to cope with the entire problem as it is perceived by the decision-makers; thus, an incomplete and insufficient routine, in turn, reinforces the time pressure due to the rigidity of any routine. Looking at the principle of routine more closely, routine simply means that decisions have already been made prior to the emergency situation. Therefore the quality of the decision, if this can be called a "decision" at all, largely depends on the quality of the planning done prior to the emergency situation. What in a crisis situation is called "surprise" is therefore nothing other than an inadequacy or inability of routine reactions to deal with a new situation presented by the acute threat. In other words, any contingency planning is very ambiguous by nature. It may help a decision but it may also create rigid constraints and precedents for future decisions. It very much depends on the quality of prior planning.

In a more general sense, the same must be said of the so-called "operational codes" which are defined as a set of generalized principles about political life, a belief-system about fundamental issues of politics (George 1969; Holsti 1975). Sometimes the actions and reactions of Governments in crises are to be seen more as the outcome of an organizational routine than as the conscious decision of a rational protagonist. The interaction between a great number of individuals within an organization requires certain rules and there exist some fixed ways of performing a given task, so-called Standard Operating Procedures (SOPs). Allison and Halperin (1972: 55) pertinently pointed out that SOPs have advantages, but also shortcomings: "Action according to standard operating procedures and programs does not constitute far-sighted, flexible adaptation to "the issue". Detail and nuance of actions by organizations are determined chiefly by organizational routines. Standard operating procedures constitute routines for dealing with standard situations. These routines allow the individuals to deal with situations without much thought, but at the price of standardization. Whereas the standardization may be adequate for ordinary situations, it may have undesirable consequences in such an exceptional situation as an international crisis.

SOPs are generally characterized by rigidity. As Smart and Vertinsky (1977: 8—9) say, SOPs ensure predictability of responses, much desired in normal situations. But the price is the introduction of rigidities into the system. Both standardization and rigidity imply the presence of a restrained set of behaviour patterns. The range of possible actions is thus restricted (Morgan 1977: 183 f.). In his pioneering study on the Cuban missile crisis, Allison (1971: 83 ff.) describes decision processes dominated by SOPs as "organizational processes". They are characterized not only by a certain rigidity; more importantly, SOPs are also resistant to change. In organizations, "assured performance requires sets of rehearsed SOPs for producing specific actions" (Allison 1971: 83). Problems arise, of course, if an unrehearsed action is demanded. This might easily happen in a crisis, because the number of programmes in a repertoire is always quite limited (*ibid.*). Even in a crisis, "the specific details of the action taken are determined in large part by standard operating procedures" (Allison and Halperin 1972: 54), or as Williams (1976: 100) puts it:

> "The organizations implementing policy could prove unresponsive to the precise needs of diplomatic management during crises. Wanting a surgeon's scalpel, policy-makers may find themselves with a butcher's knife".

But SOPs not only have the effect of limiting the range of actions possible in a crisis, they also tend to shape the perception of senior executives inasmuch as SOPs "and interests will affect what is reported" (Allison and Halperin 1972: 61). The organizational routines are important in determining (1) the information available to the central players, (2) the options that the senior players consider, and (3) the actual details of whatever is done by the Government (Allison and Halperin 1972: 55). SOPs as "implementation pathology" may even be carried so far that issues, events or orders that do not 'fit' the SOP of a given department will be discarded in favour of those that do 'fit', or will be interpreted so as to 'fit' (Smart and Vertinsky 1977: 8—9).

The implementation of decisions taken by the highest authorities during a crisis is to be supervised very carefully in order to ensure that the actions agreed on are carried out exactly as intended. The political success of crisis actions requires that the President not only make the final decisions, but monitor operational implementation to control the use of force (Head et al. 1978: 246). During the

131

Cuban missile crisis, the location of the ships for the blockade was open to some controversy. The Navy favoured a quarantine line far out in the ocean in order to be beyond the range of the Mig fighters in Cuba. The political authorities, however, wanted to give the Soviet Union some time, and consequently ordered a quarantine line much nearer to the island, so that the Soviet ships would not quickly reach this line but would have time to change their course (Allison 1971: 129—130). The line, however, seems not to have changed even on the President's order. Betts (1977: 10) describes one dramatic example of friction between political responsibility and the urge of the military for operational autonomy during the Cuban missile crisis.

> "McNamara had been spending time at the operational headquarters of the blockade, and the naval officers were irked at what they considered his interference. The secretary insisted on making detailed decisions about the operation of the blockade line, without regard to standard procedure or the chain of command. Friction mounted. McNamara then noticed that a single U.S. destroyer was standing outside the blockade line and asked Anderson what it was doing there. The secretary was anxious to make clear that the President did not want to harass any Soviet ships and wanted to allow the Russians to be able to stand off or retreat without humiliation. Anderson was reluctant to answer because some of the civilians in the secretary's party were not cleared for highly sensitive information, but he drew McNamara aside and explained that the ship was sitting on top of a Russian submarine.
> The final blowup came when McNamara demanded to know what the navy would do if a Soviet ship refused to divulge its cargo. Anderson brandished the Manual of Navy Regulations in McNamara's face and shouted, 'It's all in there'. The Secretary retorted, 'I don't give a damn what John Paul Jones would have done. I want to know what you are going to do, now'. Finally Anderson replied, 'Now, Mr. Secretary, if you and your Deputy will go back to your offices, the Navy will run the blockade' " (Betts 1977: 10).

This example highlights several problems: the problem of zones of autonomy of the military forces; the difficulties of implementing finely tuned actions in crisis, particularly signals; and the dangers of reliance on SOPs.

The deployment of nuclear weapons can also be subject to intra-service SOPs. Leitenberg (1978: 9) recalls an instructive example:

> "In two Far East countries US-piloted F-4 fighter bombers armed with nuclear weapons stood at the end of runways on 15-minute alert. Against whom? we asked. At a secret Pentagon briefing we were told the host countries initially had permitted us to station F—4 squadrons; that F—4s could carry both conventional and nuclear weapons; that F—4s were most cost-effective when nuclear armed and the most efficient mode to be so armed was on 15-minute alert".

This type of incidents leads Steinbruner to conclude that in the Cuban missile crisis, "the efforts to bring American policy under central direction must said to have failed" (Steinbruner 1979:39). This sort of thing "must be expected to happen when high crisis strikes the very complicated, inevitably decentralized, very large organizations that constitute modern strategic forces" *(ibid*:39). There is a definite distinction between explicit policy calculations and diffuse organizational reactions, and sometimes the latter seem to determine increasingly the course of a crisis (Steinbruner 1979: 46).

Similar incidents involving the armed forces of other nuclear Powers could probably also be described. The information policy with respect to events involving nuclear weapons, is, however, nowhere very extensive and is in some instances very restrictive. An illustration was given by a Soviet submarine which was assigned, in November 1981, to a mission in Swedish territorial waters close to the Karlskrona naval base and which was said to have carried torpedoes armed with nuclear warheads. Very probably, this assignment was given in the context of a typical SOP, notwithstanding the dangerous cargo the submarine was carrying.

When trying to assess the significance of SOPs as possible catalysts triggering an unintentional nuclear war, one has to ask whether SOPs concerning nuclear weapons, in a situation of crisis confrontation, would really be permitted to play the major role they have in periods of normalcy. The available evidence suggests that this is highly improbable. As soon as tension rises, the political leaders of nuclear Powers are anxious to obtain and maintain full control of any manipulations involving nuclear warheads or delivery vehicles capable of carrying nuclear warheads. The greater the tension, and the more acute the crisis, the more caution and care are applied. Every little move involving those weapons tends to be placed in the hands of the supreme authority. In situations like this, SOPs tend to be replaced by fine-tuned, reflexive orders originating from the central commanding authority.

Yet the situation may be different in prolonged crises. As Morgan (1977:188—193) notes, in situations of confrontation where no urgency and time pressure disrupts the standard routine, and if a crisis emerges only gradually, it is all the harder to contemplate alternative courses of action, so that each side's officials are reinforced in their belief that they have done what they could to avert a collision (Morgan 1977:190). In the case of the Viet Nam war one may therefore speak of an "incremental commitment".

B. The Generation of Crisis Stress by Nuclear Strategy

In examining the risks triggering an unintentional nuclear war, the central concept to be used as a starting point is stress. Stress as a state of mind becomes particularly crucial in this context if people at the upper end of the command chain dealing with nuclear weapons are affected by it. On the other hand, one must not forget that the occurrence and intensity of stress may in turn be affected by the existence of nuclear weapons and nuclear strategy. Generally speaking, stress is generated by the scale of the threat and the degree of time-pressure.

Starting from this assumption, the central question to be asked in connection with unintentional nuclear war is: are there, in the strategic system and strategic doctrines currently applied by the two major powers, any elements which are conducive to reinforcing the two factors that generate stress? There is no doubt that the answer must be affirmative. Nuclear weapons are designed for the very purpose of inflicting the maximum imaginable damage. By definition, they therefore constitute the maximum imaginable threat. As far as time-pressure is concerned, the key notion to be considered is early-warning time. The development of nuclear delivery systems has reduced the early-warning time available to almost nil. Both combat readiness and speed of the systems have been improved to a point where instant launching becomes feasible while the time available between detection of an enemy attack and the first nuclear explosion has shrunk from many hours (in the case of "classic" delivery of atomic bombs by bomber) to four to ten minutes in the case of LRTNF missiles (Lutz 1981, p. 290). These facts constantly generate a high degree of stress in "peace-time" and even more so in situations of crisis confrontation.

Therefore, it cannot be denied that international crises which might lead to full-scale hostilities, including perhaps the use of nuclear weapons, constitute intensive stress-inducing situations for the national decision-makers involved.

The perception of threat is of course not independent of certain predispositions. According to Knorr (1976: 98ff.) a threat is quickly perceived by societies that have been subject to repeated attack and military pressure or are prepared to see a threat from any State whose military strength is either great or growing relative to their own. Preconceptions within organizations can lead to a partial blindness towards evidence contradicting these pre-existing beliefs. Ideology will also tend to direct the attention of decision-makers to certain possible sources of threats while diverting it from others. The discrepancy between expectations and intelligence on threats is an additional source of propensity to distorted perceptions. Threats from outside may also be misrepresented in the political struggle within a State.

In the context of the present study the most important question is: what is the impact of modern strategic doctrines (and the strategic situation) on the decision-makers' perception of stress?

There is a broad consensus that the emergence of nuclear weapons has changed the nature of warfare. The role of these weapons is obviously different from that of conventional arms. In particular, they have made the threat of a completely new order of magnitude, having virtually a terrorizing effect by creating expectations of a danger going far beyond anything previously experienced.

The notion of "terror" as a general threat which cannot be defined or calculated is of crucial importance in this context. Terror, as it is generated by any situation at the brink or beginning of nuclear war, tends to affect deeply and to disrupt firmly established role structures and traditional patterns of perception and behaviour. It may even crush the societal and psychological bonds existing in a decision-making group, thus making it impossible or extremely difficult to think soberly and to take correct decisions. In other words, the element of terror inherent in any nuclear threat may lead to maladaptive behaviour of both decision-making individuals and organizations as a whole.

Nuclear weapons have also facilitated the emergence of a strategy based on the prevention instead of the conduct of war. This point is most clearly reflected in the strategies of deterrence, particularly in the MAD concept. Such a strategy depends to a very large extent on the invulnerability or high degree of survivability of a sufficient part of the deterrent force. Otherwise, each side may feel tempted to use its weapons first, in order to prevent their destruction by a first strike of the adversary. The survivability of the weapons assigned for a second strike after having been hit by a first strike makes the adoption of a strategy based on a quick reaction (for example launch-on-warning, LOW) unnecessary. Yet, as has been demonstrated in chapter II, technological developments in recent years have given reasons to doubt the survivability of at least the ICBMs.

As survivability and urgency of making decisions are closely interconnected, so also are strategic instability and stress experienced by decision-makers causally linked. Time pressure in a crisis situation, and consequently the propensity to uncontrolled escalation, may be reduced if both sides possess weapons capable of withstanding any first strike, if military doctrines stress the importance of delay rather than haste in employment of force (Holsti 1972 : 237). On the other hand, urgency in making decisions about the firing of nuclear weapons can have disastrous effects. Schelling (1966 : 227), writing at a time when accuracy did not yet allow anything like a disarming first strike, notes that the premium on haste is the greatest source of danger that peace will explode into all-out war. The whole idea of accidental or inadvertent war, of a war that is not entirely intended or premeditated, rests, according to Schelling, on a crucial premise — that there is an advantage in being the one to start the war. The incentive to pre-empt may change entirely the state of mind of the decision-makers. However, if there is no decisive advantage in striking an hour sooner than the enemy and no disadvantage in striking an hour later, one can afford to wait.

The dangers of cognitive distortion occurring in crisis situations may become even more marked if account is taken of the increasingly sophisticated nature of modern strategic concepts. At the time when blunt and straightforward concepts like "massive retaliation" used to govern the strategic planning of the major Powers, misjudgements and faulty conclusions with regard to the meaning of strategic principles were almost impossible. However, at a time when strategic doctrines are becoming increasingly complex and sophisticated, based on a variety of arms with different performance characteristics, considerable efforts are required to master all the subtleties of modern nuclear strategy.

The question may therefore be raised whether the political leaders of the countries concerned, in the hectic situation of a crisis emergency, will still be capable of deciding and acting fully according to the requirements of the complex logic of strategy. This question implies two aspects: first, the risk-taking behaviour of leaders; and, secondly, the cognitive mastery of the new strategic complexity.

As far as the first aspect is concerned, there are good reasons to believe that contemporary political leaders still have Hiroshima present in their minds. This will also be the case for the next generation of leaders.

This ensures a very careful attitude towards the use of nuclear weapons. No responsible leaders in our day could be inclined to consider nuclear weapons as just another weapon. They are all clearly and fully aware what the use of such weapons would imply.

On the other hand, one may ask whether they are also in a position to understand all the contingency plans and flexible and varied options offered by today's nuclear arsenal. One may assume that they are constantly briefed on these problems. In addition, it seems that they are surrounded and assisted by professional specialists who ensure a high degree of institutional continuity.

The question can of course never be answered definitely, and fortunately there has not so far been any test which would have produced evidence of the intellectual grasp of modern strategic problems by the world's leaders. Even if they are highly competent, some doubts may remain. Reinforcing these doubts is the fact that contemporary public discussion about strategic weapons exhibits a surprising amount of short-cut thinking, distortion and *simplification*. Obviously, not all people are able or inclined to apply the stringent logic required for analysing the nuclear strategic system.

In conclusion, it must be noted that the possibility of having a calm, relaxed decision-making process (by contrast to nervous, hasty decision-making under conditions of emergency) does not depend or only partly depends on the individual or organizational qualities of the decision-makers concerned. It is also contingent on a specific structure of a strategic situation. The structure of the situation determines both the issue at stake and the decision-time available. Decision-makers may become victims of emergency and fall into all or many of the pitfalls of decision-making under stress described in section A of the present chapter.

In other words, the propensity of the strategic system to become unstable has additional consequences aggravating the risk of unintentional war by increasing the chance of making inappropriate decisions. The originally bad situation has an inherent tendency to become worse. Therefore, even more care is required to avoid or retard any developments in the international strategic system that might affect crisis stability. The greater the crisis instability of the system, the greater the likelihood of a poor performance by the decision-makers. Unfortunately, there are no easy expedients to invert this relationship.

Similar conclusions must be drawn with regard to the other determinant of stress — threat. The lethality of nuclear weapons and also their sheer number have received much public attention. The emergence of nuclear weapons has to some degree even changed the minds of all those who are aware of the consequences of their use. Nuclear weapons are *the* ultimate weapons, with unsurpassed lethality. No practical experience so far gathered by any decision-maker can match the amount of stress produced by the lethality of nuclear weapons, once the decision-maker is faced with the imminent firing of nuclear weapons. Although many authors assume a particularly cautious and sober behaviour in this type of situation, the findings of comparative research on international crises reported in section A do not give many reasons for optimism. There is always a grave risk of suboptimal behaviour. What this means in practice is easy to realize: miscalculation, false perceptions, and all sorts of inappropriate reactions.

C. The Use of Force as a "Continuation of Politics by Other Means"

Ever since groups of men — tribes, nations, alliances — have confronted each other, they have tended to communicate less by words than by actions. Words become meaningless in a situation dominated by hostility and mistrust. The nuclear age has not changed this pattern. On the contrary, while the actual use of force has become increasingly risky and costly, many authors (Garnett 1975; Williams 1976: 46) have observed a growing sophistication in exploiting military power without actually using military force.

All strategic thinking in both East and West points to the more or less refined techniques that the opponents would use in order to test each other's resolve and to communicate their willingness to escalate or to compromise, in case an acute crisis breaks out between them. Negotiation is being replaced by coercive bargaining, dominated by what Williams (1976: 47ff.) aptly termed the "duality of purpose". Governments wish to protect the vital interests of their States, if necessary by military force. On the other hand, they share a mutual interest in survival, and this requires care and circumspection in order to avoid the terrible prospect of a direct armed clash. Emphasis is placed on realizing the opponents' shared risks, their mutual desire to avoid escalation, and their common interest in escaping the disaster of war (Gilbert/Lauren 1980). Many commentators make the point that the existence of nuclear weapons and, implicitly, the risk of a global nuclear holocaust, has made Governments all over the world, and particularly the Governments of the two major Powers, much more cautious.

This assertion is in fact supported by the results of empirical research. Eberwein, in his comprehensive study of serious international disputes in the 1900—1976 period, observed two contradictory trends: on the one hand, the number of confrontations has increased in the nuclear age, as compared with the pre-nuclear age; on the other hand, the relative frequency of escalation processes leading to war has declined by approximately 50 per cent (Eberwein 1981a:122f.; Eberwein 1981b:8). Additional insights are available if one combines these findings with the evidence produced by studies on the arms race. Wallace found out that, of 15 confrontations accompanied by an arms race, 11 resulted in war, whereas of 65 confrontations not linked with an arms race, only two resulted in war (Wallace 1980:6; Sonntag 1981:113). This observation urgently underlines the highly dangerous interrelationship between confrontations and arms races.

Yet again, it should be borne in mind that the risk is a product of the probability of escalation and the amount of damage caused by such a process. Even if there is the slightest probability of an escalation, should this escalation process cross the threshold to nuclear war, the result would be appalling. Therefore, the evidence of a declining relative frequency of war offers little comfort.

It is conceivable that coercive bargaining as the dominant pattern of communication carries with it great risks of misunderstanding and miscalculation and their attendant disasters (Polanyi 1980). It is also quite easy to imagine an unintentional nuclear war resulting from misunderstanding of the meaning of actions taken by each side to signal resolve to the other side.

This aspect of crisis interaction therefore requires careful and critical attention. Three questions have to be addressed in this context: (1) What for do such conventions exist, if at all, what can they accomplish and how do they function? (2) What are the risks of misunderstanding and miscalculation inherent in this type of interaction? (3) What tendency can be discerned in contemporary international politics with regard to the use of force for conveying political signals?

The "Rules of the Game"

The question of the existence and efficiency of conventions of crisis or rules of the game has attracted considerable attention in recent years. According to the latest of a very large number of studies devoted to this subject (Cohen 1981), there is a broad range of restraints by which States regulate their conduct and thereby prevent, or at least mitigate, conflict and facilitate co-operation. They might properly be called "rules of the game" (Cohen 1980 and 1981a:V). Bell (1979) proposes a set of conventions for crisis diplomacy, i.e., expected behaviour and understood signals, excluding laws, moral norms, or enforceable rules. According to Bell, the heterogeneity of world cultures does not preclude the existence of such conventions, as only a very small set of individuals are involved in crisis management, namely the highest-level officials of the countries concerned.

Bell maintains that these officials, as members of a true international "jet-set", seem often in many ways — education, life-style, experience, temperament, ability — to resemble each other more than they do the average member of their own society (Bell 1979: 167). Thus, the relative homogeneity of the people involved should allow for the following proposed conventions (Bell 1979: 173—182):

(1) Communications with the adversary must and will be maintained and should rather grow closer and more intensive as the confrontation sharpens;

(2) One should not seek to win too much, since the other side cannot afford to lose too much;

(3) One must build "golden bridges" behind the adversary to facilitate his retreat. No situation could be more dangerous in the nuclear age than to box one of the nuclear Powers into a corner;

(4) Contingency plans must not be allowed to dictate the manner in which the crisis is managed;

(5) Local crises shall be met in local terms; even a crisis of the central balance shall be met at least initially in conventional terms;

(6) The other's side of influence requires a special wariness and restraint when touched by intramural crisis in the way of dissent;

(7) The powers will not allow their signals to each other to become infected with excess or misleading ambiguities through consultation with allies;

(8) Surveillance by contemporary means is legitimate and will not be interfered with.

Other authors point to a vocabulary of signals constituting the central element of a system of "rules of the game". Preference is thereby given to the symbolic use of armed forces. Armed forces of all kinds are a particularly apt and evocative medium for the expression of attitudes and policies related to the position and security of the State and the modalities of its relations with other States (Cohen 1981a: 41). The dispatch of air squadrons, troop movements, convoys and concentrations, military parades, armed alerts, nuclear tests and so on may signal specific messages. As has been observed by Cohen, naval power has been the most ubiquitous and fine-tuned instrument of communication. Naval movements are capable of conveying a whole repertoire of meanings, such as triumph, resolution, defiance, displeasure, threat, enhancement of credibility, political support both in a qualified and unqualified way and the like (Cohen 1981: 41—48; Cohen 1981b; McConnell 1979).

As far as the descriptive aspects of this vocabulary are concerned, there is little controversy. In a critical perspective, however, at least two questions have to be asked:

(1) Is this vocabulary really sufficient to convey the signals opponents need to exchange in an acute crisis?

(2) To what extent does the symbolic use of force generate risks of escalation into bluntly "non-symbolic" uses of force? There may be highly explosive dangers lurking in this type of "conversation" employing armed forces as signals. The second question will be dealt with below.

Apart from the grammar of gestures and movements, there are what Cohen calls "tacit rules" (Cohen 1981a: 50—63), defined as

> "arrangements not arrived at by any formal process of negotiations but via a variety of expedients, including spontaneous mutual abstention by the dropping of discreet hints, through the mediation of a third party or by a process of nonverbal signalling involving the publicized or visible manoeuvering of one's forces".

Generally speaking, these tacit rules are rules of mutual restraint, whereby the parties refrain from doing certain things or from encroaching on each other or exercise mutual tolerance in certain fields (satellite inspection, for instance). Such rules are extremely fragile, particularly if they are not contingent upon each other, i.e., if the breaking of rules by one side cannot be punished by retaliation by the other side. Williams has tried to identify two principal rules applied by the major Powers in international crisis situations. The first is the unwillingness to initiate the use of deliberate violence against each other, i.e., a very careful and prudent observance of the threshold beyond which a direct clash would become inevitable (Williams 1976: 101—113).

The second rule, according to Williams, is that of non-intervention in local disputes between client states. Yet Cohen cites a number of different examples which suggest that this rule is not as rigorously applied (Cohen 1981a: 59f.). It seems therefore that the system of tacit rules is not so reliable as required if one hopes for a stable regulation of mutual interests in situations of acute international confrontation. Its utility as an instrument of crisis management is limited.

This is demonstrated by situations in which a Government appraises a step by its opponent as a serious infringement of the existing rules of the game; more often than not, such steps are perceived to be the precursor of an encompassing programme of aggression and expansion (Cohen 1981a: 144). An example of this type of threat perception is provided *(ibid*: 149f.) by the 1979/1980 Afghanistan crisis. Soviet policy and strategy in Afghanistan were perceived as a violation of the rules and therefore as jeopardizing overall relations. From the Soviet perspective, there was no such meaning implied in assisting Afghanistan. As was demonstrated by the case of the Afghanistan crisis, as soon as one side perceives events as a violation of a particular rule, this has an aggravating escalatory impact on the evolution of the crisis. As a consequence, the parties concerned react vehemently and the risks of a breakdown of order and the outbreak of direct hostilities become acute.

140

The Risk of Misunderstanding

The gravity of the risk of war resulting from the symbolic use of force depends to a great extent on the awareness of the Governments involved of the dangers with which they are confronted. If decision-makers are confident of their ability to control events, they may be more willing to take risks. There is perhaps an inverse relationship between the assessment of the probability of disaster should a crisis erupt and the willingness to risk provoking a confrontation in the first place (Williams 1976:51). In particular, two (partially overlapping) types of risks can be distinguished *(ibid.* 1976:94f.). The first is that crisis bargaining will go awry due to faulty calculations of manoeuvres, threats and counter-threats. The second is that the participants will inadvertently lose control over events, thus creating an autonomous risk. It is this second type which deserves the utmost attention.

If a crisis spills over into a process of violent interaction, the two opponents are likely to be swept along by a "logic of events" and will be powerless to resist, let alone reverse its direction (Williams 1976: 96f.). Military necessity could replace political calculation as the key to action, with the result that both sides almost inexorably commit more and more of their resources to avoiding defeat. Recognition of this problem and its dangers may lead to efforts to overcome them.

It is conceivable that the deployment of armed forces in a crisis situation may lead to direct low-level tactical engagements and possibly also to serious incidents and clashes between individual army, navy or air force units which were neither intended nor welcomed by the respective superior military commanding and political authorities. This might even involve ships or aircrafts carrying nuclear weapons. The question is whether such incidents might suffice as catalysts for triggering an unintentional nuclear war. What would happen if, for example, in the worst case a submarine carrying long-range ballistic missiles armed with multiple nuclear warheads were traced by an attack submarine and accidentally rammed or shot at and sunk? Very probably even such a very serious incident would not be able to exert a trigger function unless the overall strategic system were highly unstable and susceptible to a first-strike attack. There are reasons to suppose that even the loss of a strategic submarine or of another important weapons system, although certainly very much aggravating the crisis, would not induce the decision-makers to misinterpret this event as the opening phase of a nuclear attack. Very probably the responsible leaders in either Washington or Moscow would take a step back and think about the matter with great care. Almost certainly no unmeasured reaction would ensue.

A different problem is the possibility of inadvertent or unauthorized violence (Williams 1976: 113ff.), namely the crossing of the decisive threshold not out of deliberation but by low level action of subordinate commanders. Incidents of this kind are perhaps most likely when the relationship between the two major

Powers is juxtaposed with ongoing hostilities between their respective allies (Williams 1976: 117). If the leaders of the two major Powers do not react extremely cautiously to incidents at that level, and if they misinterpret their respective moves, a rash reaction may in fact tragically escalate the crisis. Williams, evaluating the record of crisis management in the post-war era, concludes that although this owes something to luck as well as to good judgement, it suggests a cautious optimism about the ability of statesmen to cope with international crises. It should not lead to complacency, however, as even the most strenuous attempts to maintain control have not been wholly effective *(ibid.* 118f.).

Most importantly, it is imperative that the two major Powers should be aware what it means to cross the threshold from coercion to actual violence. It seems that since the beginnings of the 1948 Berlin crisis the two major Powers have indeed carefully avoided direct violence against each other. Where the use of violence seemed imminent, as in the 1967 Middle East war, the two major Powers took great pains to assure each other via the "hot line" that they were basically adopting a stance of non-intervention and that any charges regarding intervention should not be used as a pretext for direct interference (Williams 1976: 108f.).

A considerable amount of risk arises from the fact that in situations of crisis confrontation, policy-makers tend to lose trust in verbal communication and therefore rely primarily on communication by signals and gestures which are euphemistically called "showing the flag" or, less euphemistically, "sabre-rattling." In other words, this means the symbolic use of force (Cohen 1981; Feld 1977; Franck/Weisband 1972, Kruzel 1977; McConnell 1979; Petersen 1979). The vocabulary of such signalling is extremely limited. The main signals conveyed by this technique are intended to indicate resolution or commitment in respect of a certain area or a certain subject.

The use of force without war, or the symbolic use of force, constitutes a general practice to be observed anywhere and at any time. Today, the question must be asked, however, whether there are any qualitatively new implications of this practice given the conditions of the nuclear age. To what extent does the symbolic use of force in the contemporary strategic system contribute to the generation of catalytic causes that might trigger unintentional nuclear war?

Incidents occurring during the use of force without war may get out of control and thus escalate into more serious military confrontation, finally ending in a nuclear confrontation. However, the risks become even more serious to the extent that nuclear weapons are involved. As Snyder/Diezing (1977: 454) have noted, the development of nuclear weaponry has provided several sorts of new demonstrative options — e.g., various levels of "alert" status for missiles, dispersal of bombers, putting more bombers in the air on airborne alert, deploying tactical nuclear weapons near the crisis area, putting more nuclear submarines out to sea, etc. According to Leitenberg (1980b), the United States made 27 threats involving the use of nuclear weapons since the end of the Second World War, including routine deployments of missiles, verbal threats to use nuclear weapons, increased alert levels for the nation's nuclear weapons systems and specific deployments of nuclear weapons systems during a crisis. Irrespective of the restraints used and the precautionary measures taken, the risks of a nuclear war by misunderstanding are thus considerably increased.

In addition, one has also to bear in mind that the party to which such signals are addressed may easily misinterpret their meaning; in the worst case, a signal may be interpreted as the initial step in a pre-emptive attack. In this case, nuclear disaster would become inevitable. Generally speaking, any overestimation of the meaning of signals tends to unleash a process of escalation and to accelerate it.

On the other hand, there is also the possibility of underestimating the meaning of signals; in such cases of "intelligence of stupidity" (Chan 1979) the consequences may be no less awesome, because the underestimation of the opponent's commitment and intent to resist can easily trigger events which lead to the very same outcome as in the case of overestimation: namely to sudden escalation. Salient examples of this type of misreading of signals are the failure of strategic warning on the eve of the German attack on the Soviet Union, on 22 June 1941, and the Japanese attack on Pearl Harbor on 7 December 1941. It is not sufficient to have a kind of code of conduct or a set of rules of the game in crisis situations. What matters is mutual sensitivity to the respective signals and hence the ability to interpret and "decipher" signals adequately.

Again, the rapid development of weapons technology and the shrinking of early warning time available greatly increases the risks. Potential time-pressure leads the major Powers to maintain a higher level of combat readiness than ever before and to make more frequent use of military alerts. The overall strategic system thus becomes more "nervous", generating additional stress for decision-makers in both East and West.

Several authors have referred to the 1973 Middle East crisis (Steinbruner 1979: 43; Williams 1976), in which the United States National Security Council and President Nixon ordered a world-wide alert of United States military forces involving also an increase in the state of readiness of some strategic weapons units and some movements of forces, including apparently a transfer of a number of B-52 strategic bombers from Guam to the United States. These measures served the purpose of bolstering diplomatic resistance to the Soviet intervention which seemed imminent after United States intelligence had found out that seven Soviet divisions had been placed on alert and that airlift capability was being assembled for those divisions. Apart from the problem of whether such moves were made as a consequence of explicit policy calculations or of diffuse organizational reactions (which must be examined in a different context), this incident clearly illustrates the risks inherent in the continuation of politics by the symbolic use of force in the nuclear age, once a Government starts manipulating the risks of nuclear war. There is very plausible evidence, based on a variety of available sources, that none of the key participants in the crisis took the possibility of nuclear war seriously (Blechman/Hart 1982). However, even if this is true of one party, the opponent's perception may be quite different.

As has been argued by Kruzel (1977: 84), the use of military alerts is a risky business, because a military alert may trigger similar precautionary actions by other States: "Paradoxically, an escalation of alerts may lead to the sort of military conflict which the original mobilizations were designed to prevent. At worst, opponents may engage in 'competitive mobilizations'".

So far, nothing of this kind has happened. It cannot be denied that, overall, the risks inherent in the nuclear age have given statesmen incentives to behave with much more circumspection and care whenever nuclear weapons are involved. Both the United States and the Soviet Union put more emphasis on the central control of their systems. Also, as soon as a crisis escalates, the political leadership tends to devote much more attention to even minute tactical details than in periods of "normalcy". For instance, Kissinger (1982) reports that in the 1973 crisis he insisted on even fixing the precise location of navy units sailing off the shore of Israel and Egypt. A similar prerogative of the political leadership vis-à-vis the military can be assumed to exist in the case of the Soviet decision-making structure. The degree of caution is rising.

One cannot deny that the trend of actions over the years has been towards tighter controls. As the risk of a nuclear conflict becomes more awesome, so the attention to command and control increases, more constraints are imposed, and more redundancy is created (Pugwash 1978: 8).

The various risks inherent in coercive bargaining strongly suggest that communication between the opponents is of crucial importance. According to Williams (1976: 182) communication tempers the dangers of coercive bargaining in four ways: firstly, communication can help to define the structure of the crisis so that both sides perceive accurately the relative values at stake; secondly, communication helps to establish the "rules of the game", e.g. by making clear to the opponent that refraining from a specific option provides the basis for reciprocity; thirdly, it facilitates an awareness of, and sensitivity to, the opponent's positions and problems; fourthly, it minimizes the likelihood of miscalculation.

Yet, while emphasizing the importance of communication, one must not forget the great difficulty of conveying messages credibly in a situation dominated by distrust. As a matter of fact, if mutual communication were working smoothly, the problem would simply not arise; the opponents would have better capabilities to convince each other about their values and interests than by using the blunt language of signals conveyed by the symbolic use of force and coercive bargaining. Of course, every effort must be made to ensure that all possible communication channels are open; yet it should be borne in mind that it may at best mitigate the problem without solving it.

The Use of Force : Balance and Prospects

An assessment of the risks inherent in the use of force as a "continuation of politics by other means" has to take into account the general trends to be discerned in this context.

The number of instances in which the two major Powers have used their armed forces as a political instrument is very impressive. Blechman/Kaplan (1978: 545—553) cite 215 cases in which American armed forces were used in the 1946—1975 period, and Kaplan (1981: 689—693) lists 190 incidents in which Soviet armed forces were used. Since these inventories of crises were drawn, additional cases have occurred such as President Carter's commitment to defend the Persian Gulf (Blechman/Hart 1982), and no doubt many more cases will follow. It seems that, as in the era of classic gunboat diplomacy, the diplomacy of power is again, and increasingly so, becoming a "way of life". At the least, one cannot expect a decline in the frequency with which the two major Powers employ armed forces. On the basis of empirical findings regarding the 1946—1976 period, it is possible to forecast the future evolution by applying extrapolation calculations. According to these calculations, 13 military confrontations per year must be expected in the 1982—2000 period (previous period 1946—1976: 12 confrontations). Among them are 10 limited bilateral conflicts, two limited multilateral conflicts, 0.3 bilateral wars, 0.2 multilateral wars (Eberwein 1981b: 8). According to Blechman/Kaplan (1978: 516), it is mainly when something unexpected and adverse happens, when the positive long-term political effects of the acquisition, maintenance and deployment of the armed forces break down, that decision-makers turn to military operations in attempts to mend the fabric of foreign relations. In most instances, the outcomes of such actions were favourable from the perspective of United States decision-makers — at least in the short term (*ibid:* 517). In contrast to prevailing views, the use of force by the United States was not less often successful as the Soviet Union narrowed the United States lead in strategic nuclear weapons, but it has been involved less often in such incidents since the late 1960s (*ibid:* 527). There is nevertheless a growing tendency to become involved in inter-State confrontations. Thus, the level of violence which can be threatened in a crisis is much greater than it used to be (*ibid:* 529). The danger that United States action of this sort might stimulate a Soviet military response is assessed by Blechman and Kaplan as being obvious. And in all situations there is a risk that lesser military actions may lead to pressures for greater United States involvement (*ibid:* 532). The main risk of escalation of such situations into a wider

145

conflagration stems from ambiguity (*ibid:* 534). If armed forces are used without the political objectives being made absolutely clear to political antagonists, these antagonists may act under false expectations and underestimate the degree of resolve behind United States actions.

A comparative analysis of the United States' and the Soviet use of force (Kaplan 1981:675 ff.) clearly shows that both major Powers are well aware of the risks generated by such a line of action. They tend to act with remarkable subtlety, circumspection and prudence, especially in cases in which there is or might be a direct confrontation between them. For instance, United States combat forces have never been deployed to an area where Soviet armed forces were using firepower. The Soviet Union, on the other hand, reserved actual intervention for cases in which the Soviet leadership perceived supreme interests to be at stake, and saw a high probability of United States non-involvement and a good prospect of success with moderate investment of military capital (Lambeth 1981:V).

Nevertheless, it would be premature to take the ensuing stability for granted. The adversary relationship of the United Stated and the USSR is undergoing considerable change due to both technological innovations affecting the strategic doctrines and the shift in the "correlation of forces" aimed at by the Soviet Union. A major development shaping the future style of power politics using force must be seen in the existence of quickly deployable conventional intervention forces (Kaplan 1981: 678f.). The availability of this instrument may lead the two major Powers to rely increasingly on the use of force in order to preclude or to counter the opponent's actions in a specific area of tension. An initial complication arises from the fact that the symbolic use of military force has a different meaning in different systems (Kruzel 1977, Kaplan 1981, Blechman/Kaplan 1978). On the United States side, for example, the traumatic experience of Pearl Harbor results in a long-standing preoccupation with the threat of surprise attack. This concern is constantly being increased by technological innovations which reduce to a few minutes the early-warning time available in case of an enemy missile attack. On the Soviet side, on the other hand, historical experience has taught that space can be traded for time; even Hitler's surprise attack left the Soviet Union sufficient time to organize effective resistance. Furthermore, there is less fear on the Soviet side about a possible United States surprise attack than vice-versa, because the United States open society would hardly allow preparatory steps taken for a surprise attack to be concealed whereas, on the other hand, the somewhat dissimilar nature of information available about Soviet society rightly or wrongly, in the United States perspective, seems to imply the easy possibility of launching a suprise attack without the victim being able to forestall it.

In other words, there is an asymmetrical use of signals and codes, and a signal employed by one side has not the same meaning on the other side. This fact may constitute an additional source of risks, because the interpretation of signals can easily suffer from misunderstandings. The system of signals may therefore collapse unexpectedly and give way to a dramatic escalation which was not wanted by either side.

The propensity to escalate is also a function of the ongoing arms race. As a Soviet specialist has noted, "the global arms race creates a general atmosphere intrinsically favourable for the widening of local conflicts with more great powers being involved" (Primakov 1980: 82).

There are also reasons to assume that the conventions of crisis will work smoothly in some regions but in an utterly unreliable way in other regions. Crisis spots have different "histories" — some of them quite old ones. In these cases the codes used to signal intentions are more or less clearly defined, although not articulated. This certainly applies to Europe, where the long-lasting confrontation originating in the Cold War has finally led to the establishment of rather stable zones of influence; here, obligations and responsibilities are mutually obvious. However, this may be different in new hotbeds of present-day and future crises. In these situations, the opponents often have difficulty in identifying each other's interests, and no credible codes are available to convey proper signals. This may generate incalculability and a propensity for inadvertent action, possibly precipitating unintentional escalation of a conflict.

At the same time, the increasing commitments of the major Powers in regions outside their traditional sphere of interest may lead to poorly defined situations which, in turn, may offer an incentive for at least two different types of new and escalation-prone crises (Morgan 1977: 142): the "limited probe" (a test of the limits of an ambiguous commitment); and "controlled pressure" (an attempt to erode a commitment while avoiding a frontal attack on it). Ambiguity invites provocation. Ambiguity can be overcome only if there are "rules of the game" regulating behaviour in crises. Rules of the game, however, exist only if both major Powers are present in the area concerned and both have recognized regional allies and clients (Evron 1979: 40).

Yet even in regions where crisis management seems to run smoothly, problems and dangers may arise. In the post-1945 period practically all international crises involving one or both major Powers have been solved or "managed" quite successfully. But as has been pointed out by Kahler (1979: 395f.), this feature may breed overconfidence. Just as the 1914 catastrophe was a great surprise to those who were relying on a century's smooth functioning of the international balance-of-power system, so one has to ask whether the capabilities for crisis management developed and applied since 1945 will be reliable and sufficient for the future too. Some analysts contend that the Cuban missile crisis aroused in United States policy-makers an exhilarating and dangerous overconfidence in their abilities to manage crises and to apply deterrence and coercive threats with precision. This left them vulnerable to the errors of policy in Viet Nam (Morgan 1977: 175).

There is a widespread expectation among experts that the role of force will not diminish but increase: according to Bull (1981: 19), the costs and risks of recourse to force may still be great, but the gains to be expected from it are thought increasingly to render those costs and risks acceptable.

Some authors tend to assume that there is a new spread of militarism and militarization around the globe . According to them this tendency can be observed by looking at specific types of policy orientation and execution such as (Thee 1980):

(1) High military expenditures and preferential treatment of the armed forces;
(2) Military build-up and application of military strength as an instrument of politics and diplomacy;
(3) Participation in military alliances;
(4) Imperial and neo-colonial postures;
(5) Care for police forces and participation of the army in international security operations;
(6) Military interference in shaping socio-economic goals and policy;
(7) Arbitrary decision-making processes;
(8) A return to mercantilist perceptions — i.e., the pursuit of wealth is thought to require the use of force (Bull 1981: 19);
(9) A tendency to think about the legitimacy of force to broaden the right of self-defense into a right of self-help in enforcing legal rights of many kinds (Bull 1981: 29 f.).

Although no systematic studies have been made regarding the relative growth of these symptoms as compared with prior periods, such as the inter-war period or the immediate post-Second World War period, hardly anybody would doubt the basic risks inherent in any such attitude. If used as a political means, force loses its exceptional character and becomes something like an international way of life. As long as "gunboat diplomacy" and similar, more modern forms of the use of force are highly prominent because of their exceptional and perhaps also sensational nature much caution will be applied in using these instruments.

External Commitments and "Limited Probes"

However, once the use of force becomes a generalized practice, a tendency towards carelessness may increase and thus amplify the probability of making a mistake, i.e., triggering consequences which were not intended and prove to be disastrous. This tendency is even more disquieting if one takes account of the fact that force is preferably used in third world regions. There are also additional reasons why any local and regional conflict in which there are also direct or indirect major Power interests at stake tends to become amplified and spread to other regions as well. For instance, during the Yom Kippur War in 1973 United States arms shipments to

148

Israel partly originated in stocks located in the territory of the Federal Republic of Germany. Also, United States forces stationed in other NATO countries were put on alert (Afheldt 1976: 174). If the crisis in the Middle East had not been controlled, any escalation would very probably also have affected these countries, even though they were not a party to the conflict and irrespective of the geographical distance separating Bonn or the Azores from the war theatre in the Sinai and the Golan Heights. A similar "infection" of outside regions by a local conflict can be expected in the case of a major-Power conflagration in the Persian Gulf area; this would automatically affect European and Japanese interests, given the high degree of dependency on energy supplies from the Middle East.

In other words, strategic interdependence has today reached global dimensions; if a fire breaks out at one end of the "global village" the rest of the village cannot feel safe. Powerful transmission mechanisms are at work, and decision-makers are often not aware of them since they become apparent only in situations of acute crisis.

The problem is even more serious considering that the nuclear Powers could find themselves, against their will, on a course of nuclear war as a consequence of earlier commitments and the escalation of local conflicts in which neither of them may have been directly involved. This triggering of nuclear war by one or more third Powers could well be a major source of danger in a polarized world in which defence commitments span the globe and local conflicts have great repercussions for a major nuclear confrontation.

Williams (1976: 100—101) thinks that situations where the clients of the United States and the Soviet Union are engaged in open hostilities against each other could be particularly dangerous. If the outcome looked disastrous for one side, this party might do everything possible to induce the respective major Power to intervene in order to prevent the impending disaster. In such a case it appears highly doubtful whether the other major nuclear Power, also feeling compelled to honour its commitments, would stand idly by. In this way, the major Powers could be dragged into a conflict without having made a conscious decision to engage in such a confrontation. Calder (1980: 79) describes the beginning of open hostilities involving the nuclear Powers as particularly likely if ships were to be the main combatant units. The dangers of non-verbal signalling (with aircraft carriers or other surface ships stationed near client States engaged in combat) getting out of hand seem to be increased by the relative absence of great collateral damage using nuclear weapons on the seas.

Holsti, in his research on the outbreak of the First World War, points to the effect of reduced policy options as a consequence of commitments during a crisis, "especially with partners who cannot be depended upon to view the resulting obligations as reciprocal" (Holsti 1972: 217). Ultimately, the choice may be between only two alternatives: reducing the commitment under threat, thereby seriously eroding one's credibility in the future; or backing the promise to the hilt, with the possibility of becoming a prisoner of the ally's policies *(ibid.)*.

A factor mitigating the danger of client States initiating a global conflagration is the limitation of means at the disposal of the smaller Powers. During the Cuban missile crisis, the Soviet Government made it quite clear to Washington that the missiles were strictly under their control (Williams 1976: 130). Pre-positioning of military hardware appears, in this perspective, as a rather undesirable course of action, creating the danger of interventions which were not desired and perhaps not even envisaged. The limitation of stakes in a local conflict could be attempted, at least with respect to armaments procured. Without delving deep into the problem of limited war, the danger of escalation of local conflicts must be assessed with some reservation. There have been several instances in which the major Powers have been able to contain the conflict (Freier 1979: 132), for example Korea, Viet Nam, East Africa. But there are, on the other hand, the events in the Middle East just before the cease-fire between Israel and Egypt, when unilateral intervention was threatened by the Soviet Union, and the United States increased the level of nuclear alert.

When referring to the use of force by the major Powers in the third world it would, however, be quite unsatisfactory to deplore the increasing frequency of such involvement without looking into the cause underlying this trend. A major source of past and future confrontation must be seen in the flow of conventional armaments to the third world. Arms transfers tend to create a dynamic of their own, since in a local crisis there will be a need to ship supplies, ammunition, spare parts and additional hardware. This in turn leads to a concern to secure access to the crisis spot, while the opponent may be tempted to harass the shipment of arms. In 1977 and 1978, the United States and the Soviet Union engaged in a series of talks (CAT, Conventional Arms Transfers talks) (Kearns 1981; Krause 1981). Unfortunately they ended unsuccessfully, and the international climate since the end of 1979 does not seem to be conclusive to a prompt and easy resumption of these talks. Critics also have quite pertinently deplored the absence of other (mainly European) arms producers (Kearns 1981: 5) from these talks.

Arms transfers seem to be considered, by the major Powers, as a substitute for sending troops. This was the position expressed in the so-called "Nixon doctrine" of 1969, which related to the possibility of offering military grants and credits and making cash sales to friendly nations while at the same time reducing United States overseas involvement. Similar concepts may underlie Soviet arms transfers. Yet the assumption that there is a neat trade-off between arms transfers and armed direct intervention may eventually turn out to be nothing but a fallacy. As already indicated, this point was demonstrated by the 1973 Yom Kippur War, where the commitments made by the two major Powers to provide their clients with supplies dragged them into a direct involvement and a direct confrontation close to the brink of war.

Kearns (1981: 11) argues that if the airlift operations for arms shipments from the United States and the USSR to their respective side involved in the war had been prevented by multilateral restraints, direct intervention would have been more conceivable. He suggests that, if the avenue of supporting one's client through arms transfers is closed by a multilateral agreement, alternative avenues become more likely — avenues which carry with them a greater risk of military confrontation and the spectre of nuclear war. The author of the present study cannot share this view; rather, the existence of commitments regarding arms transfers generates opportunities for a multitude of direct confrontations. If there were no such commitments, the risk of direct clash would be smaller.

Nevertheless, there is an element of truth in the opinion expressed by Kearns, which is perhaps consistent with the view of those who expect a direct confrontation due to the necessity to secure routes of access to deliver arms shipments. The underlying problem must obviously be seen in the fact that there is major Power involvement in third world regions. If the United States and the USSR were willing to abstain from pursuing and defending any interests in the third world, of course neither arms transfers nor direct intervention would take place. Yet any such proposals completely ignore political realities and are thus beside the point. A more realistic approach would be to study the possibility of reaching a kind of tacit or explicit agreement on both zones of influence and codes of conduct regarding admissible behaviour in controversial regions of the third world.

Of course, the elaboration of a code of conduct for the policies of the two major Powers in outside regions may be an utterly unrewarding task, because their interests and concepts are to a large extent downright contradictory. This does not mean, however, that the approach as such would be wrong. As a matter of fact, the two major Powers do seem to be interested in such an approach. The United States Government has repeatedly alleged "violations" of the rules of the game by the Soviet Union, thus indicating assumptions regarding the existence of such rules. On the other hand General Secretary Leonid Brezhnev in 1981 suggested the proclamation of a code of conduct comprising principles such as the prohibition of including any country in one's own sphere of interest (Lüders 1981: 111). One must, however, beware of drawing premature conclusions from this seemingly convergent interest in having a kind of code of conduct. It would be naïve to neglect the inherently competitive attitude reflected in the policies adopted by the two major Powers vis-à-vis third Powers. Moreover, competition would inevitably affect the content and basic thrust of any such rules. Hence the approaches to the actual details of such rules of conduct may well be irreconcilably different, despite the common interest in having such rules in principle.

Conclusions: International Crises as Catalytic Agents Triggering Unintentional Nuclear War

The risks:

1. *In international crisis situations, decision-makers suffer from stress which causes a number of cognitive and behavioural maladaptations (distorted perception, suboptimal decision-making). These maladaptations greatly enhance the risk of crucial decisions not being made correctly and rationally, thus leading to nuclear war by miscalculation.*
2. *Similar maladaptations may occur due to organizational problems of decision-making units: contraction of the decision-making group, information overflow, "groupthink", internal dissension and inflexible standard operating procedures may result in the decisions taken in a crisis situation being of poor quality.*
3. *Strategic vulnerability, urgency, strategic instability and crisis instability inevitably affect the performance of the responsible decision-makers. Thus, an inherently bad situation automatically worsens instead of leading to better decision-making.*
4. *The rules governing the use of force as a "continuation of policy by other means", as employed by the Powers for conveying signals, are utterly fragile and prone to misunderstandings, especially between opponents committed to systems of different ideological orientation. It may therefore be difficult to avoid fatal miscalculations regarding the use of nuclear weapons.*
5. *Crisis bargaining entails the risk of events getting out of control due to the "logic of events", military necessity, low-level actions taken by subordinate commanders and organizational routine and confusion due to the malfunctioning of C^3 systems.*
6. *The trend towards global militarization and poorly defined, ambiguous commitments in the third world fosters the inclination to use force in crisis bargaining.*
7. *The risks inherent in this trend are enhanced by a network of strategic interdependence which makes the success of efforts to localize crises doubtful. Hence there is a risk of unintentional escalation (both geographically and militarily) of international crises.*

Mitigating factors:

1. *To some extent stress experienced by decision-makers faced with a crisis situation tends to improve the perceptive and behavioural performance of decision-makers. But extreme stress has a disruptive effect in most situations.*
2. *In crisis situations, Governments try to assume full control of all details of the making and execution of decisions, thus reducing the likelihood of organizational maladaptation by involvement in and meticulous handling of all aspects.*

3. *Governments also generally tend to behave with utmost care and circumspection as soon as military force is involved in crisis bargaining.*

4. *Existing mechanisms of communication contribute to avoiding misunderstandings.*

Risk assessment:

The risks are hard to estimate. Whether positive or negative influences prevail depends to a large extent on the special circumstances of a crisis. Although the Governments concerned are generally aware of the problems and dangers involved, the unpredictable and uncertain nature of specific situations may still produce a set of circumstances which might simply override all precautionary measures.

VI. NUCLEAR ACCIDENTS AND INCIDENTS

Nuclear War by Accident?

Right from the very beginning of the nuclear arms race, considerable attention has been devoted to the problem of nuclear weapons accidents and incidents. Rightly or wrongly, authors were afraid that such incidents might start a nuclear war or at the least cause great damage at the site of accidental detonation and also over a wider area due to nuclear fall-out (Leitenberg 1970). In 1962, Herman Kahn noted a widespread concern that "an electrical circuit might shortcut, a relay stick, a switch fail, or that a button might be pressed accidentally, a message misunderstood, an aurora borealis, meteor, or flock of geese be mistaken for an attack and so on" (Kahn 1962: 40). Kahn located the sources of danger in mechanical or human error, false alarm, unauthorized behaviour or miscalculation by the people authorized to launch the nuclear weapons. There have been scenarios with a missile being fired accidentally in the East detonating in the West, and evoking a response from the proverbial nervous officer who misunderstands his orders and fires the missiles under his control (Kahn 1962: 145—150). Kahn concluded that the "current probability of inadvertent war is low, " although he pointed out that this danger may grow as a result of the proliferation of independent nuclear capabilities and the growing number of buttons that can be pressed accidentally (Kahn 1962: 40).

Such was the assessment of the probability of accidental nuclear war in 1962. It does not differ fundamentally from the appraisals made in the late 1970s or early 1980s. Dumas defines accidental war as an "exchange of weapons of mass destruction not initiated with the purposeful calculation of the governmental decision-makers in authority" (Dumas 1977:70). He also mentions that two conditions are necessary: the triggering event (faulty communications, false warnings of attack, or serious accidents involving nuclear weapons) and the situation in which it can have the catalytic effect (high level of tension, need of quick response) (Dumas 1977: 73). As far as the assessment of the risk is concerned, however, no author in East or West thinks that nuclear war by accident constitutes a central problem. It seems that the general public's awareness is to some extent misdirected when it focuses on the danger of nuclear war by accident only.

For obvious reasons the information policy of the nuclear Powers regarding accidents and incidents involving nuclear weapons is very restrictive. As one observer notes:

> "To put it euphemistically: governments are not devoting themselves to the dissemination of information about these types of accidents. The USSR, France, China and the UK have never reported any data; the USA limits its communications to those occurrences which have already attracted public attention" (Niezing 1980:71).

The discussion about nuclear accidents and incidents is almost completely restricted to United States cases. This concentration does not mean that the safeguards of other countries are to be considered superior. Although accidents are not usually fully disclosed to the public, some information is constantly being published, and there are also reports listing types, dates and specifications of accidents. There may have been about 130 accidents (Leitenberg 1977 a).

The classification of accidents and incidents has been developed up to a point where a precise terminology can be identified (Niezing 1980). A nuclear weapon accident (code name: "Broken Arrow"), according to United States sources, is any unexpected event involving nuclear weapons or nuclear components which result in any of the following:

> a) Accidental or unauthorized launching, firing or use by United States forces or United States supported allied forces of a nuclear capable weapon system which would create the risk of outbreak of war;
> b) Nuclear detonation;
> c) Non-nuclear detonation/burning of a nuclear weapon;
> d) Radioactive contamination;
> e) Seizure, theft or loss of a nuclear weapon or nuclear component, including jettisoning;
> f) Public hazard, actual or implied (Leitenberg 1977 a: 53).

On the other hand, a nuclear weapon incident (code name: "Bent Spear") is any unexpected event involving nuclear weapons or nuclear components which does not fall into the nuclear weapon accident category but which

> (a) Results in evident damage to a nuclear weapon or a nuclear component to the extent that major rework, complete replacement or examination or recertification by the Energy Research and Development Administration is required, or
> (b) Requires immediate action in the interest of safety or which may result in adverse public reaction or premature release of information.

Within the four services of the United States armed forces, the codes used for reporting such accidents and incidents, apart from "Broken Arrow" and "Bent Spear", are "Dull Sword" and "Nucflash" (Leitenberg 1977a: 83: Albertini 1981: 54; Niezing 1980: 71). The codes reflect the degree of seriousness, depending on whether

nuclear incidents occurred or whether nuclear weapons were involved (for definitions, see Leitenberg 1977a: 83—85). Among them are incidents and accidents such
as crashes of strategic bombers carrying nuclear warheads, loss of nuclear bombs
during flight, explosion of fuel tanks of an operational ICBM, misfiring of nuclear-
tipped missiles, and the like. Other incidents involve malfunctioning or misinterpretation of the early warning system thus causing erroneous alert.

In order to make a proper assessment of the dangers of the occurrence of nuclear
accidents and incidents, it is necessary to analyse their main potential causes, as well
as the system of safeguards established to prevent them. The two main sources of
thinkable accidents and incidents can be identified in the technical field and in the
human factor.

The Technical Factor

As far as the technical aspects are concerned, one cannot but agree with Beres (1980:
35) who says that "no mechanical system, however carefully constructed and monitored, can be presumed to be infallible".

The main sources of accidents are aircraft crashes, bombs being jettisoned accidentally, aircraft catching fire or exploding in the air, a submarine being lost, an
ICBM blowing up, nuclear-tipped AAMs accidentally being launched (Leitenberg
1977: 65—82). In the 1960s, many of these accidents involved crashes of nuclear
armed B-52 bombers, as far as the United States is concerned. In the well-known
Goldsboro accident, a 24-megaton bomb was jettisoned over North Carolina. The
fall set off five of the six interlocks (Leitenberg 1970: 261; Dumas 1977: 68; Beres
1980: 37). The damage caused by accidents has been limited to some radioactive
pollution, and there have been no nuclear explosions (Niezing 1980: 71). Safety devices activating the fuses during the acceleration phase after launch or during the fall
of free-fall bombs preclude the nuclear detonation of unlaunched nuclear weapons
(Leitenberg 1970: 262: Beres 1980: 42).

However, the transportation and deployment of the many thousands of nuclear
warheads may pose some dangers. For instance, it is known that the moving and
deployment of nuclear weapons in Hawaii involves moving nuclear weapons through,
over and around heavily populated civilian areas. Even the bunkers do not seem
to be ideally situated. Under tradewind conditions, planes on approach to Honolulu
International head directly toward the West Loch bunkers, then turn away only
moments prior to touchdown (Albertini 1981: 56). In this context it must be noted
that even without a nuclear detonation, the consequences of accidents involving nuclear weapons could be grave. Besides radiation pollution, the dispersal of radioactive
material has to be considered. Radioactive material could be widely dispersed by
the explosion of the conventional explosive surrounding the core, by burning or by
other accident-related means (Dumas 1977: 67). Plutonium, used beside uranium

in nuclear weapons, is very long-lived and is considered highly toxic (Beres 1980: 180—182; Dumas 1977: 67).

With regard to failure or malfunctioning of mechanical and electronic equipment, two questions seem more relevant than the problem of infallibility:

(1) To what extent do technical failures override the redundant safety systems developed following the first accidents in the 1950s and 1960s?

(2) How likely is it that—in the improbable event that all redundant safety systems fail — an accident or incident is misinterpreted by the opponent as the beginning of a nuclear attack and thus leads to a retaliation strike?

As to the first question, nothing serious has happened so far. The incidents and accidents which did occur were immediately followed by improvement of the safety system. It is interesting to note that, if one looks at the list of known accidents and incidents, hardly any type of serious accident or incident is repeated. One may conclude that the responsible authorities drew the appropriate practical conclusions.

Any nuclear accident, particularly if it becomes public knowledge, is likely to stimulate efforts for greater security and risk limitation (Niezing 1980: 72). The minor consequences of the accidents which did occur confirm the high standard of the safeguards. The C^3 precautions against unauthorized/accidental launch are also elaborate, as far as is known. There might be reduced safety in the communications between airborne command posts and missile squads located in silos and submarines (Sonntag 1982); yet as far as the American ALCS (Airborne Launch Control System) is concerned, only little information is available, and there is almost no information about the corresponding Soviet systems.

As to the second question, in the unlikely event of something serious happening, for example, an accidental launch of a ballistic missile, one has to ask whether such an event would really be capable of triggering a punitive strike due to a misinterpretation of the evidence received about the accident.

The likelihood of nuclear accidents has to be distinguished conceptually from the likelihood of an unintentional nuclear war arising therefrom. While the probability of the first is very low, the probability of the second is even lower, at least as long as the system of deterrence is not affected by potential vulnerability of second strike forces and as long as strategic capability is guaranteed. Looking at the possible occurrence of accidents alone does not mean very much.

If a possible surprise attacker does not pose an unacceptable risk to the major Powers, they will react in a calm and circumspect way, avoiding any automatic and instantaneous response leading to an unintentional war. They are not compelled to act by the pressure of urgency. They have sufficient time to clarify the situation provided that the overall strategic situation is not dominated by strategic instability. Thus the problem has to be related to the basic problem of strategic stability; that is where the crucial and fundamental factor affecting the likelihood of an unintentional nuclear war lies. In this context, however, it must be emphasized that any doctrinal developments favouring counterforce options may have a destabilizing effect, because for the persons in charge of the weapons systems the principle "use it or lose it" becomes paramount. A strategic bomber pilot, for instance, has an obvious interest in taking off with his aircraft before the airbase is hit by a counterforce strike (Sonntag 1982).

Nevertheless, it would be unwise to project this state of affairs indefinitely into the future. In the context of the current arms race the number of nuclear warheads is constantly growing and this cannot but entail an increase of the risk of accidents. The growing frequency of crisis confrontations also contributes to this tendency.

In a serious crisis, not only will accidents be more likely to cause drastic effects, but the likelihood of accidents may increase, because (a) transportation of nuclear weapons intensifies, (b) missiles are loaded on a larger scale, (c) emphasis may be placed on quick response rather than on redundant verifications and authorizations (Niezing 1980: 73). Finally it should also be borne in mind that in the course of nuclear proliferation it is conceivable that countries lacking relative invulnerability would feel forced to utilize risky command and control measures (Beres 1980: 90) typical of an unstable strategic environment.

The Human Factor

While the risk originating in technical failure may, on the whole, be said to be quite minute, the situation is different with regard to the human factor. Officers responsible for guarding, maintaining and possibly firing nuclear weapons and launching weapon carriers are, after all, also human beings and thus even less infallible than technical systems. The ultimate significance of a nuclear accident or incident caused by unauthorized action, human error or sheer madness is the same as in the case of accident or incidents caused by technical problems. As was pointed out in the preceding section, there are no grave consequences such as the triggering of an unintentional nuclear war as long as strategic stability is assured.

Nevertheless, for the sake of comprehensive analysis, the following paragraphs will inquire into the questions (1) whether there are any opportunities at all for the human factor to cause great mischief and (2) what types of dysfunctional behaviour might be expected in those circumstances if something really goes wrong.

The first question has to do with the problem of predelegation of authority to fire nuclear weapons. This problem has already been amply dealt with (pp. 16ff.). An SSBN commander may have the authority and the instructions to fire SLBMs under certain circumstances. Due to the absence of electronic locks the crew of an SSBN seems always to be able to fire the SLBMs against the intentions of the national command authorities. Beres (1980: 39) notes that nuclear missile submarines apparently comprise the only component of the strategic nuclear triad in which firing can be accomplished without activation by remote electronic switch turned on by higher command. Calder (1979: 111) also assumes that the submarine ought logically to be able to launch its missiles without receipt of explicit orders. In this context, one has to mention the fact that co-operation between a number of officers is required in order to launch SLBMs, but the basic possibility still persists: SLBMs might be launched by the crew independently of orders.

As Fried (1981: 25) writes, there is something like "involuntary or unintended delegation of power" to members of the armed forces. He illustrates this point with the example of the pilots of nuclear armed bombers and the personnel encoding and decoding messages or translating them.

In these cases, no explicit delegation of power (much less a delegation of authority) has taken place, but this personnel could find themselves in a situation where, technically, they had the possibility of deciding whether or not to fire the nuclear weapons. This applies, however, only to situations of very high tension, where the PALs are unlocked (as for the bombs carried by aircraft). The redundancy and interlocking checks in the communication from the national command authority to the missile sites will generally also preclude the possibility of sabotage by a single individual. In other words, the only time a bomber pilot or a submarine captain can "decide" or translate orders is when they are provided with the command indicators to do so.

The reliance on armed forces personnel in the use of nuclear weapons nevertheless entails some risks. Generally speaking, the orders given by the authorities may still not be executed exactly as they are meant. Steinbruner (1979: 39) concludes that "the efforts to bring American policy under central direction must be said to have failed" in the Cuban missile crisis. The central authorities set aside the other business during the days of high crisis and concentrated on the missile crisis. The United States Navy, however, did not implement their intentions in the subtle way desired. For example, the pursuit of Soviet submarines in the North Atlantic constituted "extremely strong strategic coercion and violated the spirit of the Executive Committee policy" (Steinbruner 1979: 38). At a certain point, the military forces of the United States were put on alert, but "a great deal of activity having to do with preparing military forces for combat was accomplished well before the official order to go on alert" (Steinbruner 1979: 39). This illustrates how clumsy an instrument the armed forces may be in a crisis and how subordinates may act in ways not intended by the central authorities.

The unauthorized use of nuclear weapons by officers would be much more serious than the slightly premature or clumsy implementation of executive orders. As Calder (1979: 76—77) points out, the spread of nuclear weapons to a large number of countries may increase the danger of unauthorized use of nuclear weapons by officers of the armed forces. Such a danger exists, of course, also in the generally recognized nuclear Powers, but the super-Powers have a carefully devised chain of command and control designed to prevent any misuse of nuclear weapons by junior or even senior officers (Calder 1979: 76).

These conclusions are based on the assumption that the military authorities are loyal to the civil authorities. Yet, the safeguards would perhaps be somewhat less stringent for the armed forces of a country having newly acquired nuclear weapons. Calder doubts whether the same discipline will apply to "an Israeli general who sees Arab tanks in Tel Aviv" as to his United States or Soviet counterparts in Europe. Williams (1976: 119) recalls that at the height of the Cuban missile crisis, a U-2 on a routine patrol apparently went off course, violated Soviet air space and was chased by Soviet fighters. In the event, the Soviet leaders avoided a rash response but it is not inconceivable that with intensified tension they could have interpreted the flight as a reconnaissance mission prior to a United States nuclear attack. The United States command authority also had some difficulties in actively discouraging senior officers to strike after Cuba had shot down a U-2 reconnaissance aircraft. As Keegan (1981: 149) puts it, "it took the active disallowance of President Kennedy to cancel it".

The types of potential dysfunctional behavior by officers have also been very often dealt with in the literature available. There are reports about alcoholism, drug addiction, mental illness and other related problems in the military in general; army personnel manning nuclear-capable missile batteries were arrested for possession or sale of LSD (Muller 1982). Furthermore, the routine work to be done by personnel assigned to the controls over weapons of mass destruction is known to be stress-inducing while at the same time causing boredom, due to monotony and isolation (Dumas 1981).

Existing Safeguards

On the other hand, there is an impressive array of safeguards and countermeasures i.e. negative controls of all kinds, taking into account, in a most thorough manner, all possible consequences of technical and human fallibility. The system of safeguards has been fully described in official United States Government publications as well as in the academic literature available on this subject. There is no need to repeat it in this context. Summarizing the reports about these safeguards in a few key words, the following systems are currently in operation on the United States side (cf. Ball 1981:4f.; Beres 1980:34—51; Calder 1979:84—88; Miller 1979; Foster 1981):

> Computer-constructed key codes, coding devices and interlocks;
> Sealed authenticator system (SAS);
> Permissive action links (PALs);
> Redundancy of communication systems;

161

Personnel reliability program (PRP);
Emergency destruction devices and procedures;
Command destruction (CD) design;
Two-men rule.

All these systems and procedures are deployed with much redundancy, thus reducing the likelihood of unauthorized release of nuclear weapons to almost zero.

What has been said in this section refers primarily to United States nuclear forces; in general, the United States Government is rather free in disclosing information about accidents and incidents and precautionary measures taken against such events. The general picture conveyed by the large amount of openly available United States information must be said to be quite comforting. Yet one might nevertheless ask whether this situation will not give the impression that everything is perfect while in practice it might not work as theoretically expected.

As far as the other nuclear Powers are concerned, the available information may be less exhaustive but is hardly less conclusive. According to Miller (1979: 63—65), in France, aircraft carrying nuclear weapons are equipped with "black boxes" that can be activated to neutralize the warheads. Although no authentic official information is published about Soviet safeguards, it is generally assumed that the Soviet Union practises a system of extremely tight and carefully centralized control in all branches of the armed forces dealing with nuclear weapons. According to Soviet sources, centralization constitutes a general feature of the Soviet command system, and centralization is carried out in a very rigid way from the top to the bottom.

The redundancy and efficiency of the safeguard systems led one expert to the somewhat surprising conclusion that the main danger is not to be seen in the accidental release of a nuclear weapon, and possibly in the triggering of an unintentional war; the real danger may rather lie in too much restraint (Miller 1979: 55). The safeguards are thoroughly restrictive, and if one link in the chain of procedures is missing, the whole procedure will be stopped. There were reports *(Washington Post*, 13 December 1981) that after President Reagan was shot in the assassination attempt of 30 March 1981, his secret personal code card was lost for several hours and finally found with the FBI, which had collected the clothes stripped from the wounded President as he lay on the stretcher in the emergency ward of the hospital. The card contains a series of coded numbers and words with which the Commander-in-Chief can identify himself to military officials in case of war and which activates the elaborate top-secret cryptographic Sealed Authenticator System (SAS).

One might infer from this speculation that the probability of a nuclear war by accident is lower than the probability of a self-blocking of the system once a war breaks out and a Government decides to launch a nuclear strike.

Yet this fact creates a "sinister irony", as Calder (1979:113) calls it: the more thoroughly the system prevents a Government from firing nuclear weapons without proper authority, the more tempting it is for an attacker to launch a "decapitating" strike at the national command centre that may leave the victim powerless to respond. Too many safeguards may thus contribute to vulnerability and reduce strategic stability. This conjecture is, however, grossly hypothetical. Even if some chains of command — e.g., the ones linking the supreme commanding authority with SLBM-carrying submarines — are complex and require some time to be operated, there are other systems — such as SAC — which can react more quickly without being less safe against the various types of fallibility resulting from the technical and human factors involved.

Nevertheless, it is interesting to note that, again, there is a trade-off between two tendencies promoted by technological progress. This trade-off may be expressed in the following dilemma: how can one avoid the launching of missiles when they must not be launched (negative controls) — and how can one make sure that they really go off once one decides to launch them (positive controls)? Again, there is no easy way out of this dilemma — and sooner or later the dilemma may be resolved by again favouring positive controls at the expense of negative controls (Steinbruner 1981:24).

Evaluation of the Dangers

In conclusion, it must be noted that the degree of public attention devoted to nuclear weapons accidents and incidents is in marked contrast to the evaluation of the danger as given by experts. The experts generally agree that triggering off nuclear war by technical failure or any other type of breaking of safety rules is highly improbable.

When the evidence available so far and the evaluation carried out by experts on this subject are examined, it cannot be denied that the real dangers inherent in this problem area do not correspond to the fears prevalent among the general public. It would therefore certainly be inappropriate to concentrate more than necessary on this aspect.

It would also be irresponsible to concentrate exclusively on this subject, thus neglecting other, more prominent risks and dangers existing on other levels of analysis. The focus on the risk of nuclear war by accident, according to one of the most competent specialists in this field (Leitenberg, in a letter to the author of this study), not only misrepresents the problem; it also misdirects attention from the really crucial and perhaps most dangerous concerns in this context.

The concern for nuclear weapons accidents and incidents can only be understood if seen against the background of the 1950s. Very serious and highly dangerous incidents were reported for the initial years of the nuclear era. The systems were in fact accident-prone, as were, at least potentially, political reactions to such incidents. Yet the dangers inherent in this state of technological, communicative and political evolution were correctly perceived, and practical conclusions appropriate to the requirements of the situation were drawn. As a consequence, the systems deployed in the 1960s and even more so those deployed in the 1970s were fully equipped with all kinds of controls and safeguards. This cannot be said to constitute an important issue any longer, at least not for the time being.

Still, a critical question must be raised with regard to the increasing number of nuclear warheads manufactured, stored and deployed all over the world. If, apart from missile warheads and airborne bombs, one includes nuclear shells for heavy artillery assigned to tactical nuclear warfare, the estimated number of nuclear warheads deployed probably exceeds 15,000, and it still is constantly growing (United Nations Centre for Disarmament 1981 : 8f.).

Statistically speaking, the sheer number of warheads cannot but increase the probability of accidents and incidents, even if the original risk of such an occurrence is minute and insignificant. Whether this quantitative multiplication of risks will be matched and neutralized by a corresponding improvement of qualitative safeguards cannot be answered at this point. Yet it emphasizes two imperatives: firstly, the necessity of finding ways and means to assure strategic stability with a smaller number of deployed nuclear weapons; and, secondly, the necessity of refining and upgrading the systems of existing safeguards.

Conclusions: The Risks of Nuclear War by Accident

The risks:

1. *Due to technical failure or malfunctioning, nuclear weapons may be accidentally detonated or launched. Technical malfunctioning may also lead to false alarms.*
2. *Nuclear accidents and incidents may also be caused by unauthorized action, human error or sheer madness.*
3. *Such accidents or incidents with nuclear weapons may be misinterpreted by an adversary nuclear Power and lead it to retaliate immediately.*
4. *The risks are particularly serious in countries which have a newly acquired nuclear capability but are not yet able or willing to invest in sophisticated safeguard systems.*

Mitigating factors:

1. *Redundant and efficient safeguard systems and countermeasures, although not completely infallible, practically exclude a serious accident or incident due to technical failure or malfunctioning.*
2. *C^3 systems (PAL, etc.) are designed to prevent any misuse of nuclear weapons by subordinate commanders.*

164

3. There is a general tendency to subject the release of nuclear weapons to tight control by the supreme political authority.
4. Nuclear accidents and incidents are not capable of triggering an all-out nuclear war provided that strategic stability is assured and no LOW or predelegation policies have been adopted.

Risk assessment:

Contrary to the public's perception, the risk of nuclear war by accident is minute and negligible, provided that strategic stability is assured. The focus on the risk of nuclear war by accident may misrepresent the problem and misdirect attention from more serious and crucial risks constituting a far greater danger.

VII. THE EFFECTS OF NUCLEAR PROLIFERATION ON THE RISK OF UNINTENTIONAL NUCLEAR WAR

A. Unintentional Nuclear War in an N-Powers' World

Prospects of Nuclear Proliferation

Nuclear proliferation, i.e., the acquisition of nuclear weapons by additional countries, constitutes a major concern of the debate on disarmament, and much has been written about it. The motives impelling non-nuclear States to "go nuclear" have been amply elucidated, as have the technological potential and access to nuclear fuel of the countries that are considered as candidates for becoming nuclear Powers. Isolated "garrison States" such as South Africa, Israel, Taiwan, etc., may be interested in having their own nuclear bomb as a "last-resort weapon". On the other hand, medium-size Powers may wish to pursue their aspirations for regional hegemonic status or enhanced prestige by acquiring nuclear weapons. Sometimes, domestic considerations may induce a Government to bolster its internal position by pressing on with the development of a nuclear arsenal. Finally, there are constraining laws of reaction: if, in a regional context characterized by high tension and hostility, one Power acquires nuclear weapons, its main opponent will try to follow suit immediately and undertake every possible effort to pursue the same course of action (Winkler 1980:28ff.; Waltz 1981:7f.; Primakov 1980:93f.; Kaliadine 1981:24). Some countries appear to have adopted a posture of deliberate ambiguity about their intentions and capabilities with regard to the acquisition of nuclear weapons. Such ambiguity contributes considerably to raising tension in the region concerned and it may also be a factor contributing to regional instability (United Nations General Assembly 1981c: 26f.).

In addition, the peaceful use of atoms contributes to a widespread proliferation not only of research and power reactors but of all nuclear facilities and activities involved in the fuel cycle; this also includes a widespread dissemination of knowledge of nuclear technology, thus creating increasing temptations for national Governments and agencies to acquire fissionable material and nuclear explosives (Epstein 1976: 45). This tendency is also reinforced by the increasing attractiveness of breeder reactors, which are capable of generating more nuclear fuel than they consume (Beres 1980: 76). At any rate, as pointed out by Weltman (1982: 183), since a good deal of the process of producing nuclear weapons can be carried out as a by-product of civil programmes, the marginal additional costs of the weapons decline as the civil industry expands. One cannot deny that "projects for peaceful applications of nuclear technology provided the essential expeditor, and in many cases the necessary cover, for gaining capabilities to make the bomb." (Iklé 1978: vii).

Proliferation may also take place through unorthodox ways and means: "scientific mercenaries" are readily available and willing to sell their services to any country seeking to develop nuclear weapons (Dunn 1976: 109). There are even more amazing forms of "grey marketeering", as Dunn calls this phenomenon: the sale, barter, or gift of nuclear weapons or of the "blueprints", and special material for their construction. Many countries resort to piecemeal purchases of components on the grey market (Lodgaard 1981 a: 18).

Much has also been written about the meagre record of the measures initiated to halt nuclear proliferation, such as the 1968 Treaty on the Non-Proliferation of Nuclear Weapons (NPT) and its implementation (cf. Epstein 1976: ch. 5—8). In fact, many commentators think that the NPT basically has missed the point. As he United Nations Disarmament Fact Sheet (No. 16, 1981) very aptly puts it,

> "the implications of the continued development of nuclear weapons have given rise to many complex questions, amongst which the most fundamental runs as follows: Why should non-nuclear States parties to the Non-Proliferation Treaty refrain from the development of nuclear weapons (so-called horizontal proliferation) while the nuclear-weapons States continue to increase the size and quality of their nuclear arsenal (so-called vertical proliferation) ?".

Other authors assume a more radical stance and do not hesitate to argue that third world countries, quite contrary to what is recommended in international forums should "go nuclear" in order firstly to make the weak more powerful, and secondly, to persuade the powerful to weaken themselves by giving up their arsenals. The road to military equality lies first in nuclear proliferation in third world countries, and later through global de-nuclearization for everybody (Mazrui 1980: 79). Not surprisingly, this view is intensely questioned, attention being drawn to the incredibly complex and arduous task of negotiating a treaty banning all nuclear weapons among a multitude of participants as well as to the intricate verification problems arising therefrom (Towle 1980).

More Nuclear Powers = More Nuclear Wars?

It is outside the scope of this study to discuss general problems of nuclear proliferation and efforts to contain it. The question to be asked in this context is: are there any specific risks of unintentional nuclear war generated by the fact of nuclear proliferation? Many experts (e.g., Barnaby 1980: 4) agree that generally as the number of countries with nuclear weapons increases, the probability of nuclear war will also increase. But what are the particular reasons for arriving at such a conclusion? The specialized literature on this subject offers a variety of hypotheses regarding this question. Some of these hypotheses are highly controversial.

There is wide agreement among experts that the issue of nuclear proliferation constitutes a real nightmare, bearing in mind that the new nuclear Powers may be ruled by leaders who are far more radical than the most radical of the leaders of the "classical" nuclear Powers. Much will then depend on these leaders' ability to cope with crisis situations. Moreover, the leadership of the major Powers are called upon to act in such a situation. Whether or not their commitment as mediators, allies, friends or opponents will be beneficial cannot be predetermined by any structural characteristics; it ultimately depends on the skill and quality of statesmanship.

As has been emphasized by Schütze (1979:91) these considerations do not imply an *a priori* case against all new nuclear Powers assuming that only the old nuclear Powers which have learnt "to live with the bomb" can be expected to act wisely. The point is, rather, that there will be a greater mischief-making potential for "maverick" candidates and countries with unstable or downright paranoic leaders. But it would be premature to underestimate the problems caused by lack of experience in "living with the bomb"; one may expect that as a consequence of deep hostilities, these Governments would be much readier to use nuclear weapons, and probably to use them indiscriminately against civilian populations (Wohlstetter *et al.* 1978:131). Similar fears are expressed by a Soviet author, who states "that fascist elements, rising to power in a nuclear State, could threaten the world with nuclear war" (Yefremov 1979:112).

The probability of accidental or irrational war seems to increase with the number of countries acquiring nuclear weapons.

On the other hand, one cannot deny also the existence of mitigating factors — some of them quite ironic ones, as suggested by Waltz, who thinks that in countries where political control is most difficult to maintain, governments are least likely to initiate nuclear-weapons programmes (Waltz 1981: 10). If countries governed by leaders who use wild rhetoric and seemingly behave in an irrational way acquire nuclear weapons, they are nevertheless unlikely to use them irrationally; even so-called "irrational" leaders have shown caution and sensitivity to costs (Waltz 1981: 11).

Specific Risks

A more specific hypothesis concerns the reliability of safeguard systems preventing nuclear accidents and incidents. As these systems are extremely expensive, States newly acquiring nuclear weapons might simply be unable to take such expensive measures, and it is conceivable that in some cases such safeguards may be altogether non-existent (Yefremov 1979: 111; Niezing 1980: 72; Beres 1980: 89—91). If nuclear proliferation progresses, it can be taken for granted that at least some of the nuclear Powers could afford only relatively "cheap" nuclear weapons without the costly safeguards and command and control systems devised by the major Powers (Hermann *et al.* 1974:79). For these reasons the conclusion cannot be avoided that the number of nuclear accidents and incidents will certainly not decrease as nuclear proliferation grows. This conclusion does not necessarily imply that such accidents and incidents will trigger a world-wide nuclear war. Yet there are plausible scenarios which suggest specific "paths" to general nuclear war.

A first possibility must be seen already on the eve of a nation becoming a nuclear Power. As a State develops a nuclear capability, there will be a temptation for its potential enemies to attack it before its nuclear delivery system is operational (Towle 1980: 219). Intriligator and Brito (1981: 256) argue that when there are very few nuclear nations, a further nuclear nation would tend to increase the probability of nuclear war: the new nation may be particularly inviting as a target in that it has a minimal stockpile with no retaliatory capability. One of the existing nuclear nations might then be tempted to take out this minimal stockpile by a "surgical strike".

In 1948, Bertrand Russell argued for a preventive war against the Soviet Union (Intriligator/Brito 1978: 176). Such a preventive attack was in fact executed, in 1981, by Israel against Iraq's "Osirak" research reactor; the Israeli Prime Minister explicitly justified this act as a defensive action required to assure his country's survival. As Betts (1981b: 2) argues, the destruction of "Osirak" could have implications as a precedent inasmuch as other threatened countries might more readily consider similar actions and commit deliberate attacks on nuclear installations.

In more general terms, an incentive to pre-empt may also be generated after two regional rival countries have acquired nuclear weapons. The assumption may not be mistaken that the initial delivery systems deployed will be characterized by a high degree of vulnerability. New nuclear Powers can hardly be expected to create a diversified and expensive system involving land-based nuclear missiles in silos, submarines, etc. (Beres 1980: 81f.). In other words, the history of strategic delivery systems repeats itself in different regional contexts, thus multiplying in the future the risks of strategic instability as it existed in the 1950s in major-Power relations. Again, but in a variety of situations, temptations will be created to launch deliberate pre-emptive strikes or to adopt low policies. Hence there is a high probability of "local" nuclear wars.

Some authors argue that nuclear weapons tend to raise the stakes of potential conflict and that their acquisition would make Governments more cautious and thus less likely to go to war (Intriligator/Brito 1978:175). Therefore one might expect a declining frequency of wars altogether and almost no nuclear wars, as soon as the potentially belligerent countries have nuclear weapons at their disposal. However, this argument neglects or disregards the fact that there is no such thing as a "nuclear weapon" in general. Rather, these nuclear weapons have certain characteristics — vulnerability or invulnerability for instance — and it is these characteristics which count when determining the stability of the international system after nuclear proliferation has taken place.

An additional refinement takes into account the different situations determined by the number of nuclear nations. According to Intriligator and Brito (1981: 256), with more nuclear nations an added nuclear nation would most likely reduce the probability of nuclear war, by providing an additional restraining force for all the existing nuclear nations. In particular, uncertainty over the possible reaction of the new nuclear nation may restrain the existing nuclear nations, more than offsetting the presence of an additional potential initiator and an additional target. Intriligator and Brito conclude that eventually, with a large number of nuclear nations, the probability of nuclear war among them may be reduced to virtually zero, since any one nuclear nation would fear the response of the other nuclear nations to its initiating a nuclear war.

Some authors tend even to confirm this hypothesis by pointing to specific regional contexts, such as the Middle East. In his study on a nuclear Middle East, Jabber (1979: 92) suggests as a very probable 1990 development of the current Middle Eastern situation in the nuclear realm a deployed Israeli nuclear force with a minimum of 30 to 40 devices of various kiloton yields and likewise an Arab nuclear force of 10 to 15 devices in the 20-kiloton range, deployed in Egypt, Syria, and Iraq. The main Israeli objective would be to deter an Arab resort to large-scale conventional war through the threat of escalation; the Arab purpose would be to deter an Israeli disarming first strike. According to Jabber, after an initial stage of strongly asymmetric capabilities providing strong incentives for an Israeli preventive strike— which in all probability would be prevented by a host of political considerations — the Arab-Israeli nuclear balance would become basically stable. The stability would grow out of the recognition that unacceptable damage could be inflicted on either side by even a minimal countervalue retaliation of one or two 20-kiloton bursts. Rather than a race to get in the first punch, we are likely to see in crisis situations a prudent crawl up the ladder of escalation to its highest rungs (Jabber 1979: 93).

In sum, there are many arguments which suggest a stabilizing effect of nuclear proliferation. Nevertheless, one can hardly deny that the existence of many nuclear

Powers will lead to considerable uncertainty and hence make crises less calculable (Weltman 1982:188). This *may*, in fact, compel Governments to exercise restraint in the use of nuclear weapons as a matter of self-interest. Yet the degree of uncertainty is increasing rapidly; growing caution may only be one possible reaction by Governments faced with acute crisis situations; a decisive offensive move may be another conceivable reaction to cope with uncertainty. While there seems little reason to conclude that a world in which 20 or 30 countries possessed nuclear weapons would inevitably produce a nuclear holocaust, the threat of use of nuclear weapons would be more common. Uncertainty about commitments could lead to a sequence of actions and reactions which might culminate in a large-scale use of nuclear weapons (Wohlstetter *et al.* 1978:133f.).

The Risk of Catalytic Nuclear War

Still the question remains, what would be the chance that such a "local" nuclear accident or war might ignite a general nuclear war, i.e. getting the two major nuclear Powers and possible other nuclear Powers as well involved. There is no simple answer to that question. According to Calder (1979:79), if Brazil and Argentina were to fight a nuclear war, "the Soviet and American leaders might quickly agree to let the fire burn itself out". But in a nuclear war in the Middle East, the two major powers, due to their prior commitments and naval deployments, might relatively easily be dragged in.

At any rate, one has to be aware that the possible involvement of super-Powers would work out differently in different regions. This fact augments the degree of uncertainty regarding this type of risk. Yet generally it might be premature to assume the worst case, i.e. a more or less automatic and blind spread of a local nuclear war into global dimensions. Evron (1982) confidently thinks that in case of a regional war escalating into a nuclear conflagration, the two major Powers would either try to disengage themselves as swiftly as possible or reimpose their control over the area in order to preclude or suppress the use of nuclear weapons by their clients.

The situation may be different if, assuming a widespread deployment of nuclear weapons in a multitude of countries, nuclear strikes are executed without clear identification (at least not in the initial phase) of the author State. Unidentified attacks may cause the victim to react on the basis of erroneous perceptions about the attacker. As Beres (1980:87) points out, the response by the attacked power may be directed against the wrong Power, which is suspected but has actually done nothing to precipitate nuclear war. In a world of many nuclear powers, where unidentified nuclear attacks are feasible, the deterrence provided by the possession of nuclear weapons could no longer be considered credible and "the victim state might lash out blindly, thus triggering a worldwide nuclear war" (Beres 1980:87).

172

Perhaps these conclusions are premature. In a simulation analysis of such unidentified attacks, Hermann, Hermann and Cantor (1974) found out that the ambiguity as to who is the attacker increased the likelihood of a delayed as opposed to an immediate response. As a comparable real-life case in point, the (Israeli) attack on the USS "Liberty" at the outbreak of the Middle East war of 1967 is cited (Hermann, Hermann and Cantor 1974: 87—88); in this case, the ambiguity had the effect of a delay until evidence was gathered that the ship had not been attacked by forces considered hostile to the United States.

When reviewing the abundant literature on the subject of the effect of nuclear proliferation on the risk of unintentional nuclear war one cannot fail to be quite perplexed by the amount of disagreement existing between experts. While on the one side the view is expressed that proliferation is one of the paths leading straight to global nuclear disaster, other experts conclude that with more nuclear states the world will have a more promising future, as provocatively indicated in the title of Waltz' (1981) study: "More May Be Better".

One would hardly do justice to the experts if one tried to explain their disagreements in terms of differing vested interests. Both conclusions have been reached by scholars who have all the credentials for being independent, objective researchers. Also, the distinction between "optimists" and "pessimists" is not admissible. The experts do not simply disagree about the extent of the danger inherent to specific developments. What they disagree about is, rather, the nature of the hypothetical developments themselves. They argue about what effects are to be expected from a specific case.

As has been noted previously, this feature of the discussion is very typical of the entire style of the debate about the risk of unintentional nuclear war. Fortunately, no practical experience is available in this field. However, this state of affairs gravely affects the quality of the reasoning about this subject by leaving monumental gaps of knowledge which have to be filled by speculation. Yet, as this speculation pertains to deadly risks, it would certainly be unwise to dismiss the more "pessimistic" conclusions out of hand. Dangers which are conceivable in principle are also possible in practice.

B. Nuclear Weapons Acquired by Extra-Governmental Groups

Among the worries plaguing people concerned about the dissemination of nuclear weapons and the staggering growth in the number of nuclear warheads, an important place is occupied by the possibility of fanatical non-governmental groups (extremists, insurgents, dissidents, disaffected groups, revolutionaries, terrorists) gaining access to nuclear weapons by theft, hijacking or sophisticated attacks on installations and means of transportation (MITRE 1975; Schelling 1976: 84—86; Epstein 1976: ch.19;

173

Leitenberg 1978: 40—49; Rosenbaum 1977). It is quite obvious that the opportunities for such acts increase as nuclear proliferation progresses (Intriligator/Brito 1981). Some countries which are candidates for becoming nuclear Powers may even be more vulnerable to nuclear terrorism than the traditional nuclear Powers. Also, one should not forget that the terms "deterrence" and "terrorism" have the same etymological root (Sonntag 1981: 110).

Generally speaking, there are few ways to obtain nuclear weapons suited for terrorist assaults, stealing or seizing a weapon or stealing fissionable material and then either dispersing it or trying to build a crude nuclear bomb. Nuclear bombs have been designed on the basis of unclassified material by people otherwise not involved with nuclear weapons (Epstein 1979: 114; Beres 1980: 103).

Albertini (1981: 52) describes transportation of nuclear weapons in Hawaii and complains that nuclear weapons are not adequately protected during transport (lack of armour and entry-denial devices, lack of aerial reconnaissance and surveillance, inadequate *en route* communications system). Another event confirming fears of unauthorized access to nuclear weapons is the incident in which a newspaper correspondent gained access to a SAC B-52 base by pretending to be a fencing contractor (see Albertini 1981: 53; Dumas 1980: 19—20).

The proliferation of nuclear weapons and also of civil nuclear technology may of course increase the danger of nuclear devices being used by terrorist groups. Epstein (1979: 112) argues that the weapons of additional nuclear Powers will probably be small and less well protected than those of the major Powers. Calder even envisages the possibility that nuclear weapons might be misused by subgroups within the armed forces: "The terrorists who seize the nuclear weapons may be the military officers appointed to guard them" (Calder 1980: 76).

Another potential risk is the possibility that one side in a civil war will fire a nuclear warhead at its opponent's strongholds. However, one might agree with Waltz who asserts that such a situation — which certainly cannot be said to be unlikely — "would produce a national tragedy, not an international one" (Waltz 1981: 11). It is difficult to see how domestic use in an unstable country might catalyse a nuclear world war. The two major nuclear Powers would very probably react in the same way as assumed in the preceding section (VII B) — i.e., either "let the nuclear fire burn itself out" or trying to gain control of the events. Still, in the worst case, it is conceivable that, in a situation in which two regional opponents possess nuclear weapons, a terrorist group might launch an unidentified "anonymous" attack with a stolen warhead, thus provoking one of the regional nuclear Powers to retaliate against its opponent on the false assumption that it was responsible for the unidentified attack.

Appalling as the prospects of nuclear terrorism are, in the context of the present study some doubts regarding its effects on the risk of unintentional war may still be appropriate. Terrorists may wish to exploit nuclear weapons primarily for the purpose of blackmailing. At worst, they may be willing to "honour" their commitment and in a nihilistic, suicidal Doomsday catastrophe drag millions of people into death. Given the specific psychic structure of fanatical terrorists (Dror 1974; Sonntag 1981: 110—112) this seems by no means unlikely. It would certainly amount to a national tragedy, but one is nevertheless inclined to agree with Rosenbaum (1977: 151) who concludes that "this sort of use is not likely to cause the sort of eschatological catastrophe characteristic of nuclear war between superpowers". This does not of course mean that the dangers emerging from nuclear terrorism can be in any way neglected; yet it does mean that its relevance for the problem of unintentional war is rather marginal.

Conclusions: The Effects of Nuclear Proliferation on the Risk of Unintentional Nuclear War

The risks:

1. *Nuclear proliferation contributes to the risk of "maverick" leaders gaining access to nuclear weapons and using them in an irresponsible way.*
2. *In countries newly acquiring nuclear weapons, safeguard systems preventing nuclear accidents and incidents may be insufficient or altogether non-existent.*
3. *In regions dominated by a high degree of tension, a Power may be tempted to launch a pre-emptive nuclear strike before its opponent has also gained access to nuclear weapons. For this reason and others, the initial phase of regional nuclear arms races are prone to strategic instability.*
4. *A local nuclear war may drag in the two major nuclear Powers or at least create unpredictably dangerous situations.*
5. *Unidentified nuclear strikes against a major nuclear Power may be misinterpreted and lead to a punitive strike against the wrong opponent.*
6. *Groups outside governmental control, including terrorists and criminals, may acquire access to nuclear weapons.*

Mitigating factors:

1. *The possession of nuclear weapons generally leads Governments to behave with enhanced caution and circumspection.*
2. *There are no convincing reasons to assume that in case of a local nuclear war the major Powers would fail to react with great care and try to limit the nuclear exchange, unless they had made irrevocable and firm commitments (nuclear guarantees).*

175

3. The possession of nuclear weapons by groups outside governmental control is aimed at blackmailing rather than actually using the arms; if they are used, this would amount to a national tragedy but would not necessarily entail escalation into an international nuclear war.

Risk assessment :

While nuclear proliferation may increase the risks of local or regional nuclear conflagration, it is highly unlikely that this type of nuclear war would be capable of triggering an all-out nuclear war involving the two major nuclear Powers. The possession of nuclear weapons by non-governmental groups may lead to national catastrophes but not to international ones.

VIII. EXISTING AGREEMENTS TO COUNTER THE RISK OF UNINTENTIONAL NUCLEAR WAR

Arms Control as a Stabilizing Factor

Arms control negotiations and agreements serve several aims (Holst 1982); yet the principal purpose the negotiating parties always had in mind quite evidently referred to the prevention of unintentional nuclear war. Right from the beginning of the nuclear age it was felt that, for instance, increased levels of strategic intelligence could reduce the risk of pre-emptive attacks as a consequence of miscalculation or misperception; this was the rationale for President Eisenhower's 1955 "Open Skies" proposal for reciprocal Soviet-United States aerial surveillance (Miller 1981: 137). Other efforts were directed towards limiting weapons of one kind or another.

However, a general evaluation of the arms control measures agreed upon so far tends to lead to rather gloomy conclusions. "The meagre 'partial' arms control measures have been futile, ineffective and outside the main thrust of great Power military efforts", Leitenberg (1978a: 20) writes. Other judgements sound even more radical. For instance, Epstein (1976: 36) alleges that agreements already concluded are designed "not to halt or reverse the arms race but rather to institutionalize it and regulate it so that it may continue within each country on its own momentum and under conditions of relatively less instability and insecurity for the two great powers — in other words, a blueprint for the continuation of the arms race under agreed-upon terms and conditions". This view is shared by George F. Kennan, who said that arms control negotiations "are not a way of escape from the weapons race; they are an integral part of it" (Kennan 1981: 9). United States Secretary of Defense Caspar W. Weinberger calls the history of arms control "a melancholy chapter" (DoD Annual Report, FY 1983: I—19). Scepticism is also expressed by Soviet specialists.

More specific reservations expressed about arms control point to the divergent impact which the agreements achieved so far have had on the quantitative and qualitative aspects of the arms race (Brito and Intriligator 1981). While the agreements, in many cases, resulted in quantitative limitations, they tended to accelerate the qualitative arms race and ultimately led to the introduction of new and potentially destabilizing weapons systems. Thus, they did nothing to improve the security of the States concerned.

Furthermore, arms control negotiations have also given rise to the problem of "bargaining chips" (Sharp 1981): weapons are developed with the intention of trading them off or deploying them in case an agreement prohibiting their deployment cannot be attained. The very idea of "bargaining chips" will add momentum to the technological arms race by creating incentives for the development of weapons without there being any genuine need for them.

It is hard to deny the pertinence of this criticism and others, even more so if one evaluates arms control by employing the standards of true disarmament which, in the long run, can only be general and complete disarmament (GCD). The lasting answer to the problems discussed in this study is GCD and anything short of this objective must be said to be clearly insufficient. Yet in the absence of any encouraging prospects of reaching GCD and under the conditions of the ongoing arms race, one cannot avoid dealing seriously with the efforts so far undertaken in the field of arms control.

In this chapter, the principal agreements and treaties will be briefly presented and their contribution to mitigating the risk of unintentional nuclear war will be assessed. More particularly, the question has to be asked whether these agreements and treaties are capable of (1) reducing the probability of war by stabilizing the strategic balance and by precluding situations that might generate incentives for pre-emption; (2) reducing the destructiveness and collateral damage of war in the event that peace cannot be preserved, and (3) reducing the enormous costs caused by preparations for war (cf. Garwin 1979: 98; Brodie 1976: 18f.). These aims are generally acknowledged by the Powers concerned. In the DoD Annual Report (FY 1982: 27) the United States Secretary of Defense writes:

"Equitable and verifiable international agreements that limit the size and capabilities of military arsenals can enhance our security by reducing the military threat arrayed against us, thus helping to reduce the chances of war. They can contribute to improved East-West relations by stabilizing the most dangerous prospects of that competition. And multilateral arms control agreements, such as the Non-Proliferation Treaty, can help avoid regional developments that could threaten U.S. interests".

Furthermore, Secretary of Defense Brown specifically noted that previous arms control agreements had advanced the United States' national security interests, for example the Limited Test Ban Treaty (LTBT), the Non-Proliferation Treaty (NPT), the Anti-Ballistic Missile (ABM) Treaty, SALT I, and the Outer Space and Seabed agreements (DoD Annual Report, FY 1982: 27).

In very similar fashion Soviet authors also think that in the absence of arms control agreements the strategic situation would be worse or at any rate less stable. They draw attention to the fact that, notwithstanding the sometimes meagre substantive results of the agreements, the arms control negotiations conducted in recent decades are useful because they established close contact between the Powers concerned and thus had a confidence-building effect.

There seems to be a considerable unanimity as far as this aspect of arms control is concerned. Summing up the functions of arms control, Gelb (1979) views arms control negotiations essentially as confidence-building and stability-building measures. According to Gelb the following guidelines deserve to be given attention for the purpose of successfully conducting arms control negotiations:

1. Arms control proposals and expectations should not move too far ahead of the overall state of United States—Soviet relations. Otherwise arms control will suffer from a deterioration in the climate between the major Powers, as arms control cannot be separated from the geopolitical environment and more general political considerations.

2. Arms restraint talks should be fashioned to move in small steps to do what can be done and to reach agreements expeditiously. Small steps will be easier to take, as each step entails less risk. Moreover, the hazards of deterioration in the relations between the participants, leading to delay, suspension of talks or non-ratification of agreements, may be avoided.

3. Arms control negotiations between the major Powers should focus more on tangible ways of maintaining stability and preventing destabilizing surprises than on reduction *per se*. These suggestions by Gelb emphasize that reducing the probability of war should have precedence over reducing the damage if war is to happen. Nodoby would argue that stabilization is an absolute necessity; however, the nuclear weapons stockpiles of the major Powers are such as to warrant some efforts towards their reduction, particularly in view not only of the bilateral United States—Soviet relationship but of the entire world environment.

4. Arms control negotiations should aim more at balancing asymmetries than at any formalistic equality in rights and numbers (Gelb 1979: 26). While compliance with this guideline would undoubtedly be most beneficial for arms control purposes, the existing armaments postures and interests of the negotiating Governments have to be taken into account. It is not only the facts and numbers which count, but also the perception of the opponent — and that of the whole world community. Thus, the mere appearance of having given more than the negotiating partner is apt to be politically intolerable.

There are two main groups of arms-control agreements: agreements open to accession by all States, and bilateral agreements or agreements with a limited membership. In the first group, the following are relevant for the prevention of unintentional nuclear war:

Antarctic Treaty	(1959)*
Limited Test Ban Treaty (LTBT)	(1963)
Outer Space Treaty	(1967)
Treaty of Tlatelolco	(1967)
Nuclear Non-Proliferation Treaty (NPT)	(1968)
Seabed Treaty	(1971)
Confidence-Building Measures of the CSCE Final Act	(1975)

In the other group, a number of bilateral agreements, mostly between the Soviet Union and the United States, have a bearing on problems discussed in this study. Some agreements are specifically designed to mitigate the threat of unintentional nuclear war. The following agreements will be presented in this chapter:

Hot Line Agreement	(1963)
Agreement to Reduce the Risk of Nuclear War	(1971)
Agreement on the Prevention of Incidents on the High Seas	(1972)
Basic Principles	(1972)
SALT I (Interim Agreement)	(1972)
ABM Treaty	(1972)
Prevention of Nuclear War Agreement	(1973)
SALT II	(1979)

Some treaties concluded between France and the Soviet Union and the United Kingdom and the Soviet Union supplement this group. A crucial question as far as the multilateral treaties are concerned is how many and which countries are signatories to the treaty in question. In some cases, the very States considered most crucially important have not acceded to the treaty (for example the NPT), thus decisively weakening its effect.

The Antarctic Treaty

The Antarctic Treaty was signed in 1959 and entered into force in 1961. It states that Antarctica shall be used for peaceful purposes only. Any measures of a military nature, such as the establishment of military bases and fortifications, the carrying out of military manoeuvres and the testing of weapons, are prohibited by the treaty. However, the use of military personnel or equipment for scientific research or for other peaceful purposes is allowed. Besides regulating the scientific activities to be carried out in Antarctica and calling for the exchange of information regarding scientific programmes, observations and results, and of scientific person-

---

* The dates refer to the year when the treaty was signed.

nel, the Treaty prohibits any nuclear explosions in Antarctica and the disposal there of radioactive waste material. Antarctica is defined as the area south of 60° Southern Latitude.

In order to ensure compliance with the provisions of the Treaty, each party has the right to designate observers to carry out inspections. Each observer has complete freedom of access at any time to all areas of Antarctica, including all stations, installations and equipment within those areas, and all ships and aircraft at points of discharging or embarking cargoes or personnel in Antarctica, which shall be open at all times to inspection by any observers designated by the contracting parties. The observers shall be nationals of the contracting parties which designate them, and their names have to be communicated to every other contracting party at the beginning and the termination of their appointment. The observers are subject only to the jurisdiction of the contracting party of which they are nationals in respect of all acts or omissions occurring while they are in Antarctica for the purpose of exercising their functions. (For the text of the Antarctic Treaty, see Treaty Series vol. 402: 71–102).

The Treaty had been signed by 21 States, as at 31 December 1979 (United States Arms Control and Disarmament Agency 1980: 83–91). Goldblat (1978: 5) describes this Treaty as an important preventive measure. It also has a special significance in that it was the first of its kind to be concluded after the Second World War. Goldblat mentions that parts of the Antarctic were potentially suitable for nuclear testing or basing; the Antarctic Treaty precluded such use.

More generally, however, one would conclude that this agreement was comparatively easy to reach, as the military usefulness of the Antarctic was probably not considered to be particularly important at the time it was negotiated.

With respect to the danger of unintentional nuclear war, it seems desirable to have as many and as extended nuclear-weapon-free zones as possible, to limit potentially destabilizing developments not only technologically, but also geographically (Frei 1973).

The Limited Test Ban Treaty / Threshold Test Ban Treaty / Peaceful Nuclear Explosions Treaty

In 1963, the Governments of the United States, the Soviet Union and the United Kingdom agreed to ban nuclear weapon tests in the atmosphere, in outer space and under water. The Treaty is widely known under the name "Limited Test Ban Treaty" (LTBT). According to this Treaty, the parties to the Treaty are obliged to prohibit, to prevent and not to carry out any nuclear weapon test explosion, or any other nuclear explosion, at any place under their jurisdiction or control "in the atmosphere; beyond its limits, including outer space; or under water, including territorial waters or high seas", or in any other environment if such explosion causes radioactive debris affecting areas outside the territorial limits of the participant State. Moreover, each signatory undertakes to refrain from causing, encouraging, or in any way participating in any nuclear explosion in the environments described.

The Treaty is of unlimited duration. However, each party

> "shall in exercising its national sovereignty have the right to withdraw from the Treaty if it decides that extraordinary events, related to the subject matter of this Treaty, have jeopardized the supreme interests of its country".

Three months' notice of such withdrawal is required. The LTBT is open to all States for signature. Most States are parties to it or have signed it. Conspicuous among the States which have not acceded to it are the People's Republic of China and France. (For the text of the Treaty, see Treaty Series vol. 480: 43—99; for its present status, see ACDA 1979, Arms Control 1979: 83—92.)

The Treaty between the United States and the Soviet Union on the Limitation of Underground Nuclear Weapons Tests, from 1974, commonly known as the Threshold Test Ban Treaty (TTBT), further limited nuclear test explosions. Basically, it prohibited underground nuclear weapon tests having a yield exceeding 150 kilotons from 31 March 1976 on. The parties agreed to limit the number of their underground nuclear weapon tests to a minimum and to continue negotiations towards the cessation of all underground nuclear weapon tests.

The parties rely on national technical means for verifying compliance with the provisions of the treaty; the national technical means must not be interfered with. To promote the objectives of the treaty the parties agreed to consult with each other, make inquiries and furnish information in response to inquiries.

The TTBT concerns only underground nuclear explosions carried out for military purposes. Underground nuclear explosions carried out for peaceful purposes should be governed by an agreement to be negotiated later (the Treaty on the Limitation of Underground Nuclear Explosions for Peaceful Purposes).

The duration of the TTBT was for five years. It was agreed that it should be extended unless either party notified the other of its termination no later than six months prior to the expiration of the Treaty. Each party was allowed to withdraw from the Treaty if it decided that extraordinary events related to the TTBT had jeopardized its supreme interests, but only by notification six months prior to withdrawal. (For the text of the TTBT, see Barton and Weiler 1976: 358—359.) The TTBT has not yet been officially implemented; however, the two parties are understood to observe the limitations stated in the Treaty.

In 1976, the Treaty between the United States and the USSR on Underground Nuclear Explosions for Peaceful Purposes was signed. The Treaty, known as the Peaceful Nuclear Explosions Treaty (PNET), sought to assure that underground nuclear explosions for peaceful purposes would not be used for military purposes.

Each party reserved the right to carry out explosions at any place under its jurisdiction or control outside the geographical boundaries of test sites specified and to participate in carrying out explosions in the territory of another State at the request of such other State.

The Treaty prohibits the carrying out of any individual explosion having a yield of more than 150 kilotons, any group explosion (two or more individual explosions for which the time interval between successive individual explosions does not exceed five seconds and for which the emplacement points of all explosives can be interconnected by straight line segments, each of which joins two emplacement points and each of which does not exceed 40 km) having an aggregate yield exceeding 150 kilotons except in ways that permit the identification of the individual explosions and the assessment of the yield of the individual explosions. Nuclear explosions having an aggregate yield exceeding one and one-half megatons are generally prohibited.

For the purpose of providing assurance of compliance with the provisions of the Treaty, national technical means of verification are to be used. They must not be interfered with. Moreover, information and access to sites of explosions has to be provided. A Joint Consultative Commission is proposed by the Treaty; it should furnish information in response to inquiries to assure confidence in compliance, and consider ambiguous situations and questions involving unintended interference with the means of verification. Changes in technology relevant to the Treaty and possible amendments to it would also be considered by the Commission. The two parties pledge not to carry out any explosion in the territory of a State not agreeing with the implementation of the international observation and procedures contemplated by the Non-Proliferation Treaty. The PNET was concluded for a duration of five years, to be extended for successive five-year periods unless either party notifies the other of its expiration at least six months prior to its expiration. The termination of the TTBT would allow each party to withdraw from the PNET.

A lengthy Protocol is an integral part of the PNET. It states, *inter alia*, that the party carrying out a nuclear explosion shall inform the other party of the purpose of the explosion, the location (expressed in geographical co-ordinates, with a precision of four or less kilometres), the planned date and the yield of the explosion, as well as the type of rock in which the explosion would be carried out, the degree of its liquid saturation and the technological features of the project. This information is to be given 90 days before the beginning of the emplacement of the explosives in case of an aggregate yield not exceeding 100 kilotons, and 180 days before beginning of emplacement if the explosion is to exceed an aggregate yield of 100 kilotons. Not later than 60 days before the beginning of the emplacement of the explosives, more specific information has to be provided, including the number of explosives, the planned yield of each explosive, the location of each explosive. This is the case if the aggregate yield of the explosions is to exceed 50 kilotons. For explosions exceeding 100 kilotons, more elaborate information has to be given. Nationals of the other party identified to the party carrying out a nuclear explosion have the right of access to the sites of nuclear explosions exceeding 150 kilotons (and in certain cases to sites of nuclear explosions exceeding 100 kilotons).

This designated personnel has the task of confirming the validity of the information provided and examining the circumstances of the explosion (for example, the quality of the rock, the emplacement of each explosive, etc.). Photographs are to be taken by nationals of the State carrying out the nuclear explosion, according to instructions from the designated personnel of the other party (the photographs are to be taken with cameras having built-in rapid development capability, so that the conformity with the requested photographs can be checked; if the designated personnel is not satisfied, additional photographs shall be taken immediately).

Like the TTBT, the PNET did not enter in force. (For the text of the PNET and the Protocol, see United Nations Disarmament Yearbook, vol. 1: 256—270.)

When attempting a general assessment of the measures achieved by this group of treaties (LTBT, TTBT, PNET), emphasis must be laid on the LTBT. This Treaty, however, is generally not judged particularly effective (Hussain 1981: 9). It has not slowed down the rate of innovation of systems. Underground explosions have allowed the development of new technology. The main effect has been to channel development away from very high-yield weapons and to impose some uncertainty as to the effectiveness of such weapons for exo-atmospheric ABM systems or for the destruction of fixed-site missile silos. Myrdal (1976: 95) says that the Treaty was probably never intended as a measure to curtail development of weapons. It had no restrictive effect, not even on the number and yield of tests by those nations which already possessed such weapons. Myrdal thinks that the LTBT hardly deserves being called a disarmament measure; rather, it contributed to public health by banning tests producing fall-out in the atmosphere. The LTBT is also limited in effect because the major nuclear Powers had already performed a great number of tests, while the lesser nuclear Powers are not all parties to the Treaty. Still the United Nations Department of Public Information rates the LTBT as an "important turning-point in the post-war era" (United Nations Department of Public Information 1980: 38—39). The United States Arms Control and Disarmament Agency (1980: 3) also welcomes the LTBT as having helped to deter the spread of nuclear capabilities and to have spared people world-wide harmful effects of large doses of radioactivity in the air and in the oceans.

France, not a party to the LTBT, chose to terminate its atmospheric nuclear testing in 1974, under the pressure of world public opinion and a pending suit in the International Court of Justice (Barton 1981: 108). Moral pressure may present a barrier to the violation of agreements.

The LTBT has prevented the United States and the Soviet Union from conducting nuclear explosions that might have generated empirical data about nuclear weapons effects. Such data might have been useful in resolving technical uncertainties, for example, hardness of vertical and horizontal missile shelters, nuclear effects on aircraft and surface ships or other vehicles. The limits imposed by the LTBT were considered in respect to the development of the MX missile basing modes. The lack of atmospheric nuclear weapons tests, however, is not considered to result in major technical risks (Office of Technology Assessment 1981: 313).

The TTBT faces even more severe criticism than the LTBT or the PNET. Scoville (1978: 10—11) considers these treaties not as important steps towards, perhaps even steps away from, prohibition of nuclear testing. The threshold of the TTBT is considered much too high (150 kilotons); it thus helps very little. It would be technically possible to detect nuclear explosions of very low yield. The setting of the limit at 150 kilotons is — under these circumstances — seen to be caused not by problems of verification but simply by reluctance to limit nuclear tests in any meaningful sense. The PNET also is criticized by Scoville for giving new legitimacy to peaceful nuclear explosions. This could be very insidious, because peaceful nuclear explosions are for all practical purposes indistinguishable from nuclear weapon tests.

The judgement about the TTBT test is nearly unanimous: it is much too high and does not signify any meaningful constraint (Goldblat 1978: 8; United Nations Centre for Disarmament 1977: 90; Myrdal 1976: 209). Myrdal describes the TTBT as a "disgraceful conspiracy between the two superpowers to set a ceiling for permitted nuclear-weapons tests so ludicrously high that it strangles all attempts to reach international agreements on a total ban". In sum, there are few who believe that the TTBT would place any meaningful restraints on nuclear weapons testing. The Treaty would allow the underground explosion of nuclear devices having 10 times the yield of the Hiroshima bomb. The seismic capabilities for detecting nuclear weapons explosions well below this threshold seem to exist, down to a few kilotons (Scoville 1978: 11). The TTBT, if ratified, would reduce the pressure for the Comprehensive Test Ban (CTB); this is why people favouring disarmament measures and a test ban are strongly opposed to the ratification of the TTBT and the PNET. "The two treaties were submitted to the Senate in 1976, but the Senate — in my view wisely — has refrained from ratifying them" (Epstein 1981: 4). Epstein writes that, judging from past experience with other partial treaties, if these two treaties were ratified and implemented the pressures for a CTB treaty within the United States and other nuclear nations would probably erode. It would also encourage the testing of nuclear weapons by other nuclear Powers. The potential value of peaceful nuclear explosions is not considered to be very great (Scoville 1978: 13—14). The use of such explosions for construction of a canal linking oceans does not look very promising as it would produce a great deal of debris, violating the LTBT ."The appeal of peaceful nuclear explosions is apparently waning, but several nations are not yet prepared to forego the option".

The Soviet Union, the United States, and the United Kingdom are holding discussions with a view to arriving at a CTB. The United States Arms Control and Disarmament Agency (1980: 3) noted some progress. The CTB would be "the culmination of international efforts pursued over more than a score of years" and help deter the spread of nuclear weapons to additional countries and restrict the further improvement of nuclear capabilities of the nuclear-weapon Powers.

The discussions have centred on the problem of adequate verification, with the United States placing heavy emphasis on on-site inspection. In the Carter Administration, however, the CTB was one of the most important objectives in the arms control field (United States Arms Control and Disarmament Agency 1980: 22—23), it would strengthen United States security interests by helping to prevent the proliferation of nuclear weapons. It would also show the signatory States of the NPT that the nuclear Powers were willing to accept their share of the burden.

Even a CTB would, however, not preclude some undesirable consequences of weapons testing. The testing of the delivery vehicles is to be considered as very important from an arms control perspective. The most destabilizing developments during the last few years seem to have occurred not in the development of nuclear explosives but in the accuracy of missiles and their RVs. Frye (1977: 18) proposes a missile test limitation treaty in order to diminish threats against ICBM survivability. Such a limitation could include limiting the number of tests to a small annual quota and restricting the tests to missile systems already deployed or firmly scheduled for deployment. Moreover, the tests would have to take place at agreed test ranges with prior notification of launch site, missile type and impact area. Only one missile could be launched during a 24-hour period and the testing of missiles in a depressed-trajectory mode would be prohibited.

Measures limiting the progress in lethality (yield, accuracy, numbers of missiles) are beneficial for stability and thus for mitigating the danger of unintentional nuclear war. It is highly undesirable to allow technological dynamics to shape the strategic environment. Not all technologically feasible refinements of strategic nuclear weapons are desirable. Test limitations and test bans could at least limit destabilizing developments.

The Outer Space Treaty

The Treaty on Principles Governing the Activities of States in the Exploration and Use of Outer Space, Including the Moon and Other Celestial Bodies was signed and ratified in 1967. It has important implications for the arms race and particularly for the deployment of nuclear weapons.

Besides regulating the exploration and use of outer space, the moon and other celestial bodies and providing rules for space flights, the Treaty restricts the military use of outer space:

> "States Parties to the Treaty undertake not to place in orbit around the earth any objects carrying nuclear weapons or any other kinds of weapons of mass destruction, install such weapons on celestial bodies, or station such weapons in outer space in any other manner" (article IV, first paragraph).

The Treaty stipulates that the moon and other celestial bodies are not subject to national appropriation by claim of sovereignty, by means of use or occupation, or by any other means, and shall be used for peaceful purposes only. Thus, the establishment of military bases, installations and fortifications, the testing of any type of weapons and the conduct of military manoeuvres on celestial bodies is prohibited. However, the deployment of military personnel for scientific research or for any other peaceful purposes is allowed, as is the use of any military equipment or facility necessary for peaceful exploration of the moon and other celestial bodies.

All stations, installations, equipment and space vehicles on the moon and other celestial bodies are open for inspection by representatives of other States parties to the Treaty on a basis of reciprocity; reasonable advance notice of a projected visit is required.

The remaining clauses of the Outer Space Treaty deal with questions of jurisdiction and the responsibility of States for their activities. Any State party to the Treaty can withdraw after giving one year's notification in advance. (For the text of the Outer Space Treaty, see Treaty Series vol. 610: 205—301). By 31 December 1979 the Outer Space Treaty had been signed by 110 States (United States Arms Control and Disarmament Agency 1980: 83—91). Among the great Powers, the People's Republic of China has not acceded to this Treaty.

Like the Antarctic Treaty, the Outer Space Treaty concerned an area of only limited military usefulness, at least at the time it was concluded. Technological progress has, however, made possible a range of military applications in space, some of the most prominent being ASAT and BMD. With hindsight, it may appear fortunate that a limitation was placed on the military utilization of outer space before military planners became too interested in the outer space.

However, the Treaty fails to preclude a number of military uses, as is demonstrated by large quantities of satellites launched for military purposes. Jasani (1978: 2) notes that it was believed in 1967 that outer space would, for the foreseeable future, be a "zone of peace" after the ratification of the Outer Space Treaty by the United States and the Soviet Union, as well as by 72 other States, by 1976. But this illusion has been shattered by the revolutionary advances in military space technology in the 1970s and by the realization that this Treaty prohibits only "the placing in orbit of weapons of mass destruction". There are, however, technical obstacles to the deployment of militarily effective nuclear weapons aboard Earth-orbiting platforms. These obstacles include accurate delivery of a nuclear weapon to a fixed point on the Earth and maintenance of adequate command and control over such a platform during a nuclear conflict (Office of Technology Assessment 1981: 312).

The Treaty seems to permit too many military activities, and it has left a wide margin by banning only nuclear weapons and weapons of mass destruction. Thus, under this Treaty, there is no provision against deploying killer satellites or BMD interceptors, even operating with charged-particle beams, provided that they operate without nuclear warheads. Therefore, many authors such as Frye (1977: 20—21) propose the prohibition of development and testing of satellite killers. Other proposals refer to the prohibition of the approach of one country's satellite to another country's satellite without prior notification. Besides suggesting the prohibition of high-energy laser or particle beam tests in outer space, Frye advocates the principle of mutual inspection rights comparable to the one agreed upon in the Antarctic Treaty.

A problem related to this Treaty concerns the fractional orbital missiles (FOBS, Fractional Orbital Bombardment Systems), i.e. nuclear weapons placed in orbit but flying less than one full revolution. These weapons are by definition not subject to this Treaty (Goldblat 1978: 9); however, they are dealt with in the SALT II agreements, where each party is obliged not to develop, test, or deploy systems for placing into earth orbit nuclear weapons, including fractional orbital missiles (Article IX, paragraph c). Another problem to be dealt with in this context is the destabilizing impact of ASAT developments. The United States Arms Control and Disarmament Agency writes that the development of ASAT systems by one side would very likely lead to development of such systems also by the other side. The Soviet Union is claimed to have conducted a series of tests of an ASAT system. This limited ASAT capability is perceived as representing an asymmetry that the United States cannot allow to go unchecked. "We would prefer to eliminate the asymmetry through negotiation; however, in the absence of an effective ASAT agreement, the United States will continue working to improve the survivability of its satellites and to develop an ASAT capability of its own" (United States Arms Control and Disarmament Agency 1980: 38—39). The pledge not to interfere with the national technical means of verification seems to bear some implications for ASAT activities, as this verification is performed to a certain degree by reconnaissance satellites. Interference with the early-warning satellites would constitute an event requiring immediate notification under the 1971 Agreement on Measures to Reduce the Risk of Outbreak of Nuclear War, if such an occurrence were perceived to create a risk of outbreak of nuclear war. At any rate, it now seems imperative to try to achieve a ban on testing or deploying conventional anti-satellite weapons

(Schneider 1981: 15). They may, in fact, be deployed; only their use is prohibited. This state of affairs is highly unsatisfactory because in the very situation where the temptation to use them would be strongest, the limitations of the Treaty might be disregarded. The dangers of ASAT have been recognized, and it was the stated policy of the Carter Administration that the United States sought a negotiated ban on anti-satellite weapons (Karas 1981: 17). The professed aims are: (1) to minimize or eliminate competition in ASAT systems; (2) to help maintain the survivability of satellites; and (3) to enhance stability by banning ASATs that could grant either side an advantage in a crisis or conflict.

Indeed, the Soviet Union and the United States held arms control talks on ASAT between June 1978 and June 1979. However, the United States refused to continue negotiations after the events in Afghanistan changed the political climate in a way not conducive to arms control agreements. So far no new initiative in respect to ASAT limitations has been undertaken. The United States is also conducting R&D work on ASAT, as it notes, to provide a "hedge against failure to achieve an adequate antisatellite agreement, against cheating or sudden-abrogation if an agreement were achieved".

The Treaty of Tlatelolco

The Treaty for the Prohibition of Nuclear Weapons in Latin America, commonly known as the Treaty of Tlatelolco, established a nuclear-weapon-free zone. It entered into force in 1968. Article 1 states:

> "1. The Contracting Parties hereby undertake to use exclusively for peaceful purposes the nuclear material and facilities which are under their jurisdiction, and to prohibit and prevent in their respective territories:
> (a) The testing, use, manufacture, production or acquisition by any means whatsoever of any nuclear weapons, by the Parties themselves, directly or indirectly, on behalf of anyone else or in any other way, and
> (b) The receipt, storage, installation, deployment and any form of possession of any nuclear weapons, directly or indirectly, by the Parties themselves, by anyone on their behalf or in any other way".

Moreover, the parties undertake to refrain from encouraging the testing, use, manufacture, production, possession or control of any nuclear weapon. The zone declared nuclear-weapon-free is described in geographical terms; within this zone the whole of the territories of the signatories to the Treaty are subject to its provisions.

"Nuclear weapon" is defined as any device which is capable of releasing nuclear energy in an uncontrolled manner and which has a group of characteristics that are appropriate for use for warlike purposes. Delivery systems for nuclear weapons are not included if they are separable from the nuclear device.

In order to ensure compliance with the provisions of the Treaty an organization was set up, the Agency for the Prohibition of Nuclear Weapons in Latin America, comprising the following organs: General Conference, Council, and Secretariat with a General Secretary.

Each party undertakes to negotiate multilateral or bilateral agreements with the IAEA for the application of safeguards. Semi-annual reports from the parties to the agencies (both the IAEA and the Latin American Agency created by this Treaty) are required, stating that no activity prohibited under the Treaty has occurred in the respective territories. With the authorization of the Council the General Secretary may request supplementary information regarding any event connected with compliance with the Treaty, explaining his reasons.

Inspections are to be arranged at the request of any party which suspects that some activity prohibited by the Treaty has been carried out or is about to be carried out. The party suspected of prohibited activity can also call for an inspection to be immediately arranged. The inspectors have full and free access to all places and all information which may be necessary for the performance of their duties.

The use of nuclear energy for peaceful purposes is not prejudiced by the Treaty. Nuclear explosions for peaceful purposes, however, require notification stating the nature of the nuclear device, its source, the place and purpose of the planned explosion, the expected force of the device and any possible fall-out from such explosions. Observers from the Agency may observe all preparations and the explosion of the nuclear device.

The General Conference may take note of violations of the Treaty. If the violation might endanger peace and security, the United Nations Security Council, the United Nations General Assembly and the Council of the OAS, in addition to the IAEA, shall be notified.

The Treaty is of unlimited duration. However, if a party regards events connected with the content of this treaty as having jeopardized its supreme interests, it may withdraw, the withdrawal taking effect three months after receipt of the notification.

Two Protocols constitute an integral part of the Treaty of Tlatelolco. The first is open to signature by all extra-continental or continental States having *de jure* or *de facto* international responsibility in the zone of application of the Treaty. It has been signed by France, the Netherlands, the United Kingdom and the United States.

A second Protocol is open to signature by all Powers possessing nuclear weapons. It states that the statute of denuclearization of Latin America will be respected and no use or threat to use nuclear weapons will be made against the States parties to the Treaty. This second Protocol has been signed by the People's Republic of China, France, the United Kingdom, the United States and the Soviet Uni on. As at 31 December 1979, the Treaty of Tlatelolco had been signed by 25 Latin American

States, Cuba und Guyana being conspicuously absent. (For the text of the Treaty and the Protocols, see Treaty Series vol. 634: 281—423; for the status see United States Arms Control and Disarmament Agency 1980: 83—91.)

It would be helpful, according to Beres (1980: 221), to regard the Treaty of Tlatelolco as a model for other regions of the globe. In the absence of respect for NPT commitments, nuclear-weapon-free zones appear to be a promising means of reducing the number of potential opportunities for confrontation entailing the risk of nuclear war.

The United States supports the Treaty of Tlatelolco as a valuable contribution to non-proliferation and as an example worthy of consideration in other regions (United States Arms Control and Disarmament Agency 1980: 26). This view is shared by the Soviet Government, which has put forward concrete proposals for the creation of additional nuclear-weapon-free zones. Some attempts to create "zones of peace" in other continents have not yet been successful. Rivalry between major Powers carried to distant areas appears as an impediment to the creation of more nuclear-weapon-free zones. The Treaty of Tlatelolco also offers countries which would not like to be party to the NPT an opportunity to contribute to nuclear disarmament.

When assessing the merits of this Treaty, one should, however, note that the parts of the Treaty relating to peaceful nuclear explosions seem to weaken the disarmament impact, because such explosions are not readily distinguishable from explosions for military purposes (Goldblat 1978: 11). This constitutes one of the main arguments in favour of a global CTB.

The Non-Proliferation Treaty (NPT)

One of the treaties most relevant to nuclear weapons and the danger of nuclear war is the Treaty on the Non-Proliferation of Nuclear Weapons (NPT) signed in 1968 and implemented in 1970. The NPT, which has been signed by more than 100 States, declares in article I:

> "Each nuclear-weapon State Party to the Treaty undertakes not to transfer to any recipient whatsoever nuclear weapons or other nuclear explosive devices or control over such weapons or explosive devices directly, or indirectly; and not in any way to assist, encourage, or induce any non-nuclear-weapon State to manufacture or otherwise acquire nuclear weapons or other nuclear explosive devices, or control over such weapons or explosive devices".

Similarly, each non-nuclear-weapon State Party pledges not to receive such transfers of nuclear explosive devices or the control thereof; not to manufacture or otherwise acquire nuclear weapons; and not to seek or receive any assistance in the manufacture of nuclear explosive devices.

The non-nuclear-weapon States accept safeguards for the purpose of verification of the fulfilment of their obligations under the Treaty with a view to preventing diversion of nuclear energy from peaceful uses to nuclear weapons or other nuclear explosive devices. The safeguards are to be applied on all source or special fissionable material in all peaceful nuclear activities within the territory of the State or carried out under its control anywhere.

The States parties to the Treaty undertake not to provide fissionable material or equipment designed for processing, use or production of fissionable material to any non-nuclear-weapon State for peaceful purposes, unless the material is subject to the safeguards required by the Treaty. The parties to the Treaty have the right to develop research, production and use of nuclear energy for peaceful purposes without discrimination. The exchange of equipment, materials and information for the peaceful uses of nuclear energy shall be facilitated. Potential benefits from peaceful applications of nuclear explosions are to be made available to non-nuclear-weapon States Party to the Treaty on a non-discriminatory basis. In article VI the parties agreed as follows:

> "Each of the Parties to the Treaty undertakes to pursue negotiations in good faith on effective measures relating to cessation of the nuclear arms race at an early date and to nuclear disarmament, and on a treaty on general and complete disarmament under strict and effective international control".

Amendments to the NPT require approval by a majority of the votes of all Parties, including the votes of all nuclear-weapon States Party to the Treaty and all other parties which are members of the Board of Governors of the IAEA at the date the amendment is circulated. Provision is made for the Treaty to be reviewed at five-year intervals, at the request of a majority of the parties to the Treaty. In 1995, a conference is to be convened to decide whether the Treaty shall continue in force indefinitely, or shall be extended for a fixed period.

Withdrawal from the Non-Proliferation Treaty is regulated in article X:

> "Each Party shall in exercising its national sovereignty have the right to withdraw from the Treaty if it decides that extraordinary events, related to the subject matter of this Treaty, have jeopardized the supreme interests of its country".

Notice of such withdrawal must be given to the States party to the Treaty and to the United Nations Security Council three months in advance. The notice has to include a statement of the extraordinary events leading to the withdrawal. (For the text of the Non-Proliferation Treaty, see Treaty Series vol. 729: 161—299). The safeguards postulated by the Treaty were later set down by the IAEA, including inspection and accounting controls.

Some notable absentees from the signatories of the NPT are Argentina, Brazil, the People's Republic of China, India, Israel, Pakistan, Saudi Arabia, Spain, and South Africa (status as at 31 December 1979; see United States Arms Control and

Disarmament Agency 1980: 83—91). These countries are known to be nearing the capability to develop nuclear weapons (Stanley Foundation 1981: 22).

The NPT has come in for severe criticism. Brodie (1976: 22) considers the NPT to have some grave shortcomings. First of all, not all relevant States had signed the NPT. Moreover, the Treaty "has more than its share of legal escape hatches, quite apart from the fact that it is more than usually subject to evasion or violation". Brodie's view is that the Treaty is not worthless, but not worth very much either.

The focal point of criticism, however, is the unequal sharing of the burden of non-proliferation between the non-nuclear-weapon States and the nuclear-weapon States. Myrdal (1976: 169—173) argues that the NPT was not tailored to convince the nations at which it was aimed, because no concrete give-and-take negotiations were conducted that could lead to firm commitments. As a result, the signatories of the Treaty do not include many important Powers which are considered particularly crucial because they may have the capability to go nuclear within a relatively short time. Myrdal enumerates five shortcomings: there is a one-sidedness in the fact that only the non-nuclear-weapon States have to accept safeguards (preventing the diversion of nuclear energy from peaceful uses to nuclear weapons); the nuclear Powers have failed to give the signatory States the preferential treatment promised regarding information and material aid in the nuclear field; the promised benefits from nuclear explosions conducted for peaceful purposes have not materialized; the promise of security guarantees to non-nuclear-weapon States given by the nuclear Powers was not felicitous. The main bone of contention, however, is the still unfulfilled pledge to cease the arms race. The non-nuclear-weapon States have assumed the main burden of obligation, while the nuclear-weapon States have sacrificed little, if anything (Goldblat 1978: 14). The rights and obligations are considered to be ill-balanced.

Barton (1981: 102) notes that the Treaty is fully intelligible only if viewed as a transitional step. From the perspective of the non-nuclear-weapon States the promise of disarmament given by the nuclear Powers was crucial. The failure to fulfil this obligation is not calculated to satisfy the parties, still less to appeal to States not yet parties to the NPT. The slow rate of progress towards disarmament is strongly criticized by the non-nuclear-weapon States (United Nations Department of Political and Security Council Affairs 1976: 83; United Nations Disarmament Yearbook 1976: 103).

The United States views the NPT as a foundation of its non-proliferation policy (United States Arms Control and Disarmament Agency 1980: 24—26). The United States Government is, however, forced to recognize that there is something like a linkage between the NPT on the one side and SALT II and the CTB on the other side, and that failure to ratify SALT II and complete negotiations on the CTB will be viewed as a major failure by the nuclear-weapon States to live up to their obligations. The Twelfth United Nations Procedures Conference, preparing the United Nations' second special session on disarmament (1981: 9), notes even that the "nuclear Non-Proliferation Treaty (NPT) is in jeopardy".

There are several proposals (Stanley Foundation 1981: 24f.) regarding changes in the most controversial elements of the Treaty. The non-nuclear-weapon States party to the Treaty should be assured an adequate supply of nuclear materials and equipment to meet legitimate energy needs, and this assurance should be contingent upon NPT signatory status. Critics also deplore the fact that, until now,

> "the nuclear weapon countries have actually provided more nuclear technology and materials to nonparty states (e.g. Israel, Egypt, Saudi Arabia, India, Pakistan, Brazil, and Argentina) than to party states. This sort of policy, inspired by classical principles of Realpolitik, subverts the essential underpinnings of the NPT ...". (Beres 1980: 230 f.).

Signatory status should provide preferential treatment in terms of security assistance, materials, equipment, etc. As a corollary to this preferential treatment, the safeguards of the IAEA should be upgraded.

The linkage between nuclear disarmament and the NPT may have the disadvantage of connecting setbacks of strategic disarmament attempts with the nonproliferation issue. Non-proliferation policy seems also to be eroded by the spread of civil nuclear technology. And even States party to the NPT are sometimes suspected, rightly or wrongly, of intending to construct nuclear weapons. At any rate, it seems that the risks of unintentional nuclear war generated by nuclear proliferation are hardly mitigated, let alone removed, by the NPT.

The Seabed Treaty

The Treaty on the Prohibition of the Emplacement of Nuclear Weapons and Other Weapons of Mass Destruction on the Seabed and the Ocean Floor and in the Subsoil Thereof (Seabed Treaty) was signed in 1971 and entered into force in 1972. The Treaty aims to prevent a nuclear arms race on the seabed, as expressed in article 1:

> "The States Parties to this Treaty undertake not to emplant or emplace on the seabed and the ocean floor and in the subsoil thereof beyond the outer limit of a seabed zone (...) any nuclear weapons or any other types of weapons of mass destruction as well as structures, launching installations or any other facilities specifically designed for storing, testing or using such weapons".

Moreover, the parties to the Treaty are obliged not to assist, encourage, or induce any State to carry out such activities. The seabed zone is defined as the 12-mile outer limit of the zone referred to in the Convention on the Territorial Sea and the Contiguous Zone. If doubts about compliance with the provisions of the Treaty

194

should arise, the State having doubts is to notify the other parties to the Treaty. The parties shall co-operate for verification, including inspection of objects, structures and installations. If the doubts cannot be removed, the United Nations Security Council will be notified. The verification of the Treaty provisions, however, shall not interfere with the activities carried out under international law.

A conference to review the Seabed Treaty was fixed for 1977 (five years after the treaty entered into force). Each State can withdraw from the Treaty, having given notice of its intention three months in advance and stated what extraordinary events related to the subject matter of the Treaty it regards as having jeopardized its supreme interests. (For the text of the Seabed Treaty see Goldblat 1978: 90—92.)

As at 31 December 1979, the Seabed Treaty had been signed by about 100 States. The People's Republic of China, Egypt, France and Israel have not acceded to it.

The Seabed Treaty is subjected to criticism similar to that directed against the Outer Space Treaty. Both treaties relate to areas considered — at the time of signature — to be of little military value. As far as outer space is concerned, the picture has changed, but the Seabed Treaty does not seem to be of great concern to the military planners of the major nuclear Powers. This may be due to the fact that ,'what the Seabed Treaty is supposed to prevent has never been of military interest" (Myrdal 1976: 100). As far as nuclear weapons and their delivery systems are concerned, it is not the seabed, but the surface and the subsurface that are relevant. Furthermore, the Treaty prohibits only the emplacement of nuclear weapons and any other types of weapons of mass destruction, while allowing other installations of military utility. The emplacement of missile launchers on the seabed is considered unattractive, particularly if they were to be fixed. Temporary stationing of SSBNs on the ocean floor is not covered by the Treaty. Finally it should be borne in mind that one of the ocean zones that is most highly prized from the military standpoint — the 12-mile zone along the coasts — is not covered by the Treaty.

As far as the risk of unintentional nuclear war is concerned, the impact of seabed militarization on strategic stability is rather uncertain. On the one hand, the emplacement of nuclear weapons on the seabed would be destabilizing, as warning time could be very short due to forward deployment. The accuracy would be excellent in case of fixed silos. This would result in high vulnerability of the land-based nuclear force components. In addition, such measures would call for countermeasures, thus opening up one more area of confrontation. Nevertheless, seabed basing may be interesting.

The Office of Technology Assessment of the United States Congress (1981: 312—313) evaluated the consequences of the Seabed Treaty for potential MX basing modes. The Treaty would, in effect, preclude the basing of a nuclear missile on the seabed floor, but "it does not appear that the Seabed Arms Control Treaty prohibits the deployment of the MX missile in any attractive basing mode". Mobile

195

platforms crawling on the seabed floor may offer a solution. However, preliminary studies on this subject led to the conclusion that these platforms would be detectable with underwater remote-sensing equipment and could not escape fast enough in case of attack. The ocean would provide protection against some nuclear weapon effects, but the crawlers would nevertheless remain vulnerable. Fixed silos dug into the seabed floor would be similarly vulnerable. Moreover, such deployment would be expensive and extremely difficult.

The SALT II Treaty prohibits the development, testing and deployment of fixed ballistic or cruise missile launchers for emplacement on the ocean floor, on the seabed, or on the beds of internal waters and inland waters, or in the subsoil thereof, or mobile launchers of such missiles, which move only in contact with the ocean floor, the seabed, or the beds of internal waters and inland waters (article IX, paragraph b). Thus, ratification of the SALT II Treaty would foster the objectives of the Seabed Treaty.

Confidence-Building Measures

The Final Act of the Conference on Security and Co-operation in Europe (CSCE), signed in 1975, also contains some elements relevant for the issue of preventing an unintentional nuclear war. In section 2 of the "first basket", concerning questions related to security, the 35 European States and the United States and Canada agreed on a Document on Confidence-Building Measures and Certain Aspects of Security and Disarmament. According to this document, the signatories are obliged to give prior notification of major military manoeuvres ("major manoeuvres" being defined as exercises involving more than 25,000 troops). In addition and on a voluntary basis, they may also announce smaller military manoeuvres and major military movements. Another discretionary provision refers to arrangements for observers from other States to attend military manoeuvres on a bilateral and reciprocal basis. (Alford 1979; Ruhala 1980; Ruhala 1981). The whole complex of measures is pertinently called Confidence Building Measures (CBMs).

Since the adoption of the "Helsinki CBMs" in 1975, negotiations on this matter have been continued at the Belgrade (1977—1978) and Madrid (1980—1982) meetings of the CSCE with a view to their possible future improvement. The main questions refer to the temporary effects of the measures and to the extent of the restrictions. Among the suggestions put forward are measures such as:

> Increasing the information content of prior notification of military manoeuvres;
> Drafting a code of conduct for observer activities at military manoeuvres;
> Lowering the ceiling of troops participating in military manoeuvres which are subject to prior notification;

Extending the period of notification in advance of the beginning of the manoeuvres;

Making notification concerning troop movements with the same level of commitment as regards notification of military manoeuvres;

Exchanging annual training calendars (cf. 37th Pugwash Symposium 1981).

Other proposals concern manoeuvre restrictions and other restraints and application of CBMs to nuclear weaponry. It is also conceivable to work out subregional measures whereby two or three neighbouring countries, on a voluntary basis, would agree on a system of prior notification of military manoeuvres and troop movements more extensive than the ones applied between all CSCE countries (Vetschera 1977; Brayton 1980; IPRA 1980; Pugwash Symposium 1981).

Although the significance of the CBM concept may seem quite marginal, it cannot be denied also to have some relevance for the task of preventing unintentional nuclear war. Generally speaking, the CBMs can be said to contribute to openness and predictability, at least with regard to the limited military options they concern. CBMs therefore reduce the likelihood of a surprise attack by providing early warning indicators of possible adversary preparations of aggression (Brayton 1980). In other words, they remove uncertainty and contribute to building up confidence by providing decision-makers with the subjective feeling that certain elements in the adversary relationship become less incalculable. As Alford aptly comments, "it is important for A to convince B that the genuinely innocent act *is* really innocent" (Alford 1979: 91; cf. also Karkoska 1977; Buch 1977; Klein 1980).

It must be noted, however, that CBMs so far agreed upon refer to a regional context only and practically exclude the domain of nuclear weaponry. In particular, they do not affect in any way whatsoever the central balance of deterrence. Their scope is limited to conventional armaments and manoeuvres concerning conventional warfare in Europe — and what they touch upon is actually restricted to a rather small segment in the field of conventional armaments and warfare. Thus, one might be inclined to agree with the many critics who maintain that the existing CBMs are of a symbolic nature only and highly superficial.

Yet, before any final judgement is made, it should be borne in mind that CBMs, despite their intrinsic insignificance, offer two advantages which deserve to be mentioned in addition to their impact on openness: firstly, the signatories of the CSCE for the first time agreed, on a reciprocal basis, to reduce the secrecy used to envelop all military matters and thus constantly fuelled mutual distrust. Secondly, by their very symbolic nature, CBMs may also have a political effect, contributing to an atmosphere of mutual understanding. They may thus support policies aimed at a graduated and reciprocal tension reduction without interfering with the ideological differences which exist between the parties concerned. Piecemeal step-by-step progress helps to produce a feeling of mutual reliability (Frei 1980: 20f.).

The "Hot Line" Agreement

The series of purely bilateral agreements between the two major nuclear Powers was initiated in 1963 by the United States—USSR Memorandum of Understanding regarding the Establishment of a Direct Communication Link, sometimes called the "Hot Line Agreement". It was a direct consequence of the Cuban missile crisis, when it was generally felt that the means of communication were rather slow and not adequate to the great urgency and high stakes involved.

The Memorandum stated that the Governments of the United States and of the Soviet Union agreed to establish "as soon as technically feasible" a direct communications link between the two Governments. Each Government would take the steps necessary for continuous functioning of the link and the prompt delivery of received messages to the head of Government (Barton and Weiler 1976: 330). The direct communications link consisted of two telegraph-teleprinter terminals between which communications were to be exchanged directly. The terminals included four sets of telegraph equipment, furnished from the USSR to the United States and vice versa. Messages from Moscow to Washington are transmitted in Russian, those from Washington to Moscow in English. Two telegraph circuits were part of the direct communications link, one duplex wire telegraph circuit and one duplex radiotelegraph circuit. In case the first were interrupted, the second could be used (for the text see Treaty Series vol. 472: 163—172).

In 1971, an agreement to improve the direct communications link was signed (Treaty Series vol. 806: 402 — 476). The reliability of the link was to be increased by several measures: two additional circuits were to be established, using a satellite communications system and a system of terminals to be located in the territory of each party, the locations being determined by the respective side.

The original circuits established by the first Hot Line Agreement were to be maintained until the two parties agreed that it was no longer necessary due to the new circuits based on satellites. The circuits installed on the basis of the 1963 agreement were routed Washington — London — Copenhagen — Stockholm — Helsinki — Moscow (wire), and Washington — Tangier — Moscow (radiotelegraph), whereas the new satellite-based system required only ground stations in the Soviet Union and in the United States and a communications satellite transponder. The messages transmitted via the direct communications link are encoded. The number of terminals is determined by each side; however, only one terminal location is connected to the circuits at any one time (Barton and Weiler 1976: 333—337).

In 1967, the Soviet Union also concluded an agreement on a direct communications link with the United Kingdom (Treaty Series vol. 632: 49—60). The establishment of direct communications links is generally considered as one means of reducing the risk of nuclear war by accident, miscalculation or failure of communication (Ignatieff 1979: 69). During the Middle East war of 1967, United States

President Johnson reportedly notified the Soviet Union via the direct communications link of the dispatching of United States aircraft to the eastern Mediterranean to search for survivors of the sunk U.S.S. Liberty, so that the Soviets would not misinterpret the mission of the aircraft (Caldwell 1979: 41). The use of the "Hot Line" is classified, but according to some reports it was used for the first time in 1967. During the 1973 Middle East war communication between the major Powers was intensive. " ... in contrast to previous crises, American and Soviet leaders communicated with one another quickly, effectively, and secretly throughout the October War" (Caldwell 1979: 42). Secretary of State Kissinger flew to Moscow for face-to-face diplomacy, the communications "shading in fact into consultation" (Bell 1978: 53). To maintain communications with opponents in crisis is very important in order to prevent misunderstandings and miscalculations and clarify ambiguous situations (Neuhold 1978: 9—10; Bell 1978: 53; Hermann 1978: 29—30). The means of communication have to be quick and reliable and to allow for secrecy. Hermann (1978) suggests establishing the communications systems designed for use in crises well in advance, as there may not be sufficient time during a crisis. It might be helpful to use the communications system designed primarily for crises also in periods of "normalcy". However, over-frequent use of a direct communications link such as the "Hot Line" between Moscow and Washington would reduce the effect which the use of special channels may have in a crisis. The fact that a channel will be used only in the most dire emergency will enhance the impact and may increase the credibility of the message transmitted (Jervis 1970: 91). Jervis notes that the direct communications link "is important not only because it allows authenticated messages to be transmitted instantaneously but also because it permits an unprecedented method of signalling during crises". The underlying assumption is that the use of extraordinary channels lends credibility to the message.

The establishment of direct communication links between the nuclear Powers is also beneficial in case of an accidental launch or other action which might be misinterpreted as a provocation. This is even more important in a strategic situation influenced by perceptions of force vulnerability and a felt need for quick reaction.

The Agreement to Reduce the Risk of Nuclear War

The second bilateral agreement concluded by the Soviet Union and the United States is fully concerned with the danger analysed in the present study. In the preamble to the 1971 Agreement on Measures to Reduce the Risk of Outbreak of Nuclear War, the two parties recognize the need "to exert every effort to avert the risk of outbreak of such a war, including measures to guard against accidental or unauthorized use of nuclear weapons". Among the principal provisions are an undertaking by the United States and the Soviet Union to maintain and improve organi-

199

zational and technical arrangements to guard against the accidental or unauthorized use of nuclear weapons under their control. Furthermore, the two parties are to notify each other immediately if accidental, unauthorized or any other unexplained incidents involving possible detonation of nuclear weapons occur. Moreover, the party whose nuclear weapon is involved will make every effort to render it harmless. The two parties also agree to notify each other immediately in the event of detection by missile warning systems of unidentified objects or of signs of interference with these early-warning systems, if such occurrences could create a risk of outbreak of nuclear war. If it is planned to launch a missile beyond the national territory of the involved party and in the direction of the other party, the other party must be notified. In case of unexplained nuclear incidents, each party undertakes to act in such a manner as to "reduce the possibility of its actions being misinterpreted by the other party". If prompt clarification is required or urgent information has to be transmitted, the direct communications link shall be used. The treaty is of unlimited duration (For the text, see Treaty Series vol. 807: 57—66).

Analogous agreements were concluded by the Soviet Union and France in 1976 and the Soviet Union and the United Kingdom in 1977. For obvious reasons, the paragraphs concerning early warning systems against ballistic missile attack and planned missile launches beyond the national territory were not included. In the French-Soviet agreement, the obligation to render harmless nuclear weapons involved in incidents was not included either, but further improvement of the means of communication between Paris and Moscow was envisaged (SIPRI Yearbook 1977: 398—399; Keesing's Contemporary Archives 1977: 28697).

The Agreements to Reduce the Risk of Outbreak of Nuclear War, according to Garthoff (1978c: 19), contribute to reducing the risk of war by accident, miscalculation, or escalation through inadvertence. The United States—Soviet Standing Consultative Commission (SCC) has worked out pre-positioned messages covering various contingencies, to facilitate rapid communication in crises.

The agreements are tailored to meet the problem treated in this study. They undoubtedly constitute an adequate basis for preventing an accident leading to disaster. However, they do not add very much to what one might expect to happen in such a case, even without a formal agreement. They are nevertheless of great value because they express awareness of the problem and imply a commitment by the signatories to make efforts to cope with this problem.

The Agreement on the Prevention of Incidents on the High Seas

In 1972 the United States and the Soviet Union concluded an Agreement on the Prevention of Incidents on and over the High Seas. The Agreement provided for measures to assure the safety of navigation of the ships of the armed forces of the two countries on the high seas and of military aircraft flying over the high seas. Rules of conduct for ships engaged in surveillance, for ships landing and launching aircraft and for aircraft operating near aircraft or ships of the other party were included. Specifically, ships must not simulate attack by pointing missile launchers, torpedoes or guns at ships of the other party which are passing by and not set any objects in motion towards ships passing by. The simulation of attack by aircraft against aircraft or ships is also prohibited by the Agreement. The parties are required to give three to five days notice of actions representing a danger to navigation or to aircraft in flight which are to be taken on or over the high seas, and to exchange information concerning instances of collisions, incidents causing damage or other incidents between the two parties' aircraft and ships on or over the high seas.

The duration of the Agreement was three years, to be extended each time for a further three years unless one party gives notice of its termination at least six months prior to its expiry (For the text see Treaty Series vol. 852: 151—162 , and Siegler 1973: 113—116.)

Garthoff (1978c: 19) rates this Agreement as

> "notably successful in reducing the number of such incidents; without fanfare, it has provided for periodic joint discussions on further measures to enhance its effectiveness".

The Agreement has to be viewed as very important and useful in an age when gunboat diplomacy (or aircraft carrier diplomacy) is a way of signalling intentions. It establishes some rules — not the "rules of the game", but nevertheless rules useful for preventing accidents which might lead to confrontation — which are particularly important in view of the fact that the fleets meet at various parts of the high seas in tense situations.

In sum, this Agreement serves to diminish the number of incidents and contributes to a better understanding in close-encounter situations. Comparable to the Agreement to Reduce the Risk of Outbreak of Nuclear War, it also serves to reduce the seriousness of accidents in the event they nevertheless occur.

The Basic Principles

In the 1972 text on Basic Principles of Relations between the two countries, the United States and the USSR agreed to proceed from the "common determination that in the nuclear age there is no alternative to conducting their mutual relations on the basis of peaceful coexistence". The relations should also be based on sovereignty, equality, non-interference in internal affairs, and mutual advantage.

The signatories also promised to exercise "restraint in their mutual relations" in order to prevent situations capable of causing dangerous exacerbation of their relations. The two parties pledged to do their utmost to avoid military confrontations and to prevent the outbreak of nuclear war. A central article of the text asserts that "both sides recognize that efforts to obtain unilateral advantage at the expense of the other, directly or indirectly, are inconsistent" with the objectives of the text.

The two parties agreed to do everything in their power to prevent conflicts or situations which would serve to increase international tensions from arising. Productive contacts between representatives of the two countries should be increased, and commercial and economic ties as well as co-operation in the field of science and technology are to be promoted. General and complete disarmament was viewed as the ultimate objective of the two parties' efforts. The United States and the Soviet Union would strive to continue efforts to limit armaments on a bilateral and multilateral basis. Finally, the signatories also reconfirmed the principle of sovereign equality of all states and affirmed that the development of the relations between the two parties were to be interpreted as not being directed against third countries (For the text of the Basic Principles, see Barton and Weiler 1976: 383—384.)

The text of the Basic Principles raised some anxieties about the prospects of a Soviet—United States world condominium (Barton and Weiler 1976: 205—207). The text was probably issued in mutual recognition of parity and of necessary co-operation, or at least restraints on competition, between the two States. One might argue that co-operation in order to make a world of nuclear Powers safer seems desirable. The text of the Basic Principles was an attempt to formulate the behaviour expected from the other side. However, it has not prevented negotiations on strategic nuclear disarmament from being generally unsuccessful.

Moreover, although it provides a kind of "rules of the game" which serve to reduce ambiguity and enhance predictability, it generated other ambiguities. Concepts like "non-interference" or "equality" or "unilateral advantage at the expense of the other" are extremely vague. Worse, they also tend to raise expectations which are unlikely to be met. If expectations and hopes are not met, frustration and possibly anger are the consequence. That is precisely what happened in the late 1970s. Hence the record of the decade which has passed since the Basic Principles were adopted is rather negative: perhaps the Basic Principles text was a wrong step in the right direction — wrong because it is unrealistic to start from the assumption implicit in the text that either major Power would refrain from all opportunities to promote its cause in international politics.

SALT I (Interim Agreement)

One of the cornerstones of modern arms control is the Interim Agreement on Certain Measures with respect to Limitation of Strategic Offensive Arms concluded in 1972 between the Soviet Union and the United States. Together with the ABM treaty it is commonly referred to as SALT I.

The Interim Agreement, referring to the obligations of the NPT, states that the parties undertake not to start construction of additional fixed land-based ICBM launchers after 1 July 1972 and that the United States and the Soviet Union will not convert launchers for light ICBMs or for older ICBMs (i.e., such deployed prior to 1964) into land-based launchers for heavy ICBMs deployed after 1964.

The SLBM launchers are limited by the Interim Agreement to the numbers operational and under construction on the date of signature of the agreement. The United States was allowed to deploy no more than 710 ballistic missile launchers on no more than 44 modern ballistic missile submarines. For the Soviet Union, the respective numbers were fixed at 950 SLBMs and 62 modern ballistic missile submarines (protocol to the Interim Agreement). Additional SLBMs beyond the levels given at the date of signature (operational and under construction: 656 SLBMs for the United States, 740 SLBMs for the Soviet Union) up to the levels stated were allowed as replacements for equal numbers of ballistic missile launchers of older types deployed prior to 1964 or of ballistic missile launchers on older submarines. The modernization and replacement of strategic ballistic missiles and launchers was allowed under the Interim Agreement.

The verification of compliance with the provisions of the Interim Agreement is based on the use of national technical means, with which no interference is permitted. Deliberate concealment measures were ruled out as well; however, changes in current construction, assembly, conversion, or overhaul practices were not required.

The Standing Consultative Commission established under the ABM Treaty was to be used by the parties to promote the objectives and the implementation of the Interim Agreement.

The Interim Agreement was to remain valid for a period of five years unless replaced earlier by an agreement on more complete measures limiting strategic offensive arms. The negotiation of a more comprehensive follow-on agreement was explicitly stated as an objective.

Each party retained the right to withdraw from the Interim Agreement on not less than six months' prior notice. It was stipulated that the notice of withdrawal should include a statement on the extraordinary events which the notifying party regarded as having jeopardized its supreme interests.

The Interim Agreement expired on 3 October 1977, but the United States and the Soviet Union stated that they intended to refrain from actions incompatible with its provisions or with the goals of the talks on a new agreement on strategic offensive weapons (SALT II). (For the text of the Interim Agreement and the Protocol, see Barton and Weiler 1976: 372—375; for a brief summary, see Goldblat 1978: 231—232.)

Garthoff (1978c) concludes that the Interim Agreement (together with the ABM Treaty) represented a major positive achievement, despite some shortcomings. It contributed to relaxing tensions between the United States and the Soviet Union and, in general, it advanced policies of détente. SALT I launched and provided a basis for continuing negotiations on strategic arms limitation and measures to enhance strategic stability. It also initiated a strategic dialogue between the two adversaries. However, the process of negotiation distorted the dialogue. In general, however, the SALT I negotiations contributed to better mutual strategic understanding. The explicit acceptance of the national technical means of verification as legitimate and the provisions regarding non-interference with these means must also be viewed as a significant step.

Barton and Weiler (1976: 202) agree that the Interim Agreement contributed somewhat to the stability of deterrence by setting limits on offensive nuclear armaments. SALT I not only recognized and supported deterrence but also a rough balance or parity between the two major Powers. The SALT process also had some relevance for the NPT because of the obligation of the nuclear-weapon States to cease the nuclear arms race. The conclusion of SALT I was thus one step towards fulfilling the NPT (Beres 1980: 208—210).

One of the main shortcomings of the Interim Agreement is that it did not substantially slow the arms race, and perhaps even helped accelerate it (Barton 1981: 93—94). The basic concept was a freeze. This is sometimes considered not sufficient by arms control supporters. Asymmetries were dealt with by "upward arms control", i.e., allowing each side to do what the other had already done. One example of this is the decision to allow two ABM sites in the ABM Treaty, because the Soviet Union had one centred around Moscow and the United States in Grand Forks, North Dakota. Barton assesses the impact of SALT I as "management of a continued arms competition rather than the termination of it". Other authors like Myrdal are even more sceptical:

> "By no stretch of the imagination can this be called arms limitation. Instead it is a mutually agreed continuation of the arms race, regulated and institutionalized. The competition for quality of nuclear weapons remains totally unregulated, leaving open the avenue for gaming without end" (Myrdal 1976: 106—107).

Garthoff (1978c: 7) deplores the fact that excessive public expectations caused a setback to arms control after it was realized that only modest goals had been attained. Garthoff criticizes two principal shortcomings of SALT I. The most basic shortcoming was failure to reach a comprehensive agreement limiting not only ABM systems but also strategic offensive arms. The most significant shortcoming, however, was the failure to ban MIRVs (Garthoff 1978c: 14). The United States had probably progressed too much in the development and testing of MIRVs to view their inclusion as attractive. This decision, however, was later not generally considered as very fortunate.

As far as the danger of unintentional nuclear war and strategic stability is concerned the exclusion of MIRVs from the SALT I agreement must be seen as very regrettable. MIRVing allows successful attack with only a fraction of the ICBMs the attacker can realistically expect to destroy, putting a premium on pre-emption (no self-disarmament). The neglect of MIRVs was detrimental to crisis stability and conductive to perceptions of vulnerability leading to the adoption of more risky operational procedures. The ABM Treaty did not provide either a measure against ICBM vulnerability, however, that treaty helped to stabilize the mutual strategic relationship by securing vulnerability (see the following section).

A problem arising in any major arms control agreement — and thus also in SALT I — is that of the "bargaining chips". The tendency to build prospective, or allegedly prospective, leverage by increasing or adding military programmes which could be treaded for concessions from the other side is very hazardous to arms control. The efforts to negotiate from a position of strength may lead to the realization of programmes which nobody really wanted in the first instance, yet which found a constituency in those who benefitted from the process of development. "The artificial use of potential arms control as bargaining leverage provided an argument for proceeding with military programs on which many of its advocates would probably never have agreed to 'cash in'" (Garthoff 1978c: 10, 21). The effectiveness of bargaining chip programmes is not clear. Across-the-board efforts may render arms control success rather unlikely, but some advantage of one party in a certain field balanced by an advantage of the other party in another may allow a trade-off (Barton 1981: 93). If bargaining chips are to be found in abundance on only one side, the outlook for arms control is not very bright. This is confirmed by perceptions within the Government of the United States at the present time, where there is advocacy of a catch-up before any serious new strategic arms-control attempts are undertaken.

The ABM Treaty

The 1972 Treaty between the Soviet Union and the United States on the Limitation of Anti-Ballistic Missile Systems (ABM Treaty) was intended to contribute to curbing the arms race, decrease the risk of outbreak of nuclear war, create favourable conditions for further negotiations on strategic arms and fulfil obligations under the NPT.

Each party to the ABM Treaty undertakes not to deploy ABM systems for the defence of the territory of its country, not to provide a base of such a defence, and not to deploy ABM systems for defence of an individual region.

An ABM system is defined as a "system to counter strategic ballistic missiles or their elements in flight trajectory" and consisting of ABM interceptor missiles, ABM launchers, and ABM radars. ABM system components are counted if they are operational, under construction, undergoing testing, undergoing overhaul, repair or conversion, and if they are mothballed.

The 1972 ABM Treaty allows each party to construct two ABM systems, each system deployment area having a radius of 150 km and centred one on the party's national capital, the other on a site containing ICBM silo launchers. The system centred on the capital may consist of no more than 100 ABM launchers and no more than 100 ABM interceptors, and no more than six ABM radar complexes, each complex having a diameter of no more than 3 km. The system centred on an ICBM field may also consist of no more than 100 ABM launchers and 100 ABM interceptors, but the radar configuration permitted is different: two large phased-array ABM radars and 18 smaller ABM radars (the size of the ABM radars was defined with respect to existing ones).

The limitations on deployment do not apply to ABM systems used for development or testing on agreed test ranges. However, there are no more than 15 launchers allowed on the test range. The development and deployment of sea-based, air based, space-based or mobile land-based ABM systems is prohibited. Each ABM launcher is allowed to launch only one ABM interceptor at a time. The deployment of future early-warning radars against strategic ballistic missile attack is limited to the periphery of the national territory, and the radars are to be oriented outward. The transfer of ABM systems to other States is prohibited. The parties agreed not to interfere with the national technical means of verification and not to use deliberate concealment measures.

A Standing Consultative Commission (SCC) was to be established to consider questions concerning the ABM Treaty. The 1974 protocol to the ABM Treaty limited the ABM systems to one for each party, the Soviet one being centred around Moscow, the American one in an ICBM field in North Dakota. Each party would be free to reverse its decision and decide instead to construct an ABM system centred on an ICBM site (in the case of the Soviet Union) or Washington, after notification. It was agreed that periodic reviews of the ABM Treaty would be held at 5-year intervals, beginning in October 1977. The ABM Treaty is of unlimited duration. However, article XV, paragraph 2, states:

> "Each Party shall, in exercising its national sovereignty, have the right to withdraw from this Treaty if it decides that extraordinary events related to the subject matter of this Treaty have jeopardized its supreme interests".

Six months prior notice of withdrawal is to be given to the other party, such notice to include a statement of the extraordinary events the notifying party regards as having jeopardized its supreme interests. (For the text of the ABM Treaty and the Protocol, see Starsman 1981: 58—66).

The ABM Treaty is generally considered to be one of the most useful arms control agreements. Garthoff (1978c: 12) describes this Treaty as a "notable and significant success in arms control", meeting the original interest and the main concrete objective of both sides in SALT. Garthoff mentions two effects of the Treaty: a contribution to potential restraint on offensive systems, and the saving of many millions of dollars.

Viewed in the context of deterrence theory, the ABM Treaty reduces the risk of war. Moreover, it helps to prevent a competition between ABM systems and technologies designed to penetrate these systems. The Treaty may also restrain the growth of nuclear forces and help to avoid destabilizing technological surprises (Barton 1981: 156). Also Myrdal (1976: 105), in her critique of the arms control approach and agreements, rates this treaty as relatively effective. The limitations are considered not disarmament but non-armament (as far as the prohibition of future ABM developments is concerned): "they represent the only elements of the SALT agreements which meaningfully attempt to inhibit the competitive arms race". The United States Arms Control and Disarmament Agency (1980: 11) agrees that the ABM Treaty has prevented an expensive, potentially dangerous, and unnecessary competition in ABM deployment and in offensive missile countermeasures to ABMs. Thus the Treaty is considered as a major step both in reducing competition in strategic arms and in enhancing stability.

Bertram tries to explain why the ABM Treaty is considered so effective. The Treaty led to genuine reductions (particularly the Protocol, limiting each side to one ABM site), permitted major savings, and facilitated the task of verification. The main feature distinguishing the ABM Treaty from other arms control treaties is that the Treaty limits or prohibits a specific mission instead of limiting numbers of weapons. This establishes a certain immunity against technological change (as long as no side has sufficient incentives to break out). This immunity made it possible to conclude a Treaty of unlimited duration (Bertram 1978: 18).

The conclusion of the ABM Treaty in 1972 is sometimes considered to have influenced the arms race in a qualitative way, banning the defence of missile silos and urban-industrial targets and permitting qualitative improvements in counterforce missile forces. Thus the offence-defence competition was replaced by sole reliance on offence-offence competition. The theory of mutual deterrence requires the vulnerability of valued assets to a second strike. However, there are some who advocate putting greater emphasis on defensive measures, particularly the defence of fixed-site ICBMs (Rosen 1979: 110).

There is some speculation as to whether the conclusion of the ABM Treaty signals Soviet acceptance of primarily United States strategic concepts based on mutual deterrence. To a certain degree, strategies of mutual deterrence may be considered as a result of a specific strategic situation (where the offence has major advantages over the defence), but the concept of mutual assured deterrence, in particular, is qualitatively different from passive acceptance of mutual vulnerability. Frye (1977: 10) argues that the ABM Treaty had some value as an indicator that both Powers accepted their mutual vulnerability. He has, however, some doubts about the Soviet motivation for this treaty, fostered by less pronounced strategic doctrines. The ABM Treaty may also have had the purpose of precluding a defensive arms race considered unattractive because the other party had a lead in the relevant technology. Barton and Weiler, describing the ABM Treaty as "probably the most important arms control agreement of the postwar period", say that the United States and the Soviet Union effectively accepted the mutual-hostage relationship essential for a stable deterrent relationship (Barton and Weiler 1976: 88/202; see also Garthoff 1978a, 1979). What is never pronounced in such statements is the problem of force or C^3 vulnerability. The authors seem very much preoccupied with the problem of defending urban-industrial targets and the effects of such activity on the deterrence relationship. However, from the present vantage point, almost 10 years after the conclusion of the ABM Treaty, the defence of fixed-site ICBMs is not to be dismissed as unnecessary and destabilizing, as improved accuracy and continued MIRVing, facilitating counterforce strategies, have succeeded in rendering the ICBM force somewhat unstable.

Thus, a rigid rejection of ABM (or BMD) may not necessarily serve the same purposes today as it served some years earlier. A primordial problem must probably be seen in the limitation on technology for offensive weapons. At least from an ethical perspective, defence has some aspects more acceptable than an arms race in pursuit of ever more sophisticated means of mutual annihilation. This is not to say that the foundations of mutual deterrence are obsolete; one surely has to acknowledge that a transition from a mutual-hostage relationship to deterrence by denial would entail some very delicate stages.

As was mentioned in chapter II there is a new United States interest in BMD technology. The effects of the ABM Treaty on such measures were assessed, in particular, in the context of possible basing modes for the MX ICBM. A Multiple Protective Structure (MPS) basing supported by endo-atmospheric BMD (LoADS) has been described as a useful countermeasure mitigating the effects of previous MIRVing, but the ABM Treaty does not allow for such installations (see Office of Technology Assessment 1981: chapter 12).

Rosen (1979: 119) argues that the new technology available for the defence of ICBMs against ballistic missile attack should lead the United States to consider the abrogation of the ABM treaty or the negotiation of a modified version permitting an updated short-range site defence of Minuteman silos: the abrogation could meet Soviet resistance. However, according to Rosen, the stabilizing effect of ICBM defence should be acknowledged by the Soviet Union.

Starsman (1981: 48—52) also poses the question what the United States should do with respect to the ABM Treaty. He suggests abiding by the ABM Treaty if the

Soviet Union exhibits a continued willingness to remain within the limits of SALT II through 1985 and into the post-1990 period; the United States should in this case rely on MPS basing modes, but continue development of silo-defence BMD to counter a potential SALT breakout. Starsman proposes limited modifications to the ABM Treaty during the 1982 and 1987 reviews permitting development but not deployment of a mobile BMD system.

If SALT II is not ratified and if the threat to ICBMs grows gradually beyond SALT limits, the ABM Treaty will probably not be abrogated immediately. However, some modifications are suggested for the 1982 and 1987 review conference including allowing more launchers and interceptors, a greater radius of the deployment area, mobile BMD systems and acceptance of MPS basing modes as not constituting deliberate concealment measures. In case of a clear SALT break-out, Starsman suggests not abiding by the ABM Treaty.

The Standing Consultative Commission (SCC)

In a 1972 Memorandum of Understanding, the United States and the Soviet Union established the Standing Consultative Commission on Arms Limitation (SCC). This commission was to promote the objectives and the implementation of the ABM Treaty, the Interim Agreement on Limitation of Strategic Offensive Arms (SALT I), and the Agreement on Measures to Reduce the Risk of Outbreak of Nuclear War.

Each Government was to be represented in the Commission by a Commissioner and a Deputy Commissioner. Periodic sessions would be held, at least two times per year (see Barton and Weiler 1976: 385; Sharp 1981).

The SCC is responsible for considering questions concerning compliance with the obligations assumed and related situations which may be considered ambiguous; providing, on a voluntary basis, information either party considers necessary to assure confidence in compliance with the obligations assumed; considering questions involving unintended interference with the national technical means of verification; considering possible changes in the strategic situation which have a bearing on the provisions of the SALT agreements; considering possible proposals for increasing the viability of the agreements, including proposals for amendments; and considering proposals for further measures aimed at strategic arms limitation (see United States Arms Control and Disarmament Agency 1980: 19—21). The proceedings are private. Sixteen sessions had been held by 31 December 1979. Two protocols related to the ABM Treaty and the Interim Agreement were completed by the SCC and signed in 1974 (the ABM protocol limiting ABM sites to just one for each party). The ABM Treaty was reviewed by the SCC in 1977. A 1976 protocol codified means of facilitating and speeding the transmission of the immediate notification required by the Agreement on Measures to Reduce the Risk of Outbreak of Nuclear War.

The United States raised questions related to the following areas: identification of special purpose silos of launch control facilities; concealment measures; modern large ballistic missiles; possible testing of an air defence system radar in an ABM mode; reporting of dismantling of excess ABM test launchers; ABM radar on Kamchatka peninsula; dismantling or destruction of replaced ICBM launchers; and concealment at a test range. Each time an issue was raised by the United States, the Soviet activity has either ceased or additional information has allayed United States concern. The Soviet Union raised questions about the following areas: shelters over Minuteman silos; status of Atlas and Titan 1 launchers; radar on Shemya island; privacy of SCC proceedings; dismantling or destruction of ABM radar under construction at Malmstrom AFB; and various radar deployments (Sharp 1981: 8—10).

The agreed strategic forces data base (SALT II) is also to be updated at each regular session of the SCC. The SCC is considered to perform valuable services. Garthoff (1981c: 20) confirms: "The SCC has done a very good job". The SCC provides a forum for consultation and removing ambiguity. The SCC has also worked out pre-positioned messages covering various contingencies requiring immediate notification. For a time, the SCC was by-channelled, but this seems to have ceased. However, the role of the SCC, flexibly defined in the SALT agreements, could perhaps be enlarged.

Barton (1981: 122—123) sees the SCC as a forum for private warnings that are likely to be more effective than public ones. There is a public-relations problem, however. The SCC should not give the impression that it acts differently from publicly stated policy. The disclosure of topics dealt with in the SCC seems useful. There may be an advantage in disclosing the problems only after some time, allowing for a quiet settlement but nevertheless being able to show the effectiveness of the SCC.

The value of informal negotiation and communication must be rated highly. The regular contacts are likely to facilitate a climate of confidence allowing the treatment of topics which can not be dealt with effectively in public diplomacy. More generally, SCC helped to stabilize a mutually acceptable status quo. Most importantly, it established and maintained up to date an agreed data base and provided a mechanism to resolve ambiguities about treaty compliance (Sharp 1981: 1—11).

The Prevention of Nuclear War Agreement

In the 1973 Agreement on the Prevention of Nuclear War the United States and the Soviet Union stated that an objective of their policies is to remove the danger of nuclear war and of the use of nuclear weapons. The two parties agreed to act in such a manner as to prevent the development of situations capable of causing a dangerous exacerbation of their relations and to avoid military confrontations.

The parties agreed to proceed from the premise that each party "refrain from the threat or use of force against the other Party, against the allies of the other Party and against other countries, in circumstances which may endanger international peace and security". If a situation concerning one of the two parties entails the risk of nuclear conflict, they shall engage in urgent consultations with each other and every effort shall be made to avert the risk. The provisions of this Agreement are without prejudice to the right of self-defence, the provisions of the Charter of the United Nations, and the obligations of either party towards its allies or other countries.

The Agreement on the Prevention of Nuclear War is of unlimited duration, with no provisions for withdrawal (For the text of the treaty, see for example Labrie 1979: 184—186.)

Bykov (1978: 63) says that this Agreement is of truly historic significance, because it marked a serious step towards lessening and ultimately towards removing the threat of nuclear war and the creation of a system of real guarantees of international security. George (1978) rates the Basic Principles agreement and the Prevention agreement as important first steps in the direction of preventing dangerous crises. However, the practical application of the principles is not dealt with and it is not specified when the two parties have to contact each other to co-operate. The two crisis-prevention agreements were put to a test during the Middle East war in October 1973, with rather uncertain results. George sees the Middle East war of 1973 as a negative example of conduct in a crisis. The outcome did not facilitate further agreements on crisis prevention, and no analysis of the failure has been undertaken. Caldwell (1979: 42) agrees that the agreements on crisis prevention were not successful in 1973; the support of the clients in the Middle East was judged to be of superior importance. However, crisis management nevertheless succeeded in restraining actions by the major nuclear Powers, if only after some critical period. Tight control over arms transfers was maintained, and Soviet— United States naval interaction was restrained, leading to no major confrontations during the war. Communication between the United States and the Soviet Union was smooth. Crisis management seems easier than crisis prevention, because it seems more difficult to make crisis prevention norms and procedures operational. A crisis can advance one's interests, and thus it is not always considered desirable to issue a warning to the other major nuclear Power; this could lead to alienating the States supported. Caldwell argues for agreements stated in less general terms, containing a set of norms applicable to a number of diverse situations in which crises could develop. Such norms could be very context-specific for various areas of the world.

The review of crisis prevention agreements after each crisis should help to evaluate strong and weak points of these agreements; this was, however, not done after the 1973 Middle East war.

Effective crisis prevention régimes, according to George (1978), can only be developed as part of a more general détente process. It is not only the behaviour but also the outcomes which have to be regulated, each party respecting the vital interests of the other. These vital interests should be assessed in a very differentiated manner.

The proposal to work out differentiated assessments of each major Power's interests in each area of the world where these interests may clash (George 1978: 4) may look useful for a United States or Soviet writer. However, such attempts to regulate international affairs by reference to the dominance of major nuclear Powers is not a desirable prospect for other States.

SALT II

In 1979 the SALT II agreements were signed by United States President Carter and General Secretary Leonid Brezhnev of the Communist Party of the Soviet Union. Ratification by the United States is still pending. The SALT II agreements include:

> Treaty between the United States and the USSR on the Limitation of Strategic Offensive Arms;
>
> Protocol to this Treaty;
>
> Joint Statement of Principles and Basic Guidelines for Subsequent Negotiations on the Limitation of Strategic Arms;
>
> Statement of Data on the Numbers of Strategic Arms;
>
> Agreed Statements and Common Understandings regarding the Treaty on the Limitation of Strategic Offensive Arms; and
>
> Soviet Backfire Statement.

The main provisions of the Treaty on the Limitation of Strategic Offensive Arms are as follows: the two parties undertake to limit strategic offensive arms quantitatively and qualitatively and to exercise restraint in the development of new types of strategic offensive arms. Each party limits the aggregate number of ICBM launchers, SLBM launchers, heavy bombers, and ASBMs which is not to exceed 2,400; this overall ceiling was to be reduced from 1 January 1981 to 2,250. Within this overall ceiling on strategic offensive arms, each party undertakes to limit the aggregate number of launchers of ICBMs and SLBMs equipped with MIRVs, ASBMs equipped with MIRVs, and heavy bombers equipped for cruise missiles (capable of a range in excess of 600 km) to 1,320. Within this subceiling for MIRVed systems and cruise-missile-armed heavy bombers, the aggregate number of ICBM and SLBM launchers equipped with MIRVs and ASBMs equipped with MIRVs is not to exceed 1,200. Within this aggregate number of MIRVed systems, the launchers of MIRVed ICBMs are limited to an aggregate number not exceeding 820.

The limitations apply to arms which are either operational, in the final stage of construction, in reserve, in storage, mothballed, or undergoing overhaul, repair, modernization or conversion.

ICBMs are defined as ballistic missiles launched by land-based launchers, capable of a range in excess of 5,500 km. SLBM launchers are launchers of ballistic missiles installed on any nuclear-powered submarine or launchers of modern ballistic missiles installed on any submarine. As heavy bombers, the American B—52 and B—1 and the Soviet Tu—95 and Myasishev types were identified in 1979. For the future, any bomber able to carry out the mission of a heavy bomber similarly to the types mentioned is defined as a heavy bomber. The group of heavy bombers includes also the types which are equipped for cruise missiles or for ASBMs. ASBMs are defined as air-to-surface ballistic missiles capable of a range in excess of 600 km and installed in an aircraft or on its external mountings. In the protocol, the two parties stated that they would not flight-test or deploy ASBMs.

Each party undertakes not to start construction of additional fixed ICBM launchers and not to relocate fixed ICBM launchers. Moreover, the conversion of launchers of light ICBMs or of ICBMs of older type into launchers of heavy ICBMs deployed after 1964 is prohibited. In the process of modernization and replacement of ICBM silo launchers the original internal volume of the silo may be increased by up to 32 per cent. Systems for rapid reload of ICBM launchers shall not be developed, tested, or deployed. At launch sites of ICBM launchers, storage facilities for storing ICBMs in excess of normal deployment requirements are not allowed. Each party undertakes not to develop, test, or deploy ICBMs having a greater launch-weight or throw-weight than the heavy ICBMs deployed by either side at the date of signature of the Treaty.

Each party is allowed to flight-test and deploy one new type of light ICBM in addition to those types flight-tested before 1 May 1979. Land-based launchers of ballistic missiles other than ICBMs (presumably such of shorter range) are not allowed to be converted into ICBMs. The number of RVs with which ICBMs and SLBMs may be equipped is limited. For the ICBMs, the number of RVs is limited to 10. For SLBMs, the number of RVs is not allowed to exceed 14. For ICBMs flight-tested before 1 May 1979, the number of RVs is limited to the maximum number of RVs with which it was equipped during flight-testing. Each party undertakes not to flight-test cruise missiles capable of a range in excess of 600 km; not to convert aircraft other than bombers into aircraft which can carry out the mission of a heavy bomber and not to develop, test or deploy:

> Ballistic missiles capable of a range of more than 600 km for installation on water-borne vehicles other than submarines;
>
> Fixed ballistic or cruise missile launchers for installation on the ocean floor, the seabed, or on the beds of internal waters and inland waters or in the subsoil thereof;

Systems for placing into earth orbit nuclear weapons or any other kind of weapons of mass destruction;

Mobile launchers of heavy ICBMs; and

SLBMs which have a launch-weight or a throw-weight greater than that of the heaviest of the light ICBMs deployed by either party by the date of signature of the Treaty.

MIRVed cruise missiles capable of a range in excess of 600 km are not allowed to be flight-tested or deployed. The Treaty also contains some provisions on the destruction of strategic arms in excess of the aggregate numbers agreed upon.

Each party is obliged not to circumvent the effectiveness of the Treaty. For providing assurance of compliance with the provisions of the Treaty, national technical means shall be used. Interference with these means is prohibited, as is the use of deliberate concealment measures. Notification of planned ICBM launches is required on a case-by-case basis except for single ICBM launches from test ranges or from ICBM launcher deployment areas which are not planned to extend beyond the national territory of the respective party.

It was provided that the Standing Consultative Commission, established in 1972, should consider questions, developments and problems related to this Treaty.

The Treaty was intended to remain in force through 31 December 1985, each party retaining the right to withdraw if it decides that extraordinary events related to the subject matter of the Treaty have jeopardized its supreme interests. Six months' advance notice of withdrawal is required, such notice to include a statement of the extraordinary events concerned. In the Protocol, the parties agree not to deploy mobile ICBM launchers. Common Understandings clarify the exact meaning of the different paragraphs. The Soviet Union states in a letter that it does not intend to give the Backfire bomber the capability of operating at intercontinental distances, and that it will not increase the production rate of this aeroplane as compared to the rate existing at the time of the signature of the treaty. A Joint Statement contains principles and basic guide-lines for subsequent negotiations on the limitation of strategic arms. Negotiations are to be continued in accordance with the principle of equality and equal security, leading to a reduction of numbers of strategic arms and qualitative limitation.

Strategic stability is explicitly mentioned as one of the objectives:

"In furtherance of existing agreements between the parties on the limitation and reduction of strategic arms, the parties will continue, for the purposes of reducing and averting the risk of outbreak of nuclear war, to seek measures to strengthen strategic stability by, among other things, limitations on strategic offensive arms most destabilizing to the strategic balance and by measures to reduce and to avert the risk of surprise attack".

Related objectives include reduction in the numbers of strategic offensive arms and qualitative limitations, including restrictions on the development, testing, and deployment of new types of strategic offensive arms and on modernization.

Provision is made for the verification of further limitations to be performed by national technical means, if appropriate, accompanied by co-operative measures contributing to the effectiveness of verification. (For the text of the SALT II agreements, see *Survival*, vol. 21, No. 5: 217—230.) The SALT II agreements were signed in 1979. However, international events led to the decision by the United States Government to delay the process of ratification, and it is very doubtful that this Treaty will ever enter into force in its present form.

SALT II would set not only quantitative but also qualitative limits by prohibiting several technologically feasible undertakings, including the development of certain weapons and different kinds of deployment. The arguments for the SALT II Treaty include the fact that it would set limits on the weapons systems, not only on the launchers but also on the allowed number of RVs; this would facilitate force and deployment planning of both sides in giving "a shape to the threat". The explicit prohibition of concealment measures would also tend to stabilize the strategic balance because knowledge would make it unnecessary to resort to worst-case thinking. The SALT II Treaty was for several years considered one of the centrepieces of the relations between the two major nuclear Powers. The failure to ratify the outcome of negotiations and renegotiations must necessarily have some repercussions on these relations as well.

For SALT's proponents, the Treaty eases the counterforce problem by limiting the number of RVs which each side can deploy. This is a prerequisite for MPS basing modes because it offers some assurance that the other Power will not be able to deploy sufficient RVs to saturate this defence. SALT's opponents, however, would like to attack this problem from the other side, by setting much lower ceilings for launchers and RVs (Staff of the Carnegie Panel on United States Security and the Future of Arms Control 1981a: 114).

Critics of SALT II assert that it provides very little genuine disarmament. It does not end the arms race. SALT II codifies the existing plans of the nuclear Powers; it is argued that both sides would not deploy more weapons systems even if allowed.

Yet, the SALT II Treaty offers a measure of predictability. This would be in line with the efforts aimed at preventing unintentional nuclear war. If SALT II is to be replaced by a more restrictive treaty on strategic nuclear arms, so much the better. But at present the prospects of the major nuclear States being willing to enter into negotiations with such an objective seem dim, and the feasibility of drastic reductions is questionable. The main emphasis should be placed on limits leading to stable situations. This would probably also include qualitative limits. In the absence of a more comprehensive agreement, however, the ratification of the SALT II Treaty would be beneficial. Time is running out, because more and more fields are becoming interesting for military use, and it is very hard to limit activities already under **way.**

Conclusions: The Contribution of Existing Agreements to the Prevention of Unintentional Nuclear War

1. Since the beginning of the 1960s a considerable number of multilateral and bilateral agreements have been concluded which implicitly or explicitly have a bearing upon the problem of unintentional nuclear war. They constitute a complex network of provisions eluding any generalized conclusion. Rather, the effect of each agreement on each possible risk must be assessed individually and systematically (see matrix on the next page).

2. When trying to generalize about the results of the systematic analysis (presented in the matrix) the conclusion cannot be avoided that the existing agreements cope with only a small fraction of the risks only. (Practically all symbols have to be put in parantheses and there are many cells left open in the matrix.) This diagnosis calls for additional and intensive efforts.

3. Nevertheless, it would be misleading to conclude that the existing provisions and measures are worthless. They are in fact capable of controlling some of the risks. More importantly, their existence reflects a widespread awareness of the risks involved in the contemporary strategic system.

THE RISKS (SUMMARY LISTING)

THE AGREEMENTS	Risk type 1: nuclear war initiated independently of explicit decision by legitimate authorities	Risk type 2: nuclear war initiated on false assumptions	Risk type 3: a conventional war unexpectedly escalating into a nuclear war
Antarctic Treaty			
LTBT			
Outer Space Treaty	(+)	(+)	
Tlatelolco Treaty	(+)	(+)	(+)
NPT	(+)	(+)	(+)
Seabed Treaty	(+)	(+)	
CBMs		(+)	
Hot Line	(+)	(+)	(+)
Risk of Nuclear War Agreement	(+)		
Naval Incidents Agreement	(+)		
Basic Principles			
SALT I (Interim)		(+)	
ABM		(+)	
Prevention of Nuclear War Agreement	(+)	(+)	
SALT II		(+)	

THE AGREEMENTS	arms race undermines strategic stability	secrecy induces "worst case" overreactions	arms race undermines C³ stability	disregard of arms R&D for strategic stability	erroneous assumptions underlying strategic doctrines	misunderstandings due to differing strategic concepts in East and West	misunderstandings due to Soviet surprise concepts	misunderstandings due to US counterforce doctrine	unexpected collateral damage in "limited" nuclear war	failure of deterrence	failure of rationality	instability due to non-credibility of extended deterrence	unstable commitments in the third world	crisis stress leading to misperception and misbehaviour	crisis breakdown of organization	misunderstandings due to the use of force	loss of control due to "logic of events"	overriding of "firebreak" by strategic interdependence	technical failure or malfunction	nuclear accidents due to human failure	misinterpretation of nuclear accidents by opponent	multiplication of risks due to nuclear proliferation	catalytic effects of regional nuclear war	nuclear terrorism
Antarctic Treaty	(+)																							(+)
LTBT	(−)	(++)																						(++)
Outer Space Treaty		(+)	(+)	(+)	(+)																			
Tlatelolco Treaty																						(+)	(++)	(+)
NPT										(+)	(+)											(++)	(++)	(++)
Seabed Treaty		(+)	(+)	(+)						(+)	(+)													
CBMs							(+)									(+)	(+)			(+++)	(++)			
Hot Line														(++)	(+)			(++)	(+++)	(+++)	(+++)			
Risk of Nuclear War Agreement																(++)	(+)		(+)	(+)	(+)	(++)	(+)	
Naval Incidents Agreement																(+)				(+)	(++)			
Basic Principles	(+)	(++)	(++)	(++)	(++)			(++)		(++)			(+)	(+)		(+)	(+)							
SALT I (Interim)	(−)	(++)	(++)	(++)	(++)						(+)	(−)												
ABM	(+)								(−)	(++)		(−)						(+)						
Prevention of Nuclear War Agreement													(+)	(+)	(+)		(+)					(+)		
SALT II	(+)	(+)	(+)	(+)	(+)			(+)		(+)						(+)	(+)							

Explanation of symbols:

+ The provisions of the agreement or treaty are capable of *fully* coping with the risk concerned.

(+) The provisions of the agreement or treaty *partly* cope with the risk concerned or contribute to *mitigating* it.

(−) There are doubts about the utility of the provisions of the respective agreement or treaty; they may even slightly *impede* efforts to contain the risk concerned.

− The provisions of the agreement or treaty are downright *counter-productive* to the prevention of nuclear war.

As a rule, the most optimistic judgement has been preferred. It is understood that a less benign evaluation would considerably reduce the number of (+) and probably add a series of (−) signs. As the significance of the agreements is rather ambiguous, + and − do not occur.

IX. CONCLUSIONS

A. General Evaluation

Interdependent and Independent Risks

As can be seen from the preceding chapters, an analysis of the risks underlying the present structure of the nuclear strategic system reveals a multitude of dangers and hazards pouring out of the nuclear Pandora's box. There are almost certainly more risks than one might imagine in any credible scenario which, by its very nature, usually concentrates on one single risk, such as the Dr. Strangelove syndrome or the possibility of a technical failure. Unintentional nuclear war can have a multitude of causes and origins, and the cumulative risks must be taken extremely seriously.

By contrast to the usual assumption that two risks are twice as dangerous as one risk and three risks three times as dangerous, the logical structure of cumulative risks, upon a closer examination based on probability theory, rather suggests that a sequence of risks unexpectedly piles up a deadly threat. This has been illustrated by Deutsch (1968: 128) by the scenario of a reckless car-driver getting his right of way at an intersection by simply and ruthlessly accelerating his speed:

> "A reckless driver is likely to get the right of way at the first intersection and thus to pass it quickly alive. Let us suppose that his chances of survival are 9 or 90%. Let us then suppose that he continues his reckless tactics and that his changes of survival and success at every following encounter at intersections are likewise 90%. In that case the chances of being alive after two encounters are 90% of 90% or $.9^2$ which is 81%. His chances of surviving three such encounters are 0.9^3 or 72.9% Hence, 21 successive encounters would offer our high risk player only one chance out of 8 to stay alive. 49 would give him less than one chance in 100; and 70 would leave him less than 1 chance in 1000. The fact that each single encounter offered him 9 chances out of 10 to live is almost irrelevant compared to the deadly effect of cumulative risks."

Although all the organizational and technical systems involved in the strategy of mutual nuclear deterrence are equipped with all kinds of safeguards, nobody can argue that they are 100 per cent proof. Assuming even a 99.9 per cent proof safety against failure , accident and uncontrolled manipulation this proud figure rapidly decreases when account is taken of the multitude of possible causes of risks. Assuming a sequence of 50 possible risks, the 99.9 per cent would be diminished to a mere 95.1 per cent; in other words: 50 successive dangers with a risk of unintentional nuclear war by accident of 1 per 1000 cumulate into a risk of no less than 4.9 per cent. It goes without saying that this way of reasoning has an utterly alarming dimension.

It must be noted, however, that this logic of cumulative risks relates only to situations where the various risks are *inter*dependent. In the case of safeguards against nuclear accidents and incidents, the overall design of safety rules and safety mechanisms is aimed at establishing redundancy: if one system fails, the second will react, and in the improbable event that even the second system does not work, the third will operate. If the different safeguard systems are *in*dependent from each other, the probability of an accident or incident decreases as a function of redundancy. Thus it is not the probability of survival (e.g. 99.9 per cent) that has to be multiplied. It is the overall probability of simultaneous failure that counts. If in 1 out of 1,000 cases the first system fails ($100 - 99.9$ per cent $= 0.1$ per cent) and if the same probability is also valid for the failure of the second, independent system, a simultaneous failure will occur once in 1 million cases: $(100$ per cent $- 99.9$ per cent$) \times (100$ per cent $- 99.9$ per cent$) = 0.0001$ per cent. If one calculates this value according to the degree of redundancy the outcome constitutes a rather insignificant risk. If one assumes 50 safeguard systems, checks, authorizations, etc., the ultimate probability of an accident or incident is $(100 - 99.9$ per cent$)^{50}$, or practically zero. It must be mentioned, however, that such extremely low probabilities are usually not achieved in reality: the history of accidents is a history of surprises (Sonntag 1981: 89). Nevertheless, from the standpoint of cumulative probability the arsenals of the nuclear Powers seem rather safe and proof against accidental failure and initiation of war by misjudgement or misunderstanding.

The assumption of *inter*dependent and hence cumulative risks constitutes something like an ideal type, as does the opposite, i.e., the assumption of *in*dependence among the risks. The reality may be somewhere in between. Some risks are in fact interdependent and dangerously reinforce each other. Others may be independent, thus creating additional safety based on the principle of redundancy. Accidents may override three or four safeguards at once before being brought under control by a fifth redundant safeguard.

The Three Types
of Unintentional Nuclear War Assessed

The implications of these considerations have to be assessed in relation to the three main types of unintentional nuclear war outlined in the introductory chapter of this study.

As far as the first type is concerned, i.e. the risk of nuclear war initiated independently of any explicit decision taken by the legitimate authorities, one can reasonably assume that the respective risks are largely independent from each other. Technical malfunctioning of systems and human error or infringement by subordinate officers are controlled and tamed by a tight network of safeguards. Therefore, and notwithstanding prevalent scenarios suggesting the opposite, the probability of a nuclear war being self-activated or initiated without authorized orders is practically zero.

The situation may be slightly different, however, with regard to the risk of nuclear war as a consequence of misjudgement, miscalculation or misunderstanding. One cannot avoid the conclusion that in the case of this danger the risks are not independent, but interdependent. In particular, this applies to the risks involved in the trend towards strategic instability and in the special circumstances obtaining in crisis situations. This produces a "synergistic effect" (Niezing 1980: 74) among different risks and can lead to a new order of magnitude. Or to put it differently: in acute crises things really look different. The Cuban missile crisis was a case in point. As Herman Kahn reports, people were sitting in bars and saying: "Let's have another drink, tomorrow we may all be dead." Failure of security policy was still not likely, yet it was no longer "unthinkable". The probability of disaster was definitely felt to be lower than 50 per cent, but it would be hard to argue that it was lower than 1 per cent. In other words: Acute crises tend to shift probabilities.

Misperception or inappropriate reactions or failure of complex men/machine systems under the stress of urgency might easily aggravate a critical situation. We know from experience in the civil sector that complex men/machine systems usually run smoothly under normal standard working conditions. But they are liable to fail in case of overwhelming difficulties. The accident at the nuclear power plant of Three Mile Island has been interpreted this way by ergonometric experts: hundreds of instruments indicating alarm during the accident, all functioning at the same time and with no adequate evaluation of the relative importance of the various signals, simply confused the operators. Also, complex weapon systems can hardly be tested and improved under "real" wartime conditions. Thus the liabilities of men/machine systems and malfunctions of other factors may aggravate critical situations. Failures that under conditions of "normalcy" would be overcome on a routine basis may constitute a certain danger during an ongoing crisis. The gravest threat obviously lies in the possible combination of various types of malfunctions during an acute international crisis.

A similar conclusion suggests itself with regard to the third type of unintentional nuclear war, i.e., the unexpected and unintentional escalation of a conventional war into a nuclear war. Although the nuclear threshold is generally paid the most careful attention, one cannot deny that the respective risks are closely intertwined and therefore interdependent, thus increasing the overall probability of escalation.

Still it would be unwise to dramatize the gravity of the threat of unintentional nuclear war. Assessing the individual risks, as was done in the preceding chapters, and evaluating the combined impact of these risks to the extent that they are interdependent leads to the conclusion that the overall risk of unintentional nuclear war is minimal if expressed as a percentage probability (cf. the estimations presented in the Appendix below). Yet, although the likelihood of an outbreak of unintentional nuclear war is extremely small, almost close to zero, it deserves the utmost attention and careful consideration. This conclusion is imperative bearing in mind the fact that the risk involved is composed of two elements: the chance of something happening and the amount of damage caused by such an occurrence (Niezing 1978: 13 ff.; Niezing 1980: 74). Given the terrible nature and atrocious dimensions of the possible tragedy, even the slightest chance that it might occur therefore makes it a matter of grave concern.

Appendix: A Tentative Quantitative Evaluation of the Risks of Unintentional Nuclear War

(This Appendix was written in cooperation with Dr. Philipp Sonntag, Science Centre Berlin)

Starting from the considerations outlined above it may be interesting to try to make some tentative calculations, taking into account the partly interdependent and partly independent nature of the risks involved. The following calculations are based on very crude and subjective estimates that cannot be confirmed or refuted by any empirical evidence. Still, they might offer some indications regarding the relative significance of the various risks and the logic of their interrelationship.

The following probabilities refer to the four major types of risks which will be included in the calculations:

p_1 probability of a nuclear war due to technical failure (nuclear accident or false alarm)

p_2 probability of a nuclear war due to the urge to pre-empt (timely and sufficient strike, either in a global or regional context, both strategic or tactical)

p_3 probability of aggravating impact of nuclear proliferation (additional probability of nuclear accidents and incidents), triggering or accelerating nuclear involvement by the major nuclear Powers

p_4 probability of human failure, mainly due to short-comings of men/machine systems and consequences of stress

p_m combination of a multitude of risks in a situation of acute international crisis (due to 1. the changing nature of risks when shifting from "normal" to crisis conditions, 2. triggering of one failure by another, i.e., chain reaction failure, 3. loss of confidence in routine handling of failures). It should be noted that the combination of risks is more dangerous than the mere addition of single risks.

The estimates are made with regard to both "normal" and crisis situations. They refer to a period of five years:

	Estimated probability of a major nuclear war within five years under	
	"normal" conditions	crisis conditions
p_1	.0001*	.003
p_2	.0001	.001
p_3	.0001	.0003
p_4	.0003	.001
p_m	.01	.05**

  * This probability estimate means that under "normal" conditions a nuclear war due to technical failure *alone* will occur once in 50,000 years.
  ** According to estimate suggested by Rosenkranz (1981:11)

Finally, one must bear in mind that statistical probabilities do not provide any information regarding the occurrence of specific single events. A probability of 1 unintentional nuclear war per 100 years may seem negligible; however, it looks much more menacing if one assumes that, according to this probability distribution, the disaster may already happen tomorrow and be followed by 99 years of "peace".

B. Practical Conclusions

When trying to express some policy implications of what has been expounded in the preceding chapters of this study, and to draw practical conclusions, an important preliminary remark has to be made. Considering the basic structure of the risk of unintentional nuclear war which may be generated by the unfortunate coincidence of an unstable strategic system and acute crisis confrontation, one cannot but recall and stress, first of all, the significance of any efforts undertaken with a view to stabilizing the strategic system and to defusing and solving international conflicts.

In particular, this requires the fulfilment of two tasks: first, progress in arms control and disarmament ultimately leading to general and complete disarmament, and, secondly, implementation of a working system of international conflict resolution replacing war or the threat to use force as an instrument for settling international disputes. Therefore, all practical conclusions related to disarmament and maintenance of international peace and security must also take full account of the considerations put forward in the perspective of the prevention of unintentional nuclear war. The recommendations adopted by the United Nations General Assembly at its first special session devoted to disarmament therefore also have an immediate bearing on the prevention of unintentional nuclear war; paragraphs 18 and 26 of the Final Document deserve particular mention in this context:

> "18. Removing the threat of a world war — a nuclear war — is the most acute and urgent task of the present day. Mankind is confronted with a choice: we must halt the arms race and proceed to disarmament or face annihilation".
>
> "26. All States Members of the United Nations reaffirm their full commitment to the purposes of the Charter of the United Nations and their obligation strictly to observe its principles as well as other relevant and generally accepted principles of international law relating to the maintenance of international peace and security . . ."

Although recommendations like these have been made again and again in the past hundred years, they continue to be vitally important, and despite their relatively general nature they are of the utmost relevance for the problem under consideration in the present study.

Yet, in the particular perspective of the study of unintentional nuclear war, some additional and more specific conclusions may seem appropriate, pointing out the immediate policy implications resulting from the analysis presented in the preceding chapters. The following proposals offered for further consideration are, however, highly tentative and selective.

1. Some additional arms control measures that are not yet part of the agenda of international negotiations deserve to be examined and discussed more closely and as soon as possible:

> Restriction of missile tests;
>
> Prior notification of missile tests;
>
> Prevention and prohibition of ASAT developments and deployments;
>
> Prevention and prohibition of ASW developments and deployments;
>
> Reconsideration of BMD applications with a view to enhancing ICBM invulnerability without jeopardizing strategic stability ;
>
> Discussion of the proposal regarding the creation of SLBM sanctuaries in the ocean.

2. The highly incrementalist, step-by-step nature of an arms development and deployment policy which is, to some extent, decoupled from top-level political decisions requires more efforts to establish full political control. In particular, arms control considerations deserve to be given greater prominence in the deliberations leading to decisions regarding arms development and deployment.

3. In arms negotiations and public discussions there is a strong emphasis on equality or parity in numbers of weapons. Actually, small qualitative differences (hit probabilities of attack and defence, quality of C^3 systems, etc.) are much more important than numbers. Further sophistication and technical improvements of weapons therefore deserve more attention than mere numbers. Arms control

should increasingly be directed towards the qualitative arms race, even if verification is difficult.

4. The high degree of secrecy surrounding new weapons developments and deployments leads the nuclear Powers to start from the "worst case" assumption in their arms procurement policies; this in turn constantly fuels the arms race thus jeopardizing strategic stability. Therefore, consideration should be given to the possibility of moderating the secrecy principle with a view to finding an optimum degree of secrecy which satisfies both national security interests and the cause of international strategic stability. At least the secrecy approach should be modified in respect of matters that do not contribute anything to national security.

5. It is desirable for the military leaders and experts of the two major Powers to hold discussions about their strategic doctrines and capabilities with a view to reaching a better understanding of their mutual deterrence posture and possibly also to identifying those areas of strategic doctrine in which consensus can be reached. UNIDIR may constitute an appropriate framework for this type of discussions, which should start among academic experts, but thereafter increasingly involve government experts as well.

6. Arms control negotiations are also helpful for this purpose. Even if they do not yield significant results, as is the case with the Vienna Force Reduction Talks, they offer opportunities for continued institutionalized contacts among strategic experts. Moreover, the SALT/START process deserves to be reinvigorated. The plurality of arms control and disarmament talks should therefore be maintained and increased if possible.

7. Although, in the long run, the overriding concern must be the abolition of nuclear weapons, it would be a mistake to disregard the security concerns which engage the attention of all States, and especially of the two major Powers. Having this in mind, efforts are required to stabilize the strategic system of mutual deterrence. This means making deterrence more credible or, to put it negatively, precluding any possibility that a major Power might be led to believe that it is being threatened and is left no option other than to launch a pre-emptive strike. Furthermore, if the Governments of the two major powers succeed in convincing each other that they can respond to any contingency, the risk of unintentional war can be controlled.

8. It is of course desirable that this goal should be achieved at the lowest possible level of armaments. Steps in this direction can be undertaken unilaterally and do not necessarily presuppose bilateral or multilateral negotiations and agreements.

9. In view of the enormous (and generally underestimated) collateral damage caused even by "tactical" nuclear weapons in the context of a "limited" nuclear war, it may be expedient to place more emphasis on *minimum* deterrence postures.

Minimum deterrence is also appropriate in terms of the enhanced credibility of the deterrence posture.

10. Concepts should be studied and discussed which contribute to securing strategic stability at a lower level of armaments without reducing the security of the nations concerned. The reduction of the number of nuclear weapons deployed represents a major goal, and there are realistic prospects for approaching this goal. It is important, however, to avoid any rigid and inflexible approach based on a specific percentage of the number of systems to be withdrawn. Reduction of the nuclear deterrence postures to a lower level means finding an appropriate solution not only aimed at a schematic reduction of numbers but also acknowledging the need to achieve the highest possible degree of invulnerability and survivability.

11. Particular emphasis should be laid, in this context, on regional measures. In particular, proposals for regional ceilings on numbers and types of nuclear weapons should be discussed and as appropriate negotiated, with a view to signing multilateral agreements.

12. More particularly, it is indispensable to seize every opportunity to raise the nuclear threshold. One means of doing this is to achieve a better balance of conventional forces where this balance is uneven and where the side perceiving itself to be inferior plans to fill the gap by threatening the first-use of nuclear weapons. Yet, as has been emphasized by Boserup (1981: 405), the problem of this policy is that additional defensive forces also add to the offensive capability of the side concerned and thereby fuel a further round in the arms race. More comprehensive and subtle approaches are required.

13. In practical terms, raising the nuclear threshold entails increasing the number of non-nuclear options.

14. Increasing the number of nuclear options makes fighting a nuclear war more feasible and hence reinforces the credibility of deterrence. This may in turn raise the nuclear threshold because deterrence is less liable to fail. On the other hand, transcending the nuclear threshold becomes more probable in ambiguous crisis situations.

15. In order to mitigate the problem of NATO's flexible response policy, it may seem desirable to examine the possibility of a policy of "no first *offensive* use" of nuclear weapons, as suggested by Speed (1979: 116). Such a policy would imply that the United States would not initiate nuclear strikes against the Soviet Union and vice-versa. According to Speed, a more logical version of this would entail NATO's renouncing the use of nuclear weapons on Warsaw Pact territory as long as Warsaw Pact forces do not use nuclear weapons on NATO territory; this does not imply a renunciation of the first use of nuclear weapons by NATO.

16. In the long run, a general agreement on the non-first use of nuclear weapons should be envisaged. Before such a step is taken, however, there is a need to

solve the security problem which leads to the adoption of a strategy involving the first use of nuclear weapons against conventional attacks; appropriate conventional arms control negotiations on a regional basis are required for that purpose.

17. In view of the doubtful credibility of extended nuclear deterrence or nuclear guarantees, and considering their susceptibility to being "probed" by potential opponents, it seems desirable to avoid any additional commitments of this kind. In the long run, ways and means should be found of reducing or abrogating existing nuclear guarantees by offering the parties concerned reliable equivalent security alternatives.

18. In order to reduce the risk of premature conclusious based on misjudgement and misperceptions, it is indispensable that both major Powers should constantly improve the consultation and checking procedures built into their decision-making processes for the release of nuclear weapons. This includes intra-Government consultation as well as intra-alliance consultations; the communication channels for these consultation processes must be well defined and reliable in order to avoid unnecessary loss of time which, in turn, would create a state of urgency apt to lead to premature decisions with unintended consequences.

19. It is desirable that the nuclear Powers should try to forge a common approach to the problem of C^3 vulnerability. They should at least exchange views on this subject. In addition, possible agreements limiting anti-C^3 weapons developments should be discussed.

20. By contrast to previous arms control agreements, negotiations undertaken with a view to reaching new agreements require intensive efforts to be made to find ways and means of making the verification processes more thorough and more reliable. Verification by national technical means is increasingly inadequate due to the growing complexity of the weapons systems to be verified. Therefore, some co-operative measures in the field of arms control measures are desirable.

21. The more complex and sophisticated weapons technology becomes, the less efficient are traditional means of verification by national means. However, in order to prevent miscalculations and misjudgement, effective verification is increasingly important. It is therefore imperative to study new procedures of verification on a broad basis. Bilateral verification agreements by no means constitute the only solution; new ideas regarding verification may also involve verification by proxy, verification by third parties (e.g., inspection teams from one or more neutral or non-aligned nations) and verification by international organizations (based on the successful experience in the non-military field of the IAEA safeguards system).

22. The efforts to improve Confidence and Security Building Measures (CSBMs) in Europe must not be halted or abandoned, despite the present crisis of the Madrid negotiations taking place in the context of the Conference on Security and Co-

operation in Europe (CSCE). They are capable of contributing substantially to enhancing conventional stability and thus also to strengthening overall strategic stability, mainly by allaying the fear of surprise attack.

23. As one of the dangers of coercive bargaining employed in crisis situations lies in the risk of inadvertent or unauthorized use of force by subordinate commanders, it is important to secure quick and efficient communication between the opponents in order to forestall or correct misinterpretations should such events occur.

24. More attention should be paid to the links existing between local crisis spots in Third World regions and the delicate strategic relationship of the two major Powers elsewhere. These links are even more crucial since they are not very obvious under "normal" conditions and tend to emerge in situations of acute crisis only, thus generating a considerable amount of surprise which, in turn, constitutes a risk with regard to national approaches to the crisis. Dismantling mechanisms that automatically drag third countries into local conflicts contributes to the limitation of these risks.

25. At the same time, it is desirable that the major Powers should re-examine their worldwide commitments. In particular, it is necessary that they should try to define more precisely the extent of their commitments and the responsibilities and obligations assumed by themselves and by their friends or allies. This process of clarification must be at least triangular, involving both the provider and the recipient of the guarantee as well as potential local or major Power opponents.

26. The various suggestions for holding talks among the major Powers, concerning the possibility of a "code of conduct" in third world regions deserve to be examined. It seems desirable to have at least a basic understanding about the types of commitments and actions that ought to be avoided on a mutual basis.

27. In view of the rapidly growing commitments of the two major Powers in the third world, and of the potential for crisis confrontations which results from them, efforts should be made to discuss the conventions of crisis. In these discussions, due attention should be paid to the observance of minimum standards of behaviour when using force as well as to ways and means of securing communications among adversaries in crisis situations.

28. In particular, attention should be paid to the dangers arising when the threshold from coercive bargaining to actual violence is crossed. Contingency planning for various crisis situations should be re-examined with a view to increasing the number of alternatives to the use of violence, i.e., to putting more rungs on the lower part of the escalation ladder.

29. Available technologies for enhanced communication in crisis situations (such as the "Hot Line") should be used by all countries that might become protagonists in future international crises.

30. It is desirable for the major Powers and other great Powers to discuss crisis procedure norms, i.e. to identify types of behaviour that ought to be avoided as well as types of behaviour recommended. However, it must be borne in mind that, for a number of reasons, it is very difficult to apply such norms (Caldwell 1979: 43). It would therefore be misleading to expect too much from efforts undertaken in this direction. It should also be borne in mind that any progress in this field will hardly be reached independently of the general political context; increasing political tension also necessarily narrows the scope for agreements in this field. Nevertheless, it might be useful to have talks among experts from various countries, to be arranged within the framework of international professional organizations active in the field of social sciences. These talks should be held with a view to elaborating a set of rules on which agreement seems possible, perhaps formulated in a context-specific way, i.e., focused on specific regions which seem crisis-prone. As a possible starting point an *ex post facto* analysis of past international crises may be envisaged.

31. As the rapidly growing use of force in the third world is not unconnected with the increasing flow of conventional armaments into the third world, it is desirable to resume talks on Conventional Arms Transfers (CAT) such as the ones begun in 1977—1978. Arms transfers are at the root of major Power involvement, and they create a dynamic of their own which may drag major powers into a local crisis despite a basic desire to stay out of it. The limitation of arms transfers can also reduce the need to deliver arms and to secure access in times of crisis. For obvious reasons these talks should also include European States active in arms transfers, as well as arms producers in the third world.

32. Pending the conclusion of universally applicable agreements for co-operative controls on arms transfers, efforts ought to be undertaken on a regional basis with a view to limiting or prohibiting arms transfers in general or the transfer of specific types of weapons to specific and clearly defined crisis regions. Again, it is essential to include any potential supplier in negotiations and also to make sure that potential supplies "by proxy" are covered.

BIBLIOGRAPHY

Afheldt, Horst, and Philipp Sonntag (1971): Stability and Strategic Nuclear Arms. World Law
    Fund Occasional Papers.
—   , and Philipp Sonntag (1973): "Stability and Deterrence Through Strategic Nuclear
    Arms". In: Journal of Peace Research, Vol. 10, Number 3. pp. 245—250.
—   (1976): Verteidigung und Frieden. Politik mit militaerischen Mitteln. Muenchen:
    Carl Hanser.
—   (1978): "Tactical Nuclear Weapons and European Security". In: Stockholm Inter-
    national Peace Research Institute (Ed.): Tactical Nuclear Weapons:
    European Perspectives. London: Taylor & Francis. pp. 262—295.
—   (1979): "Die Philosophie der Ruestungskontrolle am Ende". In: Spiegel, Number
    24. pp. 138—139.
Albertini, James V. (1981): "Hawaii: Life Under the Gun". In: Bulletin of the Atomic Scientists,
    Vol. 37, Number 3. pp. 50—57.
Albrecht, Ulrich, Asbjørn Eide, Mary Kaldor, Milton Leitenberg, and Julian P. Robinson (1978):
    A Short Research Guide to Arms and Armed Forces. London: Croom Helm.
—   , et al. (Eds.) (1981): Weltpolitik; Jahrbuch fuer Internationale Beziehungen 1.
    Frankfurt/Main: Campus.
Alford, Jonathan (Ed.) (1979): The Future of Arms Control, Part III: Confidence-Building Measures
    (Adelphi Papers; 149). London: International Institute for Strategic Studies.
Allison, Graham T. (1971): Essence of Decision. Explaining the Cuban Missile Crisis. Boston:
    Little, Brown.
—   , and Morton M. Halperin (1972): "Bureaucratic Politics: A Paradigm and Some
    Policy Implications". In : Raymond Tanter and Richard H. Ullman (Eds.): Theory
    and Policy in International Relations. Princeton, N. J.: Princeton University Press.
    pp. 40—79.
Anderson, J. Edward (1981): "First Strike: Myth or Reality" In: Bulletin of the Atomic Scientists,
    Vol. 37, Number 9. pp. 6—12.
Andriole, Stephen J., and Robert A. Young (1977): "Toward the Development of an Integrated
    Crisis Warning System". In: International Studies Quarterly, Vol. 21, Number 1.
    pp. 107—150.
Arbatov, Georgi A. (1979): "Forum: Remarks Made at a Special Session with the Prime Minister
    of Canada". In: Franklyn Griffiths and John C. Polanyi (Eds.): The Dangers of Nu-
    clear War. Toronto: University of Toronto Press. pp. 149—153.
—   (1981): "The Strategy of Nuclear Madness". In: Co-Existence, Vol. 18, Number 2.
    pp. 162—174.

Ball, Desmond J. (1977): "The Counterforce Potential of American SLBM Systems" In: Journal of Peace Research, Vol. 14, Number 1. pp. 23—40.
— (1980): "Research Note: Soviet ICBM Deployment". In: Survival, Vol. 22, Number 4. pp. 167—170.
— (1981): Can Nuclear War Be Controlled? (Adelphi Papers; 169) London: International Institute for Strategic Studies.
Barnaby, Frank (1978): "The Irrationality of Current Nuclear Doctrines". In: Stockholm International Peace Research Institute (Ed.): Tactical Nuclear Weapons: European Perspectives. London: Taylor & Francis. pp. 213—222.
— (1980): Prospects for Peace. Oxford: Pergamon Press.
— (1981): "Military-Scientists". In: Bulletin of the Atomic Scientists, Vol. 37, Number 6. pp. 11—12.
Barre, Raymond (1977): "Speech by Prime Minister Barre, 18 June 1977". In: Survival. Vol. 19, Number 5. pp. 225—228.
Barton, John H., and Lawrence D. Weiler (Eds.) (1976): International Arms Control —Issues and Agreements. Stanford: Stanford University Press.
— (1981): The Politics of Peace; An Evaluation of Arms Control. Stanford: Stanford University Press.
Barton, S. W., and Laurence M. Martin (1973): "Public Diplomacy and the Soviet Invasion of Czechoslovakia in 1968". In: Gregory Henderson (Ed.): Public Diplomacy and Political Change. Four Case Studies: Okinawa, Peru, Czechoslovakia, Guinea. New York: Praeger. pp. 244—314.
Batsanov Sergei (Ed.) (1982): How the USSR is Working for Disarmament at the U.N. Moscow: Novosti Press.
Baudissin, Wolf Graf von, and Dieter S. Lutz (Eds.) (1981a): Konflikte, Krisen, Kriegsverhuetung. Baden-Baden: Nomos.
—, and Dieter S. Lutz (Eds.) (1981b): Kooperative Ruestungssteuerung. Baden-Baden: Nomos.
—, and Dieter S. Lutz (1981c): "Kooperative Ruestungssteuerung in Europa". In: Wolf Graf von Baudissin and Dieter S. Lutz (Eds.): Kooperative Ruestungssteuerung. Baden-Baden: Nomos. pp. 9—40.
Baylis, John, et al. (Eds.) (1975): Contemporary Strategy: Theories and Politics. London: Croom Helm.
—, and Gerald Segal (Eds.) (1981): Soviet Strategy. London: Croom Helm.
Beaufre, André (1964a): Introduction à la stratégie. Paris: Colin.
— (1964b): Dissuasion et stratégie. Paris: Colin.
Beck, Melinda, and David C. Martin (1982): "The War Beneath the Seas". In: Newsweek, February 8, 1982. pp. 37f.
Beer, Francis (1981): Peace Against War. San Francisco: W. H. Freeman.
Belden, Thomas G. (1977): "Indications, Warning, and Crisis Operations". In: International Studies Quarterly, Vol. 21, Number, 1. pp. 181—198.
Bell, Coral (1971): The Conventions of Crisis. London: Oxford University Press.
— (1978): "Decision-Making by Governments in Crisis Situations". In: Daniel Frei (Ed.): International Crises and Crisis Management. An East-West Symposium. Farnborough: Saxon House. pp. 50—58.
— (1979): "Crisis Diplomacy". In: Laurence Martin (Ed.): Strategic Thought in the Nuclear Age. Baltimore, Md.: Johns Hopkins University Press. pp. 157—185.
Bereanu, Bernard (1981): "On the Probability of Selfactivation of the World Nuclear Weapons Stockpile". In: Methods of Operations Research, Number 44. pp. 507—520.

Beres, Louis René (1980): Apocalypse. Nuclear Catastrophe in World Politics. Chicago: University of Chicago Press.
—   (1981): "Tilting Toward Thanatos: America's 'Countervailing' Nuclear Strategy". In: World Politics, Vol. 34, Number 1. pp. 25—46.
Bertram, Christoph (1978): The Future of Arms Control: Part II: Arms Control and Technological Change: Elements of a New Approach (Adelphi Papers; 146). London: International Institute for Strategic Studies.
—   (1981a): Strategic Deterrence in a Changing Environment. London: Gower.
—   (1981b): "The Implications of Theater Nuclear War in Europe". In: Foreign Affairs, Vol. 60, Number, 2. pp. 305—326.
Bethe, Hans A. (1981): "Meaningless Superiority". In: Bulletin of the Atomic Scientists, Vol. 37, Number 8. pp. 1—4.
Betts, Richard K. (1977): Soldiers, Statesmen, and Cold War Crises. Cambridge, Mass., and London: Harvard University Press.
—   (1978): "Analysis, War, and Decision: Why Intelligence Failures Are Inevitable". In: World Politics, Vol. 31, Number 1. pp. 61—89.
—   (1981a): "Hedging Against Surprise Attack". In: Survival, Vol. 23, Number 4. pp. 146—156.
—   (1981b): "Nuclear Surprise Attack: Deterrence, Defense, and Conceptual Contradictions in American Policy". In: Jerusalem Journal of International Relations. Vol. 5, Number 3. pp. 73—99.
—   (1981c): "Nuclear Proliferation after Osirak". In: Arms Control Today, Vol. 11, Number 7. pp. 1—8.
—   (1981d): "Surprise Attack: NATO's Political Vulnerability". In: International Security, Vol. 5, Number 4. pp. 117—149.
Beukel, Erich (1979): "Soviet Views on Strategic Nuclear Weapons: Orthodoxy and Modernism". In: Cooperation and Conflict, Vol. 14, Number 4. pp. 223—237.
Birnbaum, Karl E. (Ed.) (1980): Arms Control in Europe: Problems and Prospects. Laxenburg: Austrian Institute for International Affairs.
Bittorf, Wilhelm (1981): "Schiessplatz der Supermaechte. Die sowjetische Bedrohung Westeuropas und die Nachruestung (III)". In: Spiegel, Number 30. pp. 118—120.
Blechman, Barry M., and Stephen S. Kaplan (1978): Force Without War. U.S. Armed Forces as a Political Instrument. Washington, D.C.: The Brookings Institution.
—   , and Douglas M. Hart (1982): "Nuclear Threats and the Nation's Security". In: International Security, Vol. 6 (Summer 1982).
Bonoma, Thomas V. (1975): Conflict: Escalation and Deescalation. Beverly Hills and London: Sage Publications.
Boserup, Anders (1981a): "A Strategy for Peace and Security". In: Bulletin of Peace Proposals, Vol. 12, Number 4. pp. 405—408.
—   (1981b): "Deterrence and Defense". In: Bulletin of the Atomic Scientists, Vol. 37, Number 10. pp. 11—13.
Bracken, Paul (1979): "Mobilization in the Nuclear Age". In: International Security, Vol. 3, Number 3. pp. 74—93.
Brams, Steven J. (1975): Game Theory and Politics. New York and London: The Free Press.
Brayton, Abbott A. (1980): "Confidence-Building Measures in European Security". In: The World Today, Vol. 36, Number 10. pp. 382—391.
Brecher, Michael (1974): "Research Findings and Theory-Building in Foreign Policy Behavior". In: Patrick J. McGowan (Ed.): Sage International Yearbook of Foreign Policy Studies, Volume Two. Beverly Hills and London: Sage Publications. pp. 49—122.

—   (1977): "Toward a Theory of International Crisis Behavior: A Preliminary Report"·
In: International Studies Quarterly, Vol. 21, Number 1. pp. 39—74.

—   (Ed.) (1978a): Studies in Crisis Behavior. New Brunswick. N. J.: Transaction
Books.

—   (1978 b): "'Vertical' Case Studies: A Summary of Findings". In: Michael Brecher
(Ed.): Studies in Crisis Behavior. New Brunswick, N. J.: Transaction Books.
pp. 264—276.

—   (1979): "State Behavior in International Crisis. A Model". In: Journal of Conflict
Resolution, Vol. 23, Number 9. pp. 446—480.

—   (1980): Decisions in Crisis. Israel, 1967 and 1973. Berkeley: University of California
Press.

Bremer, Stuart, J. David Singer, and Urs Luterbacher (1979): "The Population Density and War
Proneness of European Nations, 1816—1965". In: J. David Singer and Ass.: Explain-
ing War. Selected Papers from the Correlates of War Project. Beverly Hills and
London: Sage Publications. pp. 189—207.

Brennan, Donald G. (1979): "Commentary". In: International Security, Vol. 3, Number 3. pp.
193—198.

Brezhnev, Leonid I. (1981a): Report of the Central Committee of the CPSU to the XXVI Congress
of the Communist Party of the Soviet Union and the Immediate Task of the Party in
Home and Foreign Policy. Moscow: Novosti Press.

—   (1981 b): "L. I. Brezhnev's interview to 'Der Spiegel' Magazine". Moscow: Novosti Press.

—   (1982 a): "Leonid Brezhnev's Reply to the Japanese Writers". In: Press Bulletin Permanent Mission of the Soviet Union, Geneva, Number 34 (305), 1 March 1982.

—   (1982 b): "Put Concern for the Working People, Concern for Production at the Centre of
Attention of the Trade Unions". Moscow: Novosti Press.

—   (1982 c): "Speech on the occasion of the presentation of the Uzbek Soviet Socialist Republic
of the Order of Lenin". In: Press Bulletin Permanent Mission of the Soviet Union,
Geneva, Number 44 (315), 24 March 1982.

Brito, Dagobert L., and Michael D. Intriligator (1981): "Strategic Arms Limitation
Treaties and Innovation in Weapons Technology". In: Public Choice, Vol.
37. pp. 41—59.

—   (1982): "Arms Races: Behavioral and Economic Aspects". In: John Gillespie and
Dina Zinnes (Eds.): Missing Elements of Political Inquiry. Beverly Hills: Sage Publications. (forthcoming)

Brodie, Bernard (1976): "On the Objectives of Arms Control". In: International Security, Vol. 1,
Number 1. pp. 17—36.

Brown, Harold (1979): "Statement, 25 January 1979". In: Survival, Vol. 21, Number 3.
pp. 125—131.

—   (1980): "Address, 20 August 1980". In : Survival, Vol. 22, Number 6. pp. 267—269.

Buch, Heinrich (1977): "Detente and Military Behavior". In: Co-Existence, Vol. 14, Number 1.
pp. 138—147.

Buchan, Glenn C. (1981): "The Anti-MAD Mythology". In: Bulletin of the Atomic Scientists,
Vol. 37, Number 4. pp. 13—17.

Bueno de Mesquita, Bruce (1979): "Systemic Polarization and the Occurrence and Duration of War".
In: J. David Singer and Ass.: Explaining War. Selected Papers from the Correlates
of War Project. Beverly Hills and London: Sage Publications. pp. 113—138.

Bull, Hedley (1981): "Force in International Relations. The Experience of the 1970s and Prospects for the 1980s". In: Robert O'Neill and David M. Horner (Eds.): New Directions in Strategic Thinking. London: George Allen & Unwin. pp. 17—33.

Bundy, McGeorge (1979): "Maintaining Stable Deterrence". In: International Security, Vol. 3, Number 3. pp. 5—16.

Burt, Richard (1979): "A Glass Half Empty". In: Foreign Policy, Number 36. pp. 33—48.

Bykov, Oleg (1978): "The Control of Crisis Situations in Contemporary World Politics". In: Daniel Frei (Ed.): International Crises and Crisis Management. An East-West Symposium. Farnborough: Saxon House. pp. 59—70.

— (1980): "The Imperatives of Military Detente". In: Nikolai N. Inozemtzev (Ed.): Peace and Disarmament 1980. Moscow: Scientific Research Council on Peace and Disarmament, Progress Publishers, pp. 127—137.

Calder, Nigel (1980): Nuclear Nightmares. An Investigation into Possible Wars. New York: The Viking Press.

Caldwell, Dan (1979): Soviet-American Crisis Management in the Cuban Missile Crisis and the October War. Paper.

Carlton, David, and Carlo Schaerf (Eds.) (1975): The Dynamics of the Arms Race. London: Croom Helm.

Carter, Barry (1975): "Flexible Strategic Options: No Need for New Strategy". In: Survival, Vol. 17, Number 1. pp. 25—31.

Chan, Steve (1979): "The Intelligence of Stupidity: Understanding Failures in Strategic Warning". In: American Political Science Review, Vol. 73, Number 1. pp. 171—180.

Chari, P. R. (1979): "Forum: Remarks Made at a Special Session with the Prime Minister of Canada". In: Franklyn Griffiths and John C. Polanyi (Eds.): The Dangers of Nuclear War. Toronto: University of Toronto Press. pp. 153—156.

Clarke, Magnus (1981): The Nuclear Destruction of Britain. London: Croom Helm.

Clemens, Walter C. (1981): National Security and U.S. — Soviet Relations (Occasional Paper Number 26). Muscatine, Iowa: Stanley Foundation.

Cohen, Raymond (1979): Threat Perception in International Crisis. Madison: The University of Wisconsin Press.

— (1980): "Rules of the Game in International Politics". In: International Studies Quarterly, Vol. 24, Number 1. pp. 129—150.

— (1981a): International Politics. The Rules of the Game. London and New York: Longman.

— (1981b): "Whe.re are the Aircraft Carriers? Nonverbal Communication in International Politics" In: Review of International Studies, Vol. 7, Number 2. pp. 79—90:

Collins, John M.: U.S. — Soviet Military Balance: Concepts and Capabilities, 1960—1980.

Comptroller General of the United States (1980): Report to the Congress: Implications of Highly Sophisticated Weapon Systems on Military Capabilities (PSAD-80-61). Washington, D.C.: General Accounting Office.

— (1981 a): Report to the Congress: Effectiveness of U.S. Forces Can be Increased through Improved Weapon System Design (PSAD-81-17). Washington, D.C.: General Accounting Office.

— (1981b): Report to the Congress: Countervailing Strategy Demands Revision of Strategic Force Acquisition Plans (Acc Number 11 60 66, NASAD-81-35). Washington, D.C.: General Accounting Office.

— (1981c): Report to the Congress: The World Wide Military Command and Control Information System. Washington, D. C.: General Accounting Office.

235

Coutrot, Alain, et al. (1979): Le fondement doctrinaire de la stratégie soviétique. Paris: Fondation pour les Etudes de la Défense Nationale.

Daly, Judith Ayres, and Stephen J. Andriole (1979): "Problems of Applied Monitoring and Warning: Illustrations from the Middle East". In: Jerusalem Journal of International Relations. Vol. 4, Number 2. pp. 31−74.

— (1980): "The Use of Events/Interaction Research by the Intelligence Community". In: Policy Sciences: 12. pp. 215−236.

Daniel, Donald C. (Ed.) (1978): International Perceptions of the Superpower Military Balance. New York: Praeger.

Davis, Jacquelyn K. et al. (1981): The Soviet Union and Ballistic Missile Defense. Cambridge, Mass., and Washington, D. C.: Institute for Foreign Policy Analysis.

Deane, Michael J. (1978): "Soviet Perceptions of the Military Factor in the 'Correlation of Forces' ". In: Donald C. Daniel (Ed.): International Perceptions of the Superpower Military Balance. New York: Praeger. pp. 72−94.

de Foïard, Armand (1980): "Autres propos sur la dissuasion nucléaire". In: Défense Nationale, Vol. 36, March 1980, pp. 21−32.

Deibel, Terry L. (1980): Commitment in American Foreign Policy (National Defense University Monograph Series No. 80−4). Washington, D.C.: National Defense University.

Delahousse, Paul (1981): "Les conséquences du concept stratégique fondé sur la dissuasion nucléaire et la bataille". In: Défense Nationale, Vol. 37, March 1981. pp. 55−59.

Denis, Jacques-Marie (1981): "La France et les problèmes de la réponse 'flexible' ou 'graduée' ". In: Défense Nationale, Vol. 37, March 1981. pp. 85−91.

de Rose, François (1982): "Nuclear Forces and Alliance Relations". In: Survival, Vol. 24, Number 1. pp. 19−24.

Deutsch, Karl W. (1968): The Analysis of International Relations. Englewood Cliffs, N. J.: Prentice-Hall.

De Vries, Klaas G. (1979): "Responding to the SS-20: An Alternative Approach". In: Survival, Vol. 21, Number 6. pp. 251−255.

Dewitt, David B. (1979): "Breakpoints and Interstate Conflict". In: J. David Singer and Michael D. Wallace (Eds.): To Augur Well. Early Warning Indicators in World Politics. Beverly Hills and London: Sage Publications. pp. 51−107.

Dewitt, Hugh E. (1981): "On 'Military-Scientists' ". In: Bulletin of the Atomic Scientists, Vol. 37, Number 8. p. 60.

Dictionary of Basic Military Terms (1965): A Soviet View (Published under the Auspices of the United States Air Force, Translated by the DGIS Multilingual Section Translation Bureau of State Department, Ottawa, Canada). Washington, D.C.: United States Government Printing Office (first published 1965 in Moscow).

Dismukes, Bradford, and James M. McConnell (Eds.) (1979): Soviet Naval Diplomacy. New York and Oxford: Pergamon Press.

Douglass, Joseph D., Jr., and Amoretta M. Hoeber (1979): Soviet Strategy for Nuclear War. Stanford: Hoover Institution Press.

Dror, Yehezkel (1974): Crazy States. A Counterconventional Strategic Problem. Lexington, Mass.: D. C. Heath.

Dumas, Lloyd J. (1977): "Systems Reliability and National Insecurity". In: Peace Research Reviews. Vol. 7, Number 3. pp. 66−85.

— (1978): "Comments on 'A Catastrophe Surface in Mutual Deterrence Theory' ". In: Journal of Peace Science, Vol. 3, Number 2. pp. 123−128.

— (1980): "Human Fallibility and Weapons". In: Bulletin of the Atomic Scientists, Vol. 36, Number 9. pp. 15−20.

Dunn, Lewis A. (1976): "Nuclear 'Gray Marketeering'". In: International Security, Vol. 1, Number 3. pp. 107—118.

Eberwein, Wolf-Dieter (1978): Crisis Forecasting: The Data Base Problem. Paper prepared for the 15th European Conference of the PSSI, September 3—5, 1978, Geneva.

—   (1981a): Militaerische Konfrontationen und die Eskalation zum Krieg, 1900—2000 (IIVG Paper, Number 81/112). Berlin: International Institute for Comparative Social Research.

—   (1981b): Globale Sicherheitsprobleme in den naechsten Jahrzehnten (Papiere fuer die Praxis, Number 35). Bonn: Deutsche Gesellschaft fuer Friedens- und Konflikt-forschung.

Ehmke, Horst (1981): "Das Undenkbare verhindern". In: Spiegel, Number 44. pp. 196—218.

Eide, Asbjørn, and Marek Thee (Eds.) (1980): Problems of Contemporary Militarism. London: Croom Helm.

Einhorn, Robert J. (1981): "Treaty Compliance". In: Foreign Policy, Number 45. pp. 29—47.

Epstein, William (1976): The Last Chance. Nuclear Proliferation and Arms Control. New York: The Free Press.

—   (1979): "Nuclear Terrorism and Nuclear War". In: Franklyn Griffiths and John C. Polanyi (Eds.): The Dangers of Nuclear War. Toronto: University of Toronto Press. pp. 109—124.

—   (1981): "Limits on Nuclear Testing: Another View". In: Arms Control Today, Vol. 11, Number 8. pp. 4—9.

Ermarth, Fritz W. (1978): "Contrasts in American and Soviet Strategic Thought". In: International Security, Vol. 3, Number 2. pp. 138—155.

Evron, Yair (1979): "Great Power's Military Intervention in the Middle East". In: Milton Leitenberg and Gabriel Sheffer (Eds.): Great Power Intervention in the Middle East. New York: Pergamon Press. pp. 17—45.

—   (1982): "Conflicts in the Third World and their Impact on the U.S. — U.S.S.R. Balance". In: Daniel Frei (Ed.): Sicherheit durch Gleichgewicht? Militaerstrategische Tendenzen der achtziger Jahre. Zurich: Schulthess Polygraphischer Verlag. (forthcoming).

Falk, Richard (1976): "Nuclear Weapons Proliferation as a World Order Problem". In: International Security, Vol. 1, Number 3. pp. 79—93.

Fedorov, E. K., and Rem A. Novikov (Eds.) (1981): Le désarmement et l'environnement. Moscow: Nauka Publishers.

Fedorov, Yurii E. (1981): "La détente internationale, clé du problème écologique planétaire". In: E. K. Fedorov and Rem A. Novikov (Eds.): Le désarmement et l'environnement. Moscow: Nauka Publishers. pp. 76—81.

Feld, Bernard T., and Kosta Tsipis (1979): "Land-Based Intercontinental Ballistic Missiles". In: Scientific American 241, 5 (November 1979). pp. 50—61.

—   (1980): "If it Isn't one Thing it's Another". In: Bulletin of the Atomic Scientists, Vol. 36, Number 7. p. 4.

Feld, Maury D. (1977): "Military Demonstrations: Intervention and the Flag". In: Ellen P. Stern (Ed.): The Limits of Military Intervention. Beverly Hills and London: Sage Publications. pp. 197—212.

Fiscal Year 1982 Arms Control Impact Statements (FY 1982 ACIS) (1981). Statements Submitted to the Congress by the President Pursuant to Section 36 of the Arms Control and Disarmament Act. Washington, D. C.: United States Government Printing Office.

Fitts, Richard E. (1980): The Strategy of Electromagnetic Conflict. Los Altos, Cal.: Peninsula Publishing.

Ford, H., and Francis X. Winters (1977): Ethics and Nuclear Strategy. Maryknoll, N. Y.: Orbis.

Foster, Gregory D. (1981): "Unauthorized Nuclear Weapon Seizure: The Analysis of Post-Seizure Response". In: International Interactions, Vol. 8, Number 4. pp. 275—295.

Franck, Thomas M., and Edward Weisband (1972): Word Politics. Verbal Strategy Among the Superpowers. New York: Oxford University Press.

Freedman, Lawrence (1981): "NATO Myths". In: Foreign Policy, Number 45. pp. 48—68.

Frei, Daniel (1974): "Conflict Resolution by Mutual Disengagement". In: International Interaction, Vol. 1, Number 2. pp. 101—112.

—   (1977): Sicherheit; Grundfragen der Weltpolitik. Stuttgart: Kohlhammer.

—   (Ed.)(1978): International Crises and Crisis Management. An East-West Symposium. Farnborough: Saxon House.

—   (1980): Evolving a Conceptual Framework of Inter-Systems Relations (UNITAR Research Report, Number 25). New York: United Nations Institute for Training and Research.

—   (1981a): A Third-Party Role for the Neutrals in the Context of CBM Verification? (Paper presented to the 37th Pugwash Symposium). Hamburg: Institut fuer Friedensforschung und Sicherheitspolitik (mimeo).

—   (Ed.) (1981b): Definitions and Measurement of Détente. Cambridge, Mass.: Oelgeschlager, Gunn & Hain.

—   (1982a): Internationale Zusammenarbeit als kollektives Dilemma. Frankfurt/Main: Athenaeum.

—   (Ed.) (1982b): Sicherheit durch Gleichgewicht? Militaerstrategische Tendenzen der achtziger Jahre. Zurich: Schulthess Polygraphischer Verlag.

Freier, Shalheveth (1979): "Local Wars and Their Escalation". In: Franklyn Griffiths and John C. Polanyi (Eds.): The Dangers of Nuclear War. Toronto: University of Toronto Press. pp. 125—134.

Fried, John H. E. (1981): "First-Use of Nuclear Weapons — Existing Prohibitions in International Law". In: Bulletin of Peace Proposals, Vol. 12, Number 1. pp. 21—29.

Fritsch, Bruno (1981): Wir werden ueberleben; Orientierungen und Hoffnungen in schwieriger Zeit. Munich: Olzog.

Frye, Alton (1977): "Strategic Restraint, Mutual and Assured". In: Foreign Policy, Number 27. pp. 3—26.

—   (1980): "Nuclear Weapons in Europe: No Exit from Ambivalence". In: Survival, Vol. 22, Number 3. pp. 98—106.

Gallagher, Matthew P., and Karl F. Spielmann, Jr. (1972): Soviet Decision-Making for Defense. A Critique of U.S. Perspectives on the Arms Race. New York: Praeger.

Gallois, Pierre M. (1978): Soviet Military Doctrine and European Defence. NATO's Obsolete Concepts (Conflict Studies; Security Report Number 96). London: Institute for the Study of Conflict.

Garnett, John (1975): "The Role of Military Power". In: John Baylis, Ken Booth, John Garnett, and Phil Williams (Eds.): Contemporary Strategy: Theories and Politics. London: Croom Helm. pp. 50—64.

Garthoff, Raymond L. (1978a): "Mutual Deterrence and Strategic Arms Limitation in Soviet Policy". In: International Security, Vol. 3, Number 1. pp. 112—147.

—   (1978b): "On Estimating and Imputing Intentions". In: International Security, Vol. 2, Number 3. pp. 22—32.

—   (1978c): "SALT I: An Evaluation". In: World Politics, Vol. 31, Number 1. pp. 1—25.

—   (1979): "On Mutual Deterrence: A Reply to Donald Brennan". In: International Security, Vol. 3, Number 4. pp. 197—199.

Garwin, Richard L. (1976): "Effective Military Technology for the 1980 s". In: International Security, Vol. 1, Number 2. pp. 50—77.

—   (1979): "Weapons Developments and the Threat of Nuclear War". In: Franklyn Griffiths and John C. Polanyi (Eds.): The Dangers of Nuclear War. Toronto: University of Toronto Press. pp. 93—106.

—   (1980): "Launch Under Attack to Redress Minuteman Vulnerability". In: International Security, Vol. 4, Number 3. pp. 117—139.

—   (1981): "Are We On the Verge of an Arms Race in Space?". In: Bulletin of the Atomic Scientists, Vol. 37, Number 5. pp. 14—21.

Gelb, Leslie H. (1979): "A Glass Half Full ...". In: Foreign Policy, Number 36. pp. 21—32.

George, Alexander L. (1969): "The Operational Code". In: International Studies Quarterly, Vol. 13. pp. 190—222.

—   , and Richard Smoke (1974): Deterrence in American Foreign Policy: Theory and Practice. New York and London: Columbia University Press.

—   (1978): Discussion Paper: Towards a Crisis Prevention Regime in U.S.—S.U. Relations. Paper prepared for the Pugwash Workshop on Crisis Management and Prevention, Geneva, December 13—15.

—   (1980): Presidential Decisionmaking in Foreign Policy: The Effective Use of Information and Advice. Boulder, Colo.: Westview Press.

Gerasimov, Gennadi (1982): War and Peace in the Nuclear Age. Moscow: Novosti Press.

Gilbert, Arthur N., and Paul Gordon Lauren (1980): "Crisis Management: An Assessment and Critique". In: Journal of Conflict Resolution, Vol. 24, Number 4. pp. 641—664.

Gillespie, John, and Dina Zinnes (Eds.) (1982): Missing Elements of Political Inquiry. Beverly Hills: Sage Publications.

Gochman, Charles S. (1979): "Studies of International Violence: Five Easy Pieces?" In: J. David Singer and Ass. : Explaining War. Selected Papers from the Correlates of War Project. Beverly Hills and London: Sage Publications. pp. 35—55.

Goldblat, Jozef (1979): Arms Control: A Survey and Appraisal of Multilateral Agreements. London: Taylor & Francis.

—   (1981: "Nuclear Weapons — The Threat to Our Survival". In: Bulletin of Peace Proposals, Vol. 12, Number 1. pp. 30—32.

Goldhamer, Herbert (1978): "Perceptions of the U.S. — Soviet Balance: Problems of Analysis and Research". In: Donald C. Daniel (Ed.): International Perceptions of the Superpower Military Balance. New York: Praeger. pp. 3—20.

Gouré, Leon, William G. Hyland, and Colin S. Gray (1979): The Emerging Strategic Environment: Implications for Ballistic Missile Defense. Cambridge, Mass., and Washington, D.C.: Institute for Foreign Policy Analysis.

Gray, Colin S. (1977): The Future of Land-Based Missile Forces (Adelphi Papers; 140). London: International Institute for Strategic Studies.

—   (1979): "Nuclear Strategy: A Case for a Theory of Victory" . In : International Security, Vol. 4, Number, 1. pp. 54—87.

—   , and Keith Payne (1980): "Victory is Possible". In: Foreign Policy, Number 39. pp. 14—27.

—   (1981a): "A New Debate on Ballistic Missile Defence". In: Survival, Vol. 23, Number 2. pp. 60—71.

—   (1981b): "The Future of Land- Based Missile Forces ". In: Christoph Bertram (Ed.) Strategic Deterrence in a Changing Environment. London: Gower. pp. 64-94.

239

Green, Philip (1966): Deadly Logic; The Theory of Nuclear Deterrence. Columbus, Ohio: Ohio State University Press.

Griffiths, Franklyn, and John C. Polanyi (Eds.) (1979): The Dangers of Nuclear War. Toronto: University of Toronto Press.

Grosser, George H. (Ed.) (1964): The Threat of Impending Disaster. Cambridge, Mass.: Harvard University Press.

Guertner, Gary L. (1979): "Carter's SALT: MAD or SAFE?". In: Bulletin of the Atomic Scientists, Vol. 35, Number 8. pp. 28—33.

Gurr, Ted Robert, and Mark Irving Lichbach (1979): "Forecasting Domestic Political Conflict". In: J. David Singer and Michael D. Wallace (Eds.): To Augur Well. Early Warning Indicators in World Politics. Beverly Hills and London: Sage Publications. pp. 153—193.

Gvishiani, Jermen (1980): "Scientific and Technological Progress and the Problems of Preserving Peace". In: Nikolai N. Inozemtzev (Ed.): Peace and Disarmament 1980. Moscow: Scientific Research Council on Peace and Disarmament, Progress Publishers. pp. 49—63.

Haefs, Hanswilhelm (Ed.) (1980): Dokumentation zur Abruestung und Sicherheit, Vol. 16: 1978. St. Augustin: Siegler.

Halper, Thomas (1971): Foreign Policy Crisis. Appearance and Reality in Decision Making. Columbus: Charles E. Merrill.

Hamblin, Robert L. (1965): "Group Integration During a Crisis". In : J. David Singer (Ed.): Human Behavior and International Politics. Chicago: Rand McNally. pp. 220—230.

Hazlewood, Leo, John J. Hayes, and James R. Brownell, Jr. (1975): "Planning for Problems in Crisis Management: An Analysis of Post-1945 Behavior in the U.S. Department of Defense". In: International Studies Quarterly, Vol. 21, Number 1. pp. 75—106.

Head, Richard G., Frisco W. Short, and Robert C. McFarlane (1978): Crisis Resolution: Presidential Decision Making in the Mayaguez and Korean Confrontations. Boulder, Colo.: Westview Press.

Hearings on Military Posture and H.R. 2614 and H.R. 2970 Before the Committee on Armed Services, House of the Representatives, 97th Congress, First Session. Part 1 of 6 Parts, 1981. Washington. D.C.: United States Government Printing Office.

Hearings on Military Posture and H.R. 2614 and H.R. 2970 Before the Committee on Armed Services, House of the Representatives, 97th Congress, First Session. Part 4 of 6 Parts,: 1981. Washington, D.C.: United States Government Printing Office.

Henderson, Gregory (Ed.) (1973): Public Diplomacy and Political Change. Four Case Studies: Okinawa, Peru, Czechoslovakia, Guinea. New York: Praeger.

Hermann, Charles F., and Linda P. Brady (1972): "Alternative Models of International Crisis". In: Charles F. Hermann (Ed.): International Crises: Insights from Behavioral Research. New York: The Free Press. pp. 281—303.

— (Ed.) (1972a): International Crises: Insights from Behavioral Research. New York: The Free Press.

— (1972b):"Threat, Time, and Surprise: A Simulation of International Crisis". In: Charles F. Hermann (Ed.): International Crises: Insights from Behavioral Research. New York: The Free Press. pp. 182—211.

— ,Margaret G. Hermann, and Robert A. Cantor (1974): "Counterattack or Delay: Characteristics Influencing Decision Makers' Responses to the Simulation of an Unidentified Attack". In: Journal of Conflict Resolution, Vol. 18, Number 2. pp. 75—106.

— (Ed.) (1975): Research Tasks for International Crisis Avoidance and Management. Washington, D. C.: Office of Naval Research.

Hernu, Charles (1981): "Répondre aux défis d'un monde dangereux". In: Défense Nationale, Vol. 37, December 1981. pp. 5—23.

Heuer, Richard J., Jr. (1981): "Strategic Deception and Counterdeception". In: International Studies Quarterly, Vol. 25, Number 2. pp. 294—327.

Hoffmann, Stanley (1981): "NATO and Nuclear Weapons". In: Foreign Affairs, Vol. 60, Number 2. pp. 327—346.

Holloway, David (1981): "Doctrine and Technology in Soviet Armaments Policy". In: Derek Leebaert (Ed.): Soviet Military Thinking. London: George Allen & Unwin. pp. 259—291.

Holst, Johan Jørgen, and Karen Alette Melander (1977): "European Security and Confidence-Building Measures". In: Survival, Vol. 19, Number 4. pp. 146—154.

—   (1981): "Deterrence and Stability in the NATO-Warsaw Pact Relationship" In : Robert O'Neill and David M. Horner (Eds.): New Directions in Strategic Thinking. London: George Allen & Unwin. pp. 89—103.

—   (1982): "Towards a New Political Order in Europe? The Role of Arms Control". In: Daniel Frei (Ed.): Sicherheit durch Gleichgewicht? Militaerstrategische Tendenzen der achtziger Jahre. Zurich: Schulthess Polygraphischer Verlag. (forthcoming).

Holsti, Ole R. (1972): Crisis, Escalation, War. Montreal and London: McGill-Queen's University Press.

—   (1975): "Operational Codes, Belief Systems and Crisis Decision-Making". In: Charles F. Hermann (Ed.): Research Tasks for International Crisis Avoidance and Management. Washington. D.C.: Office of Naval Research.

—   (1979): "Theories of Crisis Decision-Making". In: Paul Gordon Lauren (Ed.): Diplomacy. New York: The Free Press. pp. 99—136.

—   (1980): "Historians, Social Scientists, and Crisis Management. An Alternative View". In: Journal of Conflict Resolution, Vol. 24, Number 4. pp. 665—682.

Hoole, Francis W., and Dina A. Zinnes (Eds.): Quantitative International Politics. New York: Praeger.

Hopple, Gerald W. (1980): Automated Crisis Warning and Monitoring: Exploring a Staircase Display Option. Research Memorandum Early Warning and Monitoring Project. McLean, Va.: International Public Policy Research Corporation.

Howard, Michael E. (1981): "On Fighting a Nuclear War". In: International Security, Vol. 5, Number 4. pp. 3—17.

Howard, Nigel (1971): Paradoxes of Rationality. Theory of Metagames and Political Behavior. Cambridge, Mass.: Harvard University Press.

Huntzinger, Jacques (1980): "La France et SALT III". In: Défense Nationale, Vol. 36, April 1980. pp. 15—32.

Hussain, Farooq (1981): The Future of Arms Control: Part IV: The Impact of Weapons Test Restrictions (Adelphi Papers; 165). London: International Institute for Strategic Studies.

Hyland, William G. (1981): "Soviet Theatre Forces and Arms Control". In: Survival, Vol. 23, Number 5. pp. 194—199.

Ignatieff, George (1979): "The Achievements of Arms Control". In: Franklyn Griffiths and John C. Polanyi (Eds.): The Dangers of Nuclear War. Toronto: University of Toronto Press. pp. 67—82.

Iklé, Fred Ch. (1978): "Preface". In: Albert Wohlstetter et al.: Swords from Plowshares. The Military Potential of Civilian Nuclear Energy. Chicago: University of Chicago Press.

Inozemtzev, Nikolai N. (Ed.) (1980): Peace and Disarmament 1980. Moscow: Scientific Research Council on Peace and Disarmament, Progress Publishers.

241

International Herald Tribune (1981): "NATO Chief Foresees All-Out Nuclear War In Any Exchange of Nuclear Arms". November 9, 1981. p. 2.

International Peace Research Association (IPRA), Disarmament Study Group (1980): "Building Confidence in Europe". In: Bulletin of Peace Proposals, Vol. 11, Number 2, pp. 1—17.

Intriligator, Michael D., and Dagobert L. Brito (1978): "Nuclear Proliferation and Stability". In: Journal of Peace Science, Vol. 3, Number 2. pp. 173—183.

— , and Dagobert L. Brito (1981): "Nuclear Proliferation and the Probability of Nuclear War". In : Public Choice, Vol. 37. pp. 247—260.

Jabber, Paul (1979): "A Nuclear Middle East. Infrastructure, Likely Military Postures, and Prospects for Strategic Stability". In: Milton Leitenberg and Gabriel Sheffer (Eds.): Great Power Intervention in the Middle East. New York: Pergamon Press. pp. 72—100.

Janis, Irving L., and Leon Mann (1977): Decision Making. A Psychological Analysis of Conflict, Choice, and Commitment. New York and London: The Free Press.

Jasani, Bhupendra M. (1978): Outer Space — Battlefield of the Future? (Stockholm International Peace Research Institute). London: Taylor & Francis.

Jervis , Robert (1970): The Logic of Images in International Relations. Princeton: Princeton University Press.

— (1976): Perception and Misperception in International Politics. Princeton: Princeton University Press.

— (1978): "Cooperation under the Security Dilemma". In: World Politics, Vol. 30, Number 2. pp. 167—214.

— (1979): "Deterrence Theory Revisited". In: World Politics. Vol. 31, Number 2. pp. 289—324.

Jones, General David C., Chairman of the Joint Chiefs of Staff (1981): United States Military Posture for FY 1982. An Overview; with Supplement Prepared by the Organization of the Joint Chiefs of Staff. Washington, D.C.: United States Government Printing Office.

Jukes, Geoffrey (1981): "Soviet Strategy 1965—1990". In: Robert O'Neill and David M. Horner (Eds.): New Directions in Strategic Thinking. London: George Allen & Unwin. pp. 60—74.

Kahler, Miles (1979): "Rumors of War: The 1914 Analogy". In: Foreign Affairs, Vol. 58, Number 2. pp. 374—396.

Kahn, Herman (1962): Thinking About the Unthinkable. New York: Horizon Press.

— (1965): On Escalation. Metaphors and Scenarios. New York: Praeger.

Kaliadine, A. N. (1981): "Arrêt de la course aux armements, passage au désarmement réel". In: E. K. Fedorov and Rem A. Novikov (Eds.): Le désarmement et l'environnement. Moscow: Nauka Publishers. pp. 23—28.

Kaplan, Stephen S. (1981): Diplomacy of Power. Soviet Armed Forces as a Political Instrument. Washington. D.C.: The Brookings Institution.

Karas, Thomas H. (1981): Implications of Space Technology for Strategic Nuclear Competition. Muscatine, Iowa: Stanley Foundation.

Karkuska, Andrzej (1977): Strategic Disarmament, Verification, and National Security. London: Taylor & Francis.

Kashi, Joseph (1975): "The Role of Deterrence in Disarmament: Some Theories and Some Defects". In: David Carlton and Carlo Schaerf (Eds.): The Dynamics of the Arms Race. London: Croom Helm. pp. 92—103.

Kearns, Graham (1981): "CAT and Dogma: The Future of Multilateral Arms Transfer Restraint". In: Arms Control, Vol. 2, Number 1. pp. 3—24.

Keegan, John (1981): "The Human Face of Deterrence". In: International Security, Vol. 6, Number 1. pp. 136—151.

Keeny, Spurgeon M., Jr., and Wolfgang K. H. Panofsky (1981): "MAD versus NUTS; Can Doctrine or Weaponry Remedy the Mutual Hostage Relationship of the Superpowers?". In: Foreign Affairs, Vol. 60, Number 2. pp. 287—304.

Kennan, George F. (1981): "Statement Upon Receiving the International Award from the Albert Einstein Peace Prize Foundation". In: Disarmament, Vol. 4, Number 2. pp. 5—12.

Kent, George (1967): The Effects of Threats. Columbus, Ohio: Ohio University Press.

Kissinger, Henry A. (1979): "NATO: The Next Thirty Years". In: Survival, Vol. 21, Number 6. pp. 264—268.

—   (1982): Years of Upheaval.

Klein, Jean (1979): "Stratégie de non-guerre et hypothèses du conflit nucléaire". In: Défense Nationale, Vol. 35. pp. 17—46.

—   (1980): "Die Bedeutung vertrauensbildender Massnahmen fuer die Sicherheit Europas". In: Hans-Juergen von Kries (Ed.): Friede durch Zusammenarbeit in Europa. Berlin: Berlin-Verlag. pp. 195—209.

Knorr, Klaus (Ed.) (1976a): Historical Dimensions of National Security Problems. Lawrence: National Security Education Program.

—   (1976b): "Threat Perception". In: Klaus Knorr (Ed.): Historical Dimensions of National Security Problems. Lawrence: National Security Education Program. pp. 78—119.

—   (1979): "Strategic Intelligence: Problems and Remedies". In: Laurence Martin (Ed.): Strategic Thought in the Nuclear Age. Baltimore, Md.: Johns Hopkins University Press. pp. 69—91.

Kober, Stanley H. (1981): U.S. — Soviet Approaches to Arms Control. Arlington, Va.: SRI International.

Kolkowicz, Roman (1981): "On Limited War: Soviet Approaches". In: Robert O'Neill and David M. Horner (Eds.): New Directions in Strategic Thinking. London: George Allen & Unwin. pp. 75—88.

Kousnetzov, I., V. Loukov, and Ivan Tiouline (1981): "Recommandations dangereuses des 'Braintrusts' occidentaux". In: La vie internationale, Number 10/1981. pp. 135—143.

Krause, Joachim (1981): "Die Beschraenkung konventioneller Ruestungstransfers in die Dritte Welt". In: Wolf Graf von Baudissin and Dieter S. Lutz (Eds.): Kooperative Ruestungssteuerung. Baden-Baden: Nomos. pp. 189—207.

Krell, Gert (1981): Plaedoyer fuer Ruestungskontrolle (Friedensforschung aktuell, Number 1/1981). Frankfurt/Main: Hessische Stiftung fuer Friedens- und Konfliktforschung.

Krieger, David (1975): "Terrorism and Nuclear Technology". In: Bulletin of the Atomic Scientists, Vol. 31, June 1975. pp. 28—34.

Kries, Hans-Juergen von (Ed.) (1980): Friede durch Zusammenarbeit in Europa. Berlin: Berlin-Verlag.

Kruzel, Joseph J. (1977): "Military Alerts and Diplomatic Signals". In: Ellen P. Stern (Ed.): The Limits of Military Intervention. Beverly Hills and London: Sage Publications. pp. 83—99.

Kupperman, Robert H. (1978): "Nuclear Terrorism: Armchair Pastime or Genuine Threat?". In: Jerusalem Journal of International Relations, Vol. 3. Number 4. pp. 19—26.

Kux, Ernst (1982): "Modernisierung der sowjetischen Militaerproduktion". In: Neue Zuericher Zeitung, February 12, 1982.

Labrie, Roger P. (1979): SALT Handbook. Key Documents and Issues, 1972—1979. Washington, D.C.: America n Enterprise Institute for Public Policy Research.

Lambeth, Benjamin S. (1979): "The Political Potential of Soviet Equivalence". In: International Security, Vol. 4, Number 2. pp. 22—39.
— (1981): Risk and Uncertainty in Soviet Deliberations About War. (Rand Report Number R-2687-AF). Santa Monica: Rand Corporation.
Lang, Kurt (1964): "Collective Response to the Threat of Disaster". In: George H. Grosser (Ed.): The Threat of Impending Disaster. Cambridge, Mass: Harvard University Press. pp. 58—75.
Lange, Dieter, and Michael Lucas (1981): "Atomchronik". In: Ulrich Albrecht et al. (Eds.): Weltpolitik: Jahrbuch fuer Internationale Beziehungen 1. Frankfurt/Main: Campus. pp. 172—204.
Langer, Albert (1977): "Accurate Submarine Launched Ballistic Missiles and Nuclear Strategy". In: Journal of Peace Research, Vol. 14, Number 1. pp. 41—58.
Lanzetta, John T. (1965): "Group Behavior under Stress". In: J. David Singer (Ed.): Human Behavior and International Politics. Chicago: Rand McNally. pp. 212—218.
LaRoque, Gene R. (1981): "How a Nuclear War in Europe Would Be Fought". In : Bulletin of Peace Proposals, Vol. 12, Number 4. pp. 367—369.
Lauren, Paul Gordon (Ed.) (1979): Diplomacy. New York: The Free Press.
Lebow, Richard Ned (1981a): Between Peace and War. The Nature of International Crisis. Baltimore and London: Johns Hopkins University Press.
— (1981b): "Soviet Incentives for Brinkmanship". In: Bulletin of the Atomic Scientists, Vol. 37, Number 5. pp. 14—21.
Leebaert, Derek (Ed.) (1981): Soviet Military Thinking. London: George Allen & Unwin.
— (1981 a): "The Context of Soviet Military Thinking". In: Derek Leebaert (Ed.): Soviet Military Thinking. London: George Allen & Unwin. pp. 3—27.
Legvold, Robert (1979): "Strategic 'Doctrine' and SALT: Soviet and American Views". In: Survival, Vol. 21, Number 1. pp. 8—13.
Leitenberg, Milton (1970): "Accidents of Nuclear Weapons and Nuclear Weapon Delivery Systems". In: Stockholm International Peace Research Institute (Ed.): Sipri Yearbook of World Armaments and Disarmament 1968/69. Stockholm: Almqvist & Wiksell. pp. 259—270.
— (1977a): "Accidents of Nuclear Weapons Systems". In: Stockholm International Peace Research Institute (Ed.): World Armaments and Disarmament, Sipri Yearbook 1977. Cambridge, Mass., and London: The MIT Press. pp. 52—82.
— (1977b): "Unfaelle mit Atomwaffensystemen". In: Technologie und Politik; 9, December 1977. pp. 156—214.
— (1978a): Arms Control and Disarmament: A Short Review of a Thirty Year Story". Ottawa: Carleton University (mimeo).
— (1978b): "Background Materials in Tactical Nuclear Weapons (Primarily in the European Context)". In: Stockholm International Peace Research Institute (Ed.): Tactical Nuclear Weapons: European Perspectives. London: Taylor & Francis. pp. 3—136.
—, and Gabriel Sheffer (Eds.) (1979): Great Power Intervention in the Middle East. New York: Pergamon Press.
— (1980a): "NATO and WTO Long Range Theater Nuclear Forces". In: Karl E. Birnbaum (Ed.): Arms Control in Europe: Problems and Prospects. Laxenburg: Austrian Institute for International Affairs. pp. 9—64.
— (1980b): "Threats of the Use of Nuclear Weapons since World War II". In: Asbjørn Eide and Marek Thee (Eds.): Problems of Contemporary Militarism. London: Croom Helm. pp. 388—395.

– (1981a): "Numbers and the Defence Capabilities of the West". In: Current Research in Peace and Violence, Vol. 4, Number 3. pp. 165–179.

– (1981b): "Presidential Directive (P.D.) 59: United States Nuclear Weapons Targeting Policy". In : Journal of Peace Research, Vol. 18, Number 4. pp. 309–317.

Leng, Russell J., and Robert A. Goodsell (1979): "Behavioral Indicators of War Proneness in Bilateral Conflicts". In: J. David Singer and Ass.: Explaining War. Selected Papers from the Correlates of War Project. Beverly Hills and London: Sage Publications. pp. 208–239.

Lentner, Howard H. (1972): "The Concept of Crisis as Viewed by the United States Department of State". In: Charles F. Hermann (Ed.): International Crises: Insights from Behavioral Research. New York: The Free Press. pp. 112–135.

Lewin, Guy (1980a): "L'avenir des forces nucléaires françaises". In: Défense Nationale, Vol. 36, May 1980. pp. 11–19.

– (1980b): "La dissuasion française et la stratégie anti-cités". In: Défense Nationale, Vol. 36, January 1980. pp. 23–31.

Lodgaard, Sverre (1981a): "Nuclear Proliferation: Critical Issues. Transfer of Technologies, Safeguards, and Sensitive Countries". In: Bulletin of Peace Proposals, Vol. 12, Number 1. pp. 11–20.

– (1981b): "Eurostrategic Weapons and Euronuclear Strategies". In: Bulletin of Peace Proposals, Vol. 12, Number 4. pp. 325–337.

Luebkemeier, Eckhard (1981): PD 59 und LRTNF–Modernisierung: Militaerstrategische und sicherheitspolitische Implikationen der Erweiterten Abschreckung fuer die Bundesrepublik Deutschland. Bonn: Friedrich Ebert Stiftung.

Lueders, Carl H. (1981): Ideologie und Machtdenken in der Aussen- und Sicherheitspolitik der Sowjetunion. Baden-Baden: Nomos.

Luttwak, Edward (1981): The Problem of Extended Deterrence (Adelphi Papers; 160). London: International Institute for Strategic Studies.

Lutz, Dieter S. (1981a): Der nukleare Entwaffnungsschlag als militaerischer Kraeftevergleich. Parameter, Bedingungen, Restriktionen, Strukturen (IFSH Forschungsberichte, Heft 20). Hamburg: Institut fuer Friedensforschung und Sicherheitspolitik.

– (1981b): Stabilitaet durch Vorsehbarkeit und Vertrauensbildung. Kriegsbilder, unkalkulierbare Realitaet und Worst-Case-Orientierung (IFSH Forschungsberichte, Heft 23). Hamburg: Institut fuer Friedensforschung und Sicherheitspolitik.

– (1981c): Zur Methodologie militaerischer Kraeftevergleiche (IFSH Forschungsberichte, Heft 24). Hamburg: Institut fuer Friedensforschung und Sicherheitspolitik.

– (1981d): Weltkrieg wider Willen? Die Nuklearwaffen in und fuer Europa. Reinbek bei Hamburg: Rowohlt.

Makins, Christopher K. (1981): "TNF Modernization and 'Countervailing Strategy' ". In: Survival, Vol. 23, Number 4. pp. 157–164.

Mandel, Robert (1977): "Political Gaming and Foreign Policy Making During Crises". In: World Politics, Vol. 29, Number 4. pp. 610–625.

Mandelbaum, Michael (1981): The Nuclear Revolution ; International Politics Before and After Hiroshima. Cambridge: Cambridge University Press.

Marder, Murrey (1981): "U.S., Russia: The Risk of Misperception". In: International Herald Tribune, January 22, 1981.

Markov, M. A. (1981): Science and the Responsibility of Scientists. Moscow: Nauka Publishers

Martin, Laurence (Ed.) (1979): Strategic Thought in the Nuclear Age. Baltimore, Md.: Johns Hopkins University Press.

Martin, Wayne R. (1977): "The Measurement of International Military Commitments for Crisis Early Warning". In: International Studies Quarterly, Vol. 21, Number 1. pp. 151–180.

Mazrui, Ali (1980): "Africa's Nuclear Future". In: Survival, Vol. 22, Number 2. pp. 76–79.

McGwire, Michael (1981): "Soviet Naval Doctrine and Strategy". In: Derek Leebaert (Ed.): Soviet Military Thinking. London: George Allen & Unwin. pp. 125–181.

McClelland, Charles A. (1977): "The Anticipation of International Crises: Prospects for Theory and Research". In: International Studies Quarterly, Vol. 21, Number 1. pp. 15–38.

McConnell, James M. (1979): "The Rules of the Game: A Theory on the Practice of Superpower Naval Diplomacy". In: Bradford Dismukes and James M. McConnell (Eds.): Soviet Naval Diplomacy. New York and Oxford: Pergamon Press. pp. 240–280.

—, and Bradford Dismukes (1979): "Conclusions". In: Bradford Dismukes and James M. McConnell (Eds.): Soviet Naval Diplomacy. New York and Oxford: Pergamon Press. pp. 281–316.

McGowan, Patrick J. (Ed.) (1974): Sage International Yearbook of Foreign Policy Studies, Volume Two. Beverly Hills and London: Sage Publications.

Meyer, Stephen M., and Thomas L. Brewer (1979): "Monitoring Nuclear Proliferation". In: J. David Singer and Michael D. Wallace (Eds.): To Augur Well. Early Warning Indicators in World Politics. Beverly Hills and London: Sage Publications. pp. 195–213.

Mies, Ullrich F. J. (1979): Destabilisierungsfaktoren des gegenwaertigen Abschreckungssystems. Die Implikationen der 1974er Modifikation der US-Nuklearstrategie fuer die global-strategische Stabilitaet. Frankfurt am Main: Haag + Herchen.

Miettinen, Jorma K. (1978): " 'Mini-Nukes' and Enhanced Radiation Weapons". In: Stockholm International Peace Research Institute (Ed.): Tactical Nuclear Weapons: European Perspectives. London: Taylor & Francis. pp. 223–246.

Milburn, Thomas W. (1972): "The Management of Crisis". In: Charles F. Hermann (Ed.):International Crises: Insights from Behavioral Research. New York: The Free Press. pp. 259–277.

Milgram, Stanley (1974): Obedience to Authority. New York: Harper & Row.

Miller, Gerald E. (1979): "Existing Systems of Command and Control". In: Franklyn Griffiths and John C. Polanyi (Eds.): The Dangers of Nuclear War. Toronto: University of Toronto Press. pp. 50–66.

Miller, James G. (1965): "The Individual as an Information Processing System". In: J. David Singer (Ed.): Human Behavior and International Politics. Chicago: Rand McNally. pp. 202–211.

Miller, Steven E. (1981): "Arms Control and Surprise Attack". In: Arms Control, Vol. 2, Number 2. pp. 135–156.

Minix, Dean A. (1980): "Small Group Dynamics and Decisional Quality During Crises". In: Korea and World Affairs, Vol. 4. pp. 38–56.

MITRE Corporation (1975): The Threat to Licensed Nuclear Facilities. Washington, D.C.: The MITRE Corporation.

Morgan, Patrick M. (1977): Deterrence: A Conceptual Analysis. Beverly Hills and London: Sage Publications.

Morosov, Grigory I. (1978): "International Organizations and Settlement of International Conflicts". In: Daniel Frei (Ed.): International Crises and Crisis Management. An East-West Symposium. Farnborough: Saxon House. pp. 89–100.

Muller James E. (1982): "On Accidental Nuclear War". In: Newsweek, March 8, 1982.

Myrdal, Alva (1976): The Game of Disarmament; How the United States and Russia Run the Arms Race. New York: Pantheon Books.

Nerlich, Uwe (1978): "Nukleare Abschreckung in Europa: Einige Probleme der Verbesserung der NATO-Faehigkeiten". In: Klaus-Dieter Schwarz (Ed.): Sicherheitspolitik. Bad Honnef: Osang. pp. 421—433.

Neuhold, Hanspeter (1978): "Principles and Implementation of Crisis Management: Lessons from the Past". In: Daniel Frei (Ed.): International Crises and Crisis Management. An East-West Symposium. Farnborough: Saxon House. pp. 4—18.

Newsweek (1981): "Reagan's Peace Offensive". November 30, 1981. pp. 10—14.

Niezing, Johan (1978): Strategy and Structure. Studies in Peace Research; II. Amsterdam: Swets & Zeitlinger.

—   (1980): "Broken Arrows and Bent Spears. Towards a Social Theory of Nuclear Weapon Accidents". In: Bulletin of Peace Proposals, Vol. 11, Number 1. pp. 71—78.

Nitze, Paul (1976): "Assuring Strategic Stability in an Era of Detente". In: Foreign Affairs, Vol. 54, Number 2. pp. 207—232.

—   (1977): "The Relationship of Strategic and Theater Nuclear Forces". In: International Security, Vol. 2. Number 2. pp. 122—132.

North, Robert C., Ole R. Holsti, and Nazli Choucri (1976): "A Re-evaluation of the Research Program of the Stanford Studies". In: Francis W. Hoole and Dina A. Zinnes (Eds.): Quantitative International Politics. New York: Praeger. pp. 435—462.

Office of Technology Assessment (1981): MX Missile Basing. Washington, D.C.: United States Government Printing Office.

Ogarkow, Nikolai W. (1981): "Fuer unsere sowjetische Heimat. Auf der Wacht fuer friedliche Arbeit". In: Beitraege zur Konfliktforschung, Vol. 11, Number 4. pp. 133—149. (Translated from "Kommunist" 10/1981)

O'Neill, Robert, and David M. Horner (Eds.) (1981): New Directions of Strategic Thinking. London: George Allen & Unwin.

Osgood, Charles E. (1962): An Alternative to War or Surrender. Urbana: University of Illinois Press.

Osgood, Robert E. (1979): Limited War Revisited. Boulder, Colo.: Westview Press.

Paine, Christopher (1981): "Running in Circles with the MX". In: Bulletin of the Atomic Scientists, Vol. 37, Number 10. pp. 5—10.

Pankov, Jurii (1981): "Definition and Dimensions of Detente". In: Daniel Frei (Ed.): Definitions and Measurement of Detente. Cambridge, Mass.: Oelgeschlager, Gunn & Hain. pp. 57—62.

Panofsky, Wolfgang K. H. (1981): "Science, Technology, and the Arms Buildup — I.". In: Bulletin of the Atomic Scientists, Vol. 37, Number 6. pp. 48—54.

Perry, William J. (1979): "Statement, 1 February, 1979". In: Survival, Vol. 21, Number 3. pp. 132—135.

Petersen, Charles C. (1979): "Showing the Flag". In: Bradford Dismukes and James M. McConnell (Eds.): Soviet Naval Diplomacy. New York and Oxford: Pergamon Press. pp. 88—114.

Petrovsky, Vladimir (1980): "Topical Problems of Disarmament: Soviet Initiatives".In: Nikolai N. Inozemtzev (Ed.): Peace and Disarmament 1980. Moscow: Scientific Research Council on Peace and Disarmament, Progress Publishers. pp. 146—159.

247

Phillips, Warren R., and Richard V. Rimkunas: "A Cross-Agency Comparison of U.S. Crisi s Perception". In: J. David Singer and Michael D. Wallace (Eds.): To Augur Well. Early Warning Indicators in World Politics. Beverly Hills and London: Sage Publications. pp. 237—270.

Pickert, Herwig (1980): "Satellitenabwehr". In: Aus Politik und Zeitgeschichte, Supplement to the Weekly "Das Parlament" October 11, 1980 (B 41/80).

Platig, E. Raymond (1981): "Crisis, Prevention Ideologies, and Superpower Ideologies". In: Orbis 511—524.

Poirier, Lucien (1979): "Quelques problèmes actuels de la stratégie nucléaire française". In: Défense Nationale, Vol. 35, December 1979. pp. 43—62.

Polanyi, John C. (1980): "The Dangers of Nuclear War". In: Bulletin of the Atomic Scientists, Vol. 36, Number 1. pp. 6—10.

Pollack, Jonathan D. (1981): "The Evolution of Chinese Strategic Thought". In: Robert O'Neill and David M. Horner (Eds.): New Directions in Strategic Thinking. London: George Allen & Unwin. pp. 137—152.

Pott, Andreas (1981): "Die seegestuetzte Abschreckung auf dem Weg in die Krise?". In: Wolf Graf von Baudissin and Dieter S. Lutz (Eds.): Konflikte, Krisen, Kriegsverhuetung. Baden-Baden: Nomos. pp. 209—224.

Primakov, Yevgenii (1980): "The Arms Race and the Local Conflicts". In: Nikolai N. Inozemtzev (Ed.): Peace and Disarmament 1980. Moscow: Scientific Research Council on Peace and Disarmament, Progress Publishers. pp. 81—94.

Pross, Harry (1974): Politische Symbolik. Theorie und Praxis der oeffentlichen Kommunikation. Stuttgart: Kohlhammer.

Pruitt, Dean G., and Richard C. Snyder (Eds.) (1969): Theory and Research on the Causes of War. Englewood Cliffs, N. J.: Prentice-Hall.

Pugwash Symposium (37th) (1981): Confidence-Building Measures. Report of Working Group III: "Confidence Building in Europe". Hamburg: Institut fuer Friedensforschung und Sicherheitspolitik (mimeo).

Pugwash Workshop on Political and Psychological Aspects of Crisis Management and Prevention (1978): Introduction to the Pugwash Workshop on Political and Psychological Aspects of Crisis Management and Prevention, Geneva, December 13—15, 1978.

Rapoport, Anatol (Ed.) (1974): Game Theory as a Theory of Conflict Resolution. Dordrecht: Reidel Publishing.

—   ,and Albert Chammah (Eds.) (1965): Prisoner's Dilemma. Ann Arbor: University of Michigan Press.

Rathjens, George (1975): "Slowing Down the Arms Race". In: David Carlton and Carlo Schaerf (Eds.): The Dynamics of the Arms Race. London: Croom Helm. pp. 82—91.

—   (1979): "Nuclear War between the Super-Powers". In: Franklyn Griffiths and John C. Polanyi (Eds.): The Dangers of Nuclear War. Toronto: University of Toronto Press. pp. 135—146.

—   (1981): "How the Use of Nuclear Weapons in Europe Might Arise". In: Bulletin of Peace Proposals, Vol. 12, Number 4. pp. 375—377.

Ray, James Lee, and J. David Singer (1979): "Measuring the Concentration of Power in the International System". In: J. David Singer and Ass.: Explaining War. Selected Papers from the Correlates of War Project. Beverly Hills and London: Sage Publications. pp. 273—304.

Record, Jeffrey (1977): "Theatre Nuclear Weapons: Begging the Soviet Union to Pre-empt". In: Survival, Vol. 19, Number 5. pp. 208—211.

Reychler, Luc (1979): "The Effectiveness of a Pacifist Strategy in Conflict Resolution: An Experimental Study". In: Journal of Conflict Resolution, Vol. 23, Number 2. pp. 228—260.

Roberts, Stephen S. (1979): "Superpower Naval Confrontations". In: Bradford Dismukes and James M. McConnell (Eds.): Soviet Naval Diplomacy. New York and Oxford: Pergamon Press. pp. 158—239.

Robinson, James A., et al. (1969): "Search under Crisis". In: Dean G. Pruitt and Richard C. Snyder (Eds.): Theory and Research on the Causes of War. Englewood Cliffs, N. J.: Prentice-Hall. pp. 80—94.

Rogers, Rita D. (1978): Political and Psychological Aspects of Crisis Management and Prevention. Paper prepared for the Pugwash Workshop on Political and Psychological Aspects of Crisis Management and Prevention, Geneva, December 13—15, 1978.

Rosen, Stephen P. (1979): "Safeguarding Deterrence". In: Foreign Policy, Number 35. pp. 109—123.

Rosenbaum, David M. (1977): "Nuclear Terror". In: International Security, Vol. 1, Number 3. pp. 140—161.

Rosenkranz, Erhard (1981): "Die Kernfrage unserer Sicherheitspolitik". In: Wolf Graf von Baudissin and Dieter S. Lutz (Eds.): Konflikte, Krisen, Kriegsverhuetung. Baden-Baden: Nomos. pp. 9—27.

—, and Ruediger Juette (1964): Abschreckung contra Sicherheit? Muenchen: Piper.

Rostow, Eugene V. (1981a): "Address to the Council on Foreign Relations". In: United States Daily Bulletin, Number 206, November 2, 1981.

— (1981b): "Statement of the UN Assembly; First Committee". In: United States Daily Bulletin, Number 203, October 28, 1981.

Rotblat, Joseph (1981): "The Threat Today". In: Bulletin of the Atomic Scientists, Vol. 37, Number 1. pp. 33—36.

Ruhala, Kalevi (1980): Confidence-Building Measures (IFSH Forschungsberichte Number 18). Hamburg: Institut fuer Friedensforschung und Sicherheitspolitik (mimeo).

— (1981): "Confidence-Building Measures". In: Wolf Graf von Baudissin and Dieter S. Lutz (Eds.): Kooperative Ruestungssteuerung. Baden-Baden: Nomos. pp. 139—170.

Ruina, Jack (1975): "The Arms Race and Salt". In: David Carlton and Carlo Schaerf (Eds.): The Dynamics of the Arms Race. London: Croom Helm. pp. 47—56.

— (1981): "Raketenabwehr-Technologie und Ruestungsbeschraenkung". In: Europa-Archiv, Vol. 36, Number 14. pp. 437—448.

Russett, Bruce (1974): "Assured Destruction of What? A Countercombatant Alternative to Nuclear MADness". In: Public Policy, Vol. 22, Number 2. pp. 121—138.

—, and Harvey Starr (1981): World Politics: The Menu for Choice. San Francisco: W. H. Freeman.

Sabrosky, Alan Ned (1979): "From Bosnia to Sarajevo: A Comparative Discussion of Interstate Crisis". In: J. David Singer and Ass.: Explaining War. Selected Papers from the Correlates of War Project. Beverly Hills and London: Sage Publications. pp. 139—157.

Salomon, Michael D. (1977): "New Concepts for Strategic Parity". In: Survival, Vol. 19, Number 6. pp. 255—262.

SALT II Treaty (1979). In: Survival, Vol. 21, Number 5. pp. 217—230.

Schelling, Thomas C. (1960): The Strategy of Conflict. London: Oxford University Press.

—, and Morton H. Halperin (1961): Strategy and Arms Control. New York: Twentieth Century Fund.

— (1966): Arms and Influence. New Haven and London: Yale University Press.

—, and Morton H. Halperin (1969): "Pre-emptive, Premeditated, and Accidental War". In: Dean G. Pruitt and Richard C. Snyder (Eds.): Theory and Research on the Causes of War. Englewood Cliffs, N. J.: Prentice-Hall. pp. 43—48.

—   (1981): "The Terrorist Threat of Nuclear Weapons". In: Bernard Brodie, Michael D. Intriligator, and R. Kolkowicz (Eds.): National Security and International Stability. (forthcoming)

Schilling, Warner R. (1981): "U.S. Strategic Nuclear Concepts in the 1970s: The Search for Sufficiently Equivalent Countervailing Parity". In: International Security, Vol. 6, Number 2. pp. 49—79.

Schmidt, Max (1982): "Der militaerische Faktor in den internationalen Beziehungen und der Politik der friedlichen Koexistenz". In: Daniel Frei (Ed.): Sicherheit durch Gleichgewicht? Militaerstrategische Tendenzen der achtziger Jahre. Zurich: Schulthess Polygraphischer Verlag. (forthcoming)

Schneider, Barry (1981): "Preventing Star Wars". In: Bulletin of the Atomic Scientists, Vol. 37, Number 8. pp. 13—15.

Schütze, Walter (1979): "A World of Many Nuclear Powers". In: Franklyn Griffiths and John C. Polanyi (Eds.): The Dangers of Nuclear War. Toronto: University of Toronto Press. pp. 85—92.

Schwarz, Klaus-Dieter, and William R. Van Cleave (1978): "Zur Theorie der Abschreckung" In: Klaus-Dieter Schwarz (Ed.): Sicherheitspolitik. Bad Honnef: Osang. pp. 131—149.

—   (1978a): "Amerikanische Militaerstrategie, 1945—1978". In: Klaus-Dieter Schwarz (Ed.): Sicherheitspolitik. Bad Honnef: Osang. pp. 345—372.

—   (1978b): "Sowjetische Militaerstrategie, 1945—1978". In: Klaus-Dieter Schwarz (Ed.): Sicherheitspolitik. Bad Honnef: Osang. pp. 373—396.

Schwarz, Urs, and Laszlo Hadik (1966): Strategic Terminology. A Trilingual Glossary. Duesseldorf: Econ.

—   (1981): Zwischen Krieg und Frieden. Duesseldorf: Econ.

Segal, Gerald, and John Baylis (1981): "Soviet Strategy: An Introduction". In: Baylis, John, and Gerald Segal (Eds.): Soviet Strategy. London: Croom Helm 1981. pp. 9—51.

Scoville, Herbert, Jr. (1978): "The Cessation of Nuclear Testing". In: Jane M. O. Sharp (Ed.): Opportunities for Disarmament; A Preview of the 1978 United Nations Special Session on Disarmament. New York and Washington, D. C.: Carnegie Endowment for International Peace. pp. 9—18.

Senghaas, Dieter (1981): "Questioning Some Premises of the Current Security Debate in Europe" In: Bulletin of Peace Proposals, Vol. 12, Number 4. pp. 321—324.

Sergeyev, Victor (1981): "The Dangerous Consequences of the Arms Race". In: International Affairs (Moscow), Number 12. pp. 31—40.

Sharp, Jane M. O. (Ed.) (1978): Opportunities for Disarmament: A Preview of the 1978 United Nations Special Session on Disarmament. New York and Washington, D. C.: Carnegie Endowment for International Peace.

—   (1981): Confidence Building Measures and SALT. Paper Prepared for the Pugwash Symposium on CBM, Hamburg, April 8—11, 1981.

Shlaim, Avi (1976): "Failures in National Intelligence Estimates: The Case of the Yom Kippur War". In: World Politics, Vol. 28, Number 3, pp. 348—380.

Siegler, Heinrich (1973): Dokumentation zur Abruestung und Sicherheit, Band X: 1972. Bonn: Siegler.

Sienkiewicz, Stanley (1978): "SALT and Soviet Nuclear Doctrine". In: International Security, Vol. 2, Number 4. pp. 84—100.

—   (1981): "Soviet Nuclear Doctrine and the Prospects for Strategic Arms Control". In: Derek Leebaert (Ed.): Soviet Military Thinking. London: George Allen & Unwin. pp. 73—91.

Sigal, Leon V. (1979): "Rethinking the Unthinkable". In: Foreign Policy, Number 34. pp. 35—51.

Simes, Dimitri K. (1981): "Deterrence and Coercion in Soviet Policy". In: International Security, Vol. 5, Number 3. pp. 80—103.

Singer, J. David (Ed.) (1965): Human Behaviour and International Politics. Chicago: Rand McNally.

— , and Melvin Small (1972): The Wages of War, 1816—1965. A Statistical Handbook. New York: Wiley.

— , and Ass. (1979): Explaining War. Selected Papers from the Correlates of War Project. Beverly Hills and London: Sage Publications.

— , Stuart Bremer, and John Stuckey (1979): "Capability Distribution, Uncertainty. and Major Power War, 1820—1965". In: J. David Singer and Ass.: Explaining War. Selected Papers from the Correlates of War Project. Beverly Hills and London: Sage Publications. pp. 159—188.

— , and Michael D. Wallace (Eds.) (1979): To Augur Well. Early Warning Indicators in World Politics. Beverly Hills and London: Sage Publications.

— (1979): "From A Study of War to Peace Research". In: J. David Singer and Ass.: Explaining War. Selected Papers from the Correlates of War Project. Beverly Hills and London: Sage Publications. pp. 21—34.

Siverson, Randolph M., and Joel King (1979): "Alliances and the Expansion of War". In: J. David Singer and Michael D. Wallace (Eds.): To Augur Well. Early Warning Indicators in World Politics. Beverly Hills and London: Sage Publications. pp. 37—49.

Slocombe, Walter (1981): "The Countervailing Strategy". In: International Security, Vol. 5, Number 4. pp. 18—27.

Small, Melvin, and J. David Singer (1979): "Conflict in the International System, 1816—1977: Historical Trends and Policy Futures". In: J. David Singer and Ass.: Explaining War. Selected Papers from the Correlates of War Project. Beverly Hills and London: Sage Publications. pp. 57—82.

Smart, C., and I. Vertinsky (1977): Designs for Crisis Decision Units: Pathologies and Prescriptions (Discussion Paper 77—49). Berlin: International Institute of Management.

Smith, Bruce A. (1981): "Vought Tests Small Antisatellite System". In: Aviation Week & Space Technology, November 9. pp. 24—25.

Smoke, Richard (1979): "Theories of Escalation". In: Paul Gordon Lauren (Ed.): Diplomacy. New York: The Free Press. pp. 162—182.

Snyder, Glenn H. (1972): "Crisis Bargaining". In: Charles F. Hermann (Ed.): International Crises: Insights from Behavioral Research. New York: The Free Press. pp. 217—256.

— , and Paul Diesing (1977): Conflict Among Nations. Bargaining, Decision Making, and System Structure in International Crises. Princeton: Princeton University Press.

Snyder, Jack L. (1978): "Rationality at the Brink: The Role of Cognitive Processes in Failures of Deterrence". In: World Politics, Vol. 30, Number 3. pp. 345—365.

Sonntag, Philipp (1981): Verhinderung und Linderung atomarer Katastrophen. Bonn: Osang.

Soutou, Georges-Henri (1981): "De quelques aspects politiques de negociations SALT". In: Défense Nationale, Vol. 37, July 1981. pp. 85—100.

Soviet Committee for European Security and Co-Operation, Scientific Research Council on Peace and Disarmament (1981): The Threat to Europe. Moscow: Progress Publishers.

Speed, Roger (1979): Strategic Deterrence in the 1980s. Stanford: Hoover Institution Press.

Spiegel (1980): "Zwanzig Minuten am Rand eines Atomkriegs". Number 26. pp. 102—114.

Spinney, Franklin C. (1981): Defense Facts of Life. Preliminary Study. Washington, D. C.: United States Department of Defense.

Staff of the Carnegie Panel on U. S. Security and the Future of Arms Control (1981a): Challenges for U.S. National Security: Defense Spending and the Economy ; The Strategic Balance and Strategic Arms Limitation ; A Preliminary Report. Washington, D. C.: Carnegie Endowment for International Peace.

— (1981b): Challenges for U.S. Security: Assessing the Balance: Defense Spending and Conventional Forces. Washington, D.C.: Carnegie Endowment for International Peace.

Stakh, G. (1981): "Washington's Neutron Madness". In: International Affairs (Moscow), Number 11, November 1981. pp. 86—91.

Stanley Foundation (1981a): The Multilateral Disarmament Process. Muscatine, Iowa: Stanley Foundation.

— (1981b): United Nations Second Special Session on Disarmament, Report of the Twelfth United Nations Procedures Conference, Muscatine, Iowa: Stanley Foundation.

Starsman, Raymond E. (1981): Ballistic Missile Defense and Deceptive Basing: A New Calculus for the Defense of ICBMs. Washington, D.C.: National Defense University Press.

Stein, Arthur G. (1976): "Conflict and Cohesion: A Review of the Literature". In: Journal of Conflict Resolution, Vol. 20, Number 1. pp. 143—172.

Stein, Janice (1978): "Can Decision-Makers Be Rational and Should They Be? Evaluating the Quality of Decisions". In: Michael Brecher (Ed.): Studies in Crisis Behavior. New Brunswick. N. J.: Transaction Books. pp. 316—339.

Steinbruner, John (1976): "Beyond Rational Deterrence: The Struggle for New Conceptions". In: World Politics, Vol. 28, Number 2. pp. 223—245.

— , and Thomas M. Garwin (1976): "Strategic Vulnerability: The Balance Between Prudence and Paranoia". In: International Security, Vol. 1, Number 1. pp. 131—181.

— (1978): "National Security and the Concept of Strategic Stability". In: Journal of Conflict Resolution, Vol. 22, Number 3. pp. 411—428.

— (1979): "An Assessment of Nuclear Crises". In: Franklyn Griffiths and John C. Polanyi (Eds.): The Dangers of Nuclear War. Toronto: University of Toronto Press. pp. 34—49.

— (1981): "Nuclear Decapitation". In: Foreign Policy, Number 45. pp. 16—28.

Stern, Ellen P. (Ed.) (1977): The Limits of Military Intervention. Beverly Hills and London: Sage Publications.

Stockholm International Peace Research Institute (Ed.) (1970): Sipri Yearbook on World Armaments and Disarmament 1968/69. Stockholm: Almqvist & Wiksell.

— (Ed.) (1978): Tactical Nuclear Weapons: European Perspectives. London: Taylor & Francis.

Stratmann, K.-Peter (1981): NATO-Strategie in der Krise? Militaerische Optionen von NATO und Warschauer Pakt in Mitteleuropa. Baden-Baden: Nomos.

Suedfeld, Peter, and Philip Tetlock (1977): "Integrative Complexity of Communications in International Crises". In: Journal of Conflict Resolution, Vol. 21, Number 1. pp. 169—184.

Suedfeld, Peter, Philip E. Tetlock, and Carmenza Ramirez (s.d.): War, Peace, and Integrative Complexity: UN Speeches on the Middle East Problem, 1947—1976. Paper.

Sukovic, O. (1978): "Tactical Nuclear Weapons in Europe". In: Stockholm International Peace Research Institute (Ed.): Tactical Nuclear Weapons: European Perspectives. London: Taylor & Francis. pp. 137—165.

Sullivan, Michael P. (1979): "Foreign Policy Articulations and U.S. Conflict Behavior". In: J. David Singer and Michael D. Wallace (Eds.): To Augur Well. Early Warning

Indicators in World Politics. Beverly Hills and London: Sage Publications. pp. 215—235.

Talbott, Strobe (1981): "The Dilemma of Nuclear Doctrine". In: Time, November 30. pp. 36—37.

Tammen, Ronald L. (1973): MIRV and the Arms Race. An Interpretation of Defense Strategy. New York: Praeger.

Tanter, Raymond, and Richard H. Ullman (Eds.) (1972): Theory and Policy in International Relations. Princeton, N.J.: Princeton University Press.

—   (1974): Modelling and Managing International Conflicts. The Berlin Crises (Volume 6, Sage Library of Social Research). Beverly Hills and London: Sage Publications,

Tatu, Michel (1981): "Les stratégies américaine et soviétique". In: Défense Nationale, Vol. 37. July 1981. pp. 17—25.

Thee, Marek (1980): "Militarism and Militarisation in Contemporary International Relations". In: Asbjørn Eide and Marek Thee (Eds.): Problems of Contemporary Militarism. London: Croom Helm. pp. 15—35.

Towle, P. A. (1980): "Letter to the Editor". In: Survival, Vol. 22, Number 5. pp. 219—221.

Treaty Series; Treaties and International Agreements Registered or Filed and Recorded with the Secretariat of the United Nations. New York: United Nations.

Treverton, Gregory F. (1980): "Global Threats and Trans-Atlantic Allies". In: International Security, Vol. 5, Number 2. pp. 142—158.

Trofimenko, Henry A. (1981): "Counterforce: Illusion of a Panacea". In: International Security, Vol. 5, Number 4. pp. 28—48.

Tromp, Hylke (1981): "Why a Nuclear War Could Start". In: Bulletin of Peace Proposals, Vol. 12, Number 4, pp. 371—373.

Tsipis, Kosta (1974): Offensive Missiles (Stockholm Paper; 5). Uppsala: Almqvist & Wiksell.

—   (1975a): "Anti-Submarine Warfare and Missile Submarines". In: David Carlton and Carlo Schaerf (Eds.): The Dynamics of the Arms Race. London: Croom Helm. pp. 36—46.

—   (1975b): "The Arms Race as Posturing". In: David Carlton and Carlo Schaerf (Eds.): The Dynamics of the Arms Race. London: Croom Helm. pp. 78—81.

United Nations Department of Political and Security Council Affairs (1976): The United Nations and Disarmament, 1970—1975. New York: United Nations.

—   (1977): The United Nations Disarmament Yearbook, Volume I: 1976. New York: United Nations.

United Nations Department of Public Information (1980): The United Nations Versus the Arms Race. New York: United Nations.

United Nations General Assembly (1980a): Comprehensive Study on Nuclear Weapons (A/35/392). New York: United Nations.

—   (1980b): Study on all the aspects of Regional Disarmament (A/35/416). New York: United Nations.

—   (1981a): Study of the Relationship Between Disarmament and Development (A/36/356). New York: United Nations.

—   (1981b): Study on institutional arrangements to the process of disarmament (A/36/392). New York: United Nations.

—   (1981c): Israeli Nuclear Armament (A/36/431). New York: United Nations.

—   (1981d): General and Complete Disarmament: Confidence-Building Measures (A/36/474). New York: United Nations.

—   (1981e): Study on the relationship between disarmament and international security (A/36/612e). New York: United Nations.

United Nations Office of Public Information (1980): Final Document of Assembly Session on Disarmament (23 May—1 July, 1978). New York: United Nations.

United States Arms Control and Disarmament Agency (1980): Arms Control 1979. Washington, D.C.: United States Government Printing Office.

— (annually): Documents on Disarmament. Washington, D.C.: United States Government Printing Office.

United States Department of Defense (1981): Annual Report Fiscal Year 1982 (Report by Secretary of Defense Harold Brown to the Congress on the FY 1982 Budget, FY 1983 Authorization Request and FY 1982—1986 Defense Programs). Washington, D.C.: United States Government Printing Office.

— (1982): Annual Report Fiscal Year 1983 (Report by Secretary of Defense Caspar W. Weinberger to the Congress on the FY 1983 Budget, FY 1984 Authorization Request and FY 1983—1987 Defense Programs). Washington, D.C.: United States Government Printing Office.

Ustinov, Dimitri F. (1981): Against the Arms Race and the Threat of War. Moscow: Novosti Press.

Vetschera, Heinz (1977): "Vertrauensbildende Massnahmen". In: Oesterreichische Militaerische Zeitschrift, Number 1. pp. 23—27.

Virally, Michel (1978): "The Role of International Organisations in Mitigating and Settling International Crises". In: Daniel Frei (Ed.): International Crises and Crisis Management. An East-West Symposium. Farnborough: Saxon House. pp. 71—88.

Wallace, Michael D. (1979a): "Alliance Polarization, Cross-Cutting, and International War, 1815—1964: A Measurement and Some Preliminary Evidence". In: J. David Singer and Ass.: Explaining War. Selected Papers from the Correlates of War Project. Beverly Hills and London: Sage Publications. pp. 83—111.

— (1979b): "Arms Races and Escalation: Some New Evidence". In: J. David Singer and Ass.: Explaining War. Selected Papers from the Correlates of War Project. Beverly Hills and London: Sage Publications. pp. 240—252.

— (1979c): "Clusters of Nations in the Global System, 1865—1964: Some Preliminary Evidence". In: J. David Singer and Ass.: Explaining War. Selected Papers from the Correlates of War Project. Beverly Hills and London: Sage Publications. pp. 253—272.

— (1979d): "Early Warning Indicators from the Correlates of War Project". In: J. David Singer and Michael D. Wallace (Eds.): To Augur Well. Early Warning Indicators in World Politics. Beverly Hills and London: Sage Publications. pp. 17—35.

Waltz, Kenneth N. (1981): The Spread of Nuclear Weapons: More May Be Better (Adelphi Papers ; 171). London: International Institute for Strategic Studies.

Weltman, John J. (1982): "Managing Nuclear Multipolarity". In: International Security, Vol. 6, Number 3, pp. 182—194.

Whence the Threat to Peace (1982). Moscow: Military Publishing House, USSR Ministry of Defense.

Wiegele, Thomas C. (1973): "Decision-Making in an International Crisis: Some Biological Factors". In: International Studies Quarterly, Vol. 17, Number 3. pp. 295—335.

— (1978): "The Psychophysiology of Elite Stress in Five International Crises: A Preliminary Test of a Voice Measurement Technique". In: International Studies Quarterly, Vol. 22, Number 4. pp. 467—511.

Wilkenfeld, Jonathan, Gerald W. Hopple, and Paul J. Rossa (1979): "Sociopolitical Indicators of Conflict and Cooperation". In: J. David Singer and Michael D. Wallace (Eds.): To Augur Well. Early Warning Indicators in World Politics. Beverly Hills and London: Sage Publications. pp. 109—151.

254

Wilkes, Owen (1979a): "Command and Control of the Sea-Based Deterrent: The Possibility of a Counterforce Role". In: Stockholm International Peace Research Institute (Ed.): World Armaments and Disarmament, Sipri Yearbook 1979. London: Taylor & Francis. pp. 389—420.

— (1979b): "Strategic Anti-Submarine Warfare and its Implications for a Counterforce First Strike". In: Stockholm International Peace Research Institute (Ed.): World Armaments and Disarmament, ..pri Yearbook 1979. London: Taylor & Francis. pp. 427—452.

Williams, Phil (1976): Crisis Management. Confrontation and Diplomacy in the Nuclear Age. London: Martin Robertson.

Winkler, Theodor (1980): Die Nuklearpolitik der Schwellenmaechte. Berlin: Berlin-Verlag.

Wohlstetter, Albert, et al. (1978): Swords from Plowshares. The Military Potential of Civilian Nuclear Energy. Chicago: University of Chicago Press.

Yefremov, A. Y. (1979): Nuclear Disarmament. Moscow: Progress Publishers.

Yost, Charles W. (1980): "National Security Revisited". In: Bulletin of the Atomic Scientists. Vol. 36, Number 8. pp. 20—24.

Zinnes, Dina A., et al. (1972): "Hostility in Diplomatic Communication: A Study of the 1914 Crisis". In: Charles F. Hermann (Ed.): International Crises: Insights from Behavioral Research. New York: The Free Press. pp. 139—162.

Zurhellen, J. Owen, Jr. (1981): "Arms Control: The Record of the 1970s and the Outlook for the 1980s". In: Robert O'Neill and David M. Horner (Eds.): New Directions of Strategic Thinking. London: George Allen & Unwin. pp. 246—260.